# Basic
# Engineering
# Technology

## Seán Ó Tuairisg

CJFallon

## Acknowledgements

The author and publishers wish to thank those listed below for their assistance in the publication of this book:
Brian Darlington and Kenneth Roberts of Engineering Equipment Company Ltd;
Imperial Chemical Industries PLC, Petrochemicals and Plastics Division; Lister
Machine Tools Ltd; British Steel Corporation; Loctite (Ireland) Ltd; Sureweld
International Ltd; Boxford Machine Tools Ltd; Aughinish Alumina Ltd; Arcon Mines Ltd;
Engineering teachers Joseph McGrath and Micheál Martin; and the editorial staff
at CJ Fallon for their patience and perseverance.

The author also wishes to thank his wife, Ann, and family, Eoin, Sile, Aodhán and
Cormac for their help and encouragement.

ISBN No. 978-0-7144-1621-2

Published by
CJ Fallon
Ground Floor – Block B
Liffey Valley Office Campus
Dublin 22

Revised Edition April 2002
This Reprint May 2016

## Preface

This book covers the Junior Certificate course at Ordinary and Higher levels. This revised edition contains a range of new material, including new diagrams, to provide comprehensive coverage of the course.

The in-depth coverage of techniques, processes and uses of equipment has been retained, helping the development of craft skills – an important aspect of an activity-based technology course. The widespread use of schematic diagrams makes the material easy to understand and encourages students to use sketches to convey, explain and record information.

The questions at the end of each chapter should facilitate the structuring of study and homework and minimise the need for note taking. The order in which the chapters are presented does not have to be adhered to, but their arrangement can act as a guide in drawing up a scheme of work.

A method of undertaking a design problem is given in Chapter 16. This indicates the activities involved but it does not eliminate, nor is it intended to, the need for imagination, creativity and the application of knowledge in finding a solution.

# Contents

# Properties of Materials

# 1

## Introduction

Early man was confined to the use of natural materials such as stone, wood, bone, clay and animal skins. He used these to make tools and weapons to provide food, clothing and shelter from the elements.

Today we have access to a wide range of materials such as metals, wood, concrete, plastics, glass and fabrics.

## Metals

Great advancements have been made in the development of metals by **alloying**, which is the mixing of a number of metals and sometimes other elements, and by heat treatments. Metals with improved properties such as extra strength, hardness and resistance to corrosion have been created. This has increased their use and their suitability for different applications.

**Fig 1.1**
Use of metal

## Wood

The development of manufactured boards such as plywood, blockboard and chipboard that are often laminated with a plastic material has enhanced the use of wood. Advancements have also been made in joining methods and in the development of surface coating and preservatives.

## Plastics

Mainly man-made materials, plastics have had a huge impact on our lives and have greatly improved our living standards. They possess a great variety of properties, giving them a wide range of uses from household goods to spacecraft parts.

**Fig 1.3**
Use of plastic

## Knowledge of Materials

A knowledge of materials is essential in the design of articles. We need to know the range of materials available, their properties, how they can be shaped and joined, their appearance and some idea of their cost. This will help us to make comparisons and assessments and enable us to make good selections.

## States of Matter

Matter exists as either a **gas**, a **liquid** or a **solid**. Some substances can be made to change from one state to another. Water, for example, will change from a liquid to a gas (steam) if heated sufficiently. Similarly, it will change to a solid (ice) if cooled enough.

A substance is usually classified according to the state it is in at normal room temperature and pressure.

## Gases

Gases are easily compressed because of the space between their molecules. In school workshops, gases used for heating appliances include air, propane, butane, oxygen and acetylene. Air is also used for plastic coating units, i.e. fluidising units.

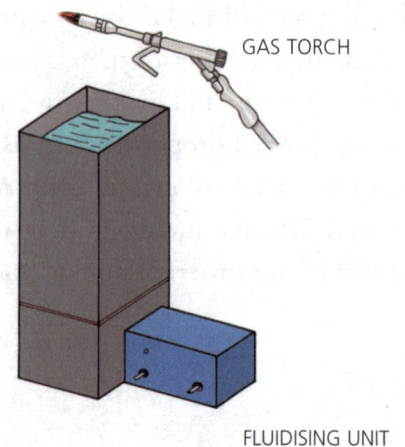

GAS TORCH

FLUIDISING UNIT

**Fig 1.4**
Use of gases in school workshop

## Liquids

Most of the molecules in liquids are in contact with one another and are therefore almost impossible to compress. Liquids have definite volumes but no definite shapes. They adopt the shapes of the containers in which they are placed. Liquids used in school workshops include water for cooling hot materials and for heat treatments, lubricating oils for machines, soldering flux, cutting fluids and adhesives.

**Fig 1.5(a)**
Liquids adopt the shapes of the containers in which they are placed

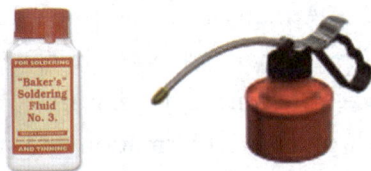

**Fig 1.5(b)**
Use of liquids in school workshop

## Solids

Solids have definite volumes. Solid materials used in school workshops include metals, plastics and wood.

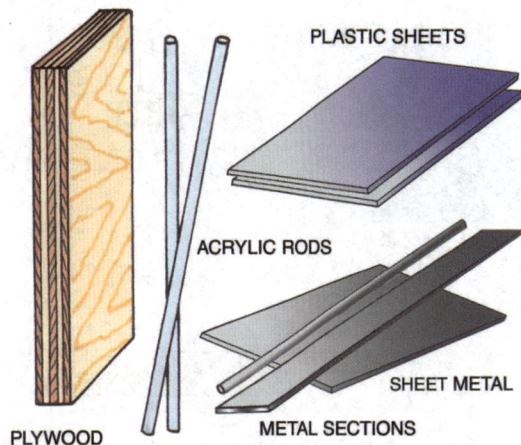

**Fig 1. 6**
Use of solids in school workshop

## Properties of Materials

● **Strength** This is the ability of a material to withstand forces of tension, compression, shear, bending and torsion.

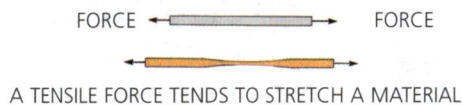

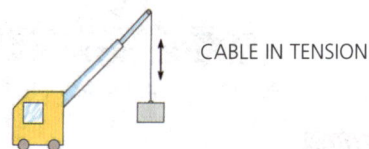

FORCE ← → FORCE

A TENSILE FORCE TENDS TO STRETCH A MATERIAL

CABLE IN TENSION

**Fig. 1.7(a)**
Tensile strength is the maximum pulling or tensile stress a material can withstand before breaking. Cables and chains need to have this property.

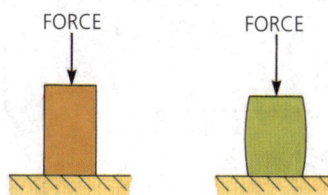

FORCE        FORCE

A COMPRESSIVE FORCE TENDS TO 'SQUASH' A MATERIAL

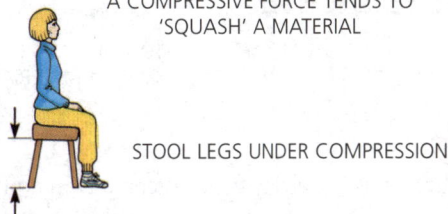

STOOL LEGS UNDER COMPRESSION

**Fig. 1.7(b)**
Compressive strength is the ability to withstand compressive forces

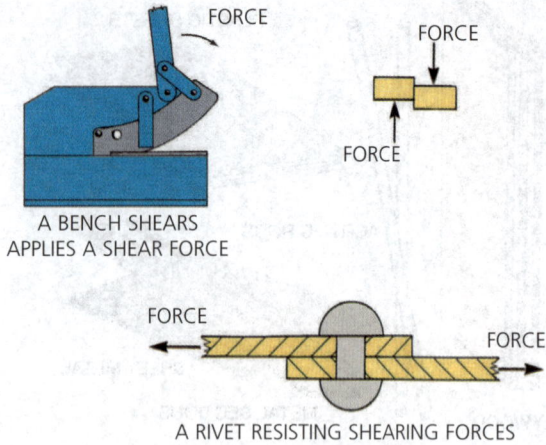

FORCE

A BENCH SHEARS
APPLIES A SHEAR FORCE

FORCE

FORCE

FORCE

FORCE

A RIVET RESISTING SHEARING FORCES

Shear strength is the ability to resist shearing forces

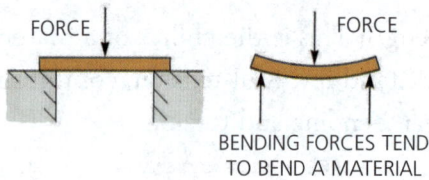

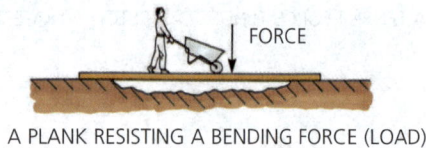

FORCE

FORCE

BENDING FORCES TEND
TO BEND A MATERIAL

FORCE

A PLANK RESISTING A BENDING FORCE (LOAD)

Bending strength is the ability to resist bending forces

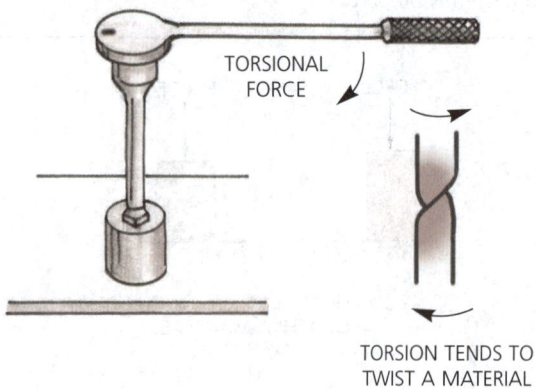

TORSIONAL
FORCE

TORSION TENDS TO
TWIST A MATERIAL

Torsional strength is the ability to withstand a twisting force or torsion

● **Hardness** The ability of a material to resist abrasive wear, indentation and scratching.

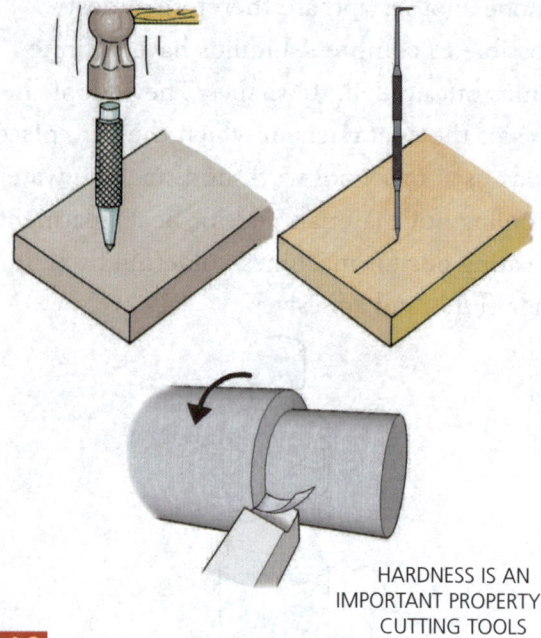

HARDNESS IS AN
IMPORTANT PROPERTY OF
CUTTING TOOLS

Hardness is the ability to resist indentation and scratching

● **Ductility** A material is said to be ductile when it can be permanently stretched, without fracture, by a tensile force. It must be plastic enough to allow deformation and strong enough not to fracture. A metal must be ductile to enable it to be drawn into wire.

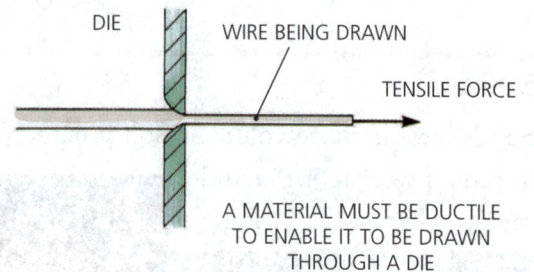

DIE

WIRE BEING DRAWN

TENSILE FORCE

A MATERIAL MUST BE DUCTILE
TO ENABLE IT TO BE DRAWN
THROUGH A DIE

Ductility

- **Malleability** This is the property that allows a material to be extended in all directions, without rupture, by rolling or hammering. The malleability of most metals is increased by heating.

A RIVET NEEDS TO BE MADE FROM A MALLEABLE MATERIAL SO THAT ITS HEAD CAN BE FORMED

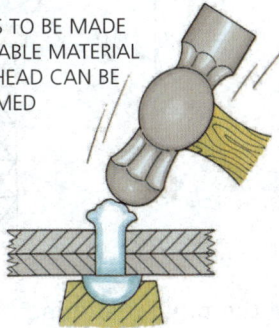

**Fig. 1.10**
Malleability

- **Toughness** This property enables a material to withstand blows or an impact. The amount of energy it takes to fracture a material is an indication of its toughness.

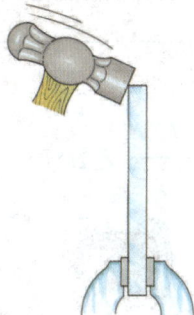

**Fig. 1.11**
Toughness enables a material to withstand impacts or blows

- **Brittleness** This is the opposite to toughness. A brittle material can easily be fractured by an impact. Glass is an example of a brittle material.

**Fig. 1.12**
Brittleness

- **Elasticity** This is the ability of a material to return to its original shape when freed from a force that was distorting it.

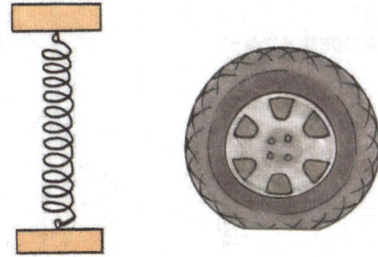

**Fig. 1.13**
Elasticity enables a material to return to its original shape after being deformed

- **Plasticity** This property enables a material to be permanently deformed, without fracture. A metal needs to be plastic when it is being forged. The plasticity of metals can be increased by heating them.

**Fig. 1.14**
Plasticity is an important property in the metals used for coins, enabling them to be embossed

- **Conductivity** This is the ability of a material to allow heat or electricity to flow through it. Silver, copper and aluminium are good conductors of heat and electricity.

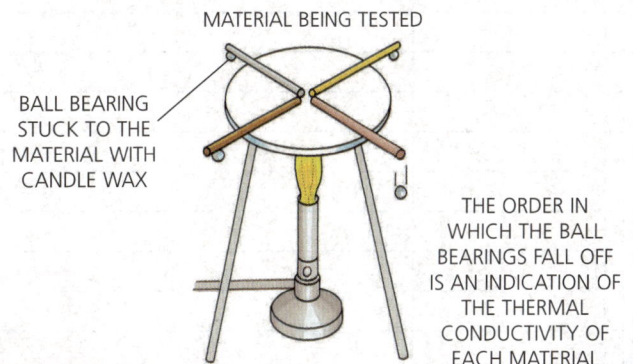

MATERIAL BEING TESTED

BALL BEARING STUCK TO THE MATERIAL WITH CANDLE WAX

THE ORDER IN WHICH THE BALL BEARINGS FALL OFF IS AN INDICATION OF THE THERMAL CONDUCTIVITY OF EACH MATERIAL

**Fig. 1.15**
Thermal conductivity

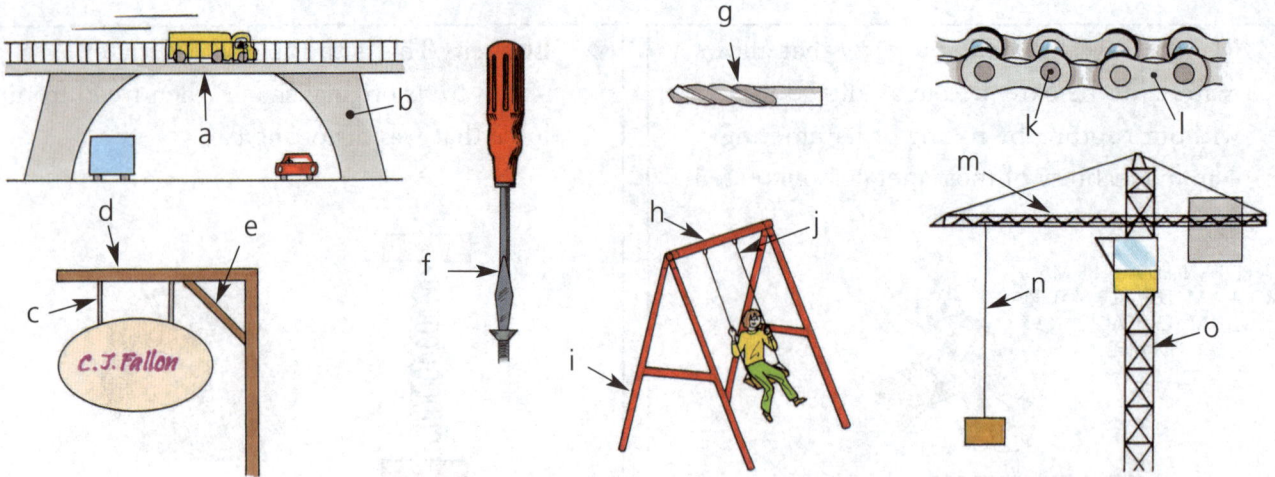

**Fig. 1.16**

## Exercises

1. List two examples of the use of gases in the school workshop.
2. List two examples of the use of liquids in the school workshop.
3. Copy the table below into your copybook and complete it by stating the type of strength (tensile, compressive, shear, bending or torsional) required by each component (a) to (o) shown in Fig. 1.16 above. The first line has been done for you.

| Component | Type of strength required |
|---|---|
| a | Bending strength |
| b | |
| c | |
| d | |
| e | |
| f | |
| g | |
| h | |
| i | |
| j | |
| k | |
| l | |
| m | |
| n | |
| o | |

4. Complete the table matching each item shown in Fig. 1.17 below with the relevant property.

| Property | Item |
|---|---|
| Ductility | |
| Conductivity | |
| Toughness | |
| Malleability | |
| Hardness | |

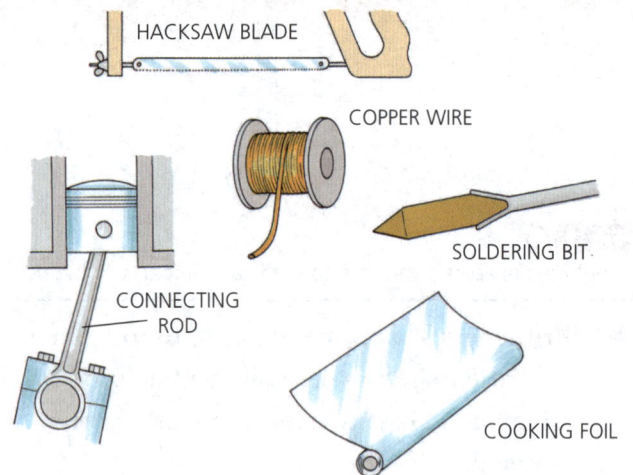

HACKSAW BLADE

COPPER WIRE

CONNECTING ROD

SOLDERING BIT

COOKING FOIL

**Fig. 1.17**

5. Complete the table matching each material listed with the appropriate property. Material: acrylic, spring steel, lead.

| Property | Material |
|---|---|
| Elasticity | |
| Plasticity | |
| Brittleness | |

## Metals

There are two main groups of metals: **ferrous metals**, which consist mainly of iron (ferrite) and **non-ferrous metals**, which contain no iron.

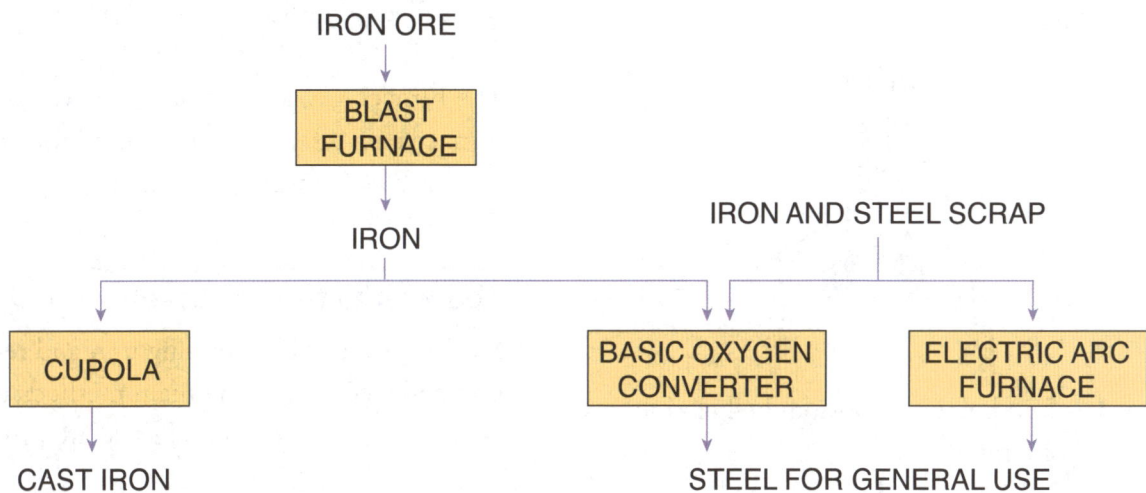

IRON ORE
↓
BLAST FURNACE
↓
IRON

IRON AND STEEL SCRAP

CUPOLA → CAST IRON

BASIC OXYGEN CONVERTER    ELECTRIC ARC FURNACE
↓
STEEL FOR GENERAL USE

**Fig. 2.1**
The various stages in the production of iron and steel

## Ferrous Metals

### Iron Ore

The main form of iron ore is iron oxide, which is iron chemically combined with oxygen. The ore also has large amounts of earthy materials, in the form of rocks, clay and sand, mixed through it. In the smelting of the ore, the unwanted elements are mostly removed, leaving a material which is mainly iron.

### The Blast Furnace

Iron ore is smelted in a blast furnace (Fig. 2.2). The iron ore, coke and limestone are fed into it from the top. Hot air is blown in through nozzles, called tuyeres, at the bottom.

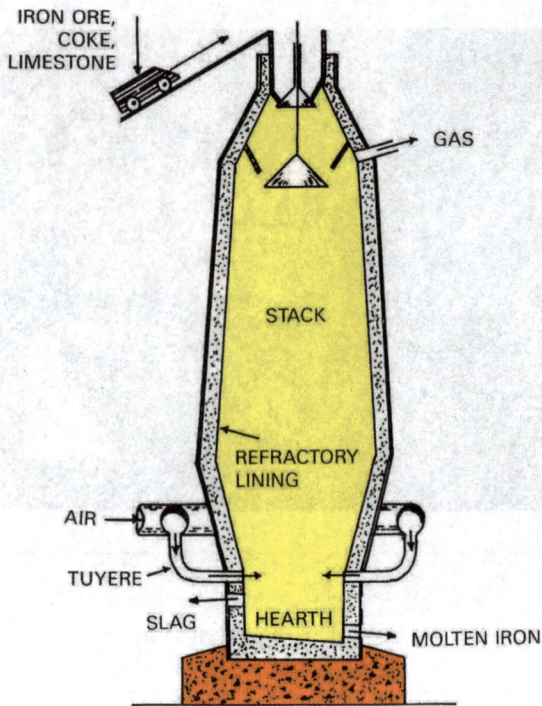

**Fig. 2.2**
The blast furnace

As the coke burns, it produces heat and carbon monoxide gas. The carbon monoxide combines with the oxygen in the ore, leaving iron. The molten iron falls to the bottom of the furnace. At the same time, the limestone combines with the earthy impurities to form a slag. This also goes to the bottom of the furnace, but it floats on top of the molten iron because it is lighter.

The slag is tapped off from time to time as it builds up. The molten iron is also tapped off at intervals as it collects beneath the slag. It is brought directly to the steel-making furnaces or sometimes cast into slabs for making into cast iron later. In the past, iron was sometimes cast into slabs before being brought to the steel-making furnace. These slabs resembled pigs and the metal was called 'pig iron'.

The furnace gas is taken off at the top of the furnace and, after cleaning, is used for pre-heating the air 'blast' entering the furnace.

## The Production of Steel

Steel is produced by refining iron and re-melting iron and steel scrap. The main methods used today are the basic oxygen and electric arc processes.

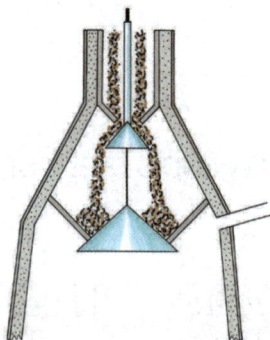

**Stage 1**    Top bell open; bottom bell closed; charge fed in

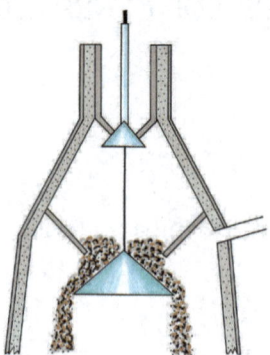

**Stage 2**    Top bell closed; bottom bell open; charge drops into furnace; escape of gases or heat kept to a minimum

**Fig. 2.3**
Charging the blast furnace

## The Basic Oxygen Process

This is the major method of producing bulk steel. In the basic oxygen process, a water-cooled lance is used for blowing oxygen into the furnace. The main portion of the charge used is molten iron, but it also involves large quantities of scrap metal. The refining is done very rapidly, resulting in a process that is much more economical than any of the earlier processes.

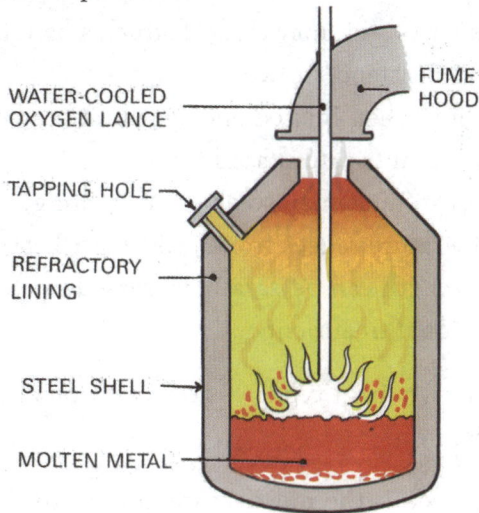

WATER-COOLED OXYGEN LANCE

FUME HOOD

TAPPING HOLE

REFRACTORY LINING

STEEL SHELL

MOLTEN METAL

**Fig. 2.4**
Basic oxygen furnace

The furnace, Fig. 2.4, is rotated to various positions during its operation, Fig. 2.5. The charge is made up of molten iron, scrap metal (iron and steel) and lime. An oxygen lance is lowered in through the mouth of the furnace and the oxygen is blown onto the surface of the molten metal at a very high speed. This burns unwanted impurities from the charge. The lime helps to produce a slag which assists the refining, and any remaining scrap is melted. During the 'blow', the temperature is checked and the molten metal analysed. When the temperature and composition are correct, the lance is withdrawn, the furnace is tilted and the molten steel is poured from underneath the slag into a ladle. The furnace is then tilted in the opposite direction in order to empty the slag.

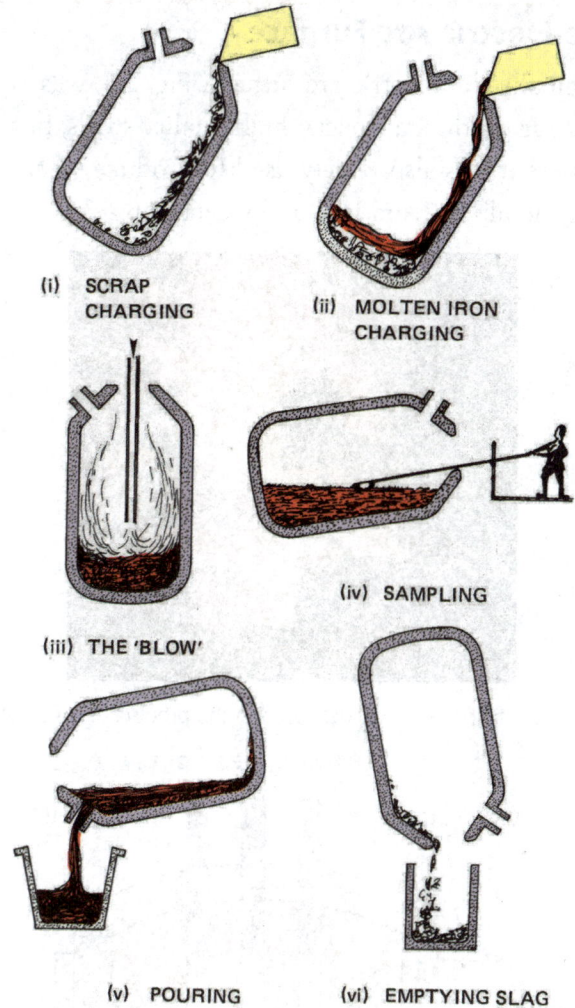

(i) SCRAP CHARGING

(ii) MOLTEN IRON CHARGING

(iii) THE 'BLOW'

(iv) SAMPLING

(v) POURING

(vi) EMPTYING SLAG

**Fig. 2.5**
Basic oxygen process

A modified process is used for iron with a high phosphorus content. In this case, finely crushed lime is blown in through the oxygen lance. The blow is in two stages, slag being produced during both. Slag is removed between the stages. This slag is rich in phosphorus and is used as a fertiliser.

9

## The Electric Arc Furnace

Originally the electric arc furnace, Fig. 2.6, was used for producing special high quality steels, but at present it is also widely used to produce steels for general use from iron and steel scrap.

Electric arc furnaces are widely used in the production of steel

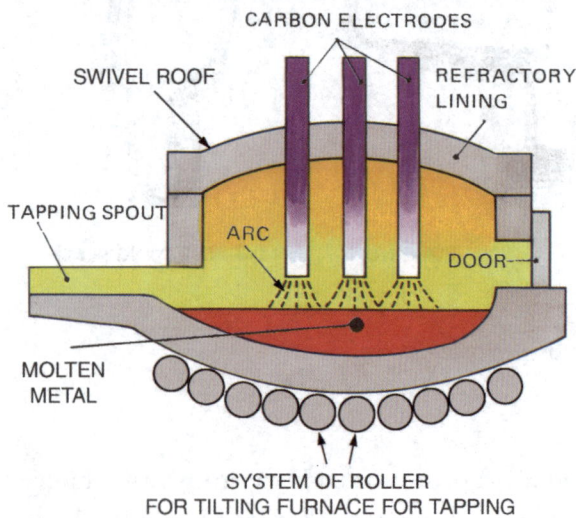

**Fig. 2.6**
Electric arc furnace

The required heat is generated by means of electric arcs produced between carbon electrodes and the charge. As well as scrap metal, lime and mill scale or iron ore are also fed into it. These latter materials combine with the unwanted elements, producing a slag. From time to time, samples are taken to check the composition of the steel. When this is correct, the slag is removed and the steel tapped by rotating the furnace on its rollers.

## Cast Iron

Cast iron is produced by refining blast furnace iron (pig iron) in a furnace called a cupola, which is similar to a blast furnace but much smaller. The inclusion of steel scrap in the charge helps to control the carbon content which is usually 2–4%. Its main properties are:

● Strength in compression but weakness in tension.

● Brittleness — it may crack if struck a hard blow.

● Good resistance to wear.

● Fluidity when melted and the ability to be cast into intricate shapes.

● Easier to melt than steel — its melting temperature ranges from 1130°C to 1250°C.

● Its strength can be greatly increased by additional treatments.

There are two main types — grey cast iron and white cast iron.

**Grey cast iron** is the most common type. Its fractured surface is grey. It is easily machined. Uses include machine beds, e.g. lathe beds, vice bodies, drilling machine tables, manhole covers, ranges and fire grates.

**White cast iron** has a white fracture. It is very hard and almost unmachinable. It is used for articles needing great hardness and good resistance to wear, such as stone crushing machinery.

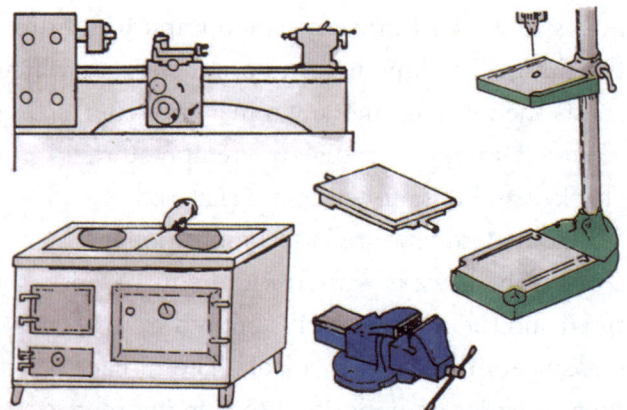

**Fig. 2.7**
Applications of cast iron include ranges, lathe beds, baths.

## Steel

Steel is an alloy of iron and carbon — the carbon content being up to about 1.5%. Although the carbon content is low, it has a great effect on the properties of the metal. Steel is available in a wide variety of shapes and properties and therefore has a wide range of uses. There are two main groups — plain carbon steels and alloy steels.

## Plain Carbon Steels

These steels are a series of iron and carbon alloys with the carbon content varying between about 0.05% and 1.4%. The main grades and examples of their uses are given in Fig. 2.8.

## Dead Mild Steel

When the carbon content of the steel is between about 0.05% and 0.15%, it is called dead mild steel. This is very ductile and easily formed.

**Common uses:** Sheets for various purposes, such as tinplate and car bodies; chains; rivets; nails; thin wire.

**Fig. 2.8**
Plain carbon steels and examples of their application

| Type of Steel | % Carbon | Uses |
|---|---|---|
| Dead mild steel | 0.05-0.15 |  |
| Mild steel | 0.15-0.30 | 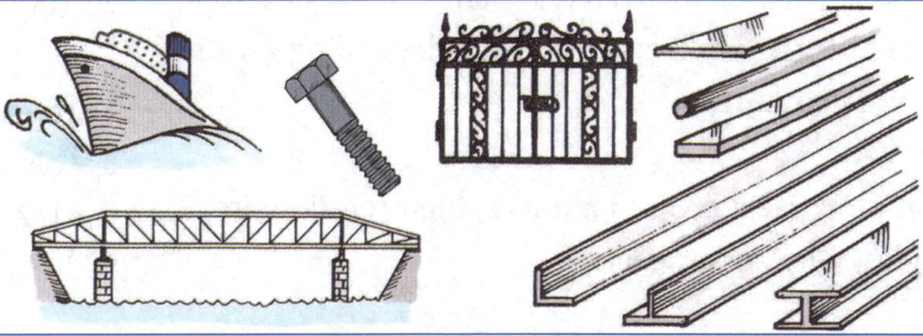 |
| Medium carbon steel | 0.3-0.6 | 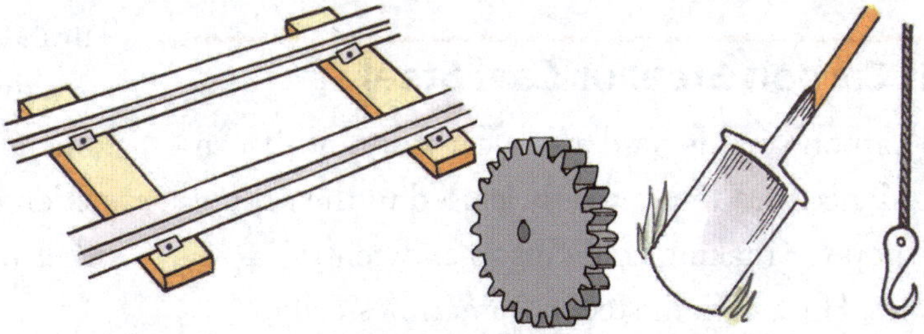 |
| High carbon steel | 0.6-1.4 | 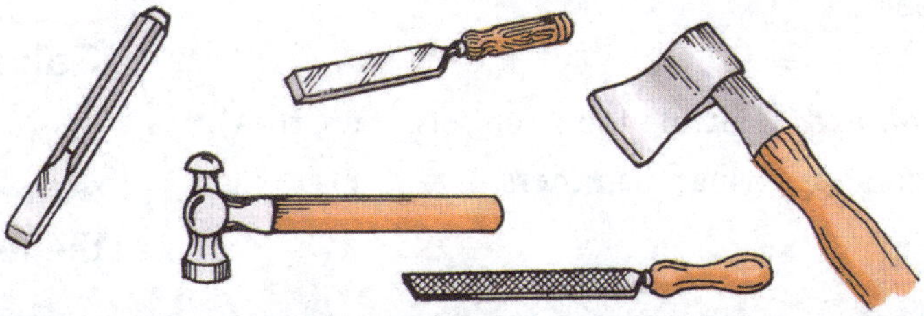 |

## Mild Steel

This is the most common type of steel and the one most used in the school workshop. It is reasonably soft and ductile, easily cut, machined and welded. It is available in bars, plates, sheets and various sections. Mild steel cannot be hardened by heating and rapid cooling, but can be case-hardened (see page 131). There are two kinds: black mild steel and bright mild steel. Black mild steel has a dark blue surface due to its being hot rolled and is less expensive. Bright mild steel has a greyish-white appearance and is finished by cold rolling or cold drawing through a die. It has a smooth surface and is accurate in size.

**Common uses:** General engineering work; structural steels (girders, etc.); nuts and bolts; plates for ship building; gates.

## Medium Carbon Steel

This has greater strength than mild steel, but it is not as ductile or malleable. It can be hardened to a certain degree by heat treatment, depending on its carbon content.

**Common uses:** Axles; railtracks; high tensile wire; spades; wire ropes; gears.

## High Carbon Steel or Cast Steel

High carbon steel is hard and wear-resistant. It can be hardened and tempered. It is used in the school workshop for making cold chisels and centre punches. High carbon steel is sometimes called cast steel.

**Common uses:** Cutting tools (chisels, saws, files); dies; punches; springs; hammers.

## Silver Steel

Silver steel contains about 1% carbon and, although it contains a small amount of chromium, it is classified as a plain carbon steel. It does not contain any silver but gets its name from its bright, silvery appearance. Silver steel is accurately ground to size and is available in round or square sections in lengths of 333mm, 1 metre and 2 metres. It can be hardened and tempered and is used in the school workshop for making scribers and screwdriver blades.

## Tool Steel

This is any steel used for making engineering tools. It can be a carbon steel or an alloy steel.

## Tinplate

Tinplate is produced by coating thin sheets of steel, containing about 0.1% carbon, with tin. Both sides are coated. The tin protects the steel from rusting as well as giving it an attractive appearance.

Care should be taken to avoid scratching tinplate, as this ruins its fine finish. If the steel is exposed, it rusts very rapidly. A hard pencil should be used for marking out on tinplate.

Tinplate is widely used for food containers. It is very suitable for this purpose because tin is non-toxic and corrosion-resistant. Tinplate is easily soldered. It is also used for containers for many other products, e.g. paints, lubricants, etc.

## Galvanised Iron

Despite its name, this is actually mild steel coated with zinc. The coating is usually done by dipping the steel article into a bath of molten zinc. Steel articles can also be zinc-coated by electroplating. Galvanising gives good protection against rusting.

The galvanising is best done when the article is finished to prevent sections becoming exposed and unprotected by further working.

Applications of galvanised iron include roofs, dustbins, buckets, barbed wire.

## Alloy Steels

Alloy steels are produced by adding various elements, such as chromium, tungsten, nickel or manganese, to the steel. These improve the properties of the steel or give it new properties, such as resistance to corrosion and the ability to retain hardness and strength at high temperatures. The elements added depend on the properties required.

High-speed steel and stainless steel are common examples of alloy steels.

## High-Speed Steels

These steels have great hardness when heat-treated and can retain their hardness at high temperatures. Because of this, high-speed steel (HSS) cutting tools can withstand the heat generated at high cutting speeds. Plain high carbon steel would soften at far lower speeds. The compositions of high-speed steels vary, but a typical example would contain about 18% tungsten, 4% chromium,

1% vanadium and 0.8% carbon. Other elements sometimes used are molybdenum and cobalt.

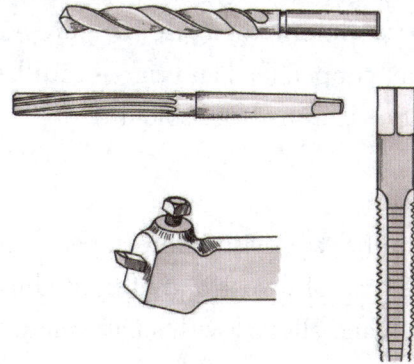

**Fig. 2.10**
Applications of high speed steel include drills, lathe cutters, reamers, taps, screw-cutting dies, hacksaw blades.

## Stainless Steels

The main property of stainless steel is its resistance to corrosion. Chromium is the main alloying element in stainless steels. There is a wide range available. Some can be hardened by heat-treatment, while others can only be work-hardened. One type contains 13% chromium and 0.3% carbon. It can be hardened by heat-treatment and is used for cutlery. Sometimes stainless steel contains nickel also. One such type is known as 18-8 stainless steel, containing about 18% chromium and 8% nickel.

**Common uses:** Cutlery; kitchen sinks; tableware; surgical instruments; scissors.

**Fig. 2.11**
Applications of stainless steel include cutlery, kitchen sinks, tableware, surgical instruments.

## Non-Ferrous Metals

This is the group of metals that do not have iron as their base. Among them are the pure metals — aluminium, copper, lead and tin — and the alloys — brass, bronze and solder.

### Aluminium

Aluminium has a greyish-white appearance. In its pure state it is soft, weak and of limited use. However, when alloyed with small amounts of other elements, its strength and hardness improve considerably, increasing its range of applications accordingly. Other properties of aluminium are:

- Lightness, having a density about one-third that of steel.
- Malleability.
- Ductility.
- Low melting point (660°C).
- Easy to cast.
- Good conductor of heat and electricity.
- Good reflector of light and heat.
- Good resistance to corrosion.

Being malleable and ductile, aluminium can be rolled into very thin sheets and drawn into fine wire.

**Fig. 2.12**

Applications of aluminium and aluminium alloys include aircraft components, bodies of buses and trucks, electric cables, cooking utensils, cooking foil, window and door frames.

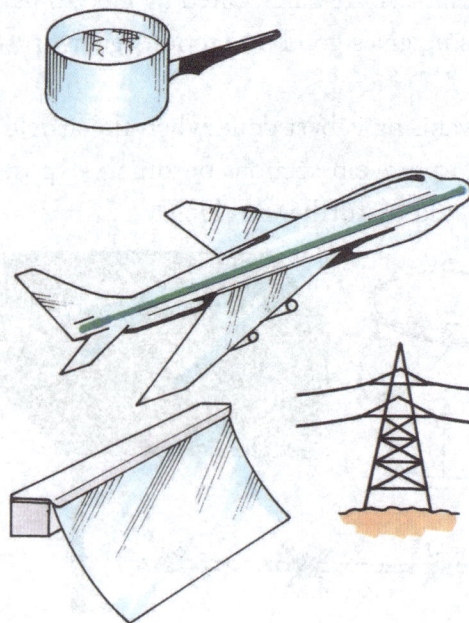

The Aughinish Alumina Limited Plant at Aughinish Island, Co. Limerick. Alumina (aluminium oxide) is extracted from bauxite ore at this plant. The alumina then goes abroad where the metal aluminium is extracted from it by electrolysis.

### Copper

Copper is easily recognised by its red appearance. It is ductile and malleable, is a very good conductor of heat and electricity and has good resistance to corrosion. It can be rolled into thin sheets and can be drawn into very fine wire. Copper is easily soldered and melts at 1083°C. It becomes work-hardened by cold-working but can be annealed (see page 128) by heating until it is dull red and then cooled in water or allowed to cool naturally.

An Irishman, Marcus Daly, played an important part in extending the mining and smelting of copper ores to meet fast-growing demands for copper in the latter half of the nineteenth century. He was born in Ballyjamesduff, Co. Cavan, and emigrated to America. He discovered rich copper ore in Montana and had a large mining and smelting operation there.

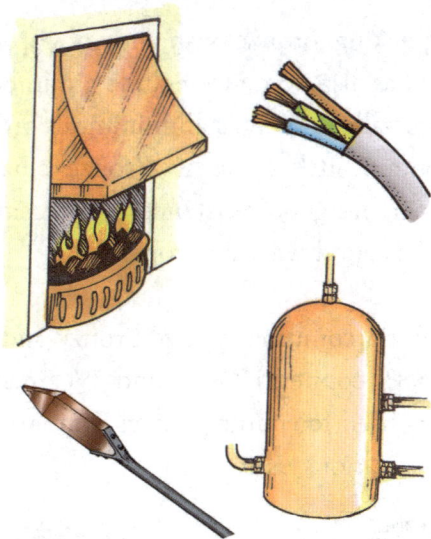

Applications of copper include electrical equipment, water tubing, domestic water heating equipment, brewery apparatus, jewellery, roofs, soldering iron bits and as a constituent in alloys such as brass and bronze.

## Lead

Lead is the heaviest of the common metals. It has a lustry, greyish-blue colour when cut but turns dull grey when exposed to the air for some time. Lead is soft and malleable, melts at 327°C, is corrosion-resistant and toxic.

Applications of lead include car batteries, coverings for electric cables, flashings around chimney stacks, protective shieldings against radiation, and it is used as a constituent in alloys such as solder.

## Zinc

Zinc has a grey colour and it melts at 419°C. It is widely used for galvanising steel articles, that is, coating them with zinc to give protection against rusting. It is also used for the casings of dry batteries and is alloyed with copper to produce brass. Zinc base alloys are widely used for die casting. Their uses include carburettors, door handles, washing machine parts and toys. Arcon Mines in County Kilkenny is an Irish example of a zinc-lead mine.

Mining of zinc-lead ore at Arcon Mines

## Tin

Tin is a soft, weak metal that has a silvery-white appearance. It has good resistance to corrosion and melts at 232°C. It is used for coating sheets of steel to make tinplate and as a constituent in the alloys bronze, soft solders, bearing metals and pewter.

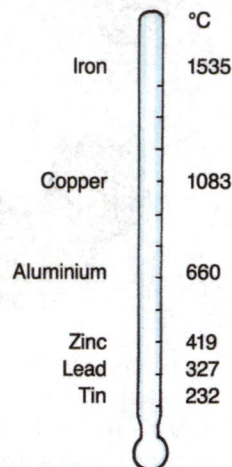

| | °C |
|---|---|
| Iron | 1535 |
| Copper | 1083 |
| Aluminium | 660 |
| Zinc | 419 |
| Lead | 327 |
| Tin | 232 |

The melting points of some common metals

## Non-Ferrous Alloys

There is also a wide range of non-ferrous alloys available. They are produced by mixing two or more metals and sometimes other elements. The purpose of alloying is to improve the properties of the metals.

### Brass

Brass is an alloy of copper and zinc. Sometimes it contains small amounts of other metals also. There are many different types produced, with varying proportions of copper and zinc. Muntz metal, containing 60% copper and 40% zinc, and cartridge brass, containing 70% copper and 30% zinc, are two common types.

Brass has a yellow colour. Its melting point varies according to its composition but is usually between 850°C and 950°C. It has very good resistance to corrosion.

Application of brass include water fittings, boat fittings, screws, musical instruments, brazing spelter, electrical fittings.

### Bronze

Strictly speaking, bronze is an alloy of copper and tin, but it has also come to include a number of copper-base alloys such as aluminimum bronze, which contains little or no tin. Bronze is harder than copper, has good resistance to corrosion, casts well and has good wearing properties.

**Gunmetal** is a common type of bronze and contains 88% copper, 10% tin and 2% zinc. It casts well and is used for pumps, valves, statuary and castings for various uses.

Applications of bronze

**Phosphor bronze** contains 4-13% tin, about 0.5% phosphorus and the remainder copper. It is used for bearings, gearwheels and springs.

Bronze is commonly used for statues

## Soft Solders

Soft solder is an alloy of lead and tin. It sometimes contains small amounts, up to 3%, of antimony. There is a range of soft solders available, with varying proportions of lead to tin. Tinman's solder, the type generally used in school workshops, contains about equal amounts of lead and tin. Plumber's solder contains about 70% lead and 30% tin. Soft solders begin to melt at 183°C but usually go through a pasty stage before being fully liquid. Plumber's solder has a pasty range of 183°C to approximately 250°C, which allows time for making 'wiped' joints.

## Corrosion

Rusting of iron and steel is the most common form of metal corrosion. Other metals corrode also, for instance the forming of a white powdery material on the surface of some unprotected aluminium alloys. Methods used to combat corrosion include:

- The application of protective coatings.
- The use of metals with good resistance to corrosion.
- Design techniques.
- Anodising.
- Use of sacrificial anodes.
- The addition of special chemicals to the water in central heating and cooling systems.

Protective coatings include paints, lacquers, plastic coatings, zinc coatings (galvanising) and tin coatings. Paints are widely used on steel articles but give only limited protection and may need to be renewed periodically.

Metals with good resistance to corrosion include stainless steel, aluminium, copper, lead and brass.

Design techniques involve the avoidance of crevices and other moisture traps, provision of draining and ventilating facilities and the spacing of members of a structure to allow for proper painting.

Anodising is an electrolytic process used for thickening the oxide on aluminium surfaces, thereby improving their resistance to corrosion.

An example of the use of sacrificial anodes is the placing of pieces of zinc close to an underground steel pipeline and joining them to the pipe with insulated cable. The pieces of zinc corrode instead of the pipe.

Methods used to remove rust before coating articles include sand blasting, wire brushing, scraping, rubbing with wire wool or emery cloth and the use of de-rusting fluids.

## Exercises

1. Fig. 2.18 shows a blast furnace.
   (a) What is the purpose of this furnace?
   (b) What does the charge consist of?
   (c) Describe briefly how it works.

**Fig. 2.18**

2. The charging mechanism for a blast furnace is shown in Fig. 2.19.
   Explain how it works.

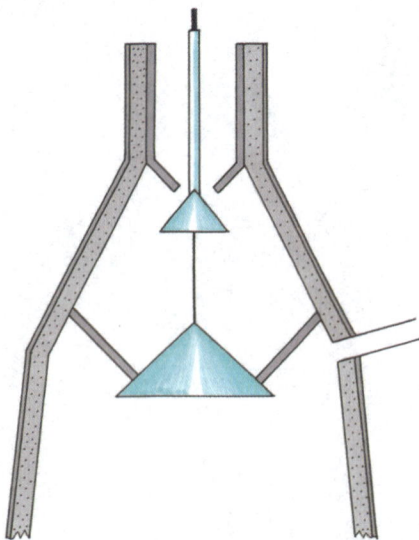

**Fig. 2.19**

3. Name two furnaces used for producing steel.

4. Fig. 2.20 shows a basic oxygen furnace. Describe briefly how it works.

**Fig. 2.20**

5. An electric furnace is shown in Fig. 2.21.
   (a) What does the charge consist of?
   (b) What is produced in it?
   (c) Name parts A and explain their function.
   (d) Name parts B and explain their function.

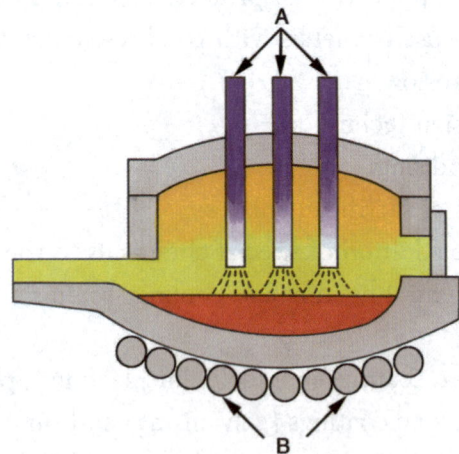

**Fig. 2.21**

6. What is meant by each of the following terms as applied to materials:
   (a) strength, (b) hardness, (c) ductility,
   (d) malleability, (e) toughness,
   (f) brittleness, (g) elasticity, (h) plasticity,
   (i) conductivity?

7. Why has black mild steel a dark blue surface?
8. Redraw the table shown below into your copybook. Complete the table listing one important property and two applications for each metal.

| Ferrous Metal | Property | Applications |
| --- | --- | --- |
| Dead mild steel | | |
| Mild steel | | |
| Medium carbon steel | | |
| High carbon steel | | |
| Cast iron | | |

9. What is tinplate made from?
10. What is galvanised iron?
11. What is an alloy?
12. Give two examples of the use of tinplate.
13. Give two applications of galvanised iron.
14. Complete the table below in your copybook listing the alloy elements, one property and two applications for each metal.

| Ferrous Alloy | Alloy Elements | Property | Applications |
| --- | --- | --- | --- |
| High-speed steel | | | |
| Stainless steel | | | |

15. Complete the table below in your copybook listing one important property and two applications for each metal.

| Non-Ferrous Metal | Property | Applications |
| --- | --- | --- |
| Aluminium | | |
| Copper | | |
| Lead | | |
| Zinc | | |
| Tin | | |

16. Complete the table below in your copybook listing the alloy elements, one property and two applications for each metal.

| Non-Ferrous Alloy | Alloy Elements | Property | Applications |
| --- | --- | --- | --- |
| Brass | | | |
| Bronze | | | |
| Soft solder | | | |

17. Name the metal you would use for each of the following and give a reason for your choice in each case:
    (a) the bit of an electric soldering iron    (b) electric cables
    (c) roof flashings    (d) bearings
    (e) cooking foil    (f) hinges for outdoor use.
18. Give three methods used for the protection of mild steel against corrosion.

# Plastics and Wood

## 3

## Plastics

Plastics are a range of materials, developed mainly in the last 100 years, which have widely varying properties. Some are soft and flexible, while others are hard and rigid. Their use is also widespread, for example, household goods, electrical articles, toys, shoes, car parts and clothes.

Natural plastics have been in use for thousands of years. **Amber**, a fossilised resin, was used for making ornaments and pipe stems. Animal **horns** were used as vessels and funnels. Other examples of natural plastics are **shellac**, which is secreted by the lac insect, and **bitumen,** which is used for road-making.
**Celluloid**, well known for its use as photographic film, could be regarded as a semi-synthetic material. It is produced by treating the naturally occurring cellulose of wood or cotton with nitric acid.

Today, some natural plastics are still in use but the vast majority are man-made. **Bakelite**, developed in 1909 from phenol and formaldehyde, was the first of the true synthetic plastics. Its commercial success encouraged further research, resulting in the development of a huge range of plastics with unique properties.

There are two main groups of plastics, **thermoplastics** and **thermosetting** plastics.

## The Structure of Plastics

The main raw material for plastics is **crude oil**. The chemicals required are obtained by refining the crude oil. These chemicals are made of molecules containing a small number of atoms. These small molecules, called **monomers**, react together to form **long chain molecules**, similar to the links of a bicycle chain. The chemical process of linking the small molecules together is called **polymerisation** (from 'poly' meaning many and 'mer' meaning unit). The product of polymerisation is called a **polymer**.

One of the simplest polymers is the plastic material **polyethylene**, or polythene. By examining how it is formed (see Fig 3.1), we can learn about the general structure of plastics and begin to understand their properties. The chemical used for making polyethylene is **ethylene**, $C_2 H_4$, sometimes called ethene. It has two carbon atoms and four hydrogen atoms. Each of the carbon atoms is linked or bonded to two hydrogen atoms and they are double bonded to each other.

The double bond is a reactive link and under suitable conditions, one link will detach and connect with another molecule. Thousands of molecules will join in this way to form each long chain polyethylene molecule. Newly formed polyethylene molecules attract one another and become tangled and twisted to form the solid material polyethylene. The forces of attraction between the molecules are called secondary bonds.

This type of polymerisation is called **addition polymerisation**. There is another type called **condensation polymerisation**. This involves two different monomers reacting together to produce the long chain molecule. An example of a polymer produced in this way is phenol formaldehyde or **Bakelite**.

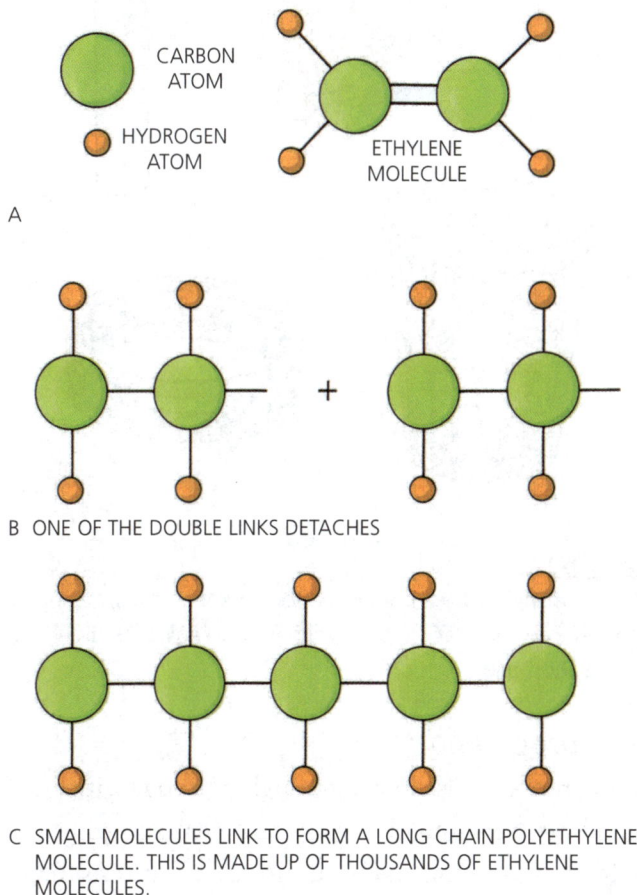

CARBON ATOM

HYDROGEN ATOM

ETHYLENE MOLECULE

A

B  ONE OF THE DOUBLE LINKS DETACHES

C  SMALL MOLECULES LINK TO FORM A LONG CHAIN POLYETHYLENE MOLECULE. THIS IS MADE UP OF THOUSANDS OF ETHYLENE MOLECULES.

**Fig. 3.1**

The polymerisation of ethylene to form polyethylene (or polythene)

## Thermoplastics

Thermoplastics soften when heated and can be moulded into required shapes when in this state. They will harden again on cooling. By heating and cooling, they can be softened and hardened over and over again.

**Fig. 3.2**

Thermoplastics

On heating, the forces of attraction between the long chain molecules become weaker, allowing them to move over one another and form a new shape under pressure. On cooling, the bonds reform again, retaining the new shape.

## Thermosetting Plastics

Thermosetting plastics undergo a chemical change during moulding and hardening and, therefore, cannot be softened again by heating. They are like eggs — they harden when heated and will not soften again by reheating.

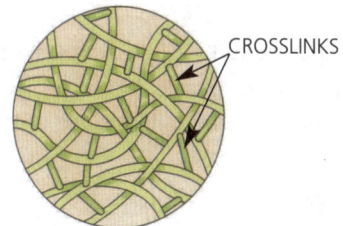

CROSSLINKS

**Fig. 3.3**

Thermosetting plastics

These undergo a chemical reaction on heating resulting in permanent crosslinking between the molecules. They cannot be softened again on heating.

## Common Thermoplastics

### Acrylic

Acrylic is commonly known by its trade name 'Perspex'. It has outstanding clarity but is more easily scratched than glass. In sheet form, it can be sawn, drilled, machined and bonded and also formed into simple shapes when heated. In granular or powder form, it can be moulded or extruded into more complex shapes. It is supplied in a wide range of colours and may be tinted or clear.

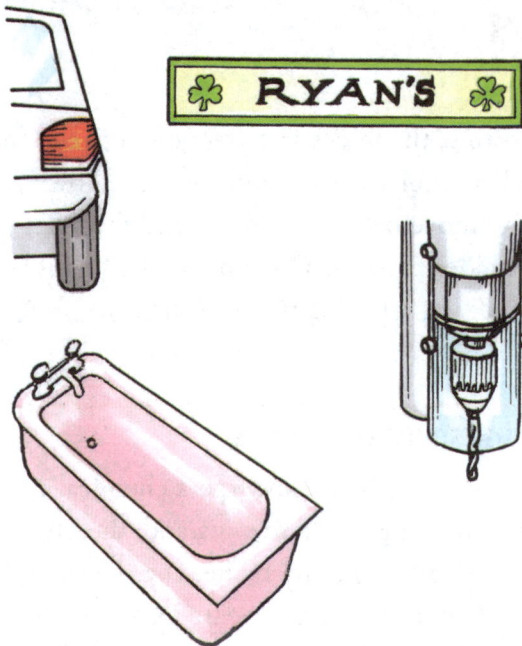

**Fig. 3.4**

**Common applications:** Rear lights lenses for cars; motorcycle windshields; machine guards; shop signs; glazing; baths; light fittings; dentures; aircraft canopies and windows; watch lenses.

### Polyethylene

This is often called polythene. It is a well-known material because of its widespread use for shopping bags and household articles. There are two basic types — low density polyethylene and high density polyethylene. Low density polyethylene is very flexible and softens at about 85°C. High density polyethylene is harder and more rigid. It has a higher softening point – about 125°C – so that articles made from it can withstand hot liquids and sterilisation in boiling waters. Polyethylene is tough, flexible and a good electrical insulator. It also has good resistance to most chemicals.

**Fig. 3.5**

**Common applications:** Bottles; bowls; baskets; basins; 'squeeze' bottles; cable insulation; pipes; film for packaging; fertilizer sacks; shop bags.

### Polypropylene

Polypropylene is a strong, tough material with good resistance to chemicals and heat and can withstand boiling water. It also has good resistance to fatigue and can be bent or flexed many times without breaking, which means that it can be formed into hinges. This enables items with hinges to be made in one piece. Like polyethylene, it is a light material and can float on water.

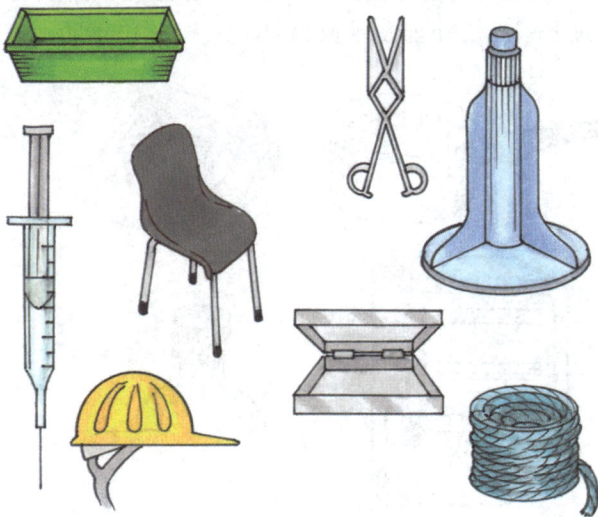

**Fig. 3.6**

**Common applications:** Stackable chair shells (as commonly used in schools); dishwasher components; washing machine agitators; hospital and laboratory ware including items needing sterilisation; containers with integral hinges; crates; toys; safety helmets; disposable cutlery; ropes; twine; fishing nets.

## Polystyrene

In its basic form, polystyrene is a clear, brittle material and can be identified by the metallic sound it makes when struck or dropped. It can be modified to improve its toughness and can also be tinted or coloured. Clarity, low cost and mouldability make polystyrene a very suitable material for display cases for cosmetics, jewellery and CDs. It also has many other applications including fluorescent light diffusers, refrigeration trays and boxes, egg boxes, toys and disposable plates.

**Fig. 3.7**
Applications of 'solid' polystyrene

**Foamed polystyrene,** which is commonly known by its trade name 'Aeroboard', is widely used as a heat insulating material in buildings and in the packaging of delicate items such as computer accessories, cameras and lenses.

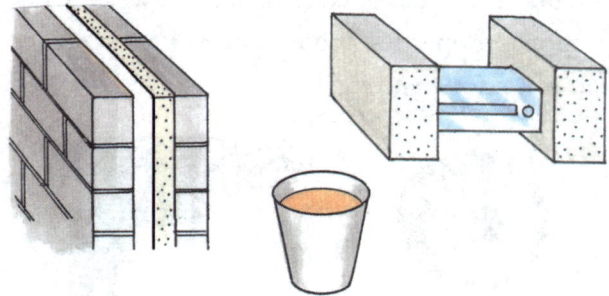

**Fig. 3.8**
Applications of 'foamed' polystyrene

## Polyvinylchloride (PVC)

This is usually called PVC. It is a tough, rigid material, but by the addition of varying amounts of other materials, called plasticisers, it can be produced in various degrees of flexibility. This greatly increases the range of applications of unplasticised PVC.

PVC has good resistance to chemicals and water and good strength. It can be produced in a great variety of colours. Unplasticised PVC is self-extinguishing.

**Fig. 3.9**
**Common applications of 'unplasticised' PVC:** Guttering; sewerage pipes; transparent bottles (such as mineral and shampoo bottles); liners for chocolate boxes.
Common applications of 'plasticised' PVC: Cable insulation; garden hoses; leathercloth for upholstery; raincoats; waterproof curtains.

## Nylon

There are various types of nylon available. They are distinguished by numbers, for example, nylon 6.6, nylon 6 and nylon 6.10. Nylon is mostly white or cream coloured, but it is available in other colours also. It has good resistance to wear, good frictional properties, good temperature resistance and it is strong and rigid.

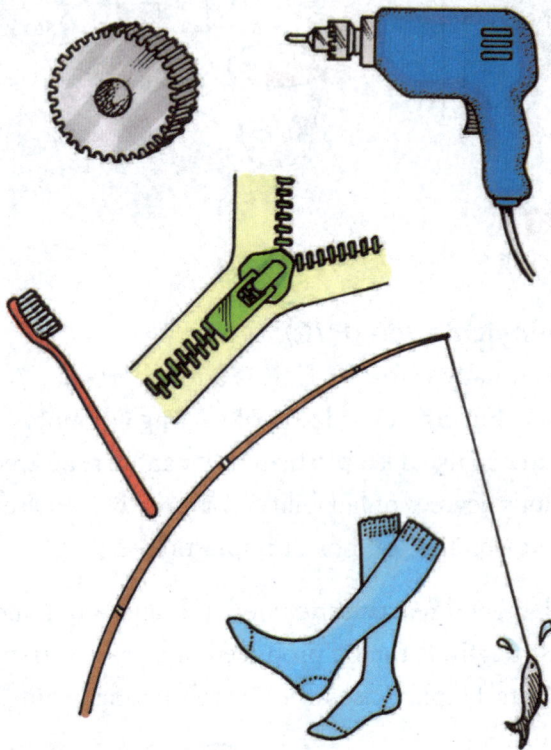

**Fig. 3.10**

**Common applications:** Bearings; gears; rollers; cams; curtain rail fittings; power tool casings; zips; bristles for brushes; fishing lines; textile fibres.

## Common Thermosetting Plastics

### Phenol Formaldehyde or Bakelite

Phenol formaldehyde was the first of the true synthetic plastics and was called 'Bakelite'. By employing different processing methods and by the use of various fillers, a range of phenolic resins is produced that has widespread applications. Phenol formaldehyde is hard and rigid, a good insulator of heat and electricity and can withstand high temperatures. It is used in dark-coloured electrical fittings, saucepan handles, ashtrays, bottle tops, brake linings and adhesives.

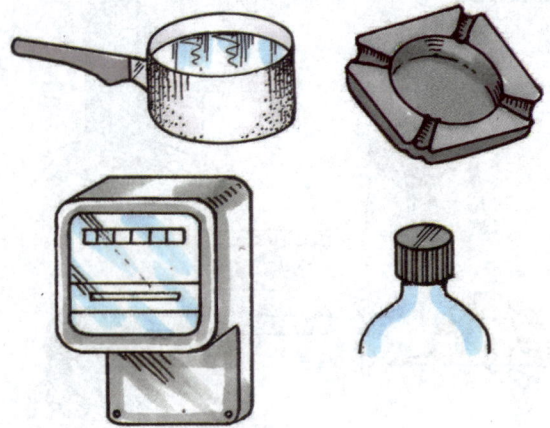

**Fig. 3.11**

Applications of phenol formaldehyde

### Urea Formaldehyde

The main properties of urea formaldehyde are strength, hardness, stiffness, brittleness and good electrical and heat resistance. It is a low-cost material that can be produced in attractive colours by adding pigments.

**Fig. 3.12**

**Common applications:** White electrical fittings such as plugs and sockets; lampshades; decorative caps and lids for bottles and other containers; buttons; as a wood adhesive in the manufacture of plywood and chipboard.

## Melamine Formaldehyde

Like urea formaldehyde, this is a strong, hard, stiff material that can be produced in a wide range of colours. It has better electrical properties, more resistance to water and more resistance to staining by tea, coffee and fruit juices than urea formaldehyde, but it is more expensive.

**Fig. 3.13**

Common applications: Tableware; laminated kitchen worktops; kitchen utensils; electrical insulation.

## Polyester Resins

Polyester plastics are often reinforced with glass fibre, which improves their strength considerably. These are often called 'fibreglass', even though the glass fibre is really the reinforcement.

Polyester resin can be set, or hardened, without external heat or pressure. This is done by adding chemicals, known as a catalyst, and an accelerator to the resin. Articles can be moulded in this way without using expensive equipment.

Great care must be taken not to mix the catalyst and the accelerator directly, because they will react violently and may even cause an explosion. Resins are often supplied pre-accelerated (with the accelerator already added), which makes them safer for school use. The hardened polyester can be transparent and may be coloured.

Do not confuse this polyester with the thermoplastic type which is often produced as a fibre (e.g. 'Terylene').

**Fig. 3.14**

**Common applications of 'reinforced' polyester:** Boats; lorry cabs; trays; storage tanks; garden pools.

**Common applications of 'unreinforced' polyester:** Ornamental castings, buttons; floorings; car body repair kits.

## Polyurethanes

Polyurethanes are available as flexible foams, rigid foams, structural foams, elastomers and surface coatings. Flexible foams are soft and spongy. Rigid foams are very good heat insulators. Structural foams are strong and rigid. Elastomers are resilient and have good resistance to wear. Surface coatings are hard and tough and have good resistance to scratching.

**Fig. 3.15**

**Common applications:** Flexible foams for upholstery and foam backings on fabrics; rigid foams for insulation in buildings and refrigerators; structural foams for furniture manufacture; elastomers for shoe soles; surface coatings for wood (varnishes and paints); adhesives for joining metals, wood and glass. Polyurethanes in various forms are used for car parts, such as seats, facias, steering wheels, panels and bumpers.

## Identification of Plastics

The tests described in the following tables are simple ones that are easily carried out. Although many plastics can be identified by these tests, it would require very specialised testing to positively identify every kind of plastic. It should be remembered that the presence of fillers, pigments or other additives can considerably alter the appearance and properties of plastics.

Special care must be observed when testing plastics, and all testing should be done under controlled conditions. If samples are being cut from bottles or other containers, they must first be thoroughly washed and dried in case they contain any residue of a dangerous substance. Some plastics give off irritating fumes, and thermoplastics can melt and drip burning molten material.

### Tests for Plastics: Identification and Properties

| Type of Plastics | Appearance<br><br>Is it transparent, translucent or opaque? Is it coloured? | Stiffness<br><br>Try bending a sample | Try cutting a sample with a knife | Drop a sample in water<br>Does it float? | Heat a sample | Try burning a small piece |
|---|---|---|---|---|---|---|
| Acrylic | Can be crystal clear; may be opaque if pigments have been added | | Splinters | | Heat | Frothing |
| Polyethylene (Polythene) | Transparent in thin film<br>Translucent in thicker sections | low density<br>high density | | | Heat | Drips<br>Burns with difficulty |
| Polyvinylchloride (PVC) | Transparent unless fillers or pigments have been added | Plasticised<br>Unplasticised | | | Heat | Self extinguishing<br>Softens and chars |
| Nylon | Opaque, except as thin film | | | | Heat | Melts to a free flowing liquid |
| Polystyrene | Transparent unless pigments have been added | Toughened | Toughened<br>Foamed crumbles | Foamed | Heat | Dark smoke bubbles at edge |
| Phenolic | Black or brown | | Splinters | | Heat | Swells and cracks |

When burning a sample, the following precautions should be taken:

- Use only a small piece of the material.
- Hold it with a gas pliers or tongs and wear protective gloves.
- Hold it over a non-flammable surface.
- Do not inhale the fumes because they can be poisonous. Ensure that there is good ventilation.

## Working with Acrylic Sheet

Acrylic sheet can be sawn, filed, drilled, tapped, polished, bonded and hot formed in the school workshop. Sheets are available in different thicknesses and in a range of colours or clear. The protective paper covering on the sheet should be left in place for as long as possible to reduce the risk of scratching the surface. Marking out, sawing, drilling and tapping can be carried out without removing the paper. Damage by vice jaws can be prevented by the use of fibre clamps or pieces of softwood. Acrylic is brittle in its cold state and easily cracked or shattered if not worked with care. Overheating and softening must be avoided during sawing and drilling operations.

### Sawing

A hacksaw or fine tenon saw can be used to cut acrylic. Curves and intricate shapes can be cut with a coping saw, fret saw or tension file. The work must be held close to the cutting line and light pressure applied to prevent chipping and fracture. Do not use a hacksaw blade with missing teeth because this can also cause fracture of the sheet.

### Filing

Double cut files work quite well on acrylic. Keep the work as low as possible in the vice.

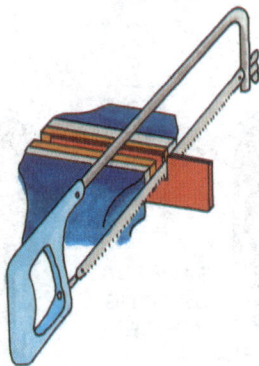

**Fig. 3.17**
When filing acrylic sheet hold it low in vice

### Drilling

Standard twist drills can be used, but the point angle should be reground to about 140°. Water can be used as a coolant. The work must be held securely and firmly supported. Use high speeds and light feeds. Do not drill through metal and acrylic held together. The drill bit could heat up going through the metal and melt the acrylic. Also, allow drills that have been used on metal to cool down before using them on acrylic.

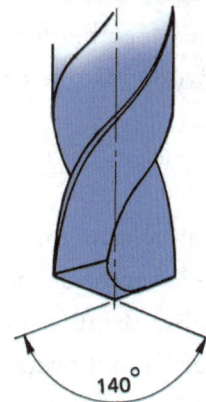

**Fig. 3.16**
Hold work so that the cut is close to vice to avoid flexing and fracture

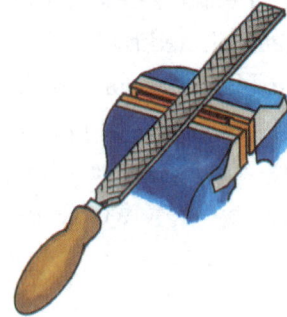

140°

**Fig. 3.18**
Drill point angle modified for acrylic

## Tapping

Coarse threads are the most suitable type for acrylic. If tapping near an edge, care must be taken to avoid fracture. Lard oil can be used as a cutting fluid.

## Polishing

A filed surface can be polished to a high degree. File marks are first removed by using progressively finer grades of emery cloth and 'wet and dry paper'. The surface can then be polished by hand or on a polishing machine. Hand-polishing is done by using a soft cloth with a special acrylic polish (or a metal polish). To prevent accidents, a polishing machine should only be used by those with experience.

## Bonding

Acrylic can be bonded using the following:
- Special acrylic cements such as 'Tensol'.
- Suitable adhesives.

Cements contain acrylic and some will fill small gaps between surfaces very well. They generally produce strong joints.

Adhesives are useful for joining acrylic to other materials. An adhesive that suits both materials must be used. Surfaces to be bonded must be clean and dry. Polished surfaces should be lightly roughened to improve their wetting properties. Apply the bonding agent to both surfaces and keep the parts pressed together for some time. Do not forget that the work must be carried out in a well-ventilated area.

## Hot Forming

Acrylic, being a thermoplastic material, will soften when heated and can then be shaped. It will retain this shape when cooled. Bending and pressing operations can be carried out using simple equipment. The acrylic sheet must be heated to about 160°C. Overheating will damage it. When

formed, it should be allowed to cool slowly to avoid distortion. Gloves or a tongs must be used to grip the hot acrylic, and care must be taken not to mark its surface.

## Bending

Unless a wide bend is required, it is better just to heat the section of the sheet where the bend is to be. This can be done using an electric strip heater. The sheet should be turned over at regular intervals to give even heating.

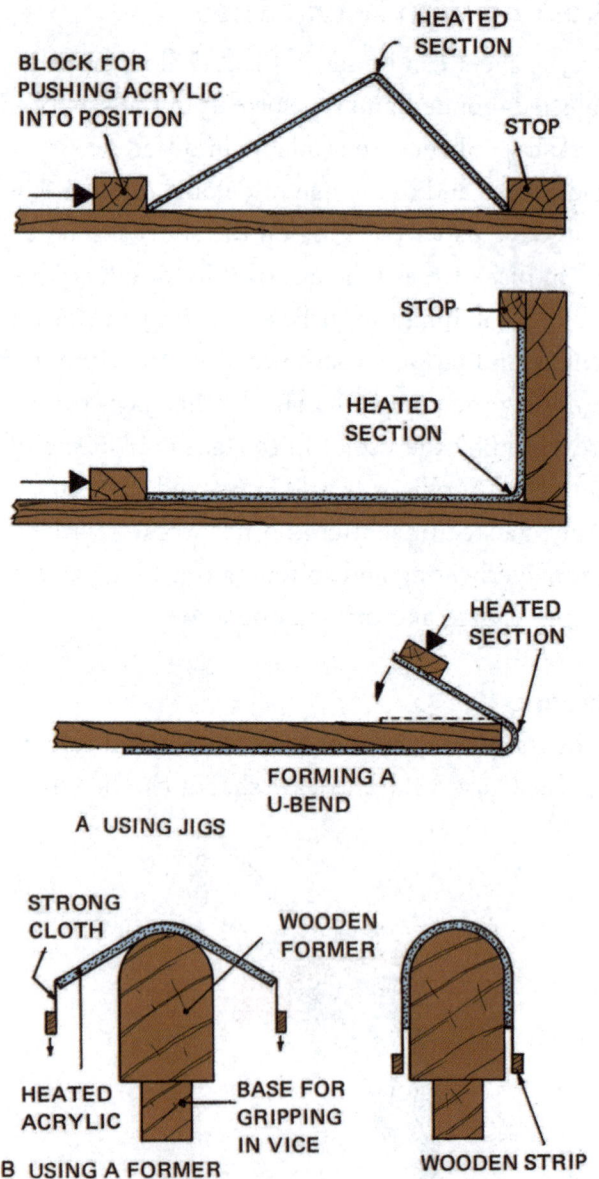

**Fig. 3.19**
Bending

If making a wide bend on a former, Fig. 3.19(B), it may be better to heat the whole sheet.

Bending jigs and formers, Fig. 3.19, can be made from wood. The surfaces of wooden jigs and formers should be smoothly finished to avoid marking the acrylic. When using a former, a piece of strong cloth can be used to bend the sheet around it. Two strips of wood, inserted into folds at the ends of the cloth, will provide a good grip.

## Pressing

Bowl and tray shapes can be produced by simple pressing techniques. One method is to place the heated sheet between matching moulds and to press them together, Fig. 3.20(A). Another method is to clamp the heated sheet over a hole in a jig, and press its central portion into the hole, Fig. 3.20(B).

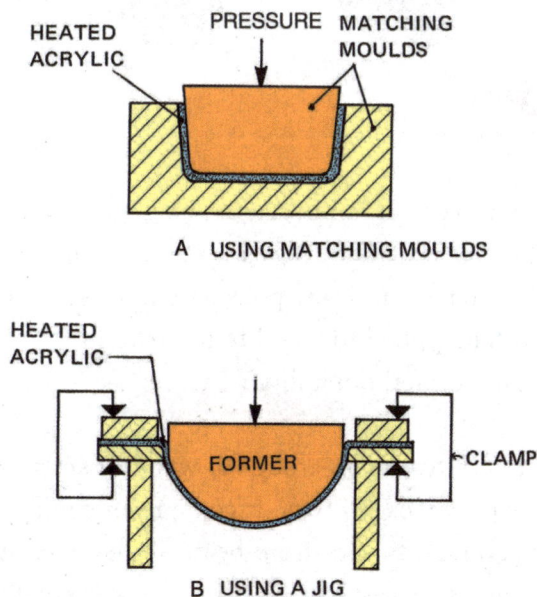

A   USING MATCHING MOULDS

B   USING A JIG

**Fig. 3.20**
Press forming

## Casting Polyester Resin

In this work, articles are formed by pouring prepared liquid resins into suitably shaped moulds and allowing them to set. Polyester resins are available in a pre-accelerated, or pre-activated, state and only require the addition of a catalyst to set, or 'cure', them. Moulds can be made from various materials. A casting can be coloured by adding a pigment to the resin. Objects such as shells, leaves, pieces of metal, plastics and wood can be embedded or encapsulated in the resin. Some objects such as flowers and insects must be specially treated before encapsulation.

There are different types of polyester resins available and manufacturers' instructions should always be followed when using them. The general procedures are as follows:

### Casting
1.  Coat the mould with a release agent to prevent the resin sticking to it.
2.  Measure out the required amount of pre-accelerated resin.
3.  Add the recommended amount of catalyst and stir well.
4.  Mix in pigment if required and allow bubbles to rise to the surface.
5.  Pour the mixture into the mould.
6.  When the casting has reached the gel stage (has become jelly-like), remove it from the mould, if possible. Place it on a polyethylene sheet to harden fully.

### Encapsulation
1.  Prepare sufficient resin to fill the mould to a depth of about 5mm.
2.  Allow this layer to gel.
3.  Place the object on this layer.
4.  Prepare the extra resin required and pour it into the mould, taking care not to disturb the object.
5.  Allow to harden as before.

## Precautions

If ever using a catalyst and accelerator, do not forget to keep them apart. Wear rubber gloves or use barrier cream to protect your hands. Work in a well-ventilated area.

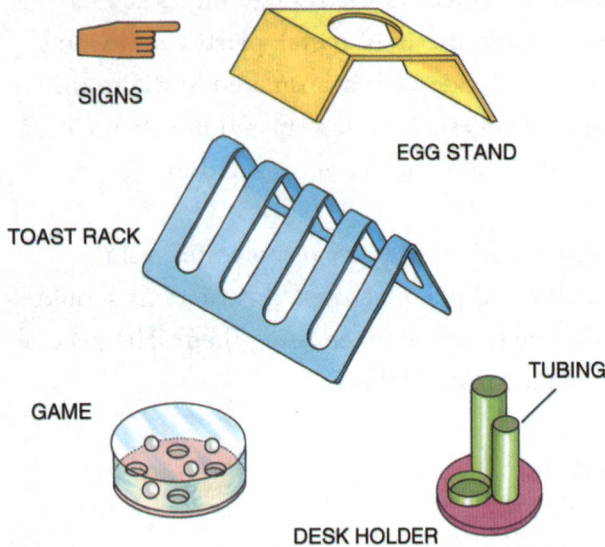

SIGNS

EGG STAND

TOAST RACK

TUBING

GAME

DESK HOLDER

**Fig. 3.21**
Projects in acrylic

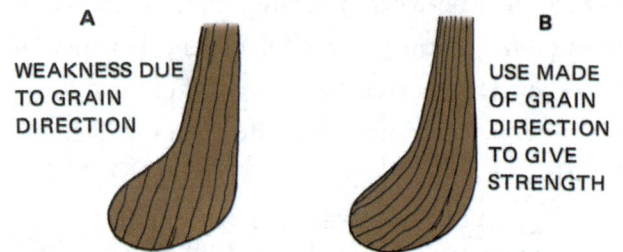

COPPER TUBE

DRILLED HOLES

ENCAPSULATION CANDLE HOLDER

PENCIL HOLDER

**Fig. 3.22**
Projects in cast resin

## Wood

Wood is widely used as a structural and finishing material. Its mechanical properties vary according to type, but, generally, wood has good resilience and shock resistance. The grain direction has a great effect on its strength. Wood is much stronger in compression and tension in the direction of the grain than across it. Also, wood has far greater resistance to shearing across the grain than along it. Wood has a relatively low specific gravity, it has good resistance to the flow of heat and electricity, and some varieties are very attractive. It is easily cut and shaped, provided sharp cutting tools are used.

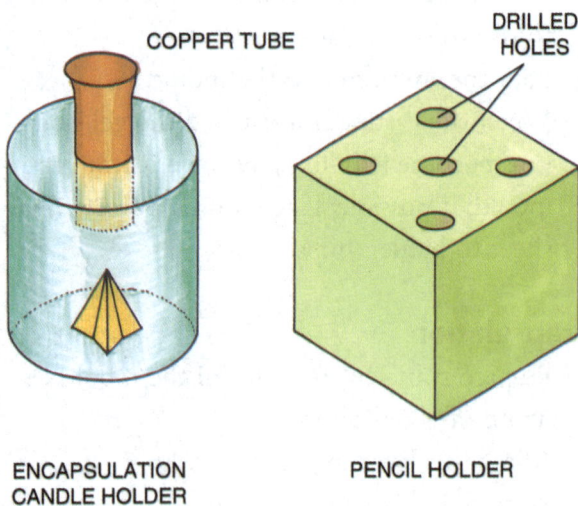

A

WEAKNESS DUE TO GRAIN DIRECTION

B

USE MADE OF GRAIN DIRECTION TO GIVE STRENGTH

**Fig. 3.23**
Effect of grain direction

Various types of joints, screws, nails, glues and metal and plastics fittings are used to join wood. Paints, stains, varnishes, polishes and preservatives are often applied to wood to improve its appearance and durability.

There are two main groups of wood — softwoods and hardwoods. Softwoods come from coniferous trees and hardwoods from broad-leafed ones. As the names suggest, the hardwoods are generally harder than the softwoods.

As well as being used in its natural form, wood may also be processed to form boards such as plywood, chipboard and blockboard.

Veneers are thin sheets of wood which are cut from logs. They are used for manufactured boards and for covering less attractive woods.

## Common Softwoods

- **Red deal** is tough and durable, easily worked and yellowish in colour. It is used for general joinery, telegraph poles and railway sleepers.

- **White deal** is lighter in colour and less durable than red deal. It is relatively cheap and is used for general joinery.

- **Parana pine** is light brown, often with streaks of pink. It is reasonably hard but easily split. Parana pine is used for ceilings, architraves (the surrounds of doors and windows), skirting boards and stairs.

- **Red cedar** is light and durable and reddish-brown in colour. It is used for windows, doors and panels. In Canada, it is used for building wooden houses.

- **Larch** has good resistance to decay and is used for outdoor articles such as boats, fences and garden seats.

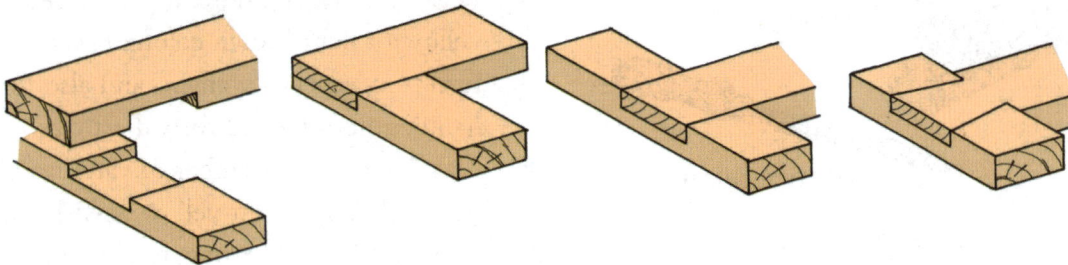

HALVING JOINTS

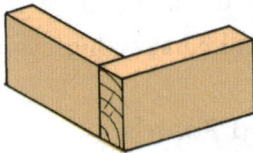

BUTT JOINT

MITRE JOINT

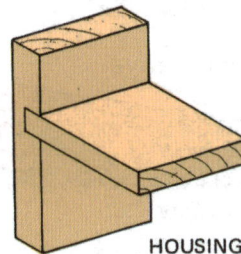

HOUSING JOINT

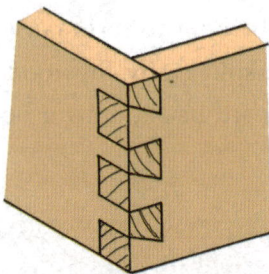

DOVETAIL JOINT

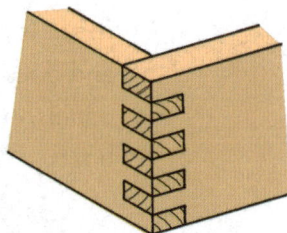

FINGER JOINT

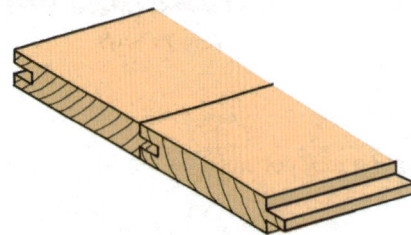

TONGUE AND GROOVE JOINT

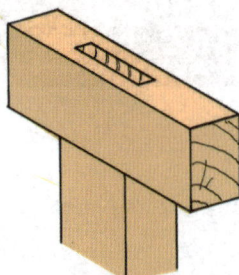

MORTICE AND TENON JOINT

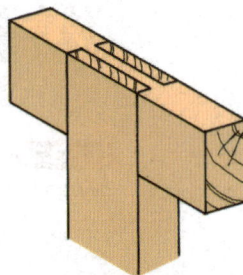

BRIDLE JOINT

DOWEL JOINT

**Fig. 3.24**
Woodwork joints

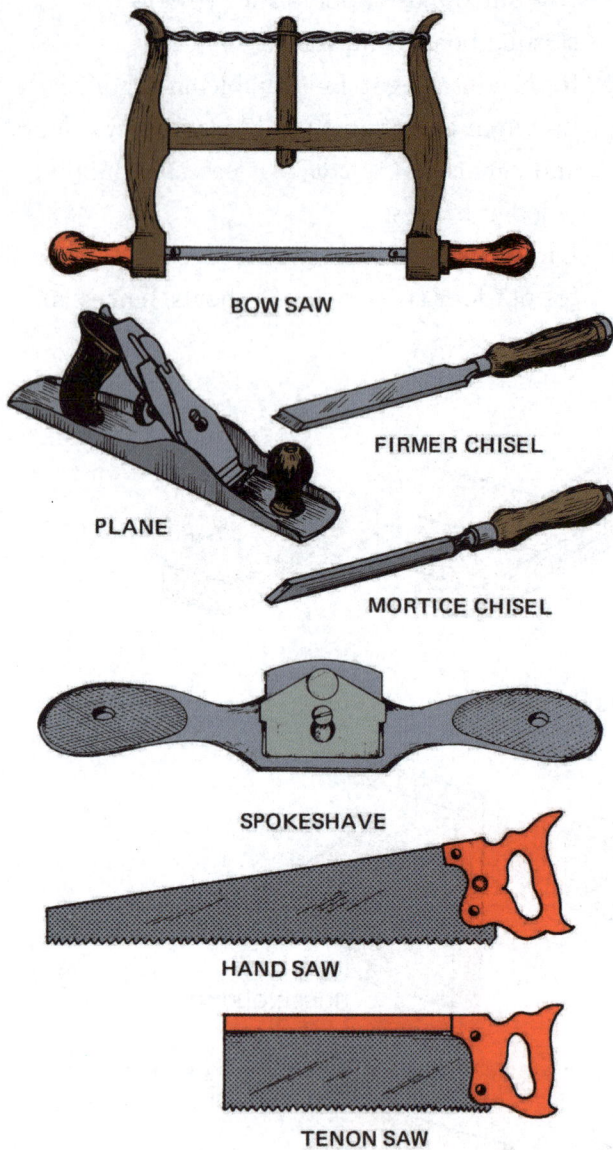

**Fig. 3.25**
Common cutting tools for wood

## Common Hardwoods

- **Mahogany** There are a number of varieties of mahogany. It has a rich, red colour and is hard and strong. Mahogany is used for furniture and high-class joinery and as a veneer for chipboard and plywood.

- **Teak** is golden brown in colour. It is hard, strong and durable, but difficult to work. Teak is used for external doors and windows, ship building and science laboratory benches.

- **Beech** is hard and durable with a reddish-yellow or light brown colour. It is used for furniture, especially chairs, and also for tool handles, flooring and turned articles.

- **Oak** There are a number of varieties of oak with colours of light yellow, light brown and brown. It is hard, strong, tough and durable and has a wide range of uses, including furniture, panelling and veneers.

- **Ash** is very resilient and tough; it is widely used for tool handles, hurleys and oars.

## Manufactured Boards

- **Plywood** is made by gluing an odd number of veneer, each at right angles to the grain of the one next to it. Plywood has greater and more uniform strength than wood in its natural form. It can be bent to form curved shapes and does not split easily. Plywood is used for panels, cupboard backs, drawer bottoms and boats.

**Fig. 3.26**
Plywood

- **Blockboard** is made up of strips of wood glued together and covered with a veneer on each side. It is used for cupboards, shelves, table tops and small doors.

**Fig. 3.27**
Blockboard

- **Chipboard** is made by gluing and compressing chips of wood. It is sometimes faced with a veneer or plastics. Chipboard is cheap but difficult to join and does not take screws well. It is used for table tops, cupboards, shelves, panels, floors and under roofing.
- **Hardboard** is made in thin sheets and is cheap. It is available plain or with various decorative finishes. Pegboard is a type of hardboard which has holes in it. Hardboard is used for cupboard backs, drawer bottoms, door panels and shop fittings.

## Exercises

1. Explain, in simple terms, the difference between thermoplastics and thermosetting plastics.
2. Give four examples of the use of plastics in each of the following cases:
   (a) in the home (b) in agriculture (c) in the construction industry
   (d) in sport and leisure.
3. Copy the table below into your copybook. Complete the table listing two properties and two applications for each type of plastic.

| Plastic Name | Properties | Applications |
|---|---|---|
| Acrylic | | |
| Polyethylene | | |
| Polyvinylchloride | | |
| Nylon | | |
| Phenol formaldehyde | | |
| Urea formaldehyde | | |
| Melamine formaldehyde | | |
| Polyester | | |
| Polyurethane | | |

4. Describe briefly five simple tests that could be carried out in the school workshop for identifying common plastics.

5. What is the purpose of the paper covering on acrylic sheets?

6. Name two types of saw that can be used to cut acrylic.

7. What precautions should be taken when sawing or filing acrylic sheets?

8. List three precautions to be observed when drilling acrylic sheets.

9. Describe how you would polish a filed acrylic edge.

10. Name two methods of bonding acrylic.

11. Explain, with the aid of a sketch, how you would make a right-angled bend in a strip of acrylic.

12. Describe, with the aid of a sketch, how you would make a small bowl from acrylic sheet.

13. Describe how you would make a cast polyester paper weight with a small object encapsulated in it.

Fig. 3.28

14. Explain how the grain direction affects the strength of wood.

15. Redraw the table below in your copybook. Complete the table listing one important property and two applications for each type of softwood.

| Softwood | Property | Applications |
|---|---|---|
| Red deal | | |
| White deal | | |
| Parana pine | | |
| Red cedar | | |
| Larch | | |

16. Redraw the table below in your copybook and give one important property and two applications for each type of hardwood.

| Hardwood | Property | Applications |
|---|---|---|
| Mahogany | | |
| Teak | | |
| Beech | | |
| Oak | | |
| Ash | | |

17. Copy the table below into your copybook and state one important property and two applications for each type of manufactured board listed.

| Manufactured board | Property | Applications |
|---|---|---|
| Plywood | | |
| Blockboard | | |
| Chipboard | | |
| Hardboard | | |

18. List four types of coating applied to wood.
19. Sketch and name four types of woodwork joint.
20. Sketch and name four cutting tools used for wood.

# Safety

## 4

Every accident has a cause, but with care and foresight, many can be avoided. The following are some of the precautions that must be observed in the school workshop.

## Clothes

Do not wear loose clothing (e.g. ties that may hang out or long, loose sleeves) that can easily get caught in machines and draw the operator in with them.

**Fig. 4.1**
Loose clothing can easily get caught in machines

## Hair

Long hair can easily get caught in a machine, especially in the drilling machine. It should be tied or clipped back and held securely in place.

**Fig. 4.2**
Long hair can get caught in a machine. If hair is long, it must be tied back. Never use a drilling machine without its guard.

## Shoes

Wear shoes with strong toe caps and strong soles, in case anything falls on your toes or in case you step on sharp or hot objects. Sandals and trainers are not suitable for the workshop.

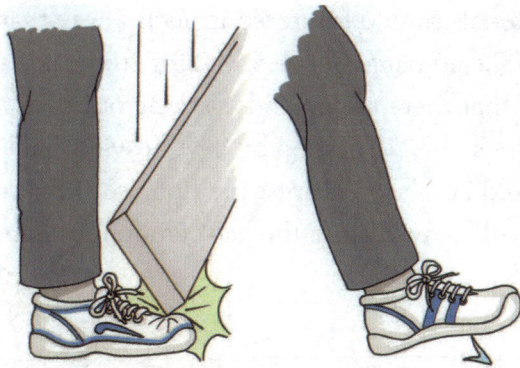

**Fig. 4.3**
Wear suitable shoes in the workshop

## Hand Tools

Never use a file with a loose handle or a hammer with a loose head. Use spanners and wrenches that are a good fit on nuts, bolts and other objects. Do not hold articles in the palm of your hand when using a screwdriver. Avoid using chisels or punches with 'mushroomed' heads as splinters may fly from them. They should be brought to the notice of the teacher to have their heads ground back and made safe.

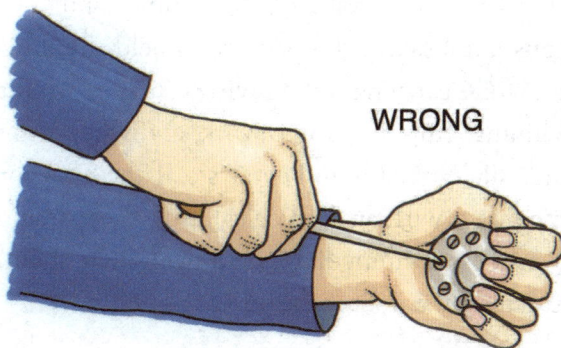

WRONG

**Fig. 4.4**
Do not hold an article in your hand when using a screwdriver on it

## Bench

Keep the bench neat and tidy with the tools laid out in an orderly fashion.

## Floor

Do not leave things that may get in the way on the floor. If oil, water or any liquid gets spilled on the floor, it must be cleaned up immediately. These simple precautions could prevent a bad fall.

OW!

**Fig. 4.5**
Keep floor free of obstruction

## Behaviour

Inappropriate behaviour in a workshop can lead to serious accidents. The workshop is no place for messing about, shouting or any behaviour that could distract another person at work, especially while operating a machine.

## Operating Machines

Never use a machine until you have been given permission to do so and until you have been shown how to operate it. The first thing to find out about a machine is the quickest way of stopping it. This should be practised at the beginning, so that you will be able to do it immediately in an emergency. Do not switch on machines between classes or at any time the teacher is not present. There should be only one student to each machine to avoid distraction or interference with controls. Never leave the key in the chuck of the lathe or drilling machine. Ensure that the work is firmly held before starting a machine.

## Machine Guards

Never use a machine without its guard in place; do not remove the guard from a machine.

## Cleaning Machine

Keep machines and the area around them neat and tidy, but never clean down a machine while it is in operation. A cleaning cloth is especially dangerous near moving machinery, because it could get wrapped around a revolving shaft so fast that you might not have time to free your fingers from it. The swarf from machines can be very sharp and sometimes very hot; don't ever touch it with your bare hands!

## Storage and Handling of Metals

Beware of sharp and jagged edges, especially on metal parts that have been cut with a shears. Wear protective gloves when handling sheets and bars. If the materials you are about to work on have any burrs, file them off.

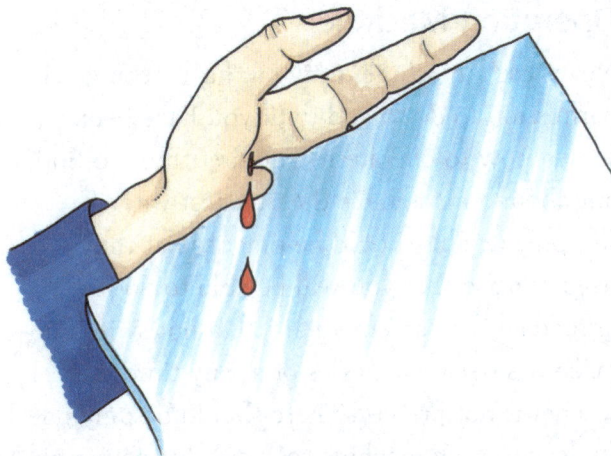

**Fig. 4.6**
Beware of sharp and jagged edges

Materials should be stored in such a way that there is no danger of them falling from the rack and that there are no ends sticking out that could injure someone passing by. The heaviest bars should be placed nearest the floor, so that if one falls off, it will cause the least amount of damage.

**Fig. 4.7**
Do not leave bars sticking out from racks

## Eye Protection

Eyes must be protected from dust, grit, flying objects (such as metal particles), fumes and various liquids. Goggles or a face shield should be worn while carrying out activities such as grinding, machining, chipping, forge work, and when using liquids such as acids and catalysts. If the eyes come into contact with an acid or catalyst, they should be washed out immediately. An eye injury should be treated by a doctor as soon as possible.

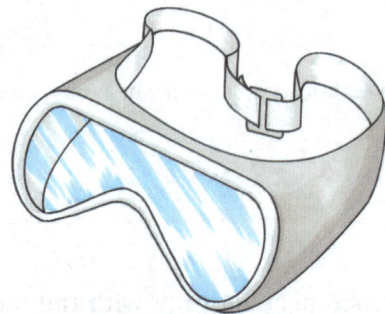

**Fig. 4.8**
Wear eye protection as required

## Skin Hazards

The skin must be protected when using resins, acids, catalysts, solvents and oil. Barrier cream, protective gloves and face shields should be worn as required. If any dangerous substance gets on the skin, it should be washed off immediately.

**Fig. 4.9**
Wear protective gloves and a face shield as required

## Dust and Fumes

Dust is produced when sanding or grinding and during the machining of cast iron and some plastics. Fumes may be produced during the heating of materials, when working with plastics and by the use of paints, sprays, aerosols and solvents. Operations where dust or fumes are produced should be carried out only in well-ventilated areas. An adequate amount of fresh air must be continually supplied. Fans are often required and you must ensure that they are switched on. Opening windows and doors also improves ventilation, and suitable respiratory masks should also be worn.

## Electricity

Do not tamper with or attempt to repair any electrical equipment. If you notice any loose or bare cables, inform the teacher immediately.

## Hygiene

Always wash your hands after finishing work and before handling food.

## Heating of Materials

It is often necessary to heat materials in the workshop, for instance, when soldering, brazing, welding, forging, heat treating and when bending acrylic sheets. Care must be taken with the heating apparatus, the tools and the hot materials.

- Do not attempt to operate a heating apparatus until you have been shown by your teacher how to use it and have been given permission to do so.
- If you are using a gas appliance, make sure it has not been left turned on without being lit. If it has, make no attempt to light it. Do not allow any flame or spark near the area. The appliance must be switched off and the place well ventilated before it is safe to use it.
- If you ever become aware of gas escaping, inform the teacher immediately. Never use a flame to check for gas leaks.
- When lighting a gas torch, always face it away from you and use a spark lighter.

**Fig. 4.10**
Make no attempt to light a gas appliance that has been left turned on

When lighting a gas torch always face it away from you

Fig. 4.12
Make sure you do not touch anyone with a hot piece of metal

Fig. 4.13
Never pick up a piece of metal without being sure it is cold

- There should be only one person at a time using the anvil. The metal must be securely gripped to prevent it flying off and hitting someone.
- Make sure you do not touch anyone with a hot piece of metal when taking it from one place to another.
- You could get a serious burn from a hot piece of metal without it being red. **Never** pick up a piece of metal without being sure it is cold. Do not leave any hot piece of metal lying about in case someone else picks it up.
- Make sure all tools are cooled before storing them.
- Beware of the steam that rises from hot metals being cooled in water. Special care must be taken when cooling a hot pipe, as a jet of steam may shoot out of it. **Always** face its end away from you.

Fig. 4.14
Beware of steam rising from metals being cooled

- When using oil for heat treatment, use a suitable kind that does not ignite easily. Make sure that all of the heated portion of the article is immersed. Use a container with an airtight lid. If the oil does catch fire, put on the lid to cut off the air supply to the fire, thus quenching the fire.

- If a hollow airtight object is heated, it may explode. This could happen when soldering or brazing a hollow handle onto some article. In such a case, a small hole must be drilled in the handle to allow the air to escape. The danger would be far greater if an airtight object containing moisture was heated.

- Goggles, face shields, leather aprons and leather gloves give good protection when working with hot materials and should be worn as required.

## Fire Hazards

Special precautions are necessary in the school workshop to prevent fires. Pupils must also be aware of the safety measures to be taken in the event of a fire. The following are some general points to be observed:

1. Any operation involving the heating of materials must be carried out in safe, specially designated areas, free of combustible materials and with adequate quenching facilities available.

2. Make sure you are aware of the safety precautions to be taken when using any heating appliance.

3. Do not carry out any work with plastics until you have received proper instructions and are familiar with any safety precautions to be observed.

4. Catalysts and accelerators must never be mixed directly as they react violently; they may even cause an explosion. For this reason, it is safer to use pre-accelerated polyester resin.

5. Catalysts and accelerators must be stored separately, in metal cupboards if possible, away from any source of heat. They should not be left in sunlight.

6. Any left-over catalysed resin should be spread out to prevent a high rise in temperature. A resin spillage should be covered with sand and removed to the open.

7. Do not use a rag to clean up different substances, as mixing of a catalyst and an accelerator may occur; this could start a fire.

8. Make sure you leave your workplace safe after you, with all heating appliances turned off, any heated material cooled and no combustible waste, especially oily rags, left lying around.

9. Make sure you know what to do if a fire does break out. Strictly follow the procedures and instructions given during evacuation drills and practices. Familiarise yourself with the contents of fire instruction notices. The building must be evacuated quickly, but in a calm and orderly manner. Panic and disorder can be more disastrous than the fire itself.

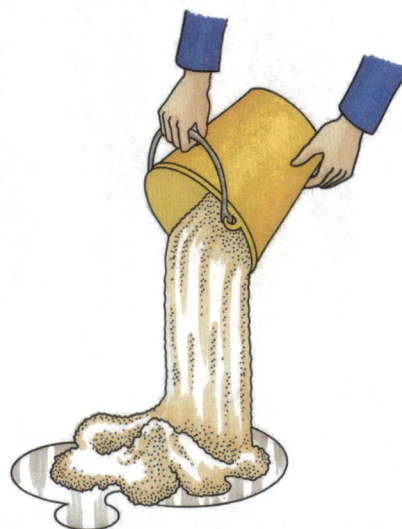

**Fig. 4.15**
A resin spillage should be covered with sand

ASSEMBLY POINT

**Fig. 4.17**
Know what to do in the event of fire

## Exercises

1. List four safety precautions to be observed as regards the clothing and shoes worn in the workshop.
2. State five safety precautions that should be taken when using hand tools.
3. List five safety precautions that should be taken when using the drilling machine.
4. List five safety precautions that should be taken when using the lathe.
5. Give five safety precautions that should be taken when storing and handling metals.
6. List five ways in which an eye accident could happen in the workshop and in each case state how the accident could be prevented.
7. Give six safety precautions to be taken when heating materials and working with hot materials.
8. State six precautions that must be observed in the school workshop for the prevention of fires and fire-related accidents.

# Marking Out and Measuring

## Marking Out

Marking out involves the drawing of lines on a blank piece of material to indicate the outline of a component. The marking out must be clear and accurate in order to produce accurate work. Bright, mild steel surfaces can be coated with a solution of copper sulfate or marking fluid to show up the scribed lines distinctly. A hard pencil or brass scriber is used for marking out on ornamental metals, such as brass, copper, tinplate and aluminium, to avoid scratching their surfaces.

Marking out is done from points, datum lines and datum edges or surfaces.

## The Scriber

The scriber is used for drawing lines on metal. It is made of high carbon steel. The points are hardened and tempered and ground to an angle of 30°. There are different types of scriber available. They can be single-pointed, Fig. 5.1 A, or double-pointed, Fig. 5.1 B, and can be made in one solid piece or have detachable points. The bent point on the double-pointed scriber is used in places which are inaccessible to a straight point. The body of the scriber is knurled to provide a good grip.

When using a scriber, you should tilt it at an angle to the straight edge, Fig. 5.2, to avoid inaccuracies. The scriber should not be used as a lever or as a punch, because the point can be easily damaged.

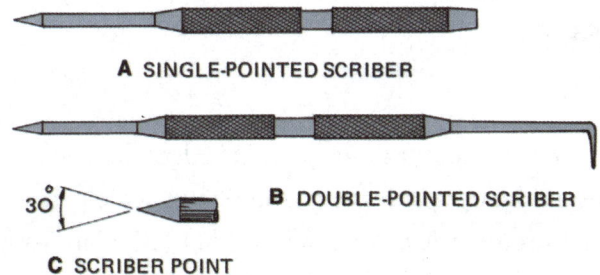

**A SINGLE-POINTED SCRIBER**

**B DOUBLE-POINTED SCRIBER**

30°

**C SCRIBER POINT**

**Fig. 5.1**
The scriber

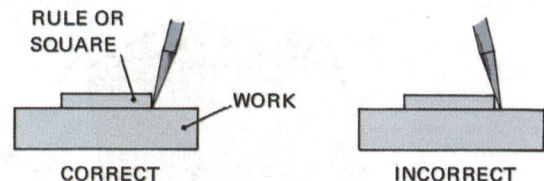

RULE OR SQUARE

WORK

CORRECT

INCORRECT

**Fig. 5.2**
Using the scriber

## The Rule

Engineer's rules are available in various lengths, but the most common types used are 150mm and 300mm. They are graduated in 10mm, 1mm and 0·5mm units. To avoid inaccuracies, the rule should be used on its edge whenever possible, Fig. 5.4 (A).

**Fig. 5.3**
Engineer's rule

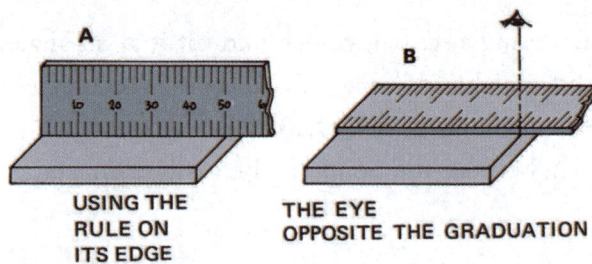

**Fig. 5.4**
Using the rule

If the rule cannot be used on its edge, the eye should be opposite the graduation at which the measurement is being read, Fig. 5.4 (B). Care must be taken not to damage the edges of the rule, as measuring is often done from its end and it is also often used as a straight edge.

**Fig. 5.5**
The tape rule is used for long measurements

## The Engineer's Try Square

The try square is made up of two parts, a stock and a blade, which are at right angles to each other.

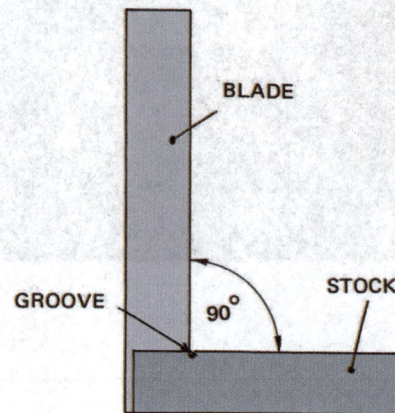

**Fig. 5.6**
The try square

The two parts are usually made separately and are held together with rivets. The blade is hardened and tempered. A small groove is cut in the stock at the inner corner to avoid errors due to burred edges. When using the try square, the stock must be pressed firmly against the edge on which it is being used. Typical uses are shown in Fig. 5.7:

**(a)** The drawing of a line at right angles to a straight edge.

**(b)** Checking a right angle with the inside of the square.

**(c)** Checking with the outside of the square.

**(d)** Using the blade as a straight edge.

**(e)** Setting a line on the end of a round bar perpendicular to a surface.

Care must be taken to maintain the accuracy of a try square. Do not strike objects with the stock, do not drop it and store it safely when it is not in use. Fig. 5.8 shows a method of testing the accuracy of a try square. Hold the stock against a straight edge of a piece of material and scribe a line along the blade. Reverse the square and draw another line. If both lines do not coincide, the square is not accurate.

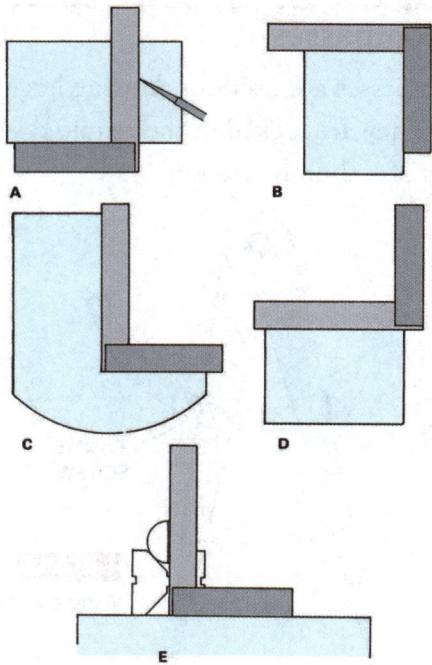

**Fig. 5.7**
Uses of a try square

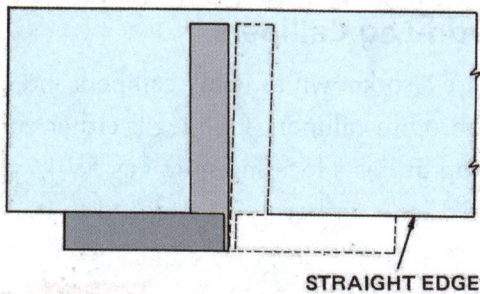

STRAIGHT EDGE

**Fig. 5.8**
Checking the accuracy of the try square

## The Centre Punch

The centre punch is used for making light indentations on lines to make them more noticeable, enabling them to be redrawn should they become obliterated. It is also used to make location marks for the point of the dividers and to mark the positions of the hole centres before drilling. The centre punch should be tilted at an angle to position the point accurately, Fig. 5.10, and then brought upright before being struck. Centre punches are mostly made from high carbon steel. The points are hardened and tempered and

ground to angles of 60° or 90°. Round ones are knurled to provide a firm grip.

Sometimes separate punches are used to mark, or 'dot', lines and to mark the positions of hole centres. In this case, the one used for making dots on a line is called a dot punch and the other a centre punch. The point of the centre punch is then ground to 90° and the dot punch to 60°. The centre punch is also heavier than the dot punch.

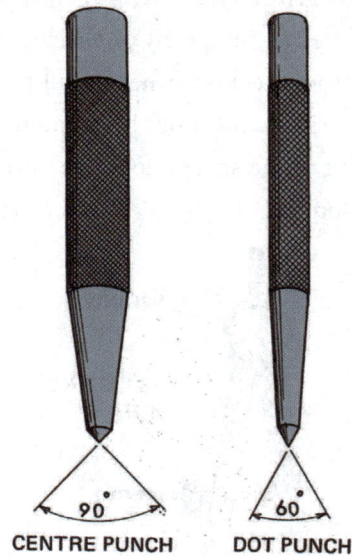

CENTRE PUNCH    DOT PUNCH

**Fig. 5.9**
Punches

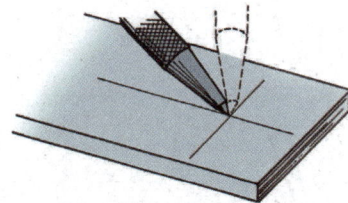

**Fig. 5.10**
Tilt the centre punch to accurately locate its point

45

## The Dividers

The dividers are used for drawing circles and arcs on metal, for transferring measurements and for carrying out geometrical constructions on metal. The dividers can be accurately set by adjusting the opening until the points fit into the required graduations on the rule, Fig. 5.12. There are two types — the spring type and a firm joint type. The spring type is the one most widely used. The size of the dividers is given by the length from the centre of the roller to the point of the leg. The legs are made from tool steel with hardened points. The points are brittle and must be treated with care. If they have to be sharpened, they must be kept the same length.

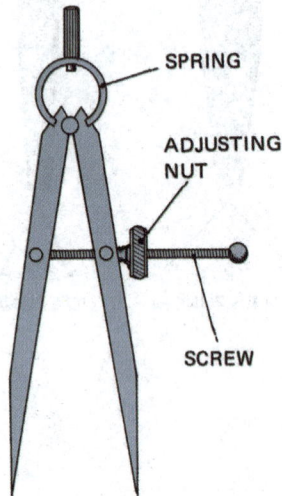

SPRING

ADJUSTING NUT

SCREW

**Fig. 5.11**
Spring dividers

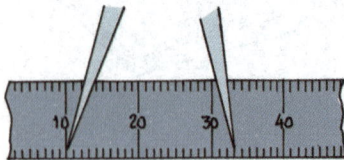

10  20  30  40

**Fig. 5.12**
Setting the dividers on the rule

## Wing Compasses

Wing compasses are used for drawing large circles and arcs. They are locked at the required setting by means of a thumb screw.

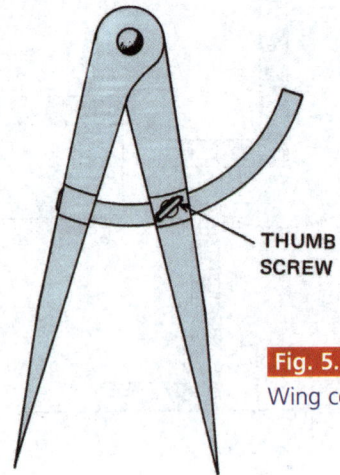

THUMB SCREW

**Fig. 5.13**
Wing compasses

## The Odd-Leg Callipers

These are also known as jenny callipers and as hermaphrodite callipers. One leg is either curved at the top or has a locating spur, Fig. 5.14, while the other has a scriber point attached to it.

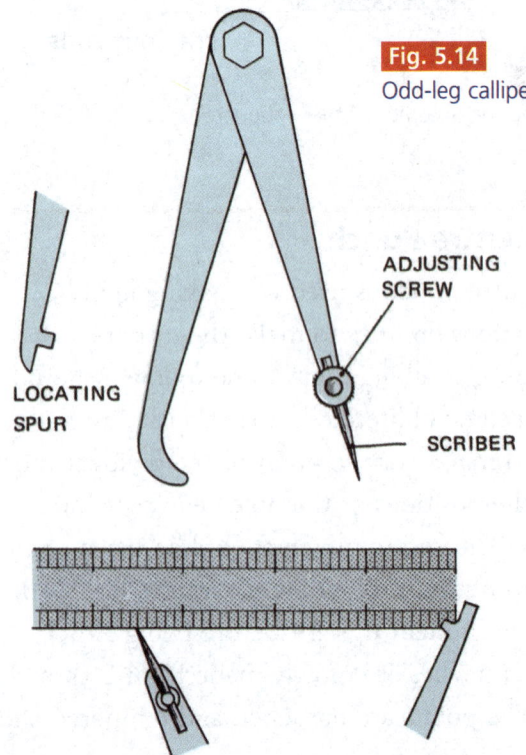

**Fig. 5.14**
Odd-leg callipers

ADJUSTING SCREW

LOCATING SPUR

SCRIBER

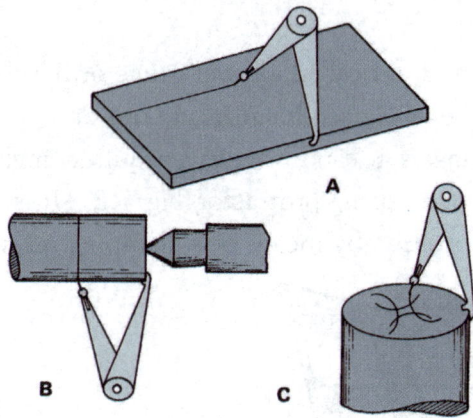

**Fig. 5.15**
Applications of odd-leg callipers

Odd-leg callipers are either set from the end of the rule or the measurements are marked on the work and the callipers set to the mark. Common applications are shown in Fig. 5.15:
(A)  Scribing a line parallel to a straight edge.
(B)  Scribing a line on a round bar on the lathe.
(C)  Locating the centre of a round bar.

They must be used with care to avoid error as shown in Fig. 5.16.

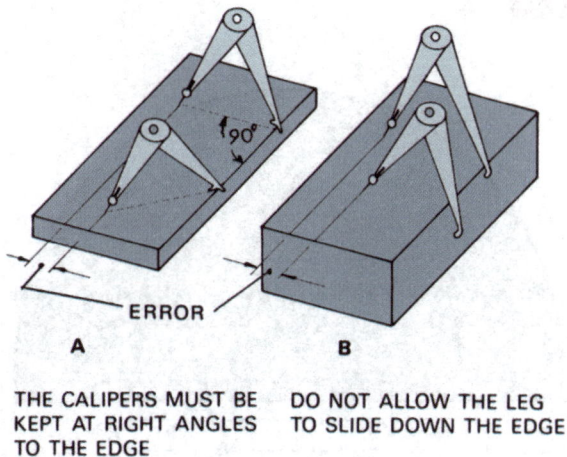

THE CALIPERS MUST BE KEPT AT RIGHT ANGLES TO THE EDGE

DO NOT ALLOW THE LEG TO SLIDE DOWN THE EDGE

**Fig. 5.16**
Using the odd-leg callipers

## The Outside Callipers

The outside callipers are used together with the rule for measuring diameters and are also used for comparing dimensions. There are spring types, Fig. 5.17 A and firm joint types, Fig. 5.17 B.

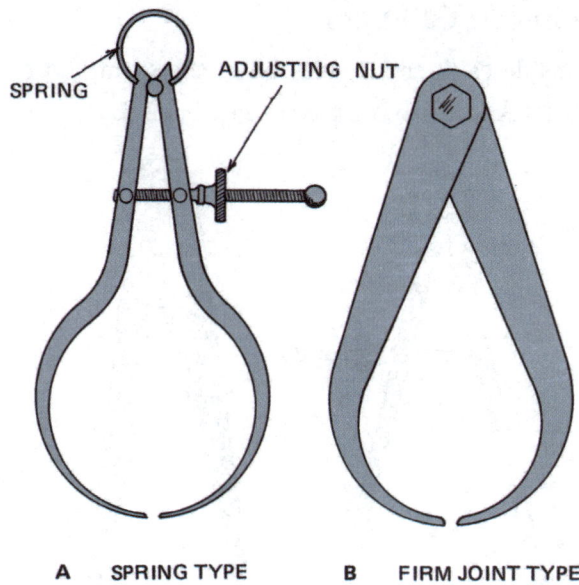

A  SPRING TYPE          B  FIRM JOINT TYPE

**Fig. 5.17**
Outside callipers

When measuring the opening, one leg should be held against the end of the rule and the measurement read at the other, Fig. 5.18 A. They are often used for checking diameters during lathe work. They can be set from the end of the rule or on an accurately finished bar or gauge of the required diameter. The diameter of the work will be correct when the callipers just slide down on it without being forced, Fig. 5.18 B.

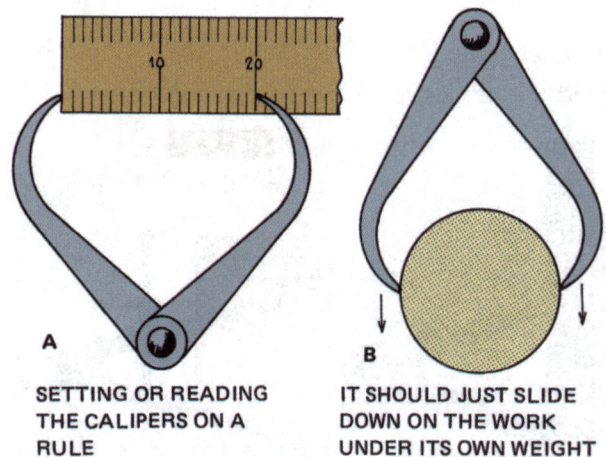

SETTING OR READING THE CALIPERS ON A RULE

IT SHOULD JUST SLIDE DOWN ON THE WORK UNDER ITS OWN WEIGHT

**Fig. 5.18**
Using the outside callipers

## The Inside Callipers

The inside callipers can also be of the spring type, Fig. 5.19 A, or firm joint type, Fig. 5.19 B.

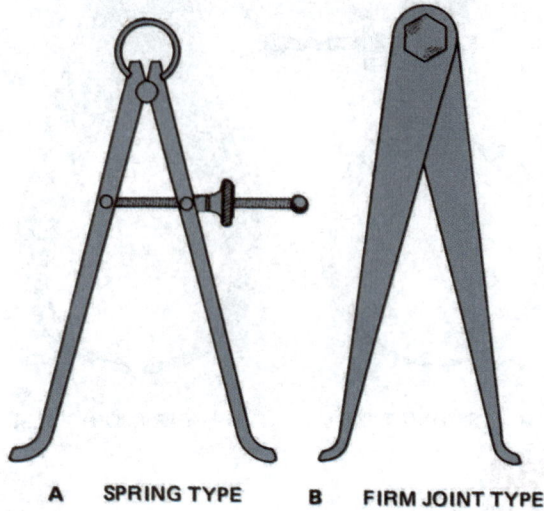

**A    SPRING TYPE      B    FIRM JOINT TYPE**

**Fig. 5.19**
The inside callipers

They are used for internal measuring and checking, such as the measuring of the diameters of holes. When using the callipers with the rule, both should be rested on a flat surface, the stock of the try square for instance, Fig. 5.20 A. They can also be set, or measurements taken from them, by means of a micrometer.

When checking internal diameters, they should be rocked on one leg as shown in Fig. 5.20 B.

**Fig. 5.20**
Using the inside callipers

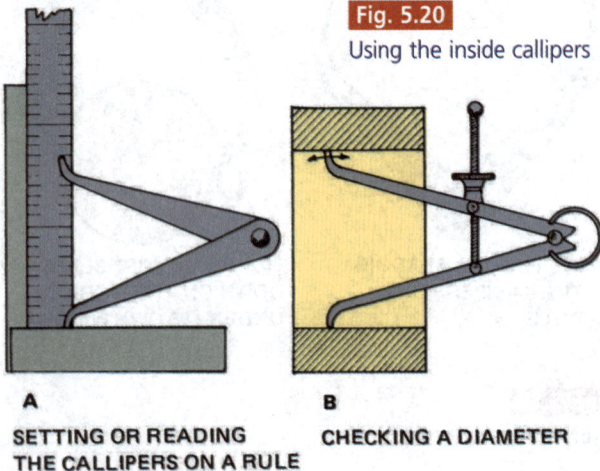

**A**
**SETTING OR READING THE CALLIPERS ON A RULE**

**B**
**CHECKING A DIAMETER**

## Bevel

This is sometimes called a bevel gauge or bevel square. A bevel is used for marking out or checking angles. It can be set to a required angle by means of a setting protractor, Fig. 5.22. It is locked in position by means of a clamping screw.

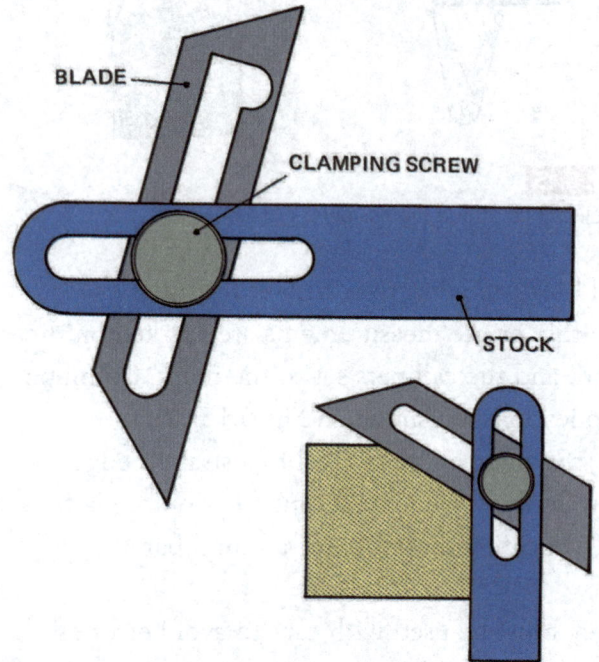

BLADE

CLAMPING SCREW

STOCK

**Fig. 5.21**
Bevel

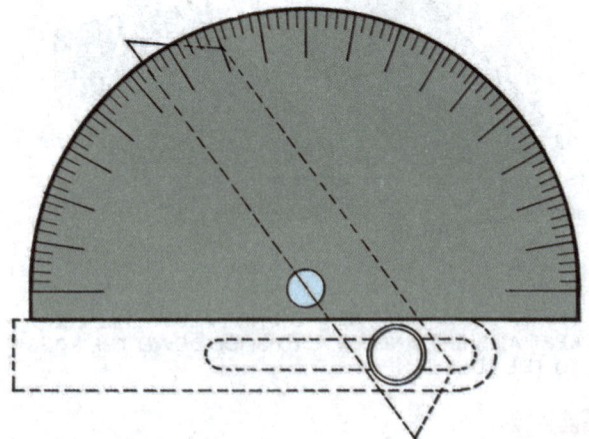

**Fig. 5.22**
Setting protractor

## Engineer's Protractor

This is another tool for marking out or checking angles. It can also be used for setting a bevel.

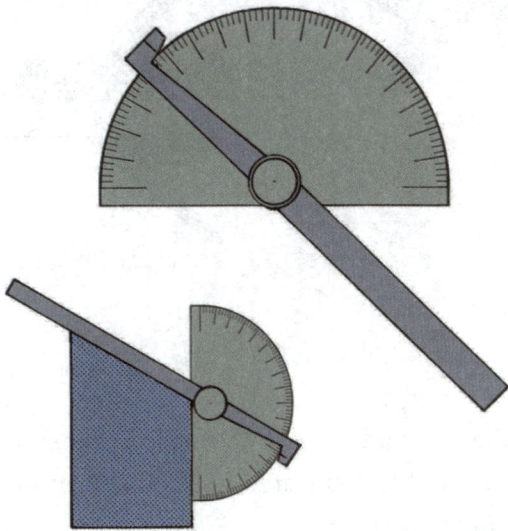

**Fig. 5.23**
Engineer's protractor

## Centre Square

The centre square is used to locate the centre of a round bar or disk. Two lines are drawn on the end of the bar and their intersection gives the centre.

**Fig. 5.24**
Centre square

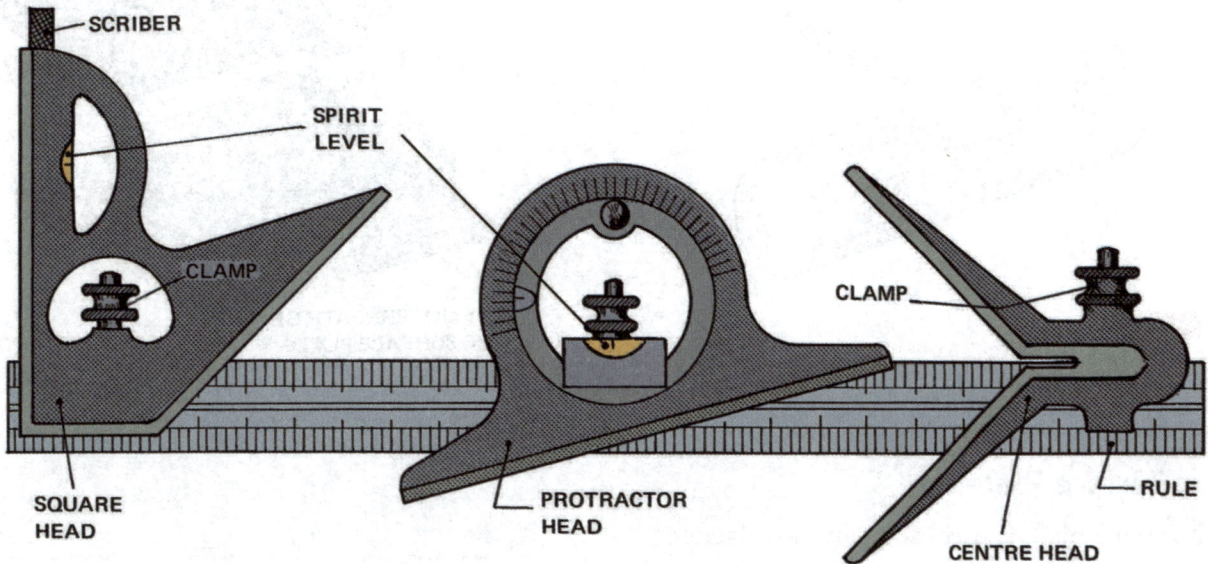

SCRIBER

SPIRIT LEVEL

CLAMP

CLAMP

SQUARE HEAD

PROTRACTOR HEAD

CENTRE HEAD

RULE

**Fig. 5.25**
The combination set

## The Combination Set

This consists of a rule and three different heads which can be attached to it. The heads are:

(a) A square head, Fig. 5.26 A, which allows it to be used for marking out and testing right angles and 45° angles and can also be used as a depth gauge.

(b) A protractor head, Fig. 5.26 B, for testing and marking out any angle.

(c) A centre head, Fig. 5.26 C, for locating the centres of round bars.

The square and protractor heads contain spirit levels.

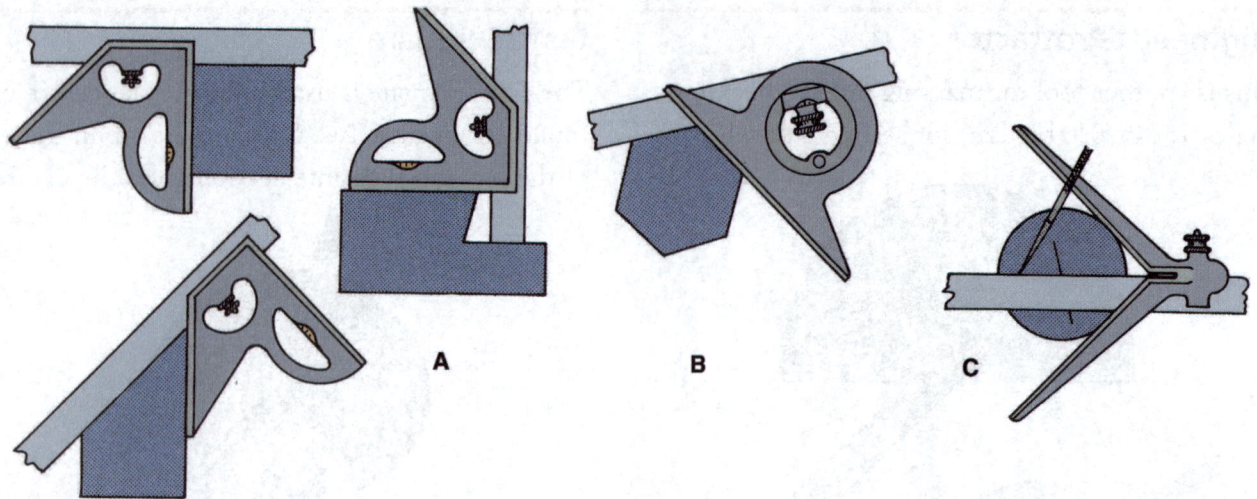

**Fig. 5.26**
Using the combination set

## Key-Seat Rule

The key-seat rule is used for drawing parallel lines on round bars, for example for marking out keyways.

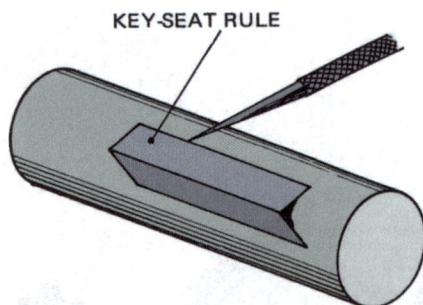

**KEY-SEAT RULE**

**Fig. 5.27**
Key-seat rule

## The Surface Plate

The surface plate is used as a datum surface for marking out and also for checking the flatness of other surfaces. The top surface is flat and accurately finished.

The sides are also accurately finished and are at right angles to each other and to the top. The underneath is ribbed to prevent distortion, and it usually has three legs so that it always remains steady. It must be kept clean and treated with care to avoid damage to surfaces. When not in use, it should be smeared with oil and protected with a wooden cover.

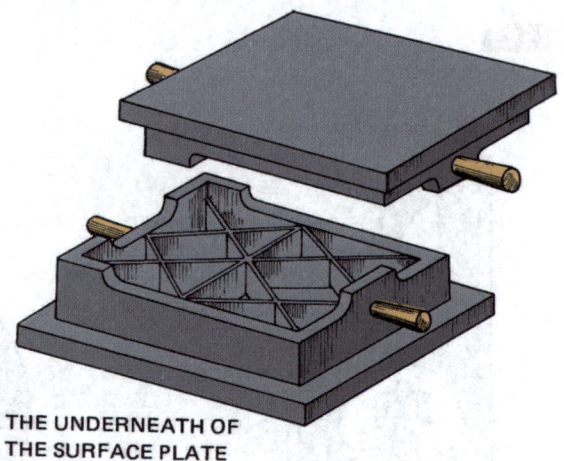

**THE UNDERNEATH OF
THE SURFACE PLATE**

**Fig. 5.28**
The surface plate

## Surface Gauge

The surface gauge or scribing block, as it is sometimes called, is commonly used with the surface plate for scribing lines parallel to the surface of the plate, Fig. 5.30 B.

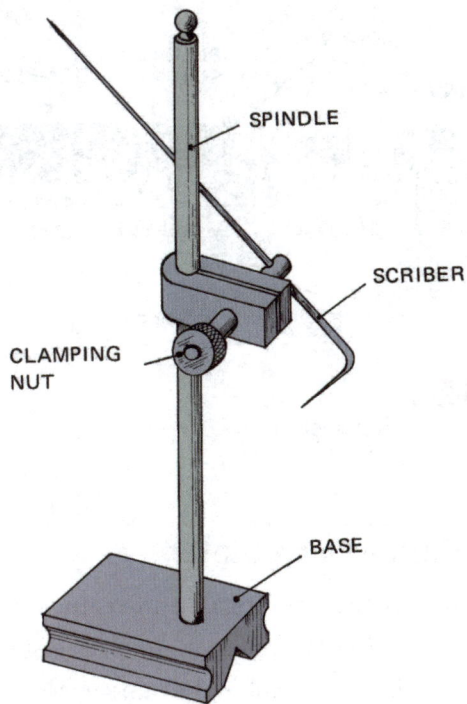

**Fig. 5.29**
Surface gauge or scribing block

SPINDLE

SCRIBER

CLAMPING
NUT

BASE

**Fig. 5.29**
Surface gauge or scribing block

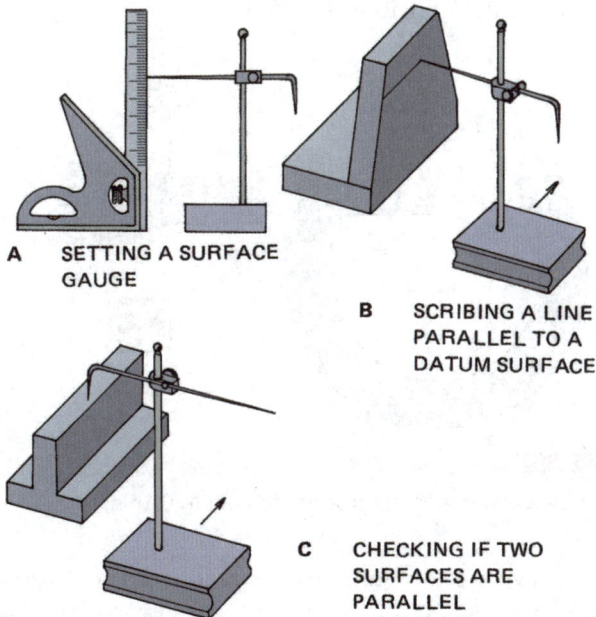

A  SETTING A SURFACE
   GAUGE

B  SCRIBING A LINE
   PARALLEL TO A
   DATUM SURFACE

C  CHECKING IF TWO
   SURFACES ARE
   PARALLEL

**Fig. 5.30**
Using a surface gauge

When setting its height with a rule, the rule must be kept perpendicular to the surface plate. This can be done by holding the rule against a square or by using the rule of combination set, Fig. 5.30 A.

By turning the bent point of the scriber downwards, the surface gauge can be used to check the parallelism of work, Fig. 5.30 C. The base may have a vee-groove in the bottom for use on cylindrical work.

## Vee Blocks

Vee blocks are used for marking out and drilling round material. They are supplied in pairs which are matched and numbered.

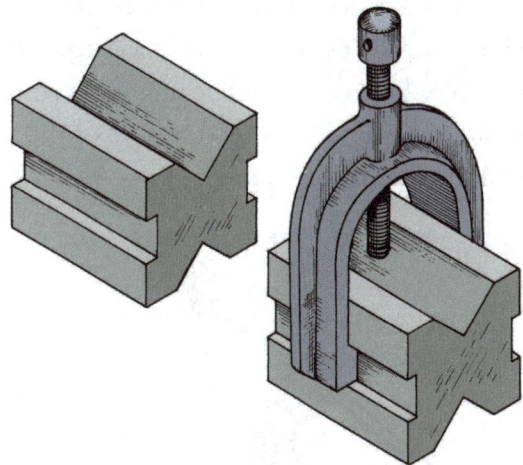

**Fig. 5.31**
Pair of vee blocks and clamp

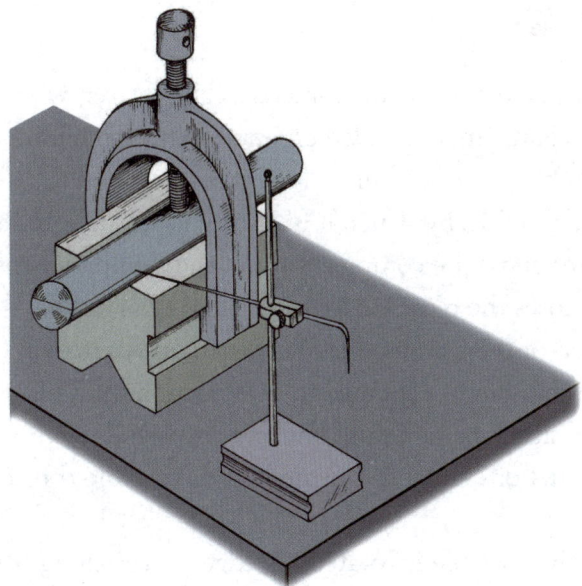

**Fig. 5.32**
Using a vee block for marking out

51

They should be stored together and used together when a pair is needed. Sometimes they have slots in their sides for clamps, as shown in Fig. 5.31. Vee blocks are made from cast iron or case hardened mild steel. Care must be taken to avoid marking them when drilling, and the work should never be struck a heavy blow while it is mounted on them.

## The Micrometer

Basically, the micrometer is like a small 'C' clamp, Fig. 5.33. As the screw is turned, the clamp is opened or closed. The micrometer has extra parts which enable the size of the opening to be read. Articles are measured between the face of the anvil and the face of the spindle.

**Fig. 5.33**

The spindle of the micrometer is like the screw of the clamp. It is threaded on one end, which allows it to be screwed in and out of the sleeve. The thimble, by which it is turned, is attached to its outer end. One complete turn of the thimble opens or closes the micrometer a distance equal to the pitch of the spindle thread. The circumference of the thimble is graduated to give fractions of a turn. The sleeve has a datum line and also a scale with graduations equal to the pitch of the spindle thread.

As the thimble is rotated, its edge moves along the scale on the sleeve. Metric micrometers have a range of 25mm and are available in sizes 0–25mm, 25–50mm, 50–75mm and so on.

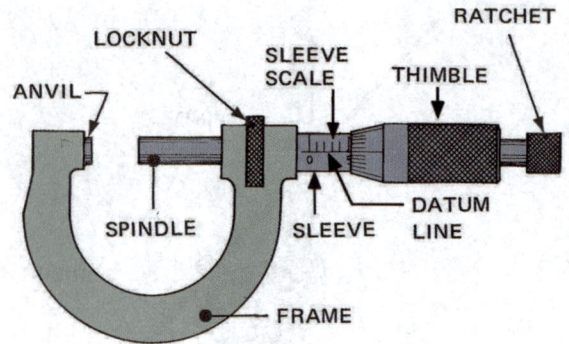

**Fig. 5.34**
Parts of the micrometer

## Reading a Micrometer

The size of the opening of a micrometer is read at the datum line, using the scale on the sleeve and the scale on the thimble. Let us say, for example, that the pitch of the spindle thread is 1mm and that the circumference of the thimble is divided into 10 equal divisions, Fig. 5.35.

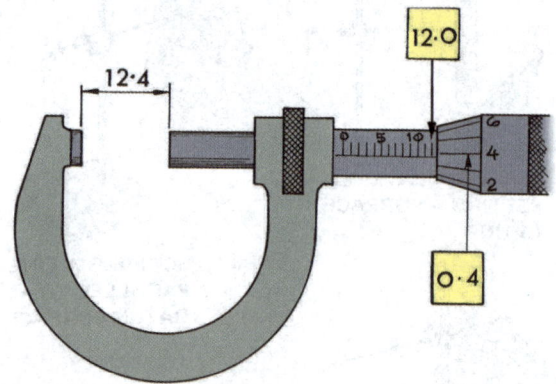

**Fig. 5.35**
Micrometer with theoretical scales to read to 0.1mm

The sleeve scale would also be graduated in 1mm units. One complete turn of the thimble would change the opening by 1mm. Turning the thimble one division would change the opening by 0.1mm. The last visible graduation on the sleeve scale will indicate the number of whole millimetres in the measurement. The line on the thimble scale opposite the datum line will indicate the number of 0.1mm units to be added. Therefore, to determine the reading shown in Fig. 5.35:

No. of 1mm units visible on sleeve
          scale is 12  =  12.0mm
No. of 0.1mm units indicated on
          thimble is 4  =  <u>0.4mm</u>
        Total Measurement  =  12.4mm

In practice, the pitch of the spindle thread on a metric micrometer is 0.5mm and the thimble circumference is divided into 50 divisions. Therefore, turning the thimble one division will change the micrometer opening by 0.5/50mm or 0.01mm. The scale on the sleeve is graduated in millimetres and half millimetres.

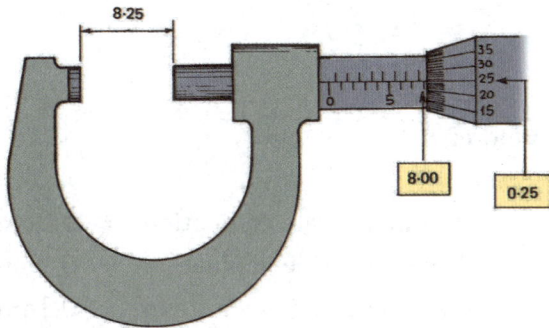

**Fig. 5.36**

In Fig. 5.36, the whole millimetres are shown below the datum line on the sleeve and the half millimetres above it. The reading shown in Fig. 5.36 is determined as follows:

    Reading on sleeve scale  =  8.00mm
    Reading on thimble scale  =  <u>0.25mm</u>
      Total Measurement  =  8.25mm

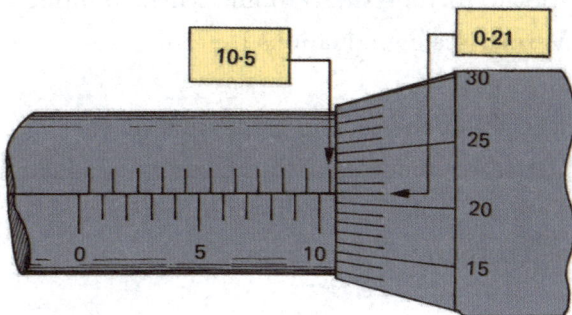

**Fig. 5.37**

To determine the measurement shown in Fig. 5.37:

Reading on sleeve scale (10 units of
    1mm + 1 unit of $\frac{1}{2}$ mm)  =  10.50mm
    Reading on thimble scale  =  <u>0.21mm</u>
      Total measurement  =  10.71mm

## Care of the Micrometer

The micrometer is a precision measuring instrument and must be handled and used with care to ensure that it retains its accuracy and shows the correct reading.

The following are some points that must be observed:

- Keep the faces of the anvil and spindle clean, and ensure that the work is clean.
- Do not overtighten the micrometer on the work. Use the ratchet, because it ensures that the same pressure is always applied and it slips before any damage is done to the instrument.
- Do not leave a micrometer lying about; take care that it does not fall on the floor. Replace it in its case after use.
- Check the zero position frequently. To do this on a 0–25mm micrometer, clean the anvil and spindle faces and then close the micrometer using the ratchet. The zero line on the thimble should then be in line with the datum line on the sleeve and, of course, the edge of the thimble should be on the zero line of the sleeve scale.

## The Vernier Callipers

These are also precision measuring instruments. They have a greater measuring range than the micrometer. Vernier callipers can be used for external measuring, Fig. 5.39 A, and internal measuring, Fig. 5.39 B. With some, the width of

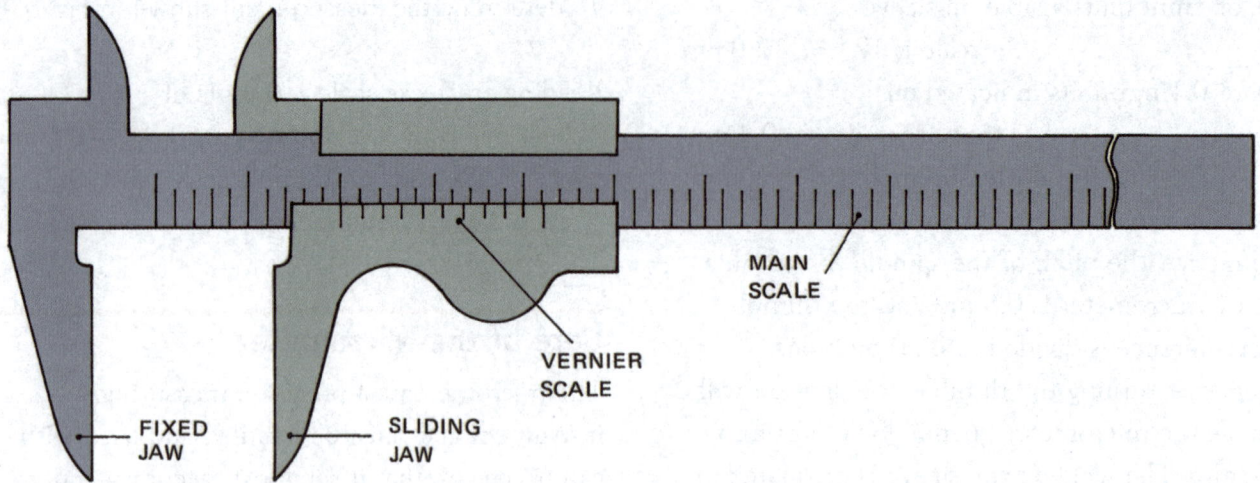

Vernier callipers

the jaws must be added to the measurement shown on the scales for internal measuring. Fine measuring is achieved by the use of two scales. The smallest unit to which a Vernier gauge can be read will be equal to the difference between the graduations on each scale.

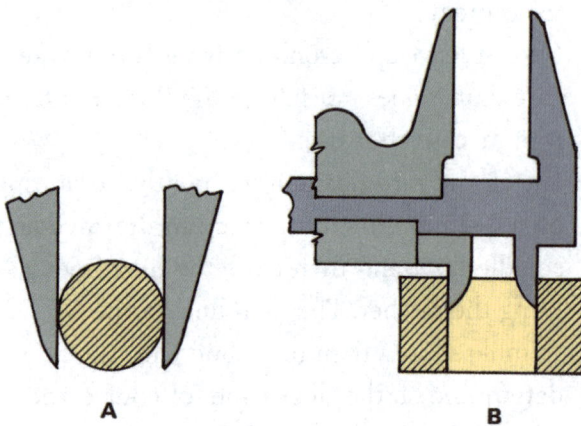

Fig. 5.39
Using a Vernier callipers

To understand the principle of the Vernier, let us first consider one with scales to read to 0.1mm, Fig. 5.40. The main scale is graduated in millimetres and the Vernier scale has a length of 9mm divided into 10 divisions so that each division is equal to $\frac{9}{10}$mm or 0.9mm.

Therefore:

| Each main scale graduation | = | 1.0mm |
| Each Vernier scale graduation | = | 0.9mm |
| Difference between them | = | 0.1mm |

When the callipers are closed, Fig. 5.40 A, the zero line on the Vernier scale coincides with the zero line on the main scale.

In Fig. 5.40 B, the sliding jaw has been moved until the first graduation on the Vernier scale is in line with the first graduation on the main scale. The callipers are therefore opened 0.1mm. (Take care not to include the zero line when counting the Vernier scale graduations.)

In Fig. 5.40 C, the second graduation on the Vernier scale coincides with the second graduation on the main scale. The callipers is therefore opened 0.1mm x 2 or 0.2mm.

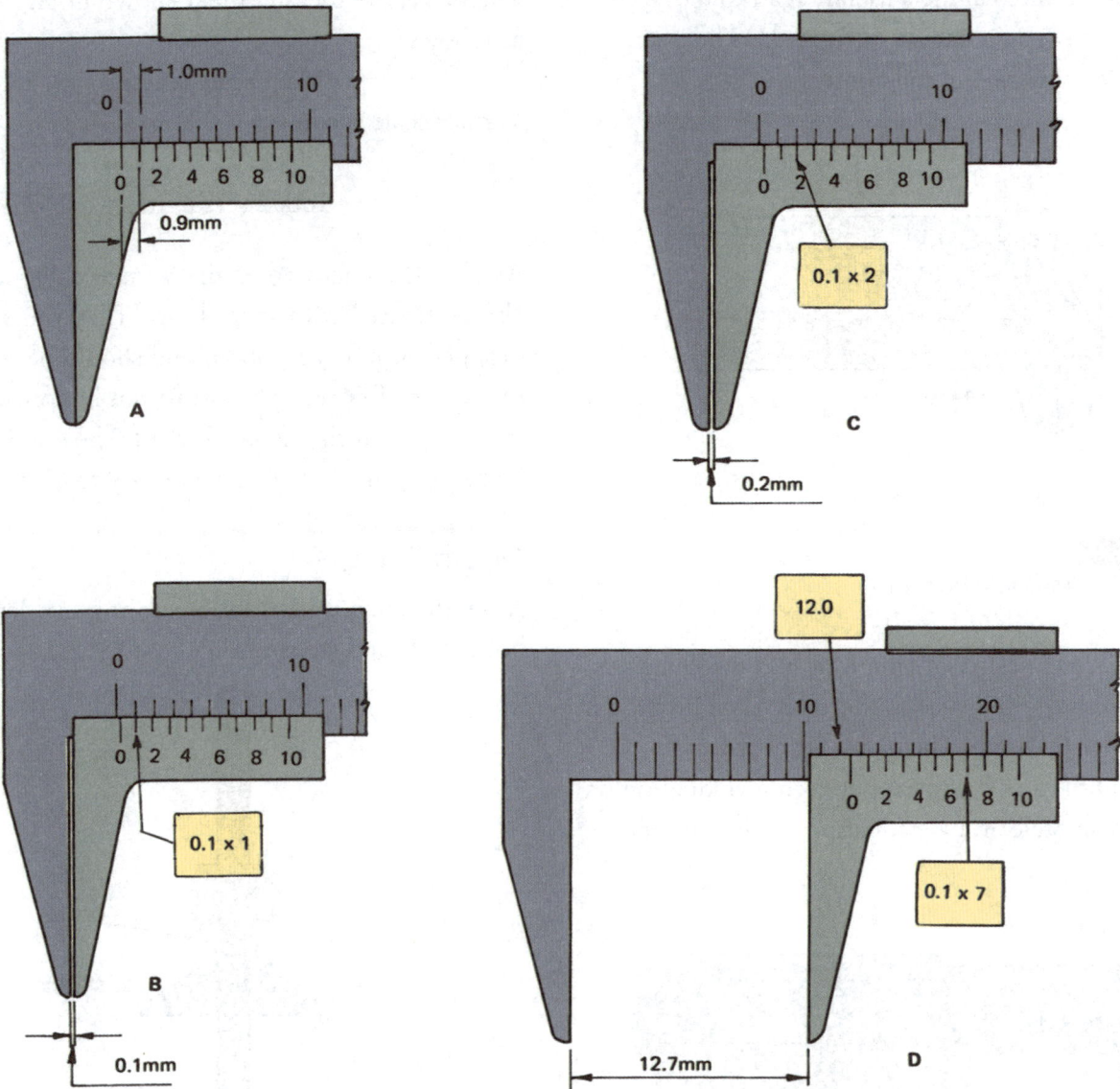

**Fig. 5.40**

Vernier scales reading to 0.1mm

If the sliding jaw is moved until the sixth graduation on the Vernier scale coincides with the sixth graduation on the main scale, the opening of the callipers will be 0.1mm x 6 or 0.6mm.

In Fig. 5.40 D, the zero line on the Vernier scale is a little past the 12.0mm mark on the main scale and the seventh graduation of the Vernier scale coincides with a graduation on the main scale.

The reading is calculated as follows:

Main scale reading  =  12.0mm
Vernier scale reading  =
0.1mm x 7  =  0.7mm
Total measurement  =  12.7mm

Therefore, to read a Vernier: First read the main scale at the last graduation before the Vernier zero, then add the reading indicated by the line on the Vernier scale which coincides with a line on the main scale.

Metric Vernier callipers usually read to 0.02mm. One such type is shown in Fig. 5.41. The main scale is graduated in millimetres.

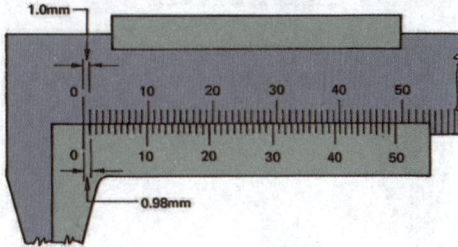

**Fig. 5.41**
Vernier scales to read to 0.02mm

The Vernier scale is 49mm long and this length is divided into 50 divisions, therefore each division is $\frac{49}{50}$mm or 0.98mm. This gives a difference of 0.02mm (1.00–0.98mm) between a graduation on the main scale and a graduation on the Vernier scale.

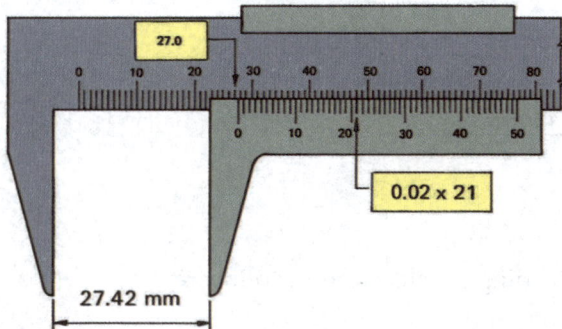

**Fig. 5.42**

In Fig. 5.42, the main scale reading is 27.00mm. The twenty-first graduation on the Vernier scale coincides with a graduation on the main scale which indicates that 0.02mm x 21 must be added.

Therefore, the measurement shown in Fig. 5.42 is as follows:

$$\text{Main scale reading} = 27.00\text{mm}$$
$$\text{Vernier scale reading} = 0.02\text{mm} \times 21$$
$$= 0.42\text{mm}$$
$$\text{Total measurement} = 27.42\text{mm}$$

As with the micrometer, the Vernier callipers must also be treated with special care. They must not be dropped or left lying about and should be returned to its case after use. They must not be forced onto the work with sliding jaw locked. The scales must be kept clean, so that they are easy to read.

## Depth Gauge

A depth gauge is used for measuring the depth of holes, slots and steps.

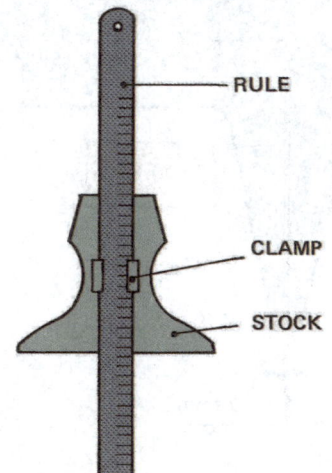

**Fig. 5.43**
Depth gauge

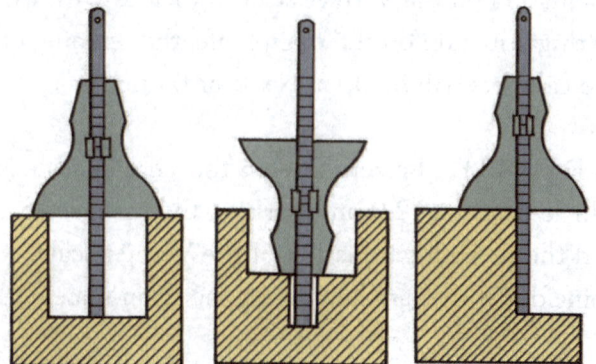

**Fig. 5.44**
Using a depth gauge

## Wire Gauge

A wire gauge is used for measuring the diameter of wire and the thickness of sheet metal. On metric gauges the sizes are shown in millimetres. When measuring the thickness of a sheet, the gauge is tried on an undamaged part of the edge until the smallest gap is found which fits on to it.

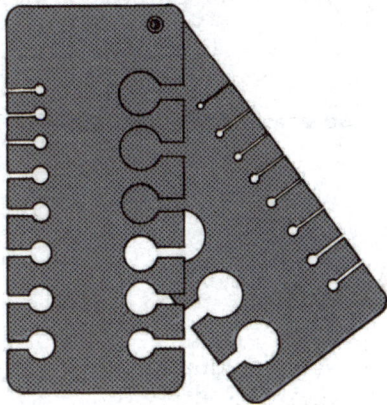

Wire gauge

## Drill Gauge

A drill gauge is used for checking drill sizes when the markings on the drill shanks have become unclear.

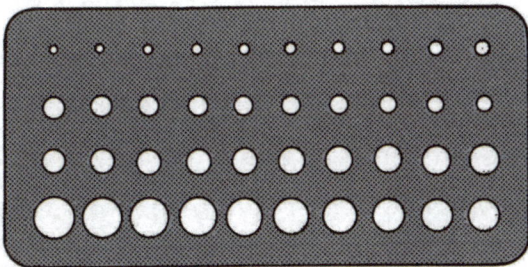

Drill gauge

## Radius Gauge

This is used for checking internal and external radii.

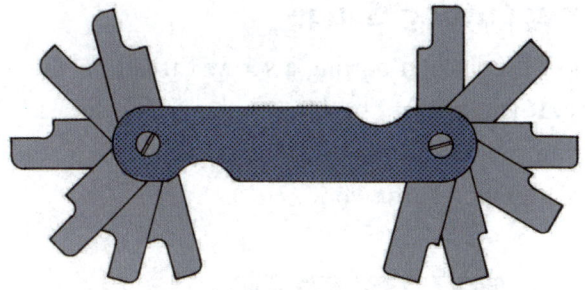

Radius gauge

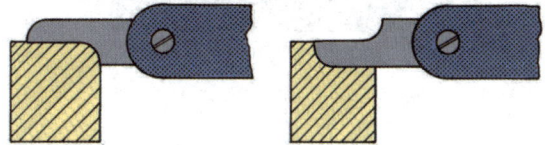

Using a radius gauge

## Screw Pitch Gauge

A screw pitch gauge is used for checking the pitch and form of screw threads on nuts and bolts.

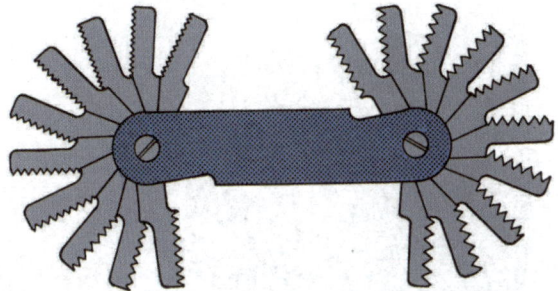

Screw pitch gauge

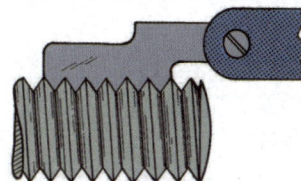

Using a screw pitch gauge

## Screw Cutting Gauge

This is used when cutting a screw thread on the lathe. It is used for checking the angle of the cutting tool and for setting the cutting tool at the correct angle to the work.

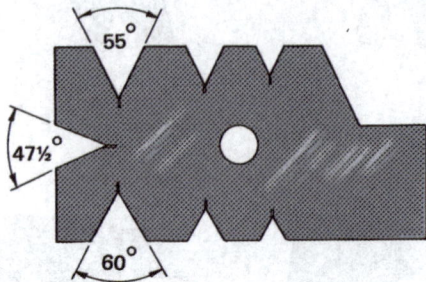

**Fig. 5.51**
Screw cutting gauge

## Feeler Gauge

This consists of a set of thin steel blades of different thicknesses, each blade having its thickness marked on it. It is used for measuring small gaps, e.g. spark plug gaps.

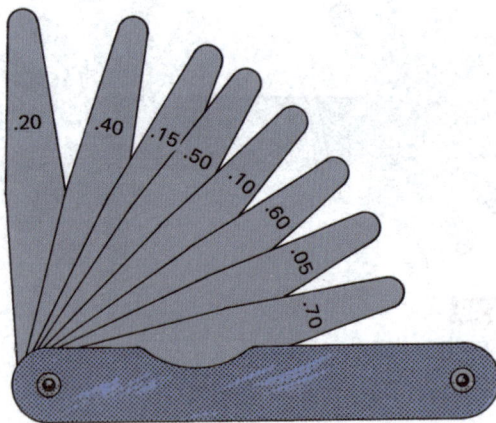

**Fig. 5.52**
Feeler gauge

## Exercises

1. What is the purpose of using marking fluid?

2. (a) What is the value of the point angle of a scriber?
   (b) What are the serrations shown at A in Fig. 5.53 called?
   (c) What is the purpose of these serrations?

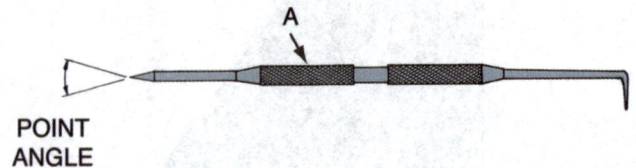

POINT
ANGLE

**Fig. 5.53**

3. (a) What graduations are marked on an engineer's rule?
   (b) Why is it better to use a rule on its edge when possible?
   (c) Why is it important to prevent the end of a rule becoming damaged?

4. A try square is shown in Fig. 5.54.
   (a) Name the parts A, B and C.
   (b) Show, by means of a sketch, how you would check the accuracy of the try square.
   (c) State three precautions that should be observed to ensure that a try square retains its accuracy.

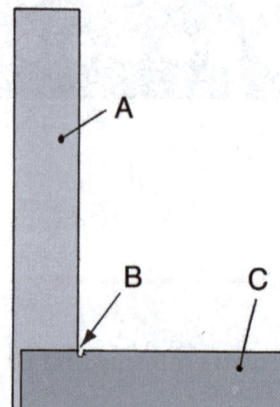

**Fig. 5.54**

5. (a) From what material is a centre punch made?
   (b) Why are round centre punches knurled?
   (c) Give three uses for a centre punch.
6. (a) Give three uses for dividers.
   (b) State two precautions to be taken to prevent damage to dividers.
7. Make a sketch of wing compasses and state their use.
8. (a) Give two uses for odd-leg callipers.
   (b) Describe, with the aid of sketches, two ways in which inaccuracies could occur when using odd-leg callipers.
9. (a) What are outside callipers used for?
   (b) Why is it incorrect to force outside callipers onto the work?
10. Describe, with the aid of sketches, how you would use inside callipers to measure an internal diameter.
11. What is a bevel used for?
12. Make a sketch of an engineer's protractor and state its use.
13. (a) Name the combination set parts 1-6 indicated in Fig. 5.55 below.
    (b) Describe the use of each head of the combination set.

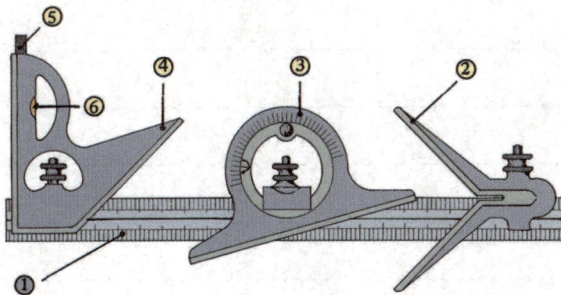

Fig. 5.55

14. What is a key-seat rule used for?

15. (a) Describe the use of a surface plate.
    (b) Why has a surface plate a ribbed underside?
    (c) How is a surface plate protected when not in use?
16. A surface gauge is shown in Fig 5.56.
    (a) Name parts A, B, C and D.
    (b) Explain, with the aid of a sketch, how you set a surface gauge to a required height.

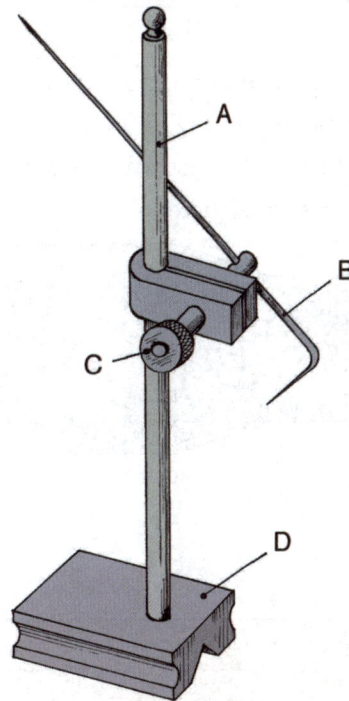

Fig. 5.56

17. Give two examples of how damage could be caused to vee blocks by misuse.
18. Describe, with the aid of a sketch, how you would mark out and drill the hole in the bar shown in Fig. 5.57 below.

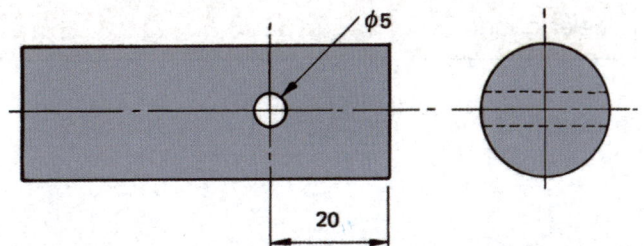

Fig. 5.57

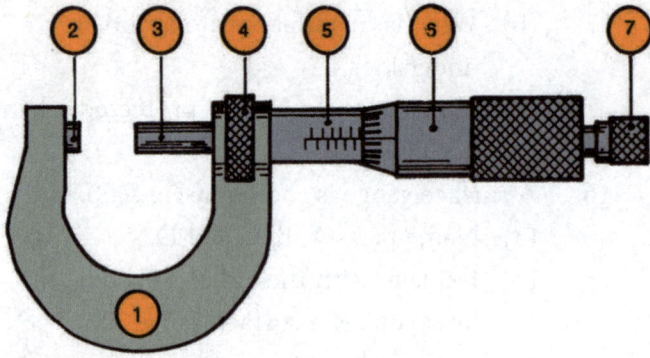

Fig. 5.58

20. Which of the following is the Vernier reading shown in Fig. 5.60 below?
   (i)  32.20mm   (iii) 32.40mm
   (ii) 52.20mm   (iv) 32.52mm

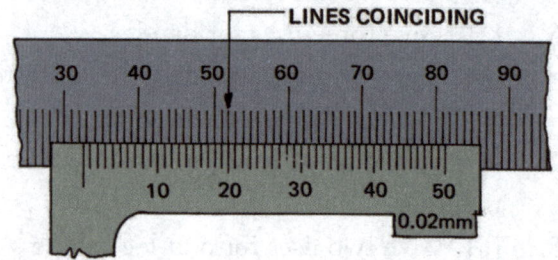

Fig. 5.60

19. (a) Name the micrometer parts 1-7 indicated in Fig. 5.58 above.
    (b) What is the micrometer reading shown in Fig. 5.59 below?

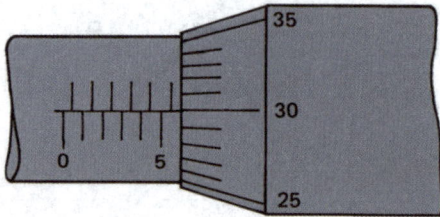

Fig. 5.59

21. Why must precision measuring instruments be treated with special care?

22. Copy the table below into your copybook and complete it giving the use of each gauge listed.

| Tool Gauge | Use |
|---|---|
| Depth gauge | |
| Wire gauge | |
| Drill gauge | |
| Radius gauge | |
| Screw pitch gauge | |
| Screw cutting gauge | |
| Feeler gauge | |

# General Benchwork

# 6

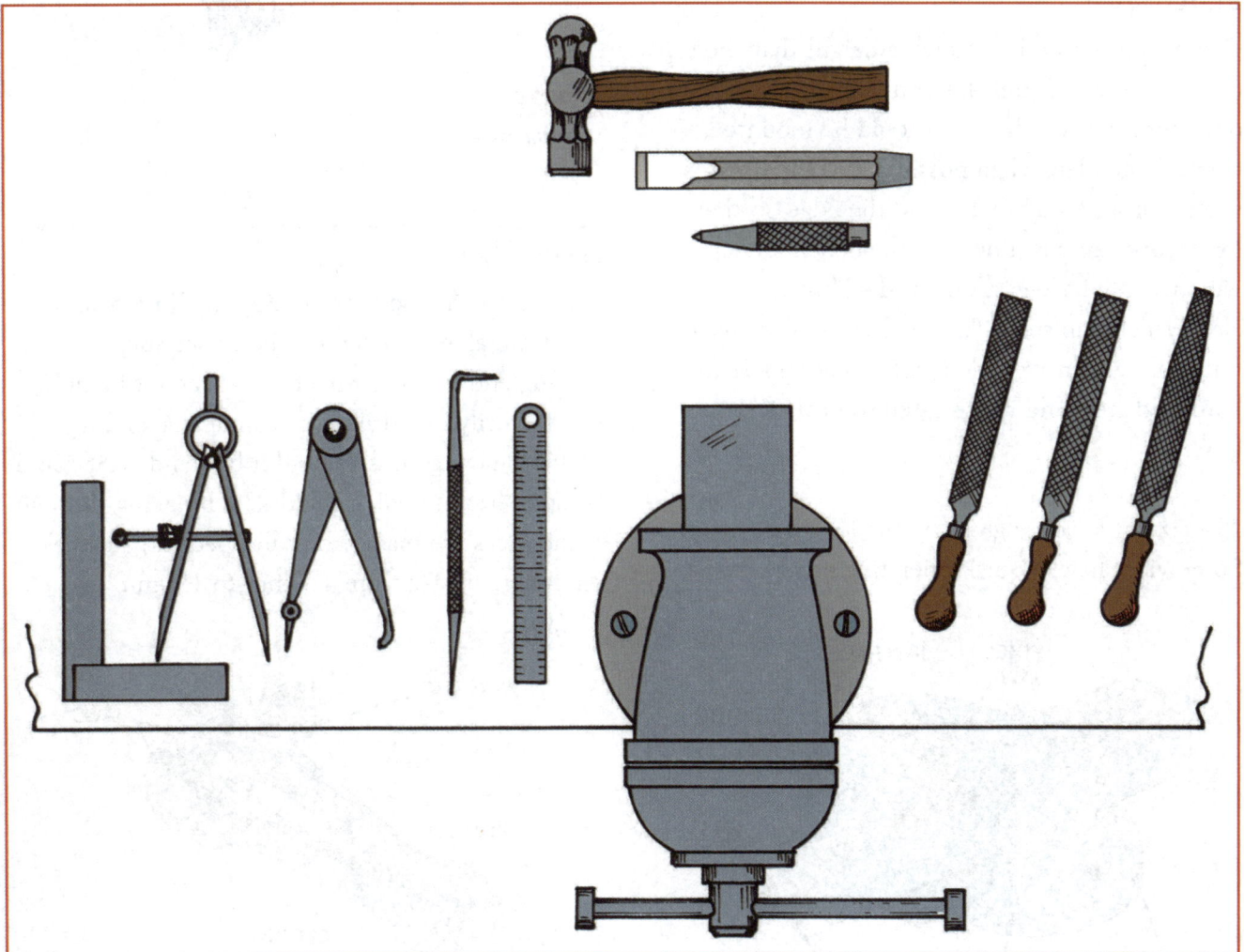

## Layout of Tools

The tools must be laid out in a definite order on the workbench. A suggested order is shown in Fig. 6.1. A left-handed person can reverse the layout, placing the files on the left-hand side and the marking tools on the right. A tool should always be returned to its proper place after use, so that the original layout is retained. If this practice is adhered to, before long a student will be able to pick up a required tool without having to look around for it.

## Bench Vice

The bench should be of such a height that the top of the vice is at about the same height as the operator's elbow. The vice should be mounted over a bench leg, when possible, and the fixed jaw should project slightly beyond the edge, so that long work can pass down by the bench. Bench vices usually have cast iron bodies, but they are also available in steel. The steel vices are stronger, but more expensive. The jaw-faces are made from hardened steel and are serrated to provide a good grip.

The size of a vice is given by the length of the jaw. Some vices have a quick-operating mechanism.

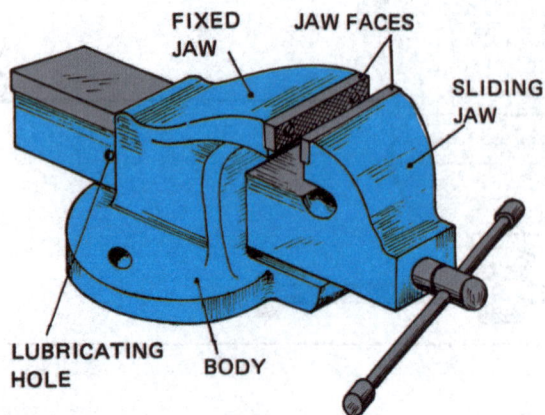

**Fig. 6.2**
Bench vice

## Vice Clamps

Vice clamps are used to prevent damage being caused to the work by the hardened and serrated jaw-faces. They can easily be made up in the workshop from copper, aluminium, brass, lead or tinplate. Fibre clamps are also available commercially. Angle iron clamps are useful when metal is either being cut with a chisel or being bent.

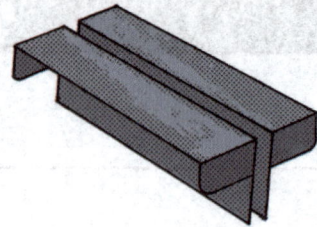

**Fig. 6.3**
Vice clamps

## Hand Vice

A hand vice is used for holding small parts and sheet metal, especially for operations such as drilling and riveting. Sheet metal cannot be held satisfactorily in a drilling machine vice and it would be dangerous to hold it by hand, as it could be spun around when the drill is breaking through. Hand vices are made from dropped forged steel and range in size from 100mm to 150mm in length.

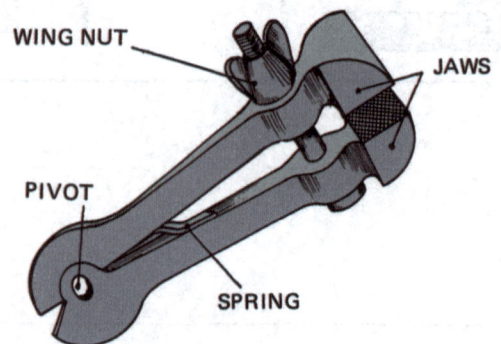

**Fig. 6.4**
Hand vice

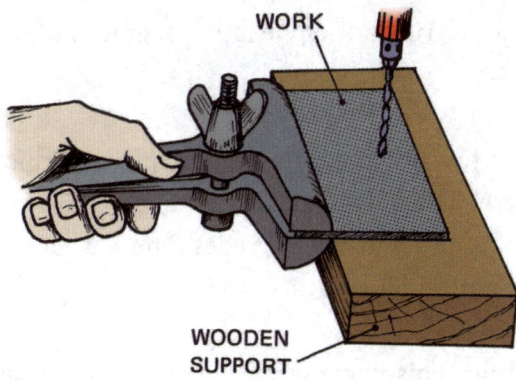

Using the hand vice

## Pin Vice

Pin vices are used for holding light section materials. Their handles are hollow so that materials of any length can be held.

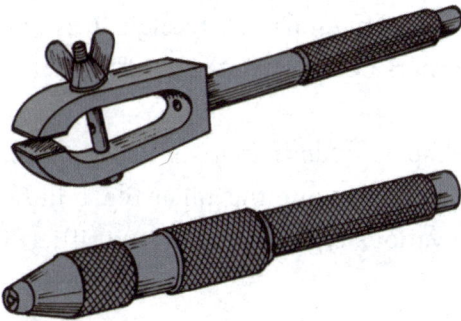

Fig. 6.6
Pin vices

## Toolmaker's Clamp

The toolmaker's clamp is useful for holding parts together for drilling and marking out, especially marking out from a template.

The jaws should be kept parallel to give a good grip and to prevent the screws being bent. They are made from case hardened mild steel.

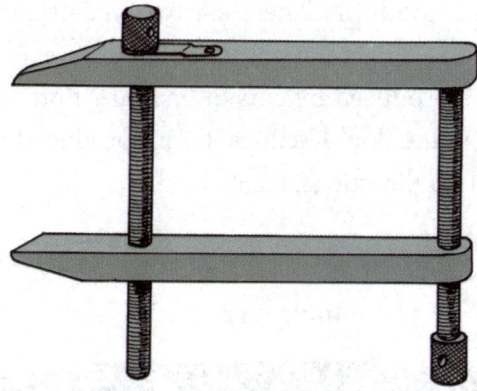

Fig. 6.7
Toolmaker's clamp

## Files

Files are made from high carbon steel. The blade is hardened but the tang is left soft. They are classified according to:

- Length
- Section and shape
- Grade of cut

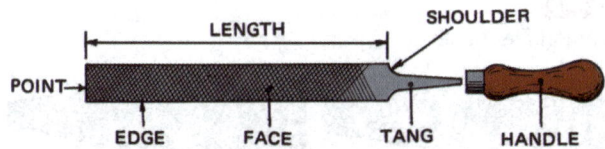

Fig. 6.8
The file

**Length** This refers to the length from the shoulder to the point and does not include the tang.

**Section and shape** This generally refers to the cross-sectional shape of the file, e.g. square, round, half-round.

**Grade of cut** This indicates the degree of coarseness of the file. There are five grades — rough, bastard, second cut, smooth and dead smooth. The coarseness of a file also varies with its length. The longer the file, the coarser it is. For example, a 250mm smooth file is coarser than a

150mm smooth file. There are two main types of file teeth — single-cut and double-cut. Single-cut teeth are produced by cuts in one direction, Fig. 6.10 A, while double-cut teeth are produced by cuts in two directions, Fig. 6.10 B.

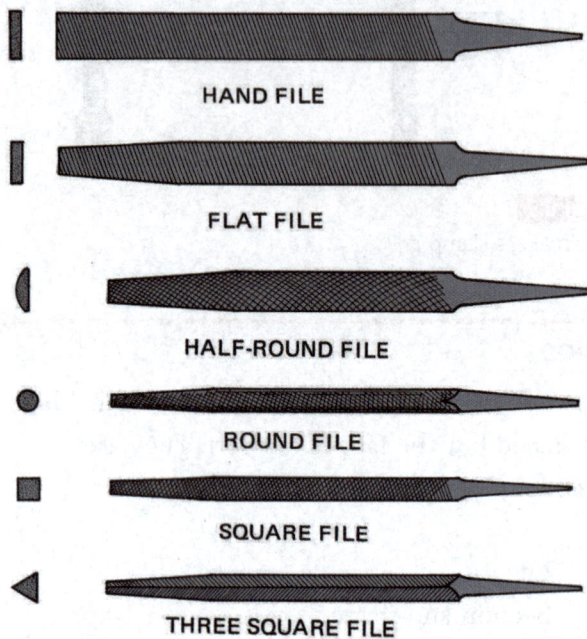

HAND FILE

FLAT FILE

HALF-ROUND FILE

ROUND FILE

SQUARE FILE

THREE SQUARE FILE

**Fig. 6.9**
Common file shapes

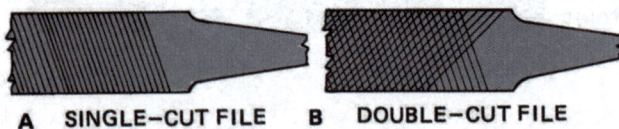

A   SINGLE–CUT FILE     B   DOUBLE–CUT FILE

**Fig. 6.10**
Single-cut and double-cut files

## Common Shapes

**Hand file** This has a rectangular cross-section. It is parallel in width but tapers in thickness over the last one-third of its length. One edge has no teeth and is called a 'safe' edge. It prevents cutting into one side of a corner while the other is being filed. Both faces are double-cut and the edge is single-cut.

**Flat file** This also has a rectangular cross-section. It tapers in width at its end. The faces are double-cut and both edges are single-cut.

**Half-round file** The cross-section of the half-round file is not a true half-circle, but a segment of a circle.

It tapers towards the point over about one-third of its length. The curved surface is single-cut except on the bastard and rough grades. The flat faces are double-cut on all grades.

**Round file** This is sometimes known as a rat-tail file. It is used for enlarging holes and for filing small curves.

**Square file** The square is used for enlarging square and rectangular holes and for filing corners and slots. It tapers over the last one-third of its length and is double-cut on all sides.

**Three square or triangular file** The cross-section of this file is an equilateral triangle. It is used for filing corners between 60° and 90°.

Other shapes of file that are not so common are the warding file, knife file, pillar file, mill saw file and the various types of needle and riffler files.

## Cross-Filing

It takes careful practice to acquire skill at filing. The following are some important points to be observed when cross-filing:

- Grip the work tightly in the vice.
- When filing to a straight line, keep the line parallel to the top of the vice.
- Stand back a little from the bench, with the feet apart, so that you can move the file horizontally and apply downward pressure on the forward stroke.
- As you move the file across the work, move it sideways also, Fig. 6.11.

- Work at a steady pace with the strokes as long as the file permits, and try to keep the file horizontal throughout each forward stroke.
- Release the downward pressure on the return stroke without lifting the file off the work.
- Hold the file as shown in Fig. 6.12.

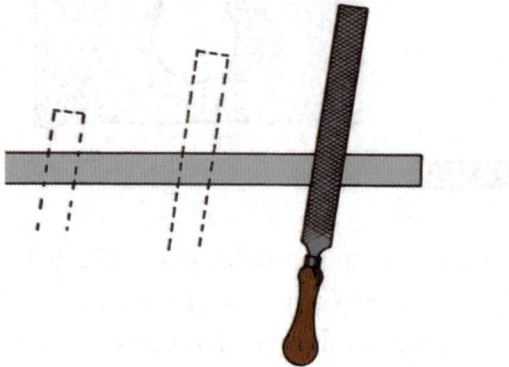

**Fig. 6.11**
File movement when cross-filing

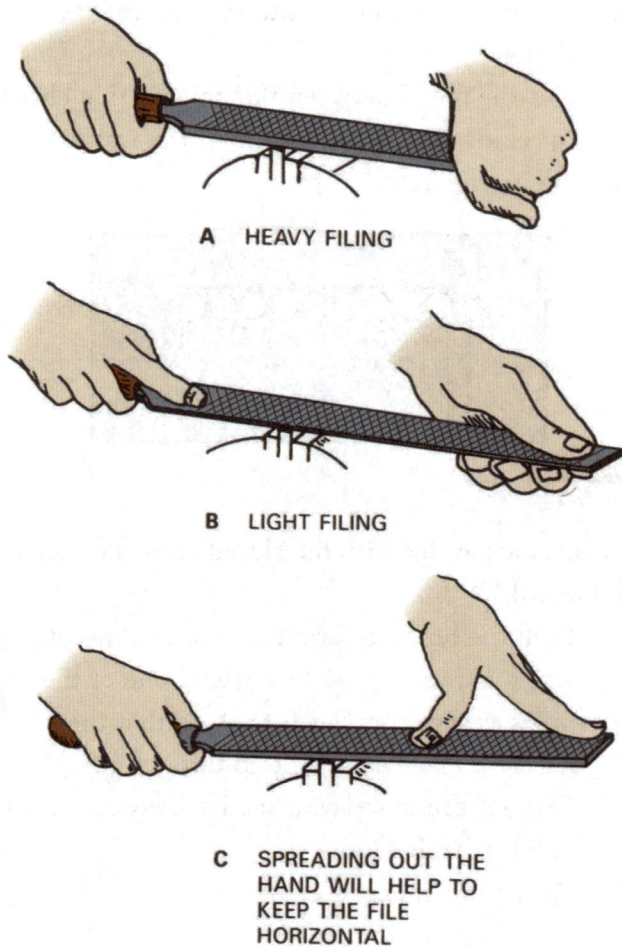

**A    HEAVY FILING**

**B    LIGHT FILING**

**C    SPREADING OUT THE HAND WILL HELP TO KEEP THE FILE HORIZONTAL**

**Fig. 6.12**
Position of hands for cross-filing

## Draw-Filing

Draw-filing is done to produce a fine finish on the work. A smooth file is placed across the work and moved forwards and backwards along the length of the work until only the fine marks of the draw-filing remain.

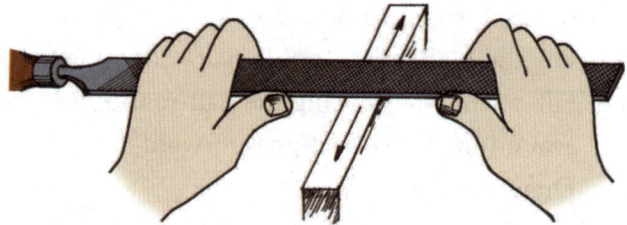

**Fig. 6.13**
Draw-filing

## Producing a Convex Profile

1. Cut close to the outline with the hacksaw.
2. File the high points until the profile is approximately the right shape.
3. File to the line by moving the file around the curve as it goes forward.
4. Draw-file the curve.
   Another method sometimes used to finish off a convex profile is shown in Fig. 6.14 D.

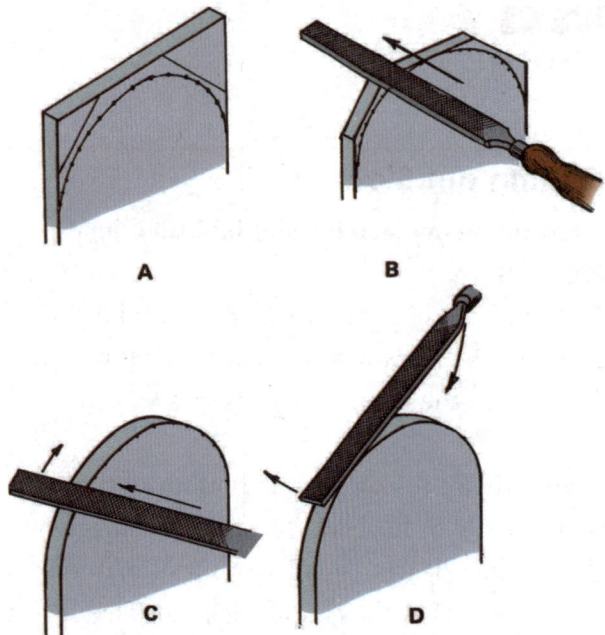

**Fig. 6.14**
Producing a convex profile

## Producing a Concave Profile

1. Drill a series of small holes close to the outline and then cut the metal between them using a chisel. The hole centres must be marked out accurately beforehand, allowing 0.5mm or a little more between the holes. In the case of shallow curves, the hacksaw can be used, Fig. 6.15 B.
2. File the high points with a half-round file.
3. File to the line, moving the half-round file around the curve as it goes forward.
4. Draw-file the curve.

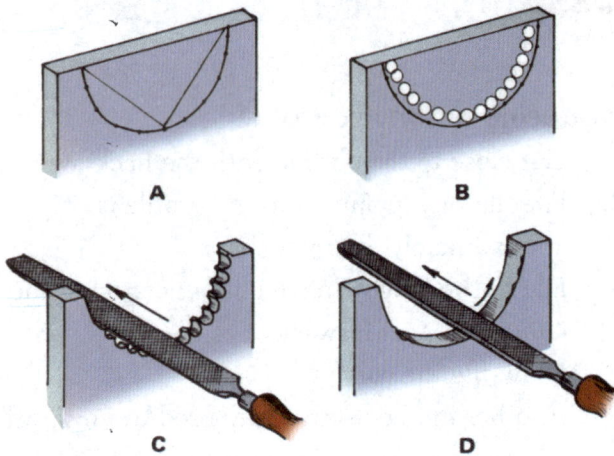

Fig. 6.16

**To cut out the slot indicated in Fig. 6.17:**

1. Drill the corner clearance holes.
2. Chain-drill the end as shown. Ensure that the holes do not run into one another or go outside the lines.
3. Cut to the end holes with the hacksaw as shown.
4. Cut the metal between the holes with a chisel to remove the main portion of the waste.
5. File to the lines.

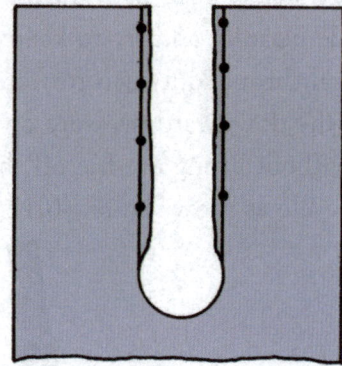

Fig. 6.15

Producing a concave profile

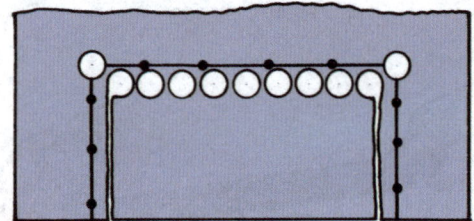

Fig. 6.17

## Cutting out Slots

To form the open-ended slot indicated in Fig. 6.16:

1. Drill the hole to form the end of the slot.
2. Cut the sides with the hacksaw as shown.
3. File to the lines.

Take care not to damage the bottom of the slot with the file or hacksaw. To prevent damage by the hacksaw, leave a small amount of material (1mm or less) at the end of each cut. Then break off the portion between the cuts by bending it backward and forward.

To cut out the slot with the closed ends indicated in Fig. 6.18:

1. Drill the holes to form the ends of the slot.
2. Using a three square file, extend one of the holes as shown in Fig. 6.18 A, so that the hacksaw blade can be fitted through it.
3. Cut out the waste with the hacksaw as shown in Fig. 6.18 B.
4. File to the lines.

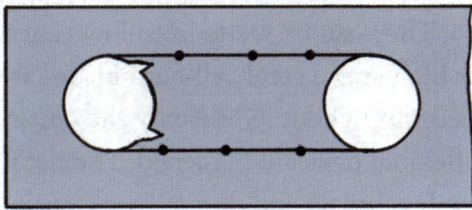

**A**

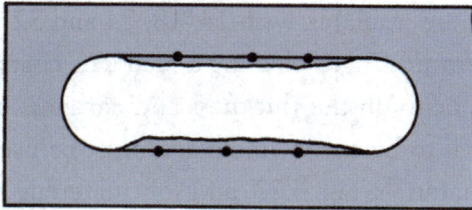

**B**

**To cut out the opening indicated in Fig. 6.19:**

1. Drill the corner clearance holes.
2. Drill two Ø12 holes in opposite corners as shown.
3. Using a three square file, extend the holes as shown to allow the hacksaw blade through.
4. Fit the blade through each hole in turn and cut out the central portion as shown.
5. File to the lines.

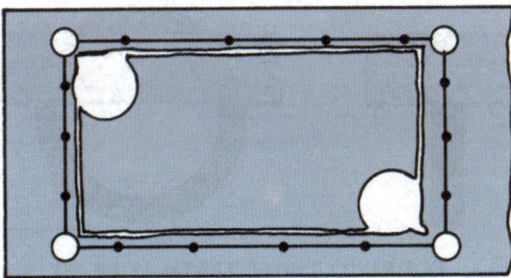

Fig. 6.19

A tension file (Fig. 6.29) can be used for cutting slots in thin metals and plastics. This will eliminate the need for both chain-drilling and the drilling of large holes for hacksaw blades when using these materials.

## Care of Files

New files should be 'broken in' on brass or machined cast iron. This wears down prominent teeth, making them level with the others. If this is not done, the prominent teeth will be broken off when the file is used on steel.

Files are very hard and brittle and the teeth are easily damaged. They should not, therefore, be allowed to rub or hit off one another. They must not be thrown on top of one another, and they should be stored in a rack separated from each other and from other tools.

The file handle must be a tight fit, must not be split and must be of a suitable size.

## Pinning

When filing soft metals or using a file with broken teeth, the teeth tend to become clogged. This is called 'pinning'. A file card, Fig. 6.20, is used for cleaning pinned files.

Fig. 6.20
File card

It should be used along the line of the teeth. Sometimes the corner of a small piece of sheet brass must be used to remove embedded particles.

## The Hacksaw

Hacksaws are available with either adjustable or non-adjustable frames and with various types of handles. The adjustable ones can take blades of different lengths.

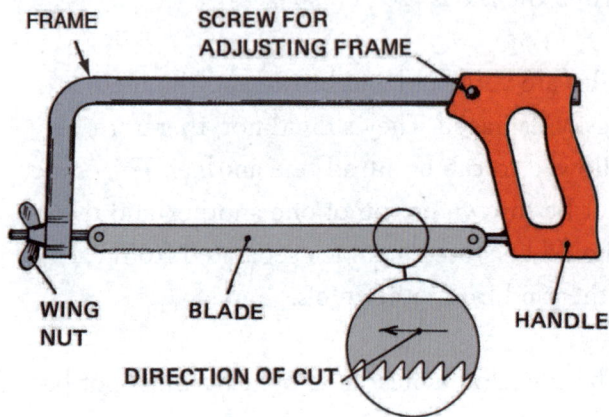

**Fig. 6.21**
The hacksaw

**Fig. 6.22**
Blade turned through 90° for a deep cut

The blade is tensioned by means of a wing nut. Care must be taken when fitting new blades to have the teeth pointing forward, that is, away from the handle. The blade can be turned through 90° for deep cuts, Fig. 6.22.

When buying blades, the following information must be given: length, material, number of teeth per 25mm and whether they are to be 'all-hard or flexible'. The usual blade lengths are 250mm and 300mm. They can be made from low tungsten steel or high-speed steel. All-hard blades are hardened throughout, while only the cutting edges of the flexible ones are hardened. The flexible ones are less brittle and do not break easily; they are, therefore, the most suitable type for beginners.

Blades are available with 14, 18, 24 and 32 teeth per 25mm. When selecting a blade, its coarseness will depend on the thickness and hardness of the material to be cut. A fine blade must be used for thin materials, Fig. 6.23, and soft materials require a coarser blade than hard materials. The following table can be used as a guide for selecting hacksaw blades.

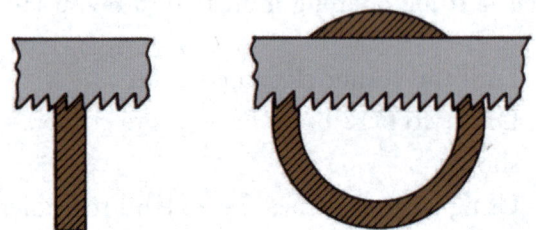

**WRONG: BLADE TOO COARSE
TEETH WILL BREAK**

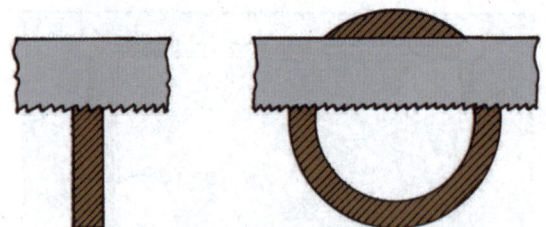

**CORRECT: THREE TEETH AT LEAST
IN CONTACT WITH THE WORK**

**Fig. 6.23**
Selecting the correct blade

## Coarseness of Blades for Different Applications

| Teeth per 25mm | Use |
|---|---|
| 14 | Soft, thick section materials e.g. aluminium, copper, brass and mild steel. |
| 18 | General use, also soft materials in thinner sections and thick section hard materials. |
| 24 | Thin section hard materials, also thick walled tubing and materials 3mm to 6mm thick. |
| 32 | Materials less than 3mm thick e.g. thin walled tubing and sheet metal. |

Hacksaw blade teeth have 'set', which enables them to make a cut wider than the thickness of the blade, Fig. 6.24 (C). This prevents the blade getting stuck in the cut.

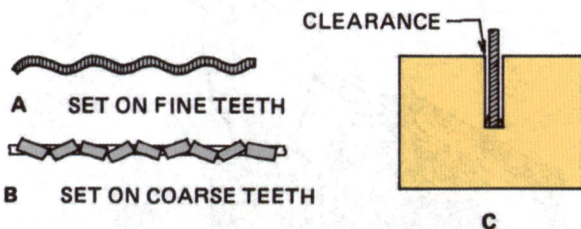

**Fig. 6.24**
Set on teeth

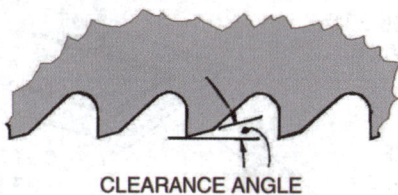

**Fig. 6.25**

## Using a Hacksaw

- Cut vertically when possible, Fig. 6.26.
- Cut close to the vice jaws.
- Use the full length of the blades.
- Cut with slow steady strokes — about 50 strokes per minute.
- Never use a new blade in an old cut. If a blade breaks, turn the work around and start again from the other side or start a new cut beside the old one.

**Fig. 6.26**
Cut vertically when possible

## Pad Handle Saw

This is used for sawing operations where the hacksaw cannot be used because of the frame. It can be used with pad saw blades or with broken hacksaw blades.

**Fig. 6.27**
Pad handle saw

## Junior Hacksaw

The junior hacksaw is useful for light work. In the type shown in Fig. 6.28, the blade is kept in tension by the spring in the frame itself. In others, the blade is tensioned by means of a knurled nut.

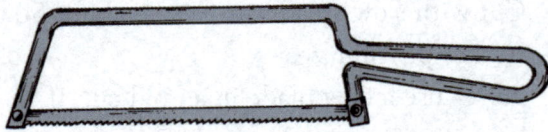

**Fig. 6.28**
Junior hacksaw

## Tension File

This is a thin, round file which is used as a sawblade. It is held in tension in a special frame or fitted to a standard hacksaw frame by means of adaptive links. The tension file is useful for cutting curves and slots in sheet metal and sheet acrylic.

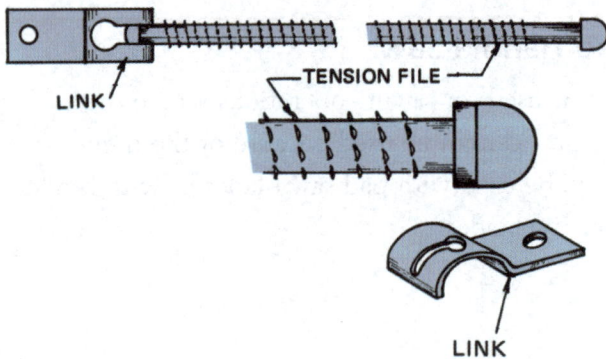

LINK

TENSION FILE

LINK

**Fig. 6.29**
Tension file with links for fitting it to hacksaw frame

## Cold Chisels

These are called cold chisels because they are used to cut cold metals. They are made from high carbon steel, with their cutting ends hardened and tempered, or from suitably heat-treated alloy steel. Some alloy steel chisels can be sharpened with a smooth file. The chisel heads are left unhardened and tend to become 'mushroomed' from the hammer blows, Fig. 6.30.

MUSHROOMED HEAD

WRONG          CORRECT

**Fig. 6.30**
Head of cold chisel

They must, therefore, be ground back from time to time. If this is not done, a particle could fly off and cause an injury. Care must also be taken to ensure that a chip of the material being cut does not fly off. The main types of cold chisel are the flat chisel, cross-cut chisel, round nose chisel and diamond point chisel.

## The Flat Chisel

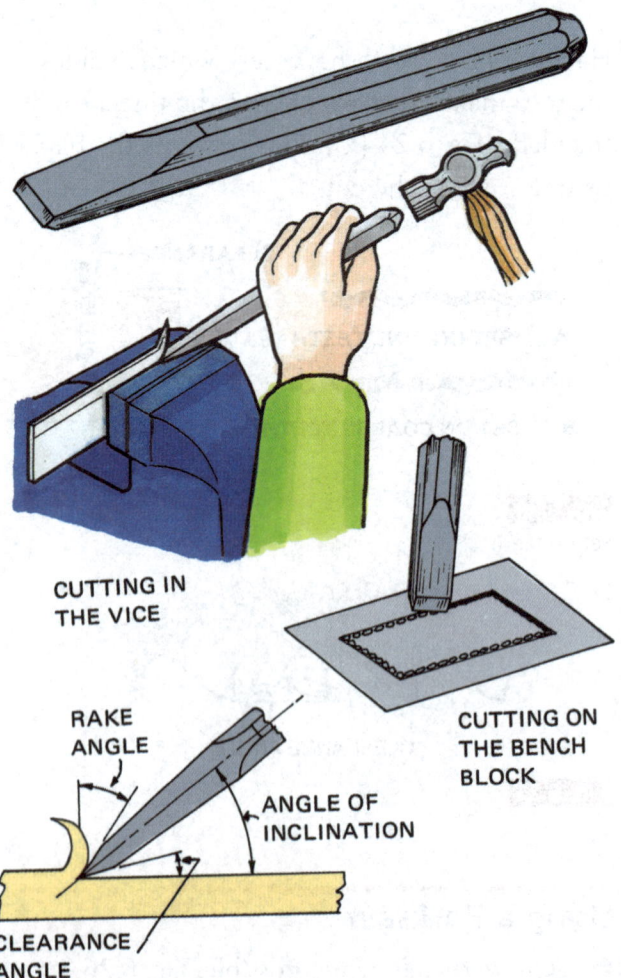

CUTTING IN THE VICE

RAKE ANGLE

ANGLE OF INCLINATION

CLEARANCE ANGLE

CUTTING ON THE BENCH BLOCK

**Fig. 6.31**
Flat chisel

## The Flat Chisel

The flat chisel is used for general work, for example cutting sheet metal, removing waste material after it has already been chain drilled and miscellaneous operations such as cutting the head off a rivet in order to remove it. When flat material is being cut, it should be gripped between angle iron clamps in the vice or supported on a bench block. Care must be taken to avoid bending the material when the waste is being cut off. The angle of the cutting edge depends on the material being cut and varies from about 30° for aluminium to about 60° for mild steel.

## Cross-Cut Chisel

This is used for cutting narrow slots and for cutting in restricted spaces.

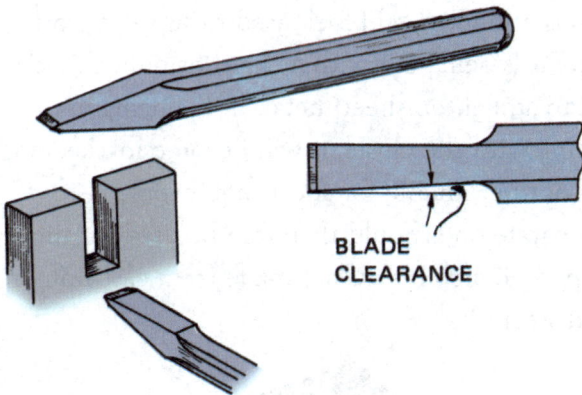

**BLADE CLEARANCE**

**Fig. 6.32**
Cross-cut chisel

## Round Nose Chisel

This is used for cutting circular grooves, such as the oil grooves in bearings.

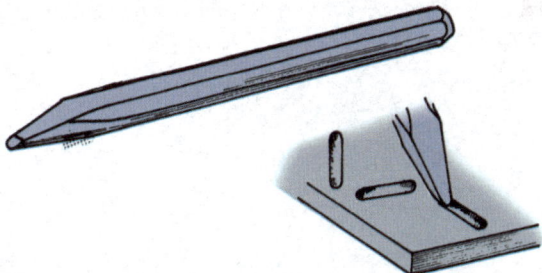

**Fig. 6.33**
Round nose chisel

## Diamond Point Chisel

This is used to produce sharp corners and to cut 'vee' grooves.

**Fig. 6.34**
Diamond point chisel

## Pin Punch

A pin punch is used for driving pins into or out of holes. It can also be used to drive out a rivet after its head has been removed. Pin punches are available in a range of sizes.

**Fig. 6.35**
Parallel pin punch

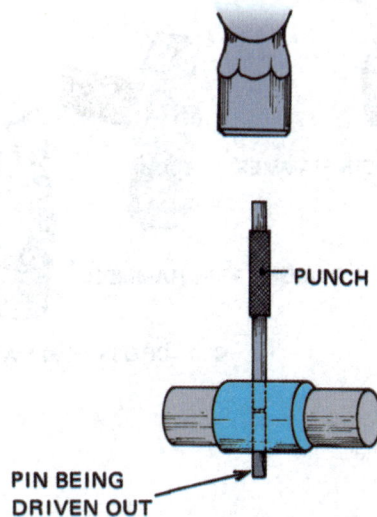

**PUNCH**

**PIN BEING DRIVEN OUT**

**Fig. 6.36**
Using a pin punch

## Engineer's Hammers

The three common types of engineer's hammer are shown in Fig. 6.37. The ball pein is the one most commonly used. Its round end is used for riveting. The straight pein and cross pein are used for hammering operations in narrow spaces. The heads are made from high carbon steel with both ends hardened and tempered, the centre around the eye being left unhardened. The handles are made from ash or hickory.

Hammers are available in different weights, a ½kg hammer is suitable for general work and 1kg for forging. The weight of a hammer refers to the weight of its head.

When using a hammer, it should be held at the end of the handle and not up near the head. Care must be taken to avoid striking the work with the edge of the face, as this will cause unsightly marks and may also lead to chipping of the edge.

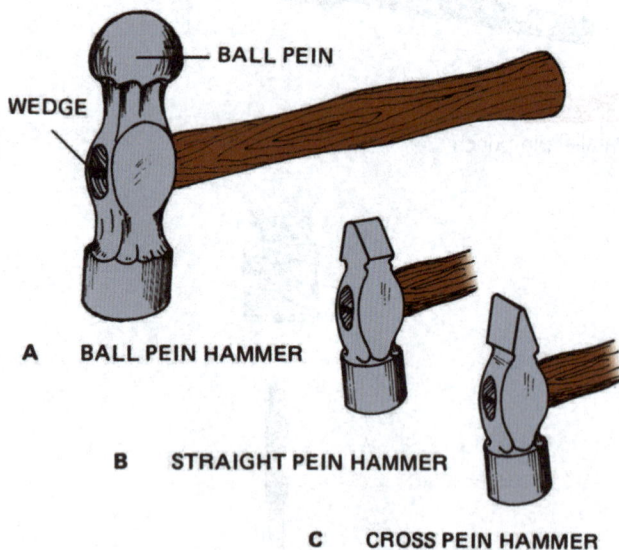

**Fig. 6.37**
Engineer's hammer

## Soft Hammers

Soft hammers are used for work on sheet metal and for assembling components in order to avoid damaging their surfaces. They are available with heads of copper, lead, rawhide or rubber.

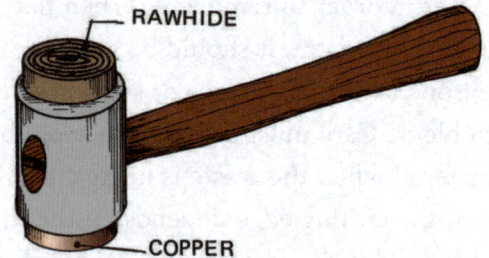

**Fig. 6.38**
A soft hammer with copper and rawhide faces

## Bench Block

This is a solid metal block used to support work while it is being cut with a chisel or punch marked and to straighten sheet metal. If it is being used for cutting with the chisel, it will become marked and will not be suitable for sheet metalwork.
A separate one should therefore be used for this purpose. Bench blocks are made from cast iron or mild steel.

**Fig. 6.39**
Bench blocks

## Exercises

1. A bench vice is shown in Fig. 6.40.
   (a) What factors must be taken into consideration when fitting a vice to a bench?
   (b) Why are the jaw-faces of a vice serrated?
   (c) What are vice jaw-faces made from?
   (d) What is the purpose of vice clamps?

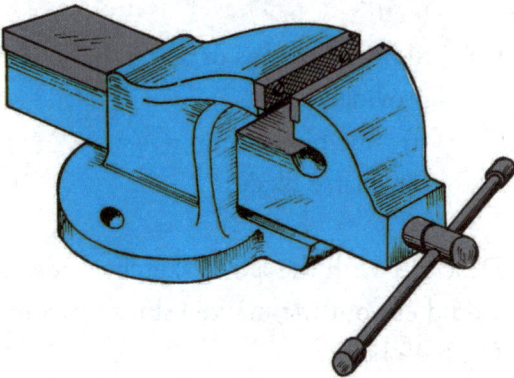

Fig. 6.40

2. Name the tool shown in Fig. 6.41 below.

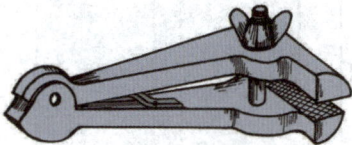

Fig. 6.41

3. When pieces of sheet metal are being drilled, why is it incorrect to hold them
   (i) by hand
   (ii) in a machine vice?

4. What is a pin vice used for?

5. Why do pin vices have hollow handles?

6. A toolmaker's clamp is shown in Fig. 6.42.
   (a) Give two uses for a toolmaker's clamp.
   (b) Why is it important to keep the jaws parallel?

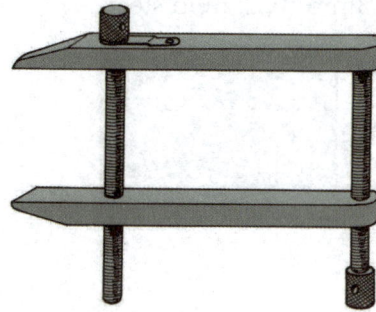

Fig. 6.42

7. A file is shown in Fig. 6.43.
   (a) Name the parts marked A, B, C, D and E.
   (b) How are files classified?
   (c) Draw a sketch of a hand file and name its parts.
   (d) Sketch six shapes of file and name each one.

Fig. 6.43

8. Name the types of file teeth shown in:
   (a) Fig. 6.44.
   (b) Fig. 6.45.
   (c) For what purpose is draw-filing carried out?

Fig. 6.44

Fig. 6.45

9. Describe, with the aid of sketches, how you would remove the waste material and finish the workpiece, shown in Fig. 6.46 below, to the curved dotted line. Assume the material to be 3mm thick mild steel.

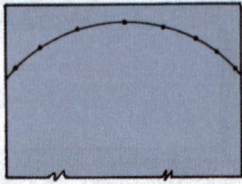

Fig. 6.46

10. Describe, with the aid of sketches, how you would produce the shape indicated by the dotted line in Fig. 6.47 below. Assume the material to be 3mm thick mild steel.

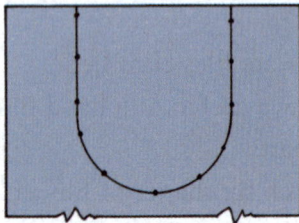

Fig. 6.47

11. (a) How is a new file 'broken in'?
    (b) What is meant by 'pinning'?
    (c) What is a file card used for?

12. A hacksaw is shown in Fig. 6.48.
    (a) Name the parts A, B, C and D.
    (b) Show, by means of a sketch, the direction in which the teeth are pointing with respect to the handle.
    (c) How is the blade tensioned in a hacksaw?

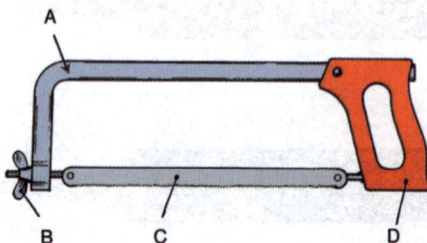

Fig. 6.48

13. (a) What details must be given when buying hacksaw blades?
    (b) When selecting a hacksaw blade for a particular job, what factors would govern its degree of coarseness?

14. (a) What is meant by:
        (i) an 'all-hard' hacksaw blade
        (ii) a 'flexible' hacksaw blade?
    (b) What is meant by the 'set' of hacksaw teeth?
    (c) Show, by means of a sketch, how set is provided on:
        (i) fine blades
        (ii) coarse blades.

15. Describe, with the aid of sketches, how you would cut out the marked slot shown in Fig. 6.49 below.

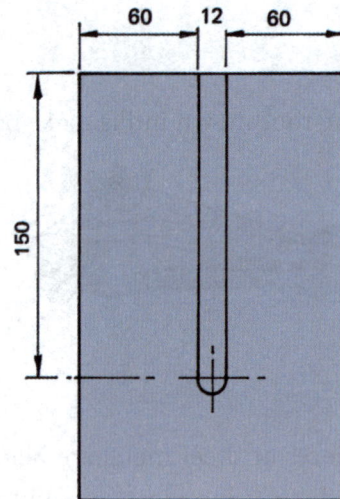

Fig. 6.49

16. When would you use a pad handle saw?

17. (a) What type of work is a junior hacksaw used for?
    (b) Describe one method used to keep the blade tensioned in a junior hacksaw.

18. (a) Name four types of cold chisels and give one use for each one.
    (b) Name one material used for making cold chisels.
    (c) Fig 6.50 shows a cold chisel being used to cut waste from a piece of metal. Name the angles A and B.
    (d) What is meant by a 'mushroom' head on a chisel?

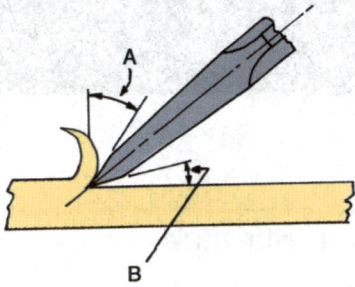

19. (a) Sketch three common types of engineer's hammer and name each one.
    (b) Give one use for the round end of a ball pein hammer.
    (c) Which of the following is given as the weight of a hammer:
        (i)   the combined weight of the head and the handle
        (ii)  the weight of the handle
        (iii) the weight of the head?
    (d) Give two reasons why the work should not be struck with the edge of the face of a hammer.

20. (a) For what purpose are 'soft hammers' used?
    (b) Name three materials from which soft hammer heads are made.

21. Give two uses for a bench block.

# Drilling

# 7

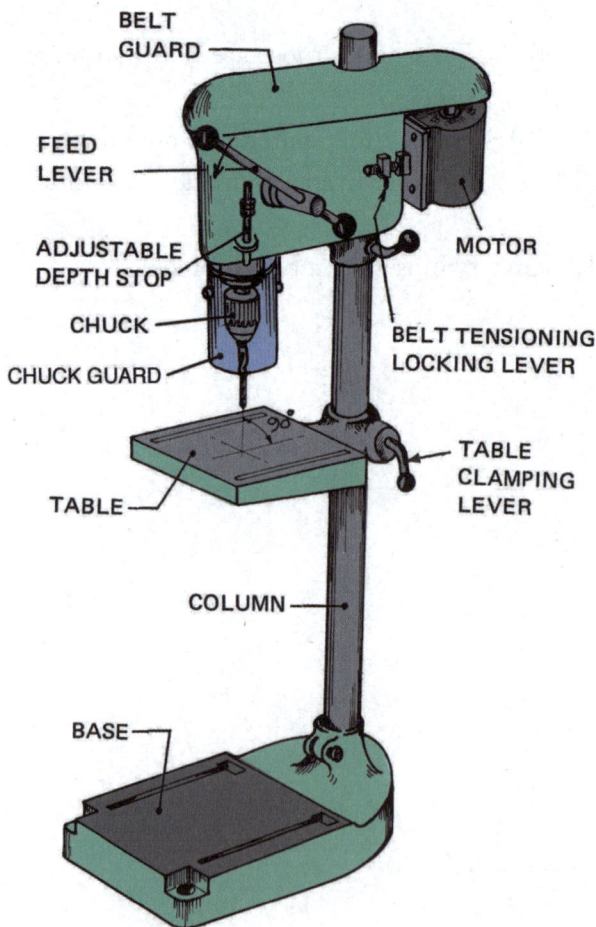

**Fig. 7.1**
Pillar drilling machine

Labels for Fig. 7.1:
- BELT GUARD
- FEED LEVER
- ADJUSTABLE DEPTH STOP
- CHUCK
- CHUCK GUARD
- TABLE
- COLUMN
- BASE
- MOTOR
- BELT TENSIONING LOCKING LEVER
- TABLE CLAMPING LEVER

## The Drilling Machine

A pillar drilling machine is shown in Fig. 7.1. This type is bolted directly to the floor. The table is at right angles to the chuck spindle. It can be raised, lowered or rotated on the column and is held in the required position by means of a clamp. The height at which the table is set depends on the height of the workpiece and the length of the drill bit being used. The table must be supported whenever the clamp is loosened, to prevent it from falling suddenly.

The upper surface of the base is machined, so that it can be used to support work which would be too high for the table. When the base is being used, the table must be swung to the side. The table and base have slots to accommodate bolts for a machine vice or for work-holding clamps.

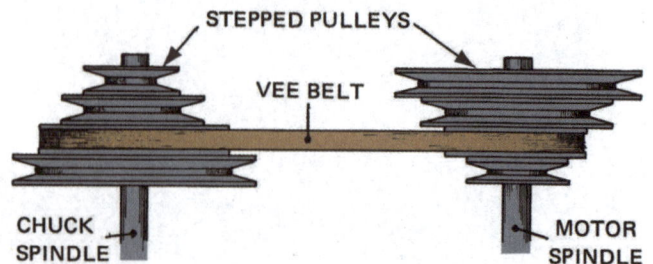

Labels for Fig. 7.2:
- STEPPED PULLEYS
- VEE BELT
- CHUCK SPINDLE
- MOTOR SPINDLE

**Fig. 7.2**
Vee belt and stepped pulleys

The drill speed can be altered by changing the position of the vee belt on the stepped pulleys. Drilling machines are also available with gear boxes which enable their speed to be changed by moving gear levers.

The chuck is lowered or raised by means of a 'rack and pinion' mechanism. The feed lever is attached to the spindle of the pinion and the chuck is lowered by turning the lever by hand. When the pressure is released, the pinion is turned in the opposite direction by means of a coil spring, thus returning the chuck to its original position.

**Fig. 7.3**
Chuck guard

A chuck guard is fitted to the drilling machine to protect the operator and the machine should *never* be used without it.

The bench drilling machine is another type of drilling machine. It is similar to the pillar type but has a shorter column and is mounted on a bench.

## Using the Drilling Machine

- Make sure there is no risk of hair or clothing getting caught in the twist drill or chuck.
- Never use the drilling machine without the chuck guard.
- When changing the vee belt, take care not to switch on the machine until the belt guard is replaced.
- Ensure that the chuck key is removed before using the machine.

- Never clean away swarf from under the twist drill by hand, as you could receive a bad cut from the point of the drill or from the swarf. If the machine is running, there is also a great risk of your sleeve getting wrapped around the drill.
- Ensure that the work is firmly gripped.
- Check that the drill speed is correct.
- Position the centre punch mark under the drill point before starting the machine. After the hole has been started, recheck its position.
- Use a cutting fluid as required.
- Reduce the pressure on the twist drill when it is breaking through, in case it binds in the hole.
- Take care not to drill into the vice or machine table.

## Holding the Work for Drilling

Fig. 7.4 shows a machine vice which is suitable for holding work to be drilled. It has a slotted base for bolting to the drilling machine table. Care must be taken to avoid marking it with the twist drill. One way of protecting the vice is to place a piece of wood under the workpiece, Fig. 7.5. The top and bottom faces of the wood must be parallel to ensure that the hole being drilled will be perpendicular to the face of the workpiece.

Various types of clamps are also used for holding work for drilling. Two methods of clamping work are shown in Fig. 7.6.

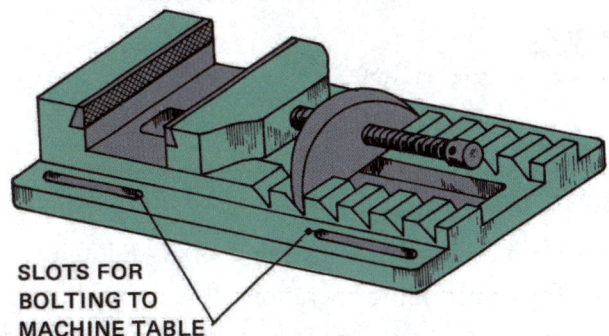

SLOTS FOR BOLTING TO MACHINE TABLE

**Fig. 7.4**
Machine vice

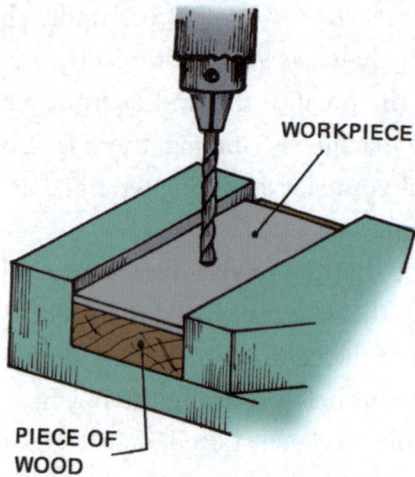

WORKPIECE

PIECE OF WOOD

**Fig. 7.5**

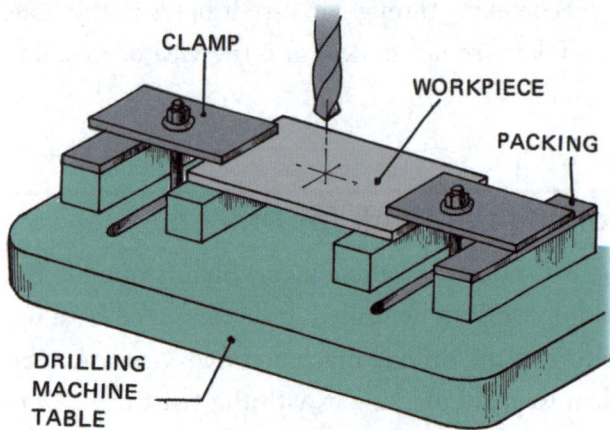

CLAMP

WORKPIECE

PACKING

DRILLING MACHINE TABLE

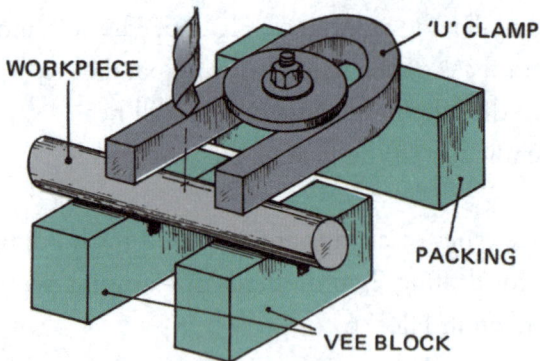

'U' CLAMP

WORKPIECE

PACKING

VEE BLOCK

**Fig. 7.6**
Methods of clamping work

## Hand Drill

The hand drill is driven by hand and is suitable only for light drilling operations. It is useful for drilling work which cannot be taken to the drilling machine or for drilling at locations where electric power is not available. It takes drills up to about 8mm in diameter. Bevel gears are used to rotate the chuck spindle. Hand drills are also available with a breast plate instead of a holding handle, which enables greater pressure to be applied to the drill bit. Battery–operated hand drills are now more commonly used.

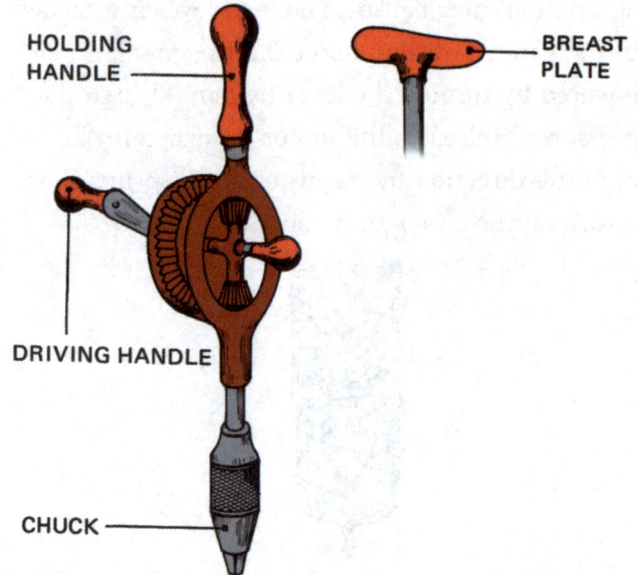

HOLDING HANDLE

BREAST PLATE

DRIVING HANDLE

CHUCK

**Fig. 7.7**
Hand drill

## Battery-Operated Hand Drill

This is powered by a rechargable battery. It can be purchased with two batteries, so that when one becomes discharged there is a spare available. The discharged battery can then be recharged.

**Fig. 7.8**
Battery-operated hand drill

In addition to drill bits, it can also grip screwdriver bits and can be operated forward or reverse. This makes it particularly useful for inserting or withdrawing screws, especially wood screws and it is widely used for this purpose. It is particularly useful for work at locations where an electric power supply is not available.

## Electric Hand Drill

This drills holes much faster and requires less effort than the hand or breast drills. It is useful for drilling work which cannot be taken to, or set up on a drilling machine and for drilling a component part of an assembly without having to dismantle it. Large electric hand drills can take drills up to 13mm in diameter.

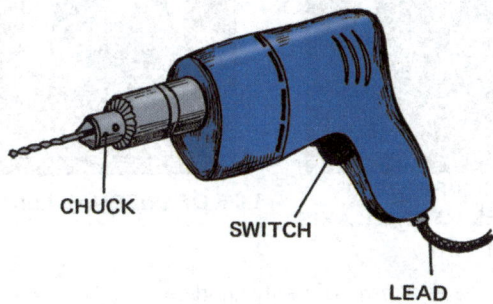

**Fig. 7.9**
Electric hand drill

## Twist Drills

Twist drills are made from high-speed steel. Drills up to 13mm usually have parallel shanks. Larger ones have taper shanks, Fig. 7.13. The parallel shank drills are held in a drill chuck. The taper shank ones are held in the taper bore of a drilling machine spindle.

The drill flutes provide the cutting lips and also a passageway for the swarf to escape and for the cutting fluid to reach the cutting edges.

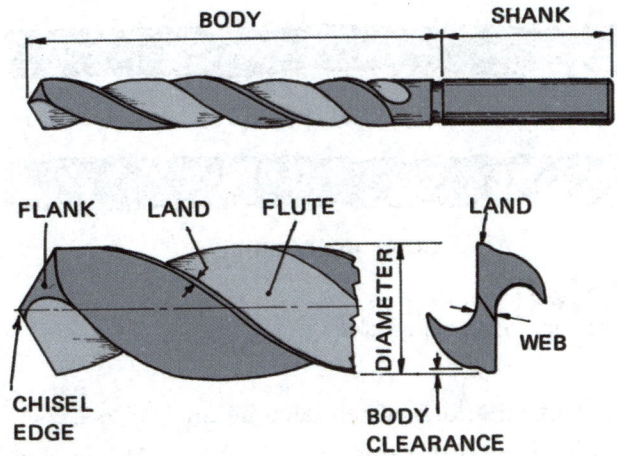

**Fig. 7.10**
Drill parts

Body clearance is provided by having the body diameter slightly less than the width across the lands. The purpose of body clearance is to reduce friction.

Standard drills have a point angle of 118°, Fig. 7.11, 59° on each side of the centre line. This is the most suitable angle for general work. The lip clearance angle is usually about 12°.

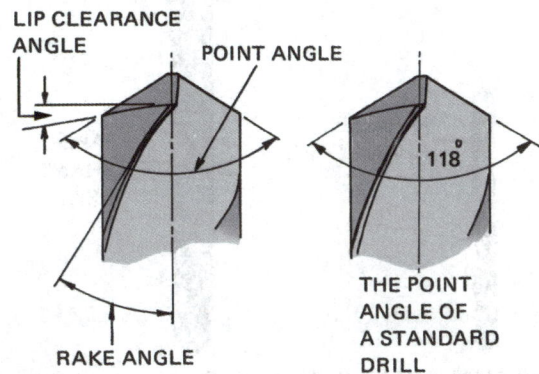

**Fig. 7.11**
The angles on the point of a drill

There are special drills available with 'slow' or 'quick' helixes, Fig. 7.12. The effect of the slow helix is to reduce the rake angle. Slow helix drills are used for drilling brass and bronze. The quick helix gives a greater rake angle, and quick helix drills are used for drilling soft materials such as copper and aluminium.

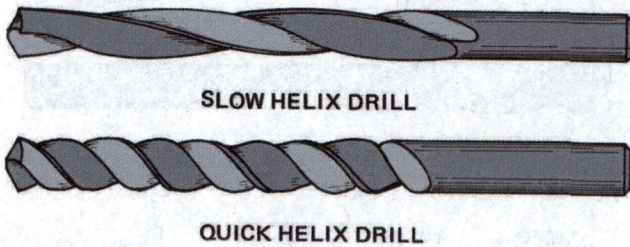

**SLOW HELIX DRILL**

**QUICK HELIX DRILL**

**Fig. 7.12**
Drills with special helix angles

Drill size markings often become unclear as a result of the drill slipping in the chuck. When this happens, the drill size must be checked with a drill gauge, Chapter 5, Fig. 5.48.

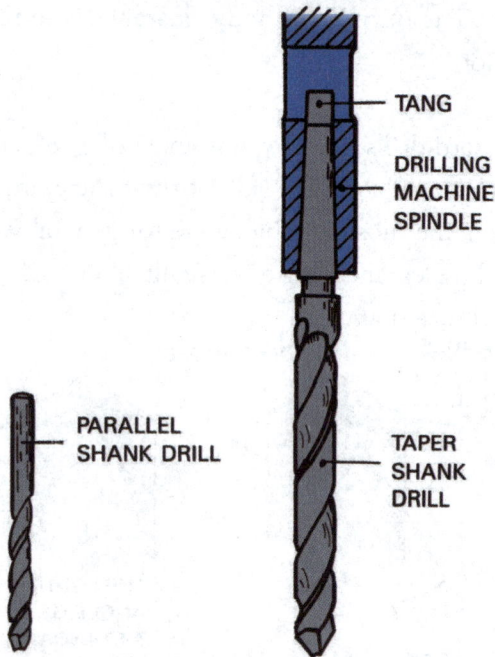

A TAPER SHANK DRILL GRIPS IN THE TAPER BORE OF THE DRILLING MACHINE SPINDLE

TANG

DRILLING MACHINE SPINDLE

PARALLEL SHANK DRILL

TAPER SHANK DRILL

A PARALLEL SHANK DRILL IS HELD IN A CHUCK WHICH IS TIGHTENED OR LOOSENED WITH A KEY

**Fig. 7.13**
Gripping drills

## Drill Grinding

Twist drills must be re-ground if the lips become blunt or chipped or if the land becomes worn away towards the point. To cut efficiently and

accurately, the clearance angle and the point angle must be correct. Both lips must be at the same angle to the drill axis and of equal length.

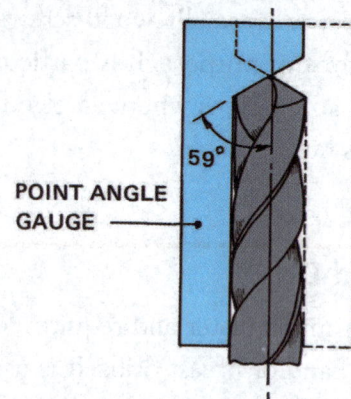

59°

POINT ANGLE GAUGE

**Fig. 7.14**
Both lips must be at the same angle to the drill axis

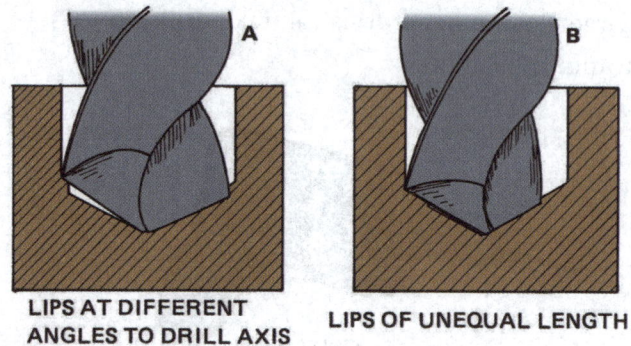

A

B

LIPS AT DIFFERENT ANGLES TO DRILL AXIS

LIPS OF UNEQUAL LENGTH

**Fig. 7.15**
Oversize holes as a result of faulty grinding

## Drill Drift

A drift is used for removing tools, such as drills reamers and arbors, from the drilling machine spindle, Fig. 7.16 A, or from taper sleeves. A small block of wood should be placed on the machine table under the tool, Fig. 7.16 B, to prevent damage to the tool and table during the removal.

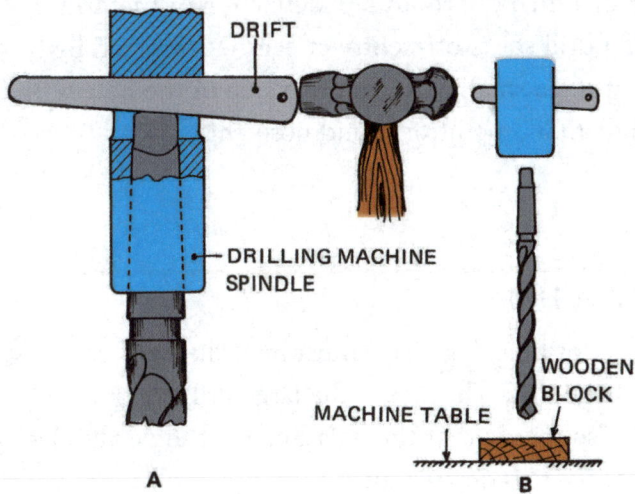

- The size of the drill: The larger the drill, the slower the spindle speed (see method of calculating below).
- The type of material being drilled: Usually, the softer the material, the higher the speed.
- The type of drill: High-speed steel drills can be run at far higher speeds than high carbon steel ones, because they retain their hardness up to a far higher temperature.
- The use of a coolant: Using a coolant when appropriate allows the drill to be operated at a higher speed.

## Morse Taper Sleeves

Morse taper sleeves are used when the taper shank of a tool is too small for the machine socket in which it is to be used. The shank of the tool is inserted into the sleeve, which is then inserted into the tapered socket of the machine, Fig. 7.17 B. Sometimes, more than one sleeve is required. They are commonly used for holding such tools as taper shank drills and reamers in drilling machine spindles and in lathe tailstocks.

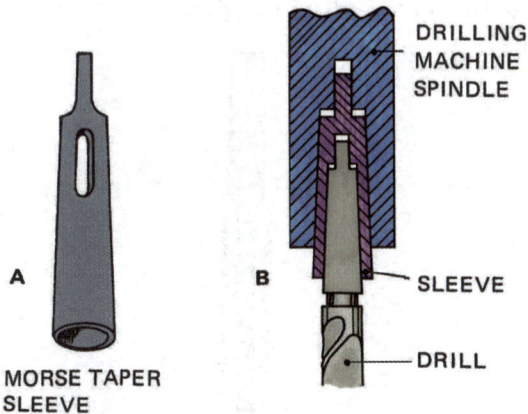

**Fig. 7.17**

## Spindle Speed of Drilling Machines

The spindle speed (revolutions per minute) of a drilling machine depends on:

## Cutting Speed

Cutting speeds for tools are given in metres per minute. To calculate the spindle speeds (or rotational speed of drills), the following formula can be used:

$$N = \frac{S \times 1000}{\pi \times D} \text{ rev/min}$$

where   N = Spindle speed in rev/min.
S = Cutting speed in metres/min.
D = Diameter of drill in millimetres/min.

**Example:**  Calculate the drilling machine spindle speed in rev/min to drill a 6mm diameter hole in a material whose recommended cutting speed is 30m/mm.
(For these calculations, it is usually sufficiently accurate to take π as 3.)

$$N = \frac{S \times 1000}{\pi \times D}$$

S = 30m/mm
D = 6mm

$$\therefore N = \frac{30 \times 1000}{3 \times 6} \text{ rev/min}$$

= 1,667 rev/min to nearest revolution.

## Feed

Feed is the rate at which the drill penetrates the material being drilled. If too much pressure is applied to the feed lever, there is a danger that the drill will overheat, bind in the hole or break. If the pressure is too little, the drill may just rub without cutting, which may cause it to lose its edge. The feed should be reduced when the drill point is breaking through the material.

## Drilling Sheet Metal

Care must be taken not to apply too much pressure to the feed lever when drilling through sheet metal. There is a danger of the drill catching in the work and carrying it around. It is also difficult to get the hole circular. These difficulties can be overcome by clamping the sheet metal between two thicker pieces of material, marking the position of the hole on the upper one and then drilling through the three of them. Making the drill point angle more obtuse also helps when drilling sheet metal.

## Locating a Hole Centre

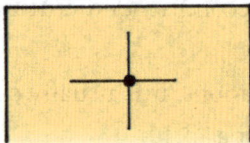

Fig. 7.18
Locating a hole centre

Locate the position of the hole centre by means of intersecting lines, Fig. 7.18. Lightly centre-punch the intersection. If the punch mark happens to be slightly off, it should be drawn over with the centre-punch before deepening it with a heavier blow. The work must be so positioned on the drilling machine that the drill point fits into the punch mark without any deflection of the drill. If a drill starts off-centre, it can be corrected by cutting a small groove at one side of the hole with a diamond point or round nose chisel.

## Pilot Hole

A pilot hole, Fig. 7.19, must be drilled before using a large drill. This keeps the large drill central, and it also means that the chisel edge of the drill does not have to do any cutting.

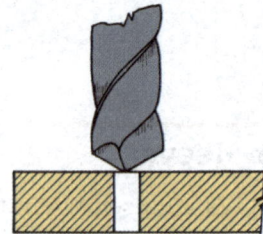

Fig. 7.19
Pilot hole

## Tapping Size Hole

This is a hole that is drilled prior to cutting an internal thread. It must be smaller than the tap to allow for the depth of the thread.

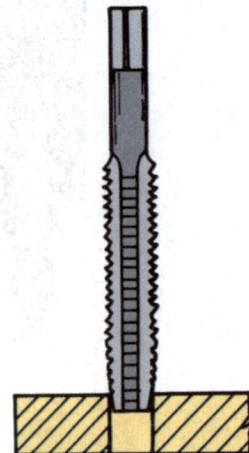

Fig. 7.20
Tapping size hole

## Clearance Hole

A clearance hole is slightly larger than the bolt, stud or screw that passes through it. When two parts are to be bolted together, Fig. 7.21 A, both must have clearance holes.

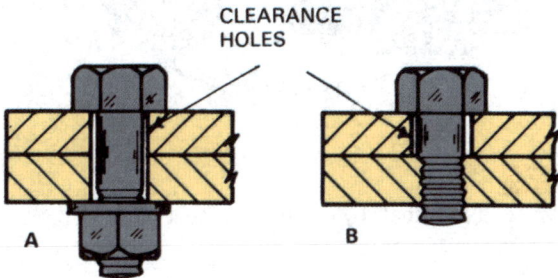

**Fig. 7.21**
Clearance holes

When a part is secured to another by means of screws, Fig. 7.21 B, the outer one must have clearance holes. The clearance enables bolts to be inserted quickly. Without clearance, all bolts cannot be inserted if any one of the holes is slightly out.

## Blind Hole

This is a hole that does not go all the way through a part. When it is not practical to have a bolt going through a part, a blind hole can be drilled in it, then tapped and a stud or screw used. This is done on engine blocks.

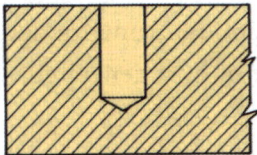

**Fig. 7.22**
A blind hole

## Countersinking

Countersinking is the enlarging of the mouths of holes to accommodate the heads of countersunk head screws and rivets. Countersinking cutters have point angles of either 60° or 90°, Fig. 7.23.

A twist drill can also be used, but the point must be ground to the required angle.

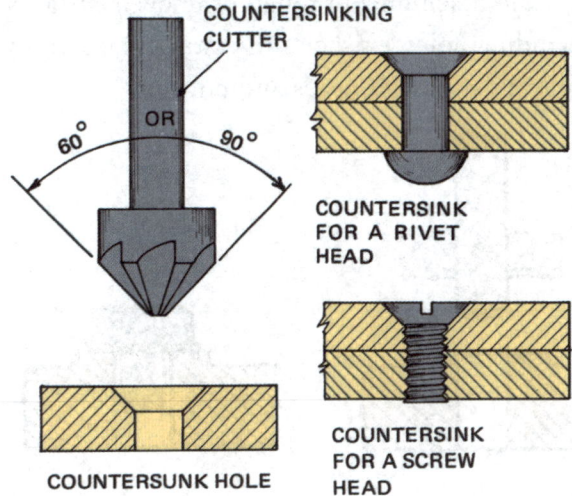

**Fig. 7.23**
Countersinking

## Counterboring

This is the increasing of hole diameters to certain depths, usually to accommodate the heads of screws, such as allen screws and cheese head screws. It allows the head to be flush with or below the surface of the part. A counterboring cutter, Fig. 7.24, is used for this work.

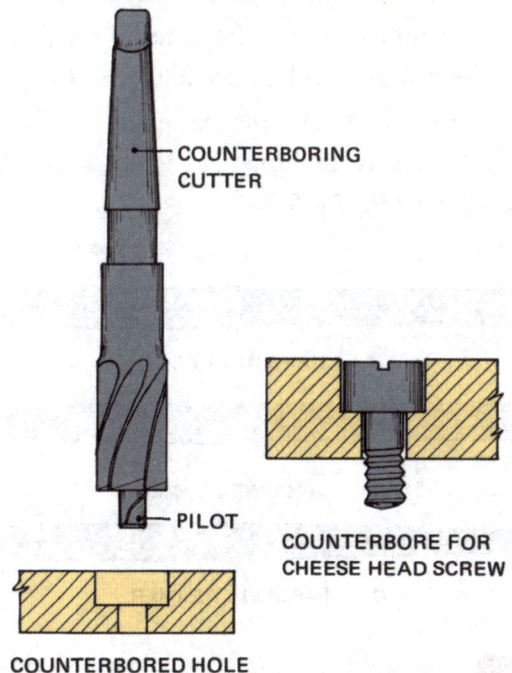

**Fig. 7.24**
Counterboring

83

## Spot Facing

This is the machining of rough or uneven surfaces surrounding holes, e.g. holes in casting. It provides a flat seating for bolt heads and nuts.

**Fig. 7.25**
Spot facing

## Reamers

Reamers are used for finishing holes smoothly and accurately. A slightly undersize hole is first drilled and the reamer is then used to finish it to size. Reamers are usually made from high-speed steel. There are various types available. A hand reamer, Fig. 7.26 A, has a square end for a tap wrench and can have either straight or helical flutes. Fig. 7.26 B, shows a machine reamer. It has a taper shank and is held in the drilling machine spindle or in the tailstock of the lathe. A taper pin reamer is shown in Fig. 7.26 C. It is used to enlarge and taper a hole to suit a taper pin, Fig. 7.27.

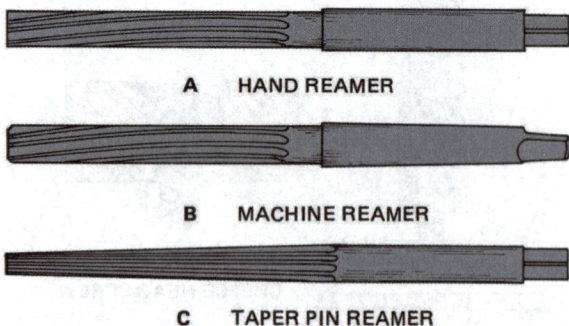

A    **HAND REAMER**

B    **MACHINE REAMER**

C    **TAPER PIN REAMER**

**Fig. 7.26**
Reamers

A reamer must always be turned clockwise, whether being entered or withdrawn from a hole, and a cutting fluid should be used as appropriate.

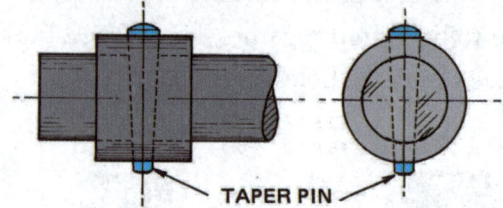

**TAPER PIN**

**Fig. 7.27**
A collar fixed to a shaft by means of a taper pin

## Cutting Fluids

Cutting fluids, sometimes called 'coolants' or 'cutting lubricants', are used to aid machining operations, for instance drilling and turning. The following are advantages that can be gained by use of a cutting fluid:

- The cutting tool lasts longer.
- The machining can be carried out at a higher speed.
- A better surface finish is produced.
- The chips are carried away.

A cutting fluid works in two ways:

1. As a coolant, carrying away the heat generated and keeping the tool and workpiece cool.
2. As a lubricant, reducing friction and thereby the amount of heat generated.

The type of fluid to be used depends on the type of material being cut and on the type of operation. Some metals, cast iron and brass for instance, can be machined dry. A common cutting fluid used is a mixture of soluble oil and water. The mixture can be about one part oil to thirty parts water, but it is better to follow the supplier's instructions. This cutting fluid is good for cooling and has many applications. Mineral and lard oil compounds are also widely used. They have good lubricating properties and are especially suitable for slow, heavy machining.

A pump, driven by the machine, is the most efficient way of supplying the cutting fluid to the cutting tool and workpiece. The cutting fluid returns to the pump reservoir through a filter so that it can be continuously circulated. If a pump is not fitted, a drip or small brush can be used.

The table below shows the cutting fluids that are suitable for general machining operations using high-speed steel tools.

| Material | Cutting Fluid |
|---|---|
| Mild Steel | Soluble oil |
| High Carbon Steel | Soluble oil; Paraffin |
| Cast Iron | Dry; Compressed air to cool |
| Brass | Dry; Soluble oil |
| Aluminium | Soluble oil; Paraffin |
| Copper | Soluble oil; Lard oil |

## Exercises

1. A drilling machine is shown in Fig. 7.28. Name the parts 1 to 9 indicated.

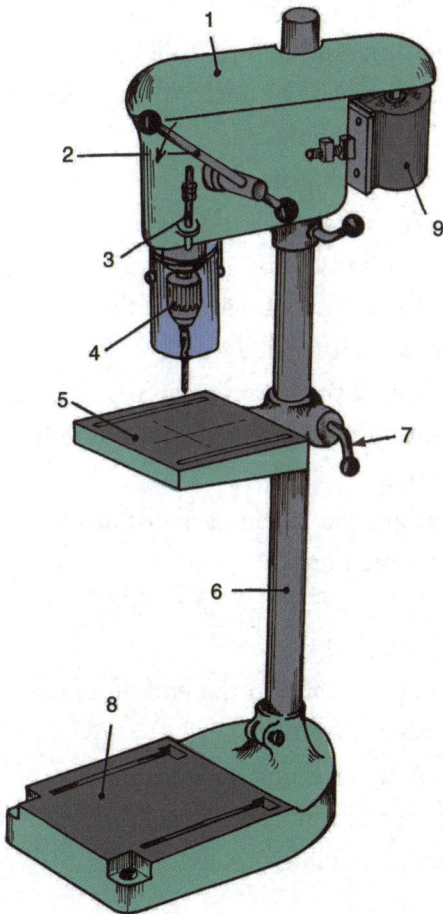

Fig. 7.28

2. What is the function of the stepped pulleys on a drilling machine?

3. Why must the table of a drilling machine be at right angles to the axis of the drill?

4. What is the purpose of the slots in a drilling machine table?

5. Why is it sometimes necessary to change the position of the table on the drilling machine column?

6. What is the function of the depth stop on a drilling machine?

7. Give two methods of holding work on the drilling machine.

8. A piece of wood is sometimes placed under the workpiece when a hole is being drilled.
   (a) What is the reason for this?
   (b) If the top and bottom faces of the piece of wood are not parallel, what effect would it have on the drilled hole?

9. State two occasions when you would use a hand drill rather than the drilling machine.

10. What advantages has an electric hand drill over a manually-operated hand drill?

11. (a) Why do battery-operated hand drills often have a spare battery?
    (b) Give one advantage of a battery-operated hand drill over a conventional electric hand drill.

12. Name the parts of the twist drill indicated in Fig. 7.29 below and state the function of each one.

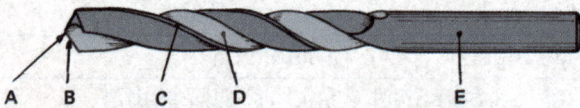

**Fig. 7.29**

13. With reference to Fig. 7.30 below, name the angles A, B and C indicated.

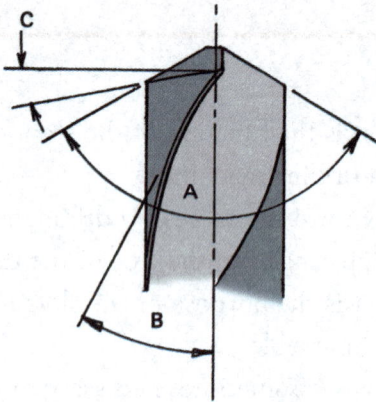

**Fig 7.30**

14. What is the value of the point angle on a standard drill?

15. What is the function of each of the following drill angles?
(a) lip clearance angle; (b) rake angle.

16. When would each of the following be used?
(a) A slow helix drill
(b) A quick helix drill

17. After grinding a drill it is discovered that it makes oversize holes. Give two possible causes for this.

18. (a) Name the drill bits A and B shown in Fig. 7.31.
(b) Describe how each drill bit is held in a drilling machine.

**Fig. 7.31**

19. Make a sketch showing how a taper shank drill is held in the drilling machine.

20. Why is a piece of wood placed on the drilling machine table when removing a taper shank drill?

21. What is a drill drift used for?

22. Sketch a taper sleeve and state its use.

23. What factors govern the spindle speed of a drilling machine?

24. A 5mm hole is to be drilled in a material whose recommended cutting speed is 30m/min. Calculate the drilling machine speed in rev/min required. (Take $\pi$ as 3.)

25. (a) What is meant by drill feed?
(b) Why is the feed reduced when the drill is breaking through the material?

26. Why is the position of the centre of a hole punch-marked before drilling?

27. What is meant by each of the following?
(a) A pilot hole
(b) A tapping size hole
(c) A clearance hole
(d) A blind hole

28. What is countersinking and for what purpose is it carried out?

29. Explain, with the aid of a sketch, what is meant by counterboring, and state its purpose.

30. What are the advantages of finishing a hole with a reamer?

31. What is the function of each of the following?
(a) The square on the end of a parallel shank reamer.
(b) A taper shank on a reamer.

32. List four advantages of using a cutting fluid when machining metals.

# Fitting and Assembly 1: Screwing, Tapping and Riveting

## 8

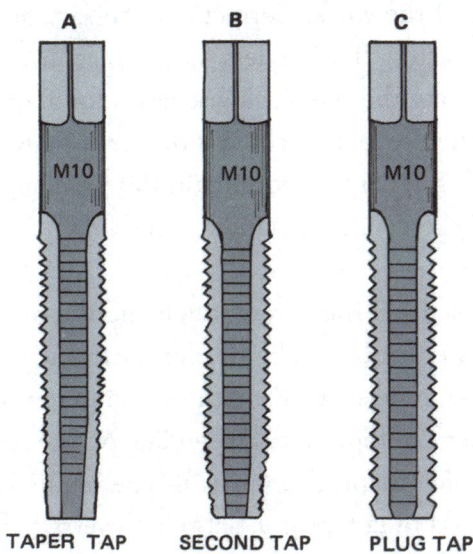

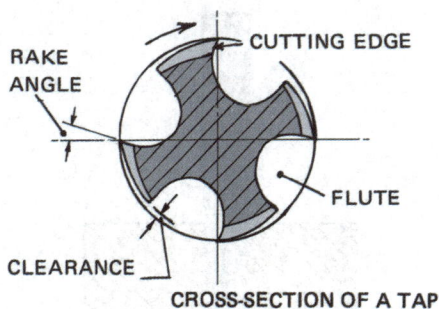

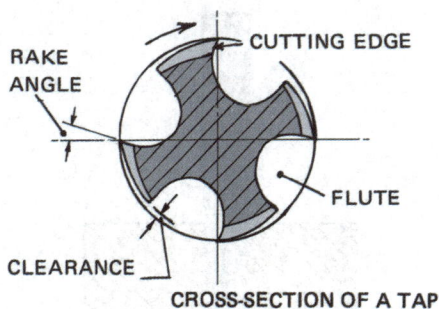

**Fig. 8.1**

Taps

## Taps

Taps are used for cutting internal threads, such as the thread on a nut. This is called tapping. There are three kinds of tap: taper tap, second or intermediate tap and plug or bottoming tap.

**Taper tap** This is tapered over the first 8 to 10 threads, allowing it to enter the hole and gradually cut to the full thread depth.

**Second tap** This is tapered over the first four threads or so and is used after the taper tap when tapping a blind hole.

**Plug tap** This has only a short taper — one or two threads. It is used for finishing the thread at the bottom of a deep or blind hole.

Taps are made from high-speed steel. They are hard and brittle and must be used with care to avoid breaking them, especially the smaller ones. The flutes along the body provide the cutting edges. The flutes also provide spaces for the chips being cut and passageways for the cutting fluid to reach the cutting edges. The ends are square for gripping in a tap wrench. Taps should always be cleaned after use.

## Tap Wrench

A tap wrench is used to rotate taps. There are two types shown in Fig. 8.2.

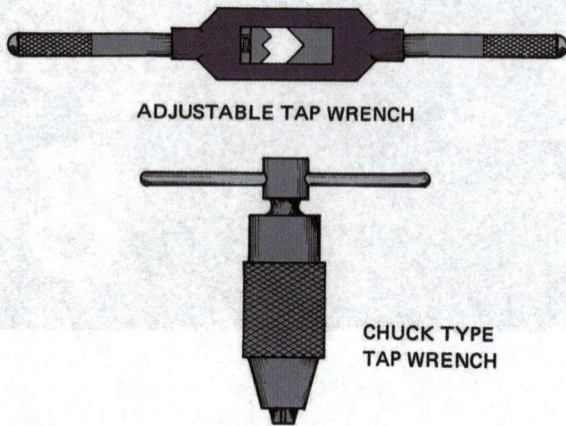

ADJUSTABLE TAP WRENCH

CHUCK TYPE
TAP WRENCH

**Fig. 8.2**
Tap wrenches

## Tapping

When mating parts are being tapped and screwed, the tapping should be done first.

The reason for this is that the size of the tap is fixed, but the die for cutting an external thread can be adjusted slightly, so that the thread on the bar can be progressively deepened until it just fits the tapped hole.

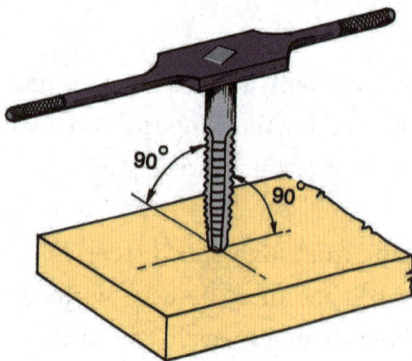

90°

90°

**Fig. 8.3**
Tapping

Before tapping, a 'tapping size' hole is drilled. This is smaller than the size of the tap. The drill size can be obtained from a table. If a table is not available, it may be obtained by trying the taper tap in the drill gauge until the hole is found into which it fits to a depth of three threads. Another method is to select the drill which just passes through a nut with the same size and type of thread.

To tap the hole, grip the taper tap in the tap wrench and enter it in the hole. Apply a slight downward pressure, keeping the tap in line with the hole, and turn it clockwise until it starts to cut. When it has just gripped, check if it is square with the face of the work. Correct, if necessary, and apply a cutting fluid, unless tapping cast iron or brass. Rotate the tap clockwise again for about half a turn, then reverse it about a quarter of a turn to break off the chips. Continue in this manner, gradually screwing the tap into the hole.

If the hole is all the way through and the material is thin, the thread can be finished with the taper tap. If the material is thick, the second tap must be used after the taper tap. Depending on the depth of the hole, the plug tap may also be required. The second and plug taps must also be reversed about every half turn to break off chips.

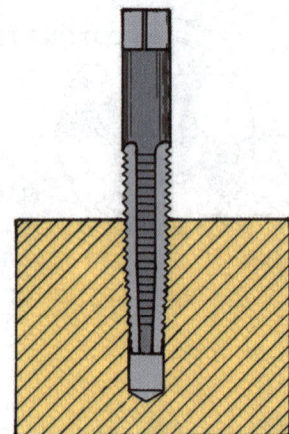

**Fig. 8.4**
Tapping a blind hole

## Tapping a Blind Hole

A blind hole cannot be threaded at its bottom with a taper tap. Therefore, the second and plug taps must also be used. The taper tap is used first, then the second tap and finally the plug tap to finish the thread to the bottom. During the tapping, the tap must be withdrawn from time to time to remove swarf from the hole and from the tap flutes. Care must be taken to avoid forcing the tap against the bottom of the hole as this could cause it to break. If the blind hole is shallow, it may not be possible to start the thread with the taper tap.

It should therefore be drilled deeper than the required length of thread, if possible. If not, it may be started with the second tap, but special care must be taken.

**Examples of common tapping faults and their possible causes are given in the table below:**

| Fault | Causes |
|---|---|
| Broken tap | Tapping hole too small. Not reversing tap to break off chips. Tap not in alignment with hole. Not starting with taper tap. Attaching wrench while tap is in hole. |
| Shallow thread | Tapping hole too big. |
| Stripped thread | Not reversing tap. Tap flutes clogged. Lack of cutting fluid. |
| Rough thread | Lack of cutting fluid. Tap flutes clogged. |
| Bolt not square with work face | Hole not drilled square with work face. |

## Stocks and Dies

Stocks and dies are used for cutting external threads on round bars and on pipes. This is called screwing. The dies are made from high carbon steel or from high-speed steel. They are held in stocks to rotate them.

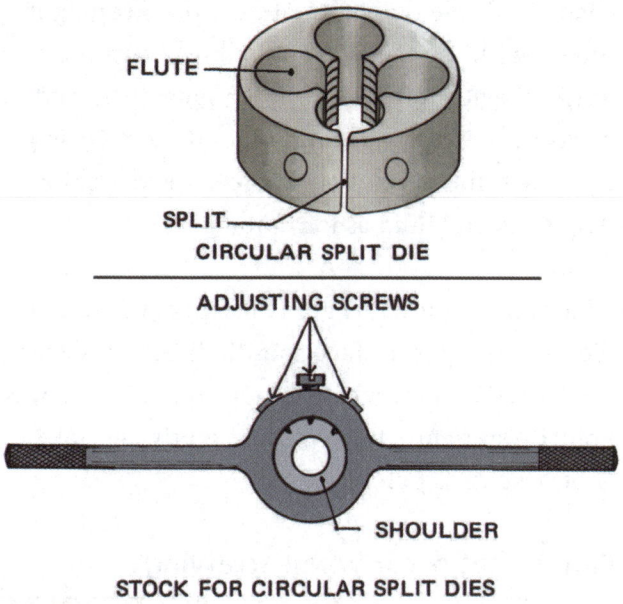

Fig. 8.5

There are different forms of stocks and dies available. Circular split dies are the ones most commonly used in school workshops. The split permits a small amount of opening and closing of the die. The point of the central adjusting screw in the stock fits into the split in the die. To open the die, the screws at either side are loosened and the centre one tightened. After adjusting, the side screws are retightened to lock the die in the stock. To close the die, the centre screw is loosened and the side screws tightened. The first two or three threads on one side of the die are chamfered to make starting easier.

Before fitting the die, the stock recess must be thoroughly cleaned out to allow the die to seat properly. When fitted, the die chamfer must be on the underside and the stock retaining shoulder on top.

## Screwing

The end of the bar should be chamfered to help start the die. If using a circular split die, it should be opened fully to take a light first cut.

Place the die on the end of the bar with its chamfered side down. Rotate the die, keeping it square with the bar, and apply downward pressure until it begins to cut. Check for squareness and correct if necessary. Continue rotating, reversing after each full revolution to break off the chips. Apply cutting fluid as for tapping.

When the required length is reached, remove the die by turning it in the opposite direction. Clean the thread and try a nut on it, or try it in a tapped hole. If too tight, close the die slightly and take another cut, as before.

The deepening of the thread must continue until the nut can be just screwed on by hand without any slackness.

## Die Nut

A die nut is used for clearing the grooves of damaged or rusted threads. It is rotated with a spanner. It is not intended for cutting new threads.

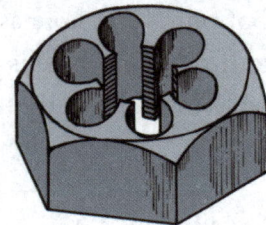

**Fig. 8.6**
Die nut

### Faults that occur when screwing

| Fault | Cause |
|---|---|
| Broken die teeth | Oversize bar |
| | Jerking the die |
| | Not starting with chamfered side of die |
| | Die not square with bar |
| | Not reversing die |
| Stripped thread | Cut too heavy |
| | Deepening the cut after it has been started |
| | Lack of cutting fluid |
| | Not reversing die |
| | Clogged flutes |
| 'Drunken' thread (bar going from side to side as it is screwed into tapped hole) | Not starting die square with bar |
| Difficulty in starting die square | Uneven chamfer on bar |
| | Broken teeth on starting side of die |
| Rough threads | Lack of cutting fluid |
| | Cut too heavy |
| | Clogged flutes |
| Bar end twisted off | Oversize bar |
| | Cut too heavy |

## Screw Thread Terms

**Crest** The most prominent part of the thread.

**Root** The bottom of the thread groove.

**Flank** The straight part of the thread between the root and the crest.

**Pitch** The distance between corresponding points on adjacent threads, measured parallel to the axis.

**Lead** The distance the screw moves along its axis in one revolution. On a single-start thread, the lead is equal to the pitch. On a double-start thread, it is twice the pitch.

**Major Diameter** The largest diameter of the screw thread. On a screw, it is the diameter at the crests.

**Minor or Core Diameter** This is the smallest diameter of a screw thread. It is equal to the major diameter minus twice the thread depth.

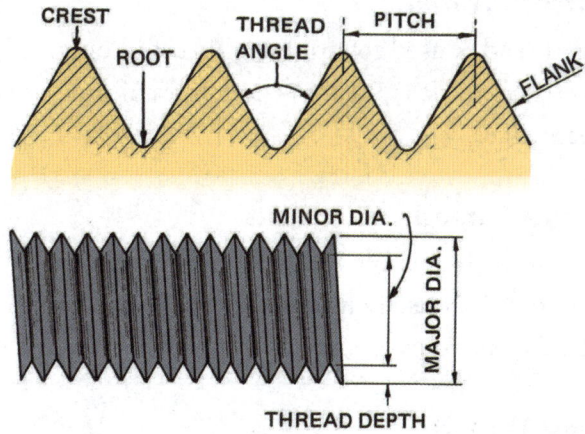

**Fig. 8.7**
Screw thread terms

## Types of Screw Threads

### ISO Metric Threads

This is an international screw thread system, which has been adopted in this country instead of now obsolete BSW, BSS and BA threads. The old threads are, however, still used occasionally. There is a fine and coarse series in the system. The coarse series is for general use and the fine for special applications. ISO metric threads are designated by the letter M, followed by the nominal size and pitch, both in millimetres.

**Examples**
(i) MIO x 1.25 — this indicates a nominal size of 10mm and a pitch of 1.25 mm (this is in the fine series).
(ii) MIO x 1.5 — this indicates a nominal size of 10mm and a pitch of 1.5 mm (this is in the coarse series).

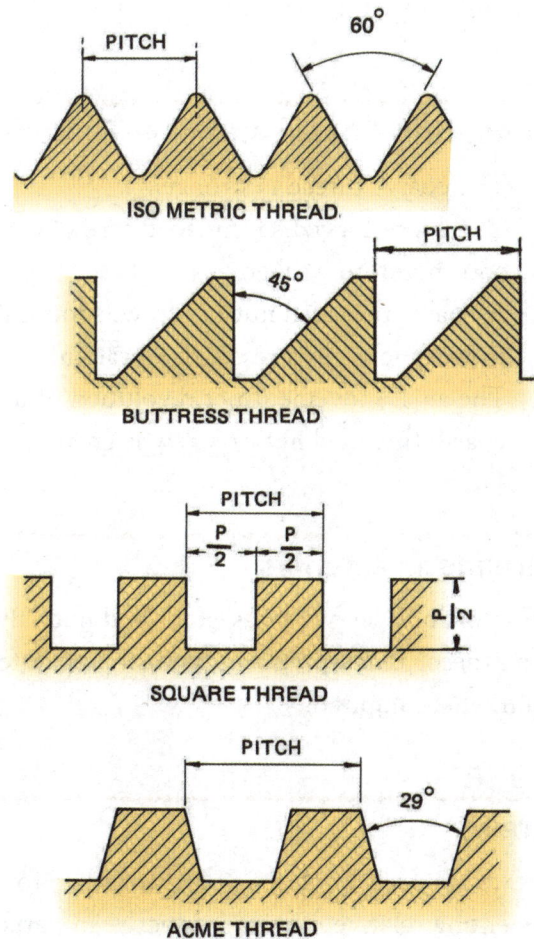

**Fig. 8.8**
Types of screw threads

When the thread is in the coarse series, it is not necessary to give the pitch. For instance, MIO x 1.5mm can be given as MIO.

## Buttress Thread

This thread is used for applying thrust in one direction only. It is used on the screws of quick release vices.

## Square Thread

This thread is suitable for applying thrust in both directions. It is used on screw jacks, vices, clamps and valve spindles.

## Acme Thread

The sloped flanks of this thread allow easy engagement of half nuts. It is used on the leadscrews of lathes.

## Comparing Coarse and Fine Threads

- The coarse thread is stronger.
- The core of a coarse threaded screw is smaller and therefore weaker.
- A coarse threaded nut or screw is more likely to work loose as a result of vibration.
- The axial movement per revolution of a coarse threaded nut or screw is greater.

## Threaded Fasteners

These include screws, bolts, studs and nuts. By using these, joined parts can be easily separated again when required.

## Screws

Screws are used for joining parts together, for preventing relative movements between parts and for adjustment purposes. When used for joining two parts, the screw passes through a clearance hole in the outer one and is screwed into a tapped hole in the inner one. It therefore does not require a nut. There are many different types of screw available.

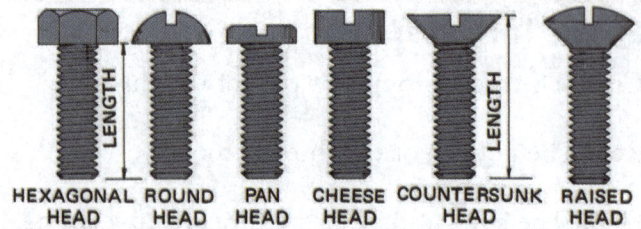

**Fig. 8.9**
Set screws

HEXAGONAL HEAD · ROUND HEAD · PAN HEAD · CHEESE HEAD · COUNTERSUNK HEAD · RAISED HEAD

**Set screws** are threaded for their full length and are available with various shapes of head, Fig. 8.9.

**Grub screws** are used to prevent relative movement between parts, such as a collar on a shaft, Fig. 8.10. They can be screwed below the surface. Therefore, when used on a revolving shaft, there is no danger of them striking anything.

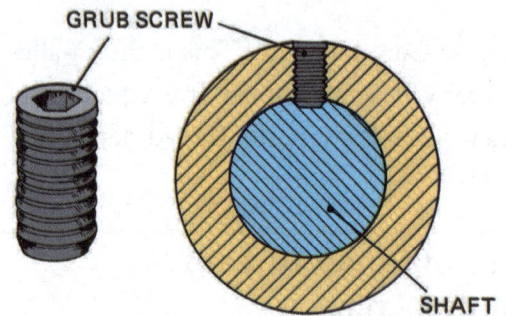

**Fig. 8.10**
Grub screw

**Thumb screws** are tightened and loosened by hand. They are often used for locking tools, such as wing compasses, at particular settings.

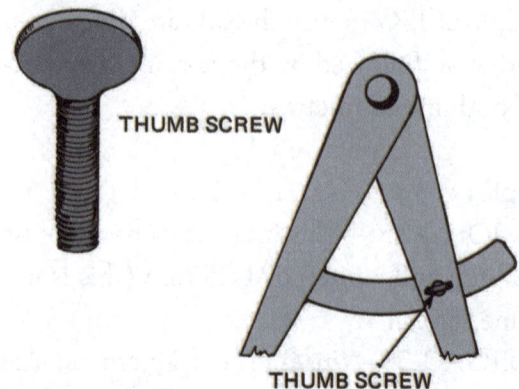

**Fig. 8.11**
Thumb screw

**Self-tapping screws** are used for sheet metal. There are various types available.

**Fig. 8.12**
Self-tapping screw

## Bolts

Bolts and nuts are often used for joining parts together. Bolts are usually threaded for only part of their length. They are available with various shapes of head, such as hexagonal, square and round. They are specified by their diameter, type of thread, length, material, finish and shape of head e.g. M10 x 50mm long, mild steel, sherardised and hexagonal head.

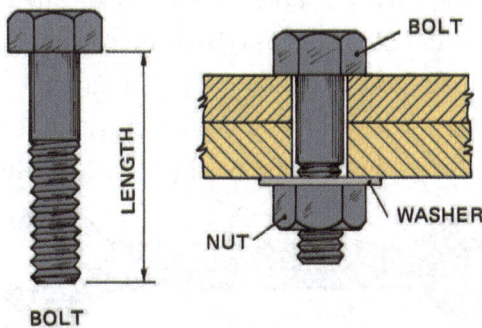

**Fig. 8.13**

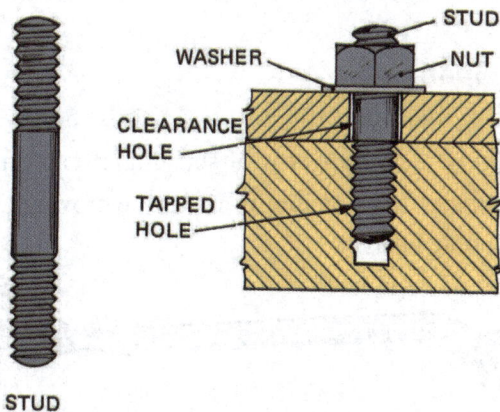

**Fig. 8.14**

## Studs

Studs are threaded at both ends. One end is screwed into a tapped hole in the main component and a nut is screwed onto the other end to tighten the parts together. If the main component is made from soft material, such as aluminium, the end being screwed into it can have a coarse thread. A coarse thread is less likely to strip. The other end can have a fine thread, so that there is less risk of the nut coming loose.

## Nuts

The thread on a nut must suit the bolt or stud on which it is to be used. They are usually hexagonal or square in shape. Special looking nuts are sometimes used to prevent loosening by vibration. They include a thin nut used with a plain nut, a castle or slotted nut used together with a split pin and nuts with nylon or fibre inserts. Wing nuts are tightened or loosened by hand. They are quick and easy to use but are suitable only where a high degree of tightness is not required, as for tensioning hacksaw blades.

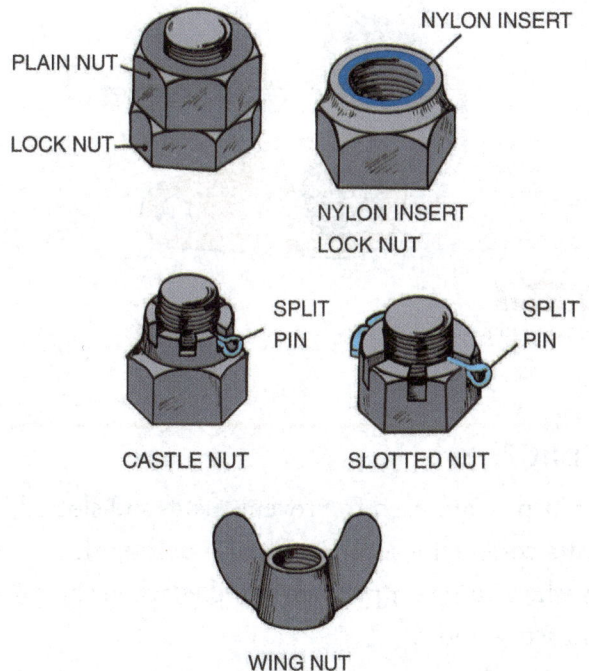

**Fig. 8.15**
Nuts

## Washers

Plain washers prevent damage to the surfaces of components when tightening nuts, bolts or screws. Spring washers, toothed washers and tab washers are locking devices.

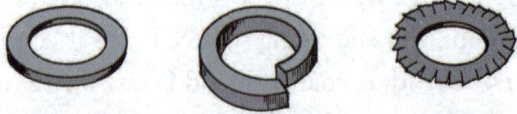

PLAIN WASHER   SPRING WASHER   TOOTHED WASHER

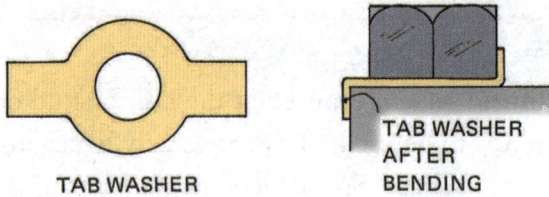

TAB WASHER

TAB WASHER AFTER BENDING

**Fig. 8.16**
Washers

## Locking Plate

This is another locking device. It fits over the nut or screw head and is secured to the component by a small screw.

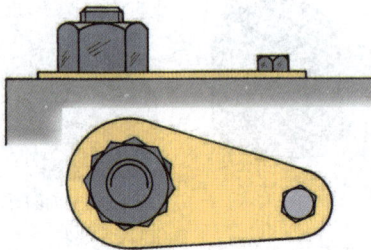

**Fig. 8.17**
Locking plate

## Split Pins

Split pins are used to prevent castle and slotted nuts coming loose. They are also used with washers to retain parts on spindles when the axial thrusts are low.

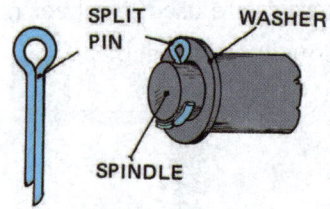

SPLIT PIN   WASHER

SPINDLE

**Fig. 8.18**
Split pin

## Spanners

Spanners are used for tightening and loosening nuts, bolts and screws of square or hexagonal shape. They are available in various sizes to fit standard nuts and bolts. The correct size spanner should always be used; otherwise, it may slip and cause an injury to the user or damage the nut or bolt corners.

### Open-Ended Spanners

These are usually double-ended and are the type most commonly used. The jaws are usually at an angle of 15° to the shank and by turning the spanner over it will be at a different angle to the nut. This enables it to be used in restricted spaces.

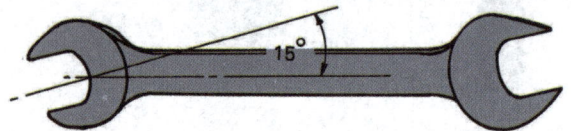

**Fig. 8.19**
Open-ended spanner

### Ring Spanner

This fits all around the nut, and if it is the correct size, there is no danger of it slipping. It can only be used where it is possible to fit it down over the nut or bolt head.

**Fig. 8.20**
Ring spanner

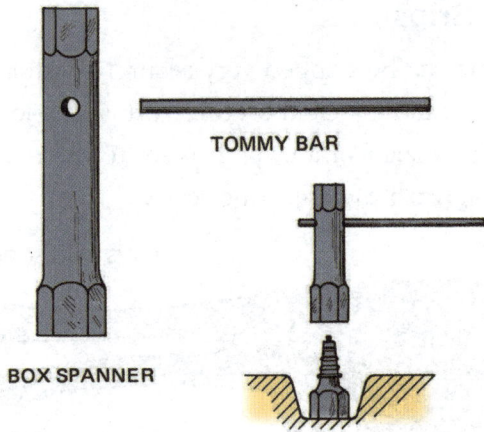

**TOMMY BAR**

**BOX SPANNER**

## Box Spanner

This is used on nuts in deep recesses, where there is insufficient room to turn other types of spanner. A common application is the removal and fitting of spark plugs. It is turned by means of a tommy bar.

## Socket Spanner

This fits down on the nut, like a ring or box spanner. A handle is attached to the other end to turn it. Sets are available, consisting of sockets in a wide range of sizes, different types of handles including a ratchet one, extensions of various lengths and a universal joint. These enable the work to be done quickly and can be used in confined places.

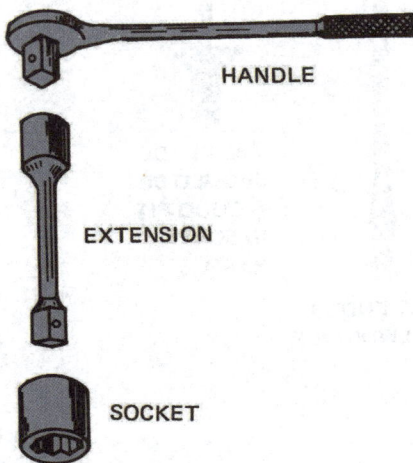

**HANDLE**

**EXTENSION**

**SOCKET**

Fig. 8.22
Socket set

## Adjustable Spanner

This can be adjusted to fit different size nuts and bolts. As there is a greater risk of it slipping, it should be used only when the correct size open-ended or ring spanner is not available.

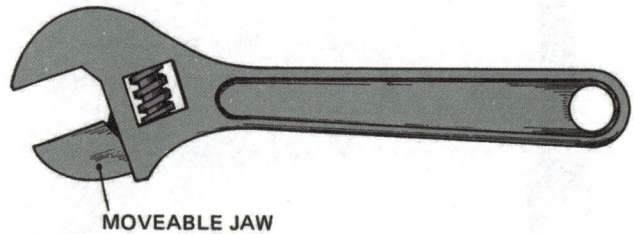

**MOVEABLE JAW**

Fig. 8.23
Adjustable spanner

## Adjustable Wrench

This is also used for tightening and loosening nuts and bolts. There are different types available.

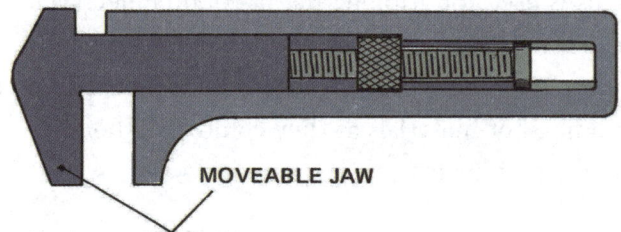

**MOVEABLE JAW**

Fig. 8.24
Adjustable wrench

## Stillson Wrench

This is also adjustable. It is used for turning pipes and cylindrical objects. It should be fitted so that it tightens on the object when turned. As the jaws are serrated, it should not be used on nuts or bolts as it would damage their corners.

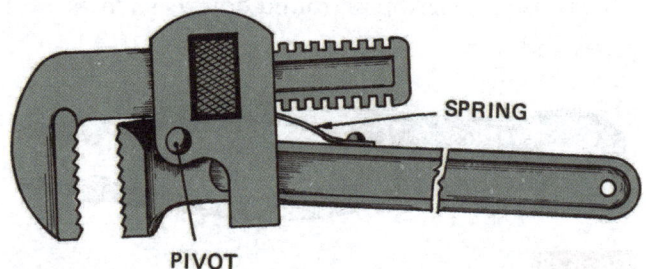

**SPRING**

**PIVOT**

Fig. 8.25
Stillson wrench

## Allen Key

Allen keys are used for turning hexagonal socket head screws.

Allen key

## Combination Pliers

This is used for gripping flat or round objects and also for cutting wire. The jaws are hardened and tempered. Therefore, they should not be used for holding hot materials as they could lose their hardness if heated.

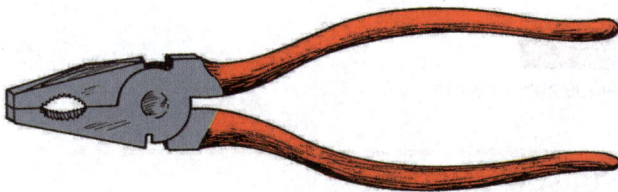

Fig. 8.27
Combination pliers

## Gas Pliers

This is used for gripping round objects such as pipes and bars.

Fig. 8.28
Gas pliers

## Vice Grips

Objects can be gripped very securely with a vice grips. It can be locked on the work and released again by means of a lever. It is set to the required opening with the adjusting screw.

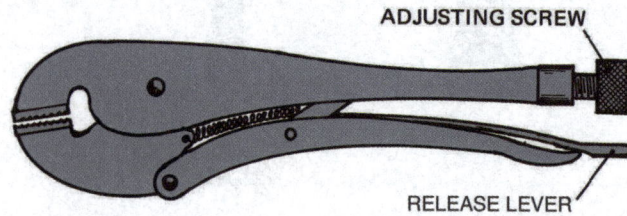

ADJUSTING SCREW

RELEASE LEVER

Fig. 8.29
Vice grips

## Screwdrivers

There are two main types of screwdriver — the flat-ended type and the Phillips type. The flat-ended screwdriver, which is the most common type, is used for turning slotted screws. The Phillips screwdriver is used for turning screws with cross-shaped recesses. Some screwdrivers are fitted with a ratchet device — this allows the screw to

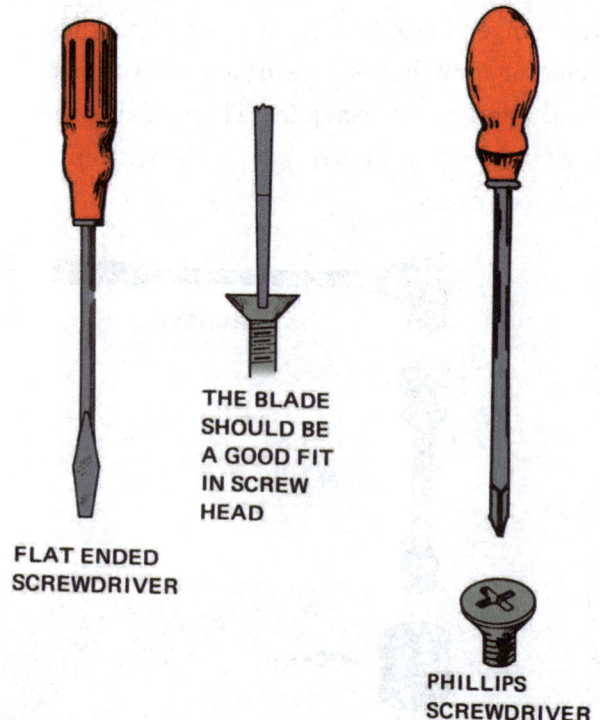

THE BLADE
SHOULD BE
A GOOD FIT
IN SCREW
HEAD

FLAT ENDED
SCREWDRIVER

PHILLIPS
SCREWDRIVER

Fig. 8.30
Screwdrivers

be turned all the way without removing the screwdriver from the slot. Screwdriver blades are made from alloy or high carbon steel, with the ends heat treated. The end must be a good fit in the screw head. When grinding the blade, care must be taken not to overheat the end, as it may lose its hardness.

## Rivets

Rivets are used for making permanent joints. A loose joint, such as that of a tongs, can be made by using a single rivet. Rivets are available in different materials, such as mild steel, aluminium, copper and brass. It is usually better to use rivets of the same material as the parts being joined. Rivets are classified according to their head shape, material, diameter and length.

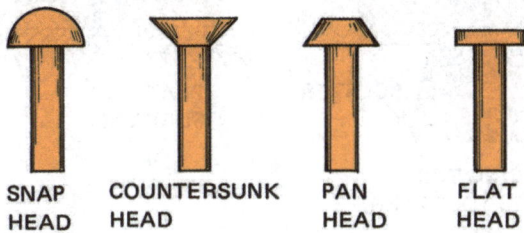

SNAP HEAD    COUNTERSUNK HEAD    PAN HEAD    FLAT HEAD

**Fig. 8.31**
Common rivet head shapes

Rivets are worked hot or cold. Hot rivets have the advantage that they shrink on cooling, thereby drawing the parts tighter together. In years gone by, rivets were widely used for gate-making, shipbuilding and structural steelwork, but this type of riveting has now been replaced by electric welding.

**Pop rivets**, Fig. 8.32, are very useful for light work. The second head is formed by drawing a pin with a head through the rivet, using a pop riveting pliers. This enlarges the end of the rivet, and as the drawing continues, the pin breaks, leaving its head behind. This type of riveting has the advantage that it can be carried out where only one side of the joint is accessible.

POP RIVETING PLIERS

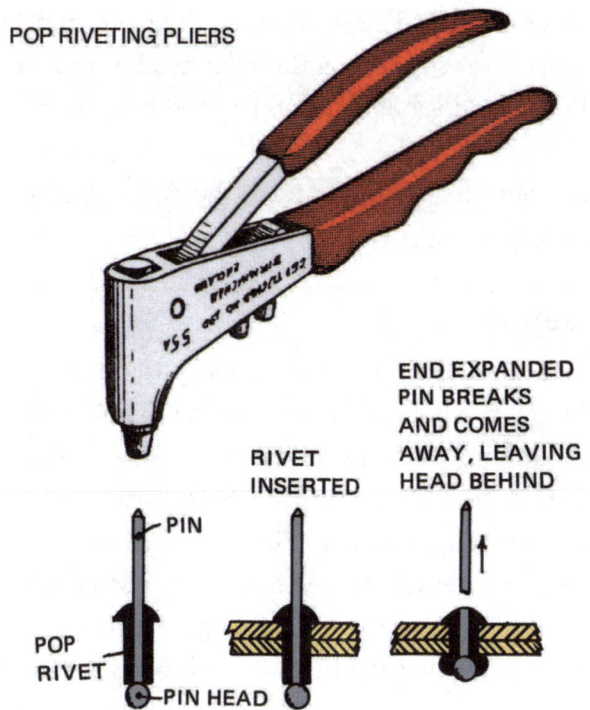

RIVET INSERTED

END EXPANDED PIN BREAKS AND COMES AWAY, LEAVING HEAD BEHIND

PIN

POP RIVET

PIN HEAD

**Fig. 8.32**
Forming a pop rivet head

## Riveting Tools

**Rivet Snap** This is used for finishing off a snap head after it has been roughly shaped with a ball pein hammer.

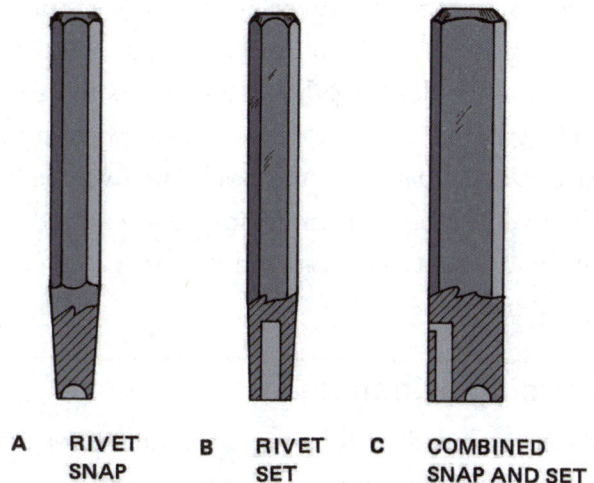

A    RIVET SNAP    B    RIVET SET    C    COMBINED SNAP AND SET

**Fig. 8.33**
Riveting tools

**Bolster or Dolly** This is similar to the rivet snap, but it is used for supporting the snap head of a rivet while a head is being formed on the other end.

**Rivet Set** This is used to force the parts together before riveting.

## Riveting

When more than one rivet is being used for a joint, all the holes should be drilled in one part first and only one in the other part. This allows one rivet to be fitted through both parts and assists in lining them up. They can then be clamped together and the remainder of the holes drilled by passing the drill through the first holes. This ensures that the holes in both parts are in line.

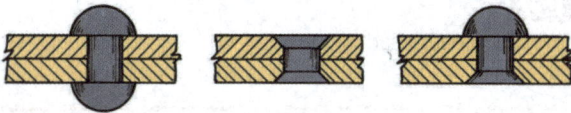

**Fig. 8.34**
Methods of using rivets

Clearance holes should not be drilled for cold rivets but are necessary for hot rivets. Any burrs or swarf must be removed from the parts to ensure that they fit close together. If a rivet has to be cut to length, the waste part should be gripped in the vice to avoid damaging the head. The two heads of the rivet can be of different shapes if required, e.g. one could be a snap head and the other a countersunk head.

## Forming a Snap Head

A certain length of the rivet shank must protrude beyond the parts to form the rivet head. The length required for forming a snap head is one and a half times the rivet diameter, Fig. 8.35 A. If the rivet diameter is 5mm, the length required $= 5 \times 1\frac{1}{2} = 7\frac{1}{2}$ mm. The rivet must be suitably supported before the forming commences, Fig. 8.35 B.

If it has a preformed snap head, it must be supported in a bolster, which can be held in the vice. Care must be taken to ensure that the head remains in the bolster throughout. A countersunk head must be supported on a flat surface, such as a bench block. The parts are then forced together with a rivet set. The ball pein of the hammer is used to form the head roughly to shape. The blows should be struck around the rivet edge as well as its centre, Fig. 8.35 C, taking care not to damage the surface of the work.

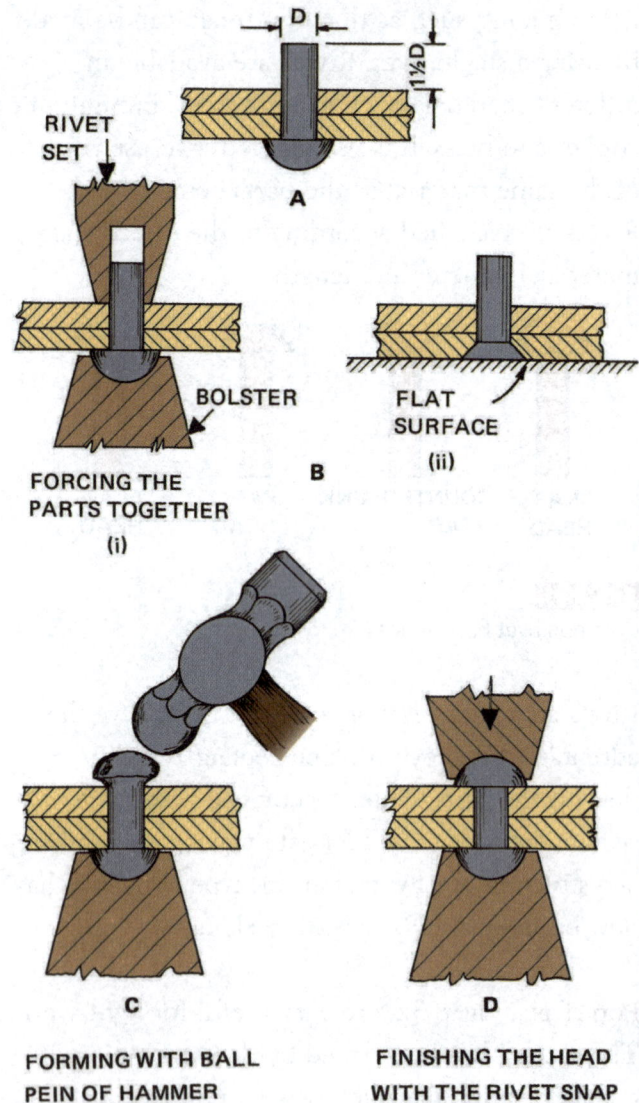

**Fig. 8.35**
Forming a snap head

The head is finished off with the rivet snap by striking it a few sharp blows, Fig 8.35 D.

The riveting tools must be of the correct size for the rivets being used.

## Forming a Countersunk Head

The rivet hole must be countersunk for a countersunk head. If the preformed rivet head is a countersunk one, it can be used as a guide for the angle and depth of the countersinking.

A length equal to the diameter of the rivet must be left protruding for forming a countersunk head, Fig. 8.36 A.

Again, the rivet must be suitably supported and the parts forced together with the rivet set, Fig. 8.36 B. The ball pein of the hammer is used to widen the rivet end and fill the countersink, Fig. 8.36 C. The hammering is completed with a few blows using the flat face of the hammer. After this, the head can be filed down flush with the surface of the work. The surface can then be drawfiled, leaving the formed head almost invisible.

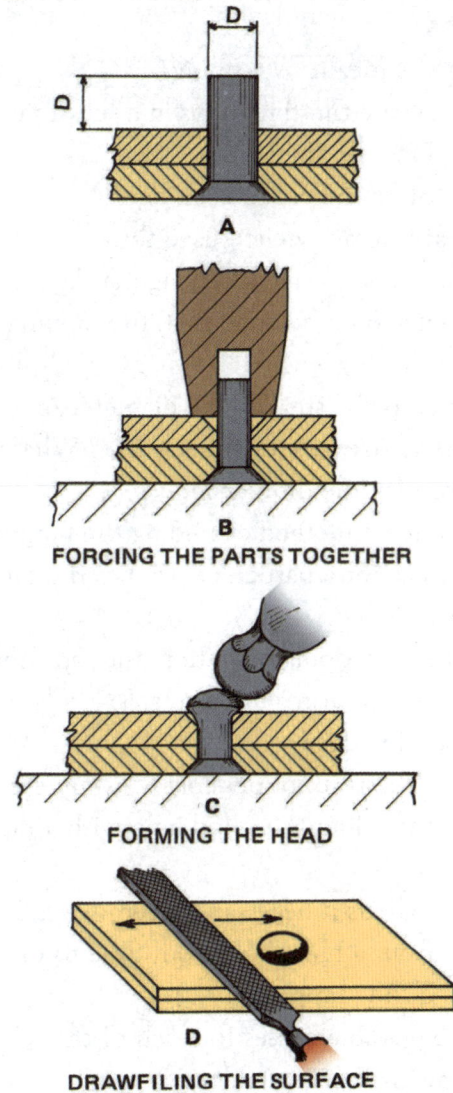

**A**

**B**
FORCING THE PARTS TOGETHER

**C**
FORMING THE HEAD

**D**
DRAWFILING THE SURFACE

**Fig. 8.36**
Forming a countersunk head

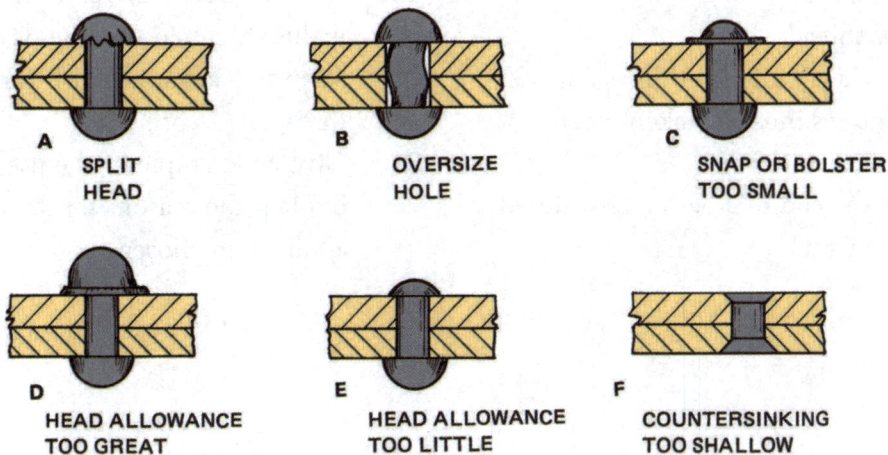

**A** SPLIT HEAD

**B** OVERSIZE HOLE

**C** SNAP OR BOLSTER TOO SMALL

**D** HEAD ALLOWANCE TOO GREAT

**E** HEAD ALLOWANCE TOO LITTLE

**F** COUNTERSINKING TOO SHALLOW

**Fig. 8.37**
Riveting faults

## Exercises

1. What is meant by tapping?
2. (a) Name the three taps in a set of taps.
   (b) How do they differ?
   (c) State the use of each one.
3. What is a tap wrench used for?
4. When tapping and screwing mating parts, which should be done first, the tapping or the screwing?
5. Which is the smaller, the diameter of a tapping size hole or the tap size? What is the reason for the difference?
6. Describe a method of finding the tapping drill size for a particular size tap if tables are not available.
7. During a tapping operation, the tap should be reversed at regular intervals. Explain the reason for this.
8. (a) Why is it not possible to complete the threading of a blind hole with a taper tap?
   (b) Why is it necessary to remove the swarf from a blind hole from time to time during tapping?
9. Give possible causes for each of the following tapping faults:
   (a) A broken tap
   (b) Stripped thread
   (c) Rough thread
   (d) Shallow thread
10. Describe how a circular split die is adjusted.
11. What precautions must be taken when fitting a die in a stock?
12. Why should the end of a bar be chamfered before threading it?

13. Give possible reasons for each of the following screw-cutting faults:
    (a) Broken die teeth
    (b) Stripped thread
    (c) 'Drunken' thread
    (d) Rough thread
    (e) Bar end twisted off
14. What is a die nut used for?
15. Name the thread elements A to E in Fig. 8.38 below.

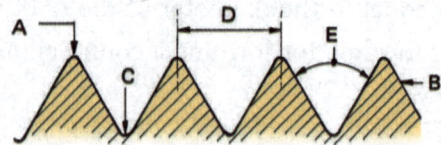

Fig. 8.38

16. Name the diameters A and B shown in Fig. 8.39 below.

Fig. 8.39

17. Sketch the ISO metric thread form and give the value of the thread angle.
18. Explain what is meant by M6 x 0.75 in relation to screw threads.
19. An ISO metric thread is indicated as M8. Is this thread in the fine or coarse series?
20. State two advantages of using a coarse thread.
21. Give an example of the use of a fine thread. Explain the reasons for its preference for the application chosen.

22. In Fig. 8.40 below:
    (a) Name each of the three thread forms.
    (b) Give the values of the thread angles X and Y.
    (c) Give one use for each thread form.

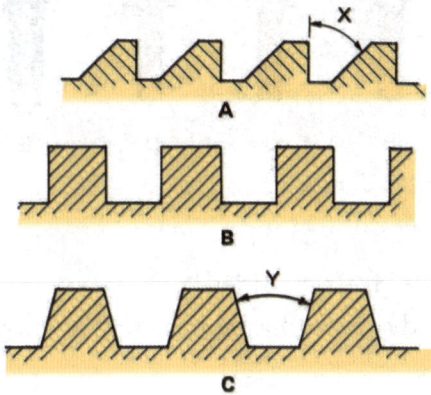

Fig. 8.40

23. Describe two methods of joining parts whereby they can be readily separated again, if required, without damaging the parts.

24. Name three permanent types of joint.

25. Name the set screws A to E shown in Fig. 8.41.

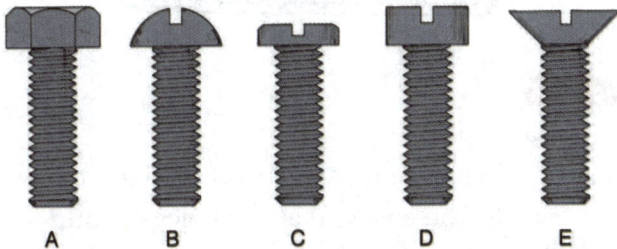

Fig. 8.41

26. If purchasing 100 of the bolts shown in Fig. 8.42 below, state the information that would need to be given.

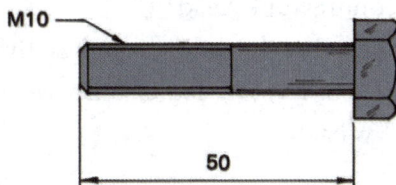

Fig. 8.42

27. (a) Name the threaded fastners A, B and C shown in Fig. 8.43.
    (b) Give a use for each one in the school workshop.

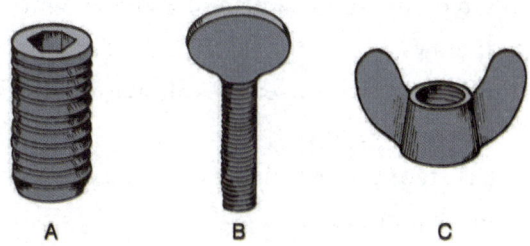

Fig. 8.43

28. Sketch a stud.

29. Describe, with the aid of sketches, four locking methods for nuts.

30. Make a sketch of a split pin and give one example of its use.

31. Name the spanners A, B, C and D shown in Fig. 8.44.

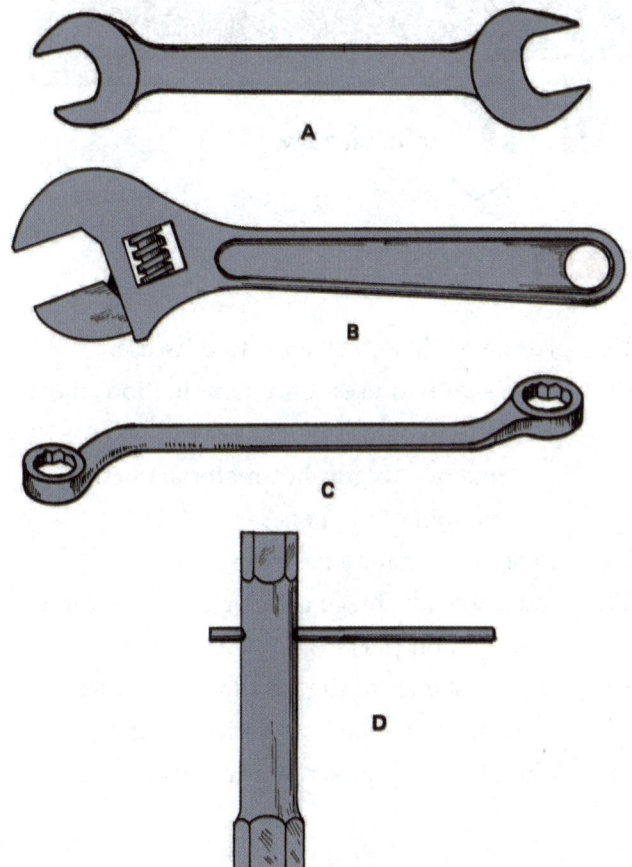

Fig. 8.44

32. What advantage has a ring spanner over an open-ended spanner?

33. Give two reasons why a spanner should be a good fit on a nut.

34. Give one disadvantage of using an adjustable spanner.

35. As regards the wrenches shown in Fig. 8.45:
    (i) name each one,
    (ii) state the use of the one shown in illustration A.

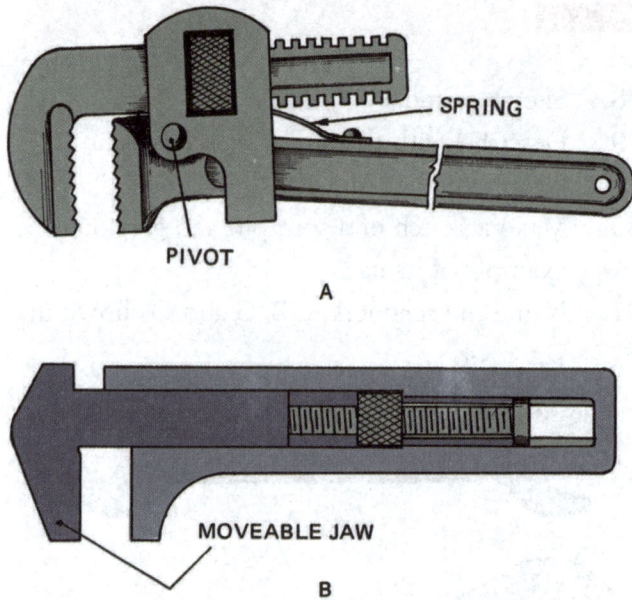

Fig. 8.45

36. Sketch an Allen key and state its use.

37. (a) Give two uses for a combination pliers.
    (b) Why would it be considered bad practice to grip hot materials with a combination pliers?

38. Give one use for a gas pliers.

39. State one advantage a vice grips has over a combination pliers.

40. Make a sketch of the tip of a flat-ended screwdriver to show its correct shape.

41. What is a Phillips screwdriver used for?

42. Name the rivets A, B, C, D and E shown in Fig. 8.46.

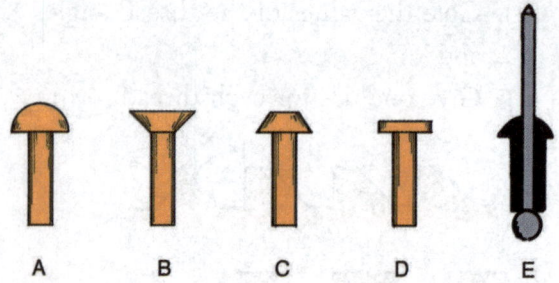

Fig. 8.46

43. How are rivets classified?

44. What advantages has hot riveting over cold riveting?

45. Give one advantage of using pop rivets rather than ordinary cold rivets.

46. Name the riveting tools A and B shown in Fig 8.47.

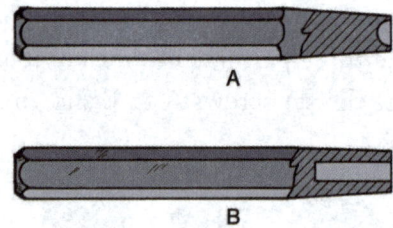

Fig. 8.47

47. If using more than one rivet for a joint, how would you ensure that the holes in both parts were directly opposite one another?

48. Why is it usually better to use rivets of the same material as the parts being joined?

49. If using 6mm diameter rivets, what length of shank should be left protruding to form:
    (i) a snap head
    (ii) a countersunk head?

50. Describe, with the aid of sketches, five examples of riveting faults and give a likely cause for each one.

# Fitting and Assembly 2: Soldering, Brazing and Adhesives

# 9

## Soft Soldering

This is a method of making permanent type joints in metals. It is used where the forces and temperatures to which the joint is subjected are low. Soft solder is an alloy of lead and tin. There is a range of soft solders available with varying proportions of lead and tin. They begin to melt at 183°C (see Chapter 2, page 17). Soft soldering does not require high temperatures or elaborate equipment and, if undertaken properly, it is usually relatively easy to carry out. Soft solder is mainly used for joining thin metals where high strength is not required.

## Fluxes

Fluxes are used to remove oxides from the surfaces of the parts being soldered and to prevent further oxidation when the parts are heated. The surfaces must be free of oxides to allow the solder to alloy with the materials at the surfaces, thereby ensuring sound bonding. There are various types available to suit different types of metals and different types of work. They are usually in either liquid or paste form.

There are two groups of fluxes — passive and active. The passive fluxes prevent oxidation during the soldering but do not actually clean the surfaces. The active fluxes remove oxides from the surfaces and prevent further oxidation during soldering. The active fluxes are corrosive and the joint must be thoroughly washed when completed.

Zinc chloride is a common type of active flux. It is sometimes called 'killed spirits'.

Resin-based fluxes are examples of the passive ones. Since they are non-corrosive, they are suitable for electrical and electronic work and other applications where it is not possible to wash the joint afterwards. Resin-cored solder is used for electronic work. It has a core of flux running along its length and no further flux is required.

Some common soft soldering fluxes and their applications are given in the table below:

| Flux | Uses |
| --- | --- |
| Zinc Chloride | Brass, copper, tinplate, steel |
| Dilute Hydrochloric Acid | Zinc and galvanised iron |
| Resin-based flux | Electrical and electronic |
| Tallow | Lead |

## Soldering Irons

Soldering irons are used for applying solder and heating the surfaces to be joined. The bit or head is made of copper, and as copper is a good conductor, the heat transfers rapidly to the work. Also, copper has an affinity for solder and the point is therefore easily 'tinned' or coated with solder. The handle is made from wood, which is a good heat insulator, and does not heat up. Soldering irons are available with various shapes of bit. The **straight bit**, Fig. 9.1 A, and **hatchet bit**, Fig. 9.1 B, are the most common types. The straight bit iron is used for general work and the hatchet bit is used for corners not easily reached with the straight type. They are available in different weights. A large one stores more heat and remains hot longer than a small one, but if it is too heavy, it will be awkward to use. A soldering iron will be at the correct temperature for use when the heating flame turns green.

Fig. 9.1 C shows an electric soldering iron. These are mostly used for light work, such as the soldering of electrical and electronic equipment.

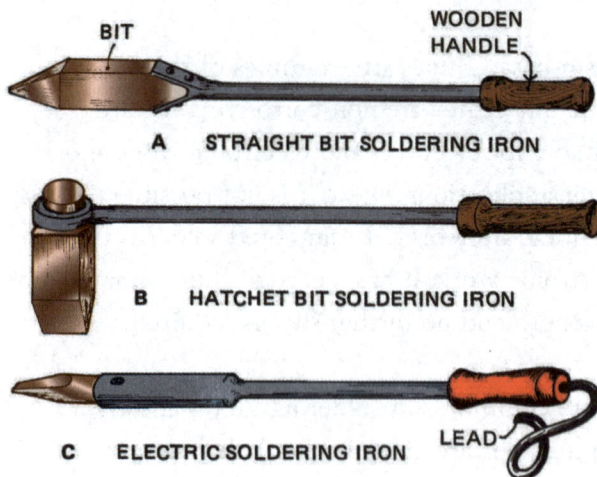

**Fig. 9.1**
Soldering irons

New soldering irons and irons that have had their coating of solder burned off by over-heating must be tinned before use. To do this, the bit is heated to its working temperature and the tip quickly filed and dipped in flux. It is then rubbed on a piece of solder until the tip is coated on all sides. The least amount possible should be filed off the bit and an old file should always be used. A new file would become clogged up with solder and be of little use for any other purpose.

## Heating Appliances

Common heating appliances used for soldering are gas torches, soldering stoves, blow lamps and electric elements in the case of electric soldering irons. When heating a soldering iron with a blow lamp or gas torch, the flame should be directed towards the centre of the bit and not its tip. This will ensure faster heating and a cleaner tip. Since copper is a good conductor, the heat will travel quickly to the tip. Two soldering irons at a time can be heated in a soldering stove.

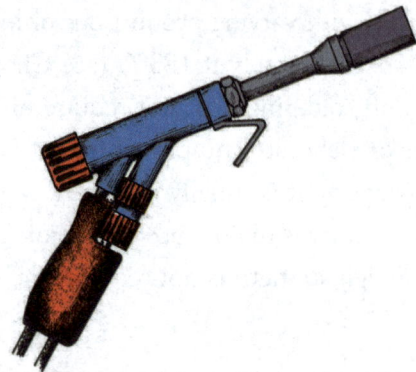

**Fig. 9.2**
Gas torch

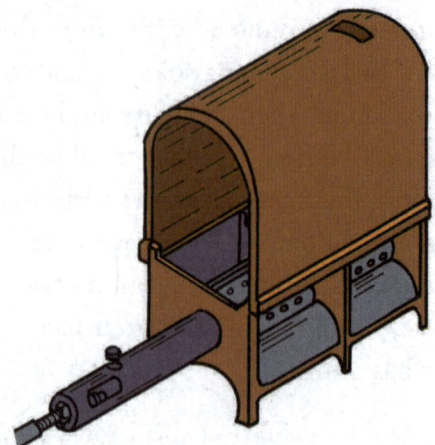

**Fig. 9.3**
Soldering stove

## Cleaning the Surfaces

Whether the flux being used is active or passive, the surfaces must be cleaned mechanically before soldering, except when using tinplate.

Non-ferrous metals can be cleaned with emery cloth or wire wool. Black mild steel must be filed to remove the scale from its surface.

## Soldering Procedures

**Example 1:** Soldering of the butt joint shown in Fig. 9.4.

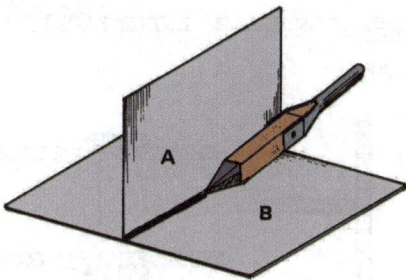

**Fig. 9.4**
Butt joint

1. Ensure that the parts fit closely together to allow the solder to be drawn in between them by capillary action.
2. Mark the position of part A on part B.
3. Clean the areas to be soldered.
4. Coat the cleaned areas with flux.
5. Heat the soldering iron until a green flame appears around it, dip it quickly in flux and apply solder to its tip.
6. Position part A on part B. Hold it with a piece of cloth or by means of a gas pliers.
7. Draw the heated soldering iron slowly along the joint allowing time for the parts to reach the melting temperature of the solder.
   The molten solder will be drawn in between the parts and should appear on the other side.
8. Wash the joint thoroughly if an active flux has been used.

## Sweating

When the joining is over large areas, a method known as 'sweating' can be used. By this process, the surfaces are tinned, the parts are then placed together and heated until the solder on both remelts and unites.

**Example 2:** The soldering of the lap joint shown in Fig. 9.5.

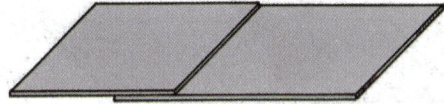

**Fig. 9.5**
Lap joint

1. Ensure that both parts fit closely together.
2. Mark the positions of the parts on one another.
3. Clean the facing surfaces.
4. Coat the areas to be tinned with flux. It is better to confine the flux to the exact areas required in order to prevent solder disfiguring the remainder of the surfaces.
5. Tin the surfaces. The solder can be applied with a soldering iron. A thin coating is sufficient.
6. Reflux the tinned area.
7. Position the parts. They can be held in position by means of a steel bar.
8. Heat the parts until the solder remelts and unites. Press the parts together so that molten solder appears all around the joint. Maintain the pressure until the solder solidifies, taking care not to move the parts. The heating can be done with a soldering iron or by means of a weak flame. A flame should not be used on tinplate as it could damage the tin surface.

9. If an active flux has been used, wash the joint thoroughly.

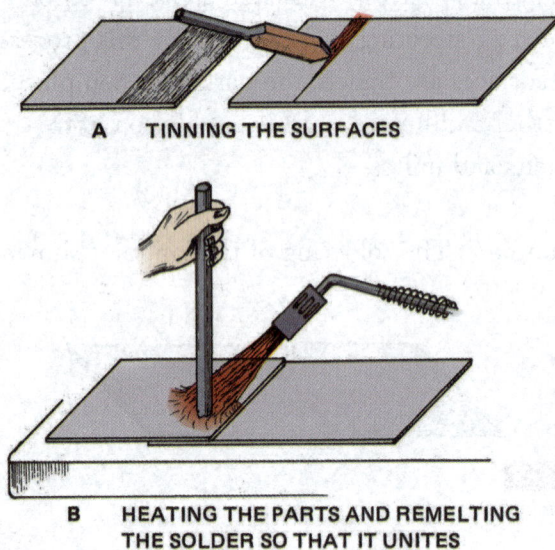

**A    TINNING THE SURFACES**

**B    HEATING THE PARTS AND REMELTING THE SOLDER SO THAT IT UNITES**

**Fig. 9.6**
Sweating

## Hints on Soldering

- The parts must be close fitting.
- Facing surfaces must be clean.
- Areas to be soldered must be coated with flux.
- The parts must be heated above the melting temperature of the solder.
- The work should be placed on a heat insulator to reduce loss of heat.
- Reheat the soldering iron if it is not melting the solder fully. The solder will be pasty and have a rough surface if not sufficiently heated.
- Do not file the joint after soldering. If the work has been carried out properly and is free of excess solder, it will be smooth and neat on solidifying. Filing the joint would also damage the file.
- The thinner the layer of solder between the parts, the stronger the joint.

## Hard Soldering and Silver Soldering

Silver soldering and sometimes brazing are classed as hard soldering. Silver solders are mainly alloys of silver, copper and zinc. There is a wide range of silver solders available. Their melting temperatures vary between 600°C and 830°C, depending on their composition. Silver solders make stronger joints and can withstand higher temperatures than soft solders. There are different types of flux available to suit the various grades of solder. Silver soldering is carried out in a similar way to brazing. There are special silver solders available for silver work that must meet hallmarking standards. These contain high percentages of silver.

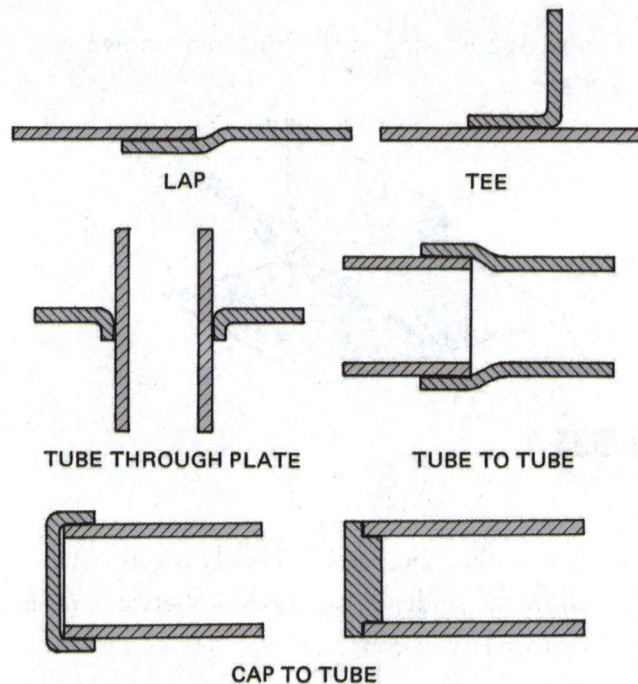

**LAP**

**TEE**

**TUBE THROUGH PLATE**

**TUBE TO TUBE**

**CAP TO TUBE**

**Fig. 9.7**

Typical examples of joint designs for silver soldering and brazing

## Brazing

Brass is the joining metal used in brazing. It requires a higher temperature and provides a stronger joint than silver soldering. The parts must be heated above the melting point of the joining material and, for this reason, it is difficult to braze copper or brass. The heating could also anneal these metals. As with soldering, the brass alloys with the parts being joined at their surfaces.

## Spelter

The brass used for brazing is called spelter. There are a number of grades available with varying proportions of copper and zinc. Their melting points are between about 850°C and 900°C, depending on composition. A common example is the one containing 60% copper and 40% zinc, which melts at about 900°C. Spelter is available in rod, strip and granular form.

## Brazing Flux

Different types of flux are used for brazing. They are mostly supplied in powder form but are often made up into a paste before use by mixing a small amount of water with the powder.

## The Brazing Hearth

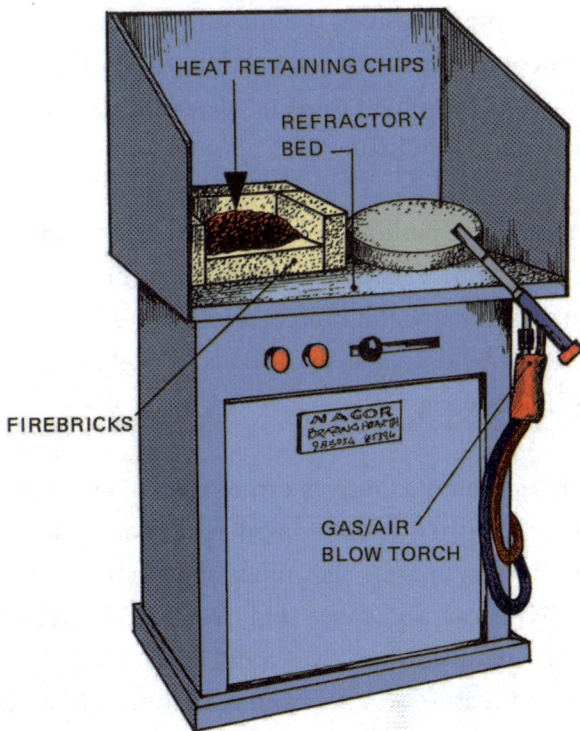

Brazing hearth

Brazing is usually carried out in a brazing hearth, Fig. 9.8. The work is heated by means of a gas-air torch. The hearth has a refractory bed and the work should be surrounded with heat retaining chips and firebricks to reduce heat loss and ensure rapid heating.

## Preparing the Parts

The surfaces must be cleaned as for soldering. The parts must fit close enough together to enable a film of molten spelter to be drawn in between them by capillary action. They must not be allowed to move during the brazing. For this reason, they are sometimes pinned together.

### Procedure

1. Coat the surfaces with flux.
2. Assemble the parts in the brazing hearth, ensuring that they will not move during the brazing.
3. Surround the work with heat resisting chips and firebricks, allowing access to the joint.
4. Use a weak flame at the beginning, so as not to blow away the flux. When the flux begins to melt, the joint can be heated quickly to red heat. If the parts are of unequal thickness, the flame should be directed mainly towards the bulkiest part so as to heat both evenly.
5. Heat the end of the brazing rod and dip it in flux. The required amount will stick to the rod.
6. Apply the rod to the joint so that it melts and is drawn in between the parts. The work must be hot enough to melt the spelter on contact with it. There will be sufficient spelter on the joint when there is a neat fillet all round.
7. Allow the work to cool naturally. If cooled rapidly, the spelter may crack.
8. Remove the flux residues when the brazing is finished.

If granular spelter is used, it should be mixed with flux and sprinkled on the joint.

## Adhesives

There is a wide range of adhesives available. They can join similar or dissimilar materials, e.g. metal to metal or metal to plastic. Joints can be air and water tight and are often quick and economical to make. Adhesives are also useful for joining metals which are difficult to solder. They are supplied in liquid, paste, solid and powder form.

Methods of hardening include the use of a hardener, heat, pressure and the evaporation of a solvent. Some adhesives are first melted by heating, then applied to the surfaces and solidify on cooling.

The choice of adhesives depends on the materials being joined and the conditions they have to withstand. Thermoplastic adhesives would not be suitable for high temperature conditions. If heat is required to harden an adhesive, the materials must be able to withstand the temperatures involved. The adhesive must also be able to withstand the forces to which the joint is subjected. To bond the parts, the adhesives must be able to wet the surfaces.

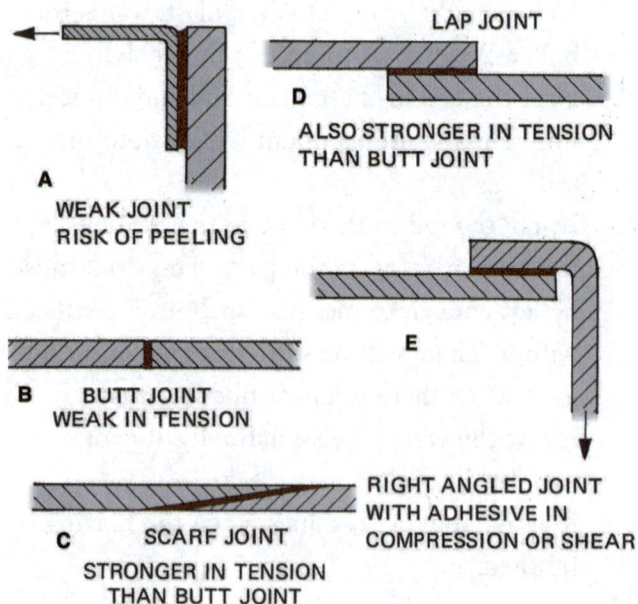

## Types

**Epoxy** adhesives are used for a wide range of applications. There are many types available. They are often used for joining dissimilar materials.
**Phenolic** adhesives are used for metal, wood and glass.
**Cyanoacrylates**, known as 'super glues', harden rapidly. They are used for materials such as metal, rubber and plastics.
**Acrylic** adhesives are good for metals, ceramics and some plastics.
**Anaerobic** adhesives are good for metals and ceramics.
**Urethane** adhesives are good for metals, ceramics and plastics.
**Polyvinyl acetate**, **casein** and **urea** adhesives are used for wood.

## Using Adhesives

When using adhesives, the manufacturers' instructions should be followed carefully. The surfaces to be joined must be clean, dry, free of grease and close fitting.

A joint made with an adhesive is stronger under a shearing, compression or tensile force than if subjected to a peeling force. Joints should therefore be designed so as to avoid peeling if possible, see Fig. 9.9.

**Caution:** Some adhesives can bond skin and eyes rapidly. If either of these happen, do not try to pull the skin apart — get medical assistance. Adhesives can also cause skin irritation. Therefore, contact with skin and eyes must be avoided. Do not breathe vapours from adhesives and use in well-ventilated areas.

LAP JOINT

D

ALSO STRONGER IN TENSION THAN BUTT JOINT

A

WEAK JOINT RISK OF PEELING

B  BUTT JOINT WEAK IN TENSION

E

C  SCARF JOINT STRONGER IN TENSION THAN BUTT JOINT

RIGHT ANGLED JOINT WITH ADHESIVE IN COMPRESSION OR SHEAR

**Fig. 9.9**

Designing joints for adhesive bonding

## Exercises

1. What is meant by:
   (a) A permanent joint
   (b) A detachable joint?
2. Why is a flux necessary when soldering?
3. What is the difference between an active flux and a passive flux?
4. What type of flux should be used for electronic work? Give the reason for your choice.

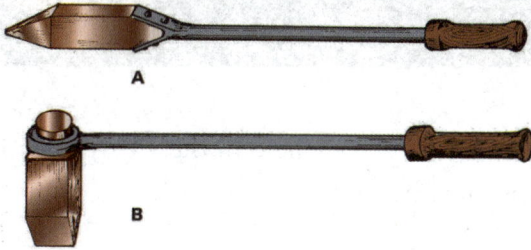

**Fig. 9.10**

5. Fig. 9.10 shows two soldering irons A and B.
   (a) Name each one.
   (b) Give two reasons why copper is used for soldering iron bits.
   (c) (i) Describe how a soldering iron is tinned.
       (ii) What is the purpose of this?
   (d) (i) Why should the flame be directed towards the centre of the bit when heating a soldering iron with a torch?
       (ii) How would you know when a soldering iron is hot enough for use?

**Fig. 9.11**

6. (a) Name the soldering iron shown in Fig. 9.11.
   (b) What type of work would this soldering iron be used for?
   (c) Why does this type of soldering iron have a plastic handle?
   (d) (i) What is cored solder?
       (ii) What type of work would cored solder be used for?

7. List four points to be observed to ensure a good soldered joint.
8. Name two types of heating appliances used for soldering.
9. What is meant by the terms:
   (a) tinning      (b)    sweating
10. Why should the work be placed on a heat insulating material when soldering?
11. Explain the difference between hard soldering and soft soldering.
12. If you have to decide whether to soft solder or to braze two metal parts together, on what factors would your choice depend?

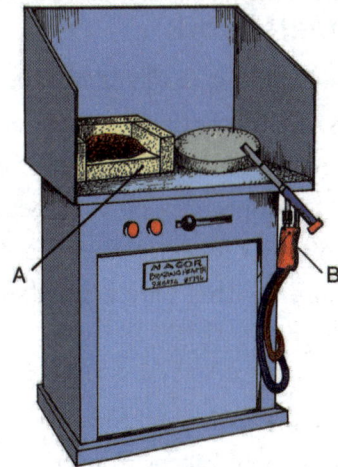

**Fig. 9.12**

13. A brazing hearth is shown in Fig. 9.12.
    (a) Name the components A and B.
    (b) What is a spelter?
    (c) Describe one method of holding parts together when brazing.
    (d) How would you know if parts had reached a high enough temperature for brazing?
    (e) Why is it bad practice to cool a brazed joint rapidly?
    (f) List four points to be observed to ensure a good joint when brazing.
14. Give three advantages of using an adhesive to join parts.
15. Give two important factors that must be considered when selecting an adhesive for a particular application.
16. List three types of adhesive.

# Cold Forming of Metals

# 10

## Sheet Metalwork

In this work, use is made of various sheet materials, including tinplate, copper, brass, mild steel, aluminium and galvanized iron. It involves drawing developments, cutting, bending and various joining processes. Sheet metal thicknesses are measured with a wire gauge (see Chapter 5, page 57).

A snips or shears is used for cutting sheet metal. Do not cut small pieces from a sheet as this can cause wastage and damage to the sheet. Instead, a strip should be cut off the width or length of the sheet and the pieces cut from this. Machines are used for mass production of sheet metal articles, but high standards can also be achieved by using hand tools. To avoid damaging their surfaces, marking out on tinplate and non-ferrous metals should be done with a 2H pencil, except when drawing lines to be cut. These can be scribed. Simple developments can be drawn directly on the material, but more complicated ones are often drawn on paper first. The shape is then cut out and can be used as a template. The template can be placed on the material and a line drawn around it or the template may be stuck onto the material. When drawing developments, allowances must be made for joints and edges.

If sheet metal is being held in the vice, protective clamps must be used.

Special care must be taken when drilling sheet metal (see Chapter 7, page 82).

## Snips

Snips are used for cutting thin sheet metal by hand. When cutting out a particular shape with a snips, the material should be cut accurately along the line, without leaving any waste to be filed. It is difficult to file thin sheet metal.

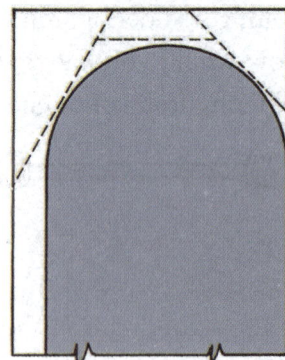

Fig. 10.1

When there is a large amount of waste to be removed, Fig. 10.1, it is better to cut off the main portions first, because it is then easier to cut along the line. When cutting, the snips should never be closed fully, as this would leave a kink in the material. Gripping one handle between clamps in the vice gives more control for many cutting operations. Snips should never be used to cut wire, as this would damage the blades.

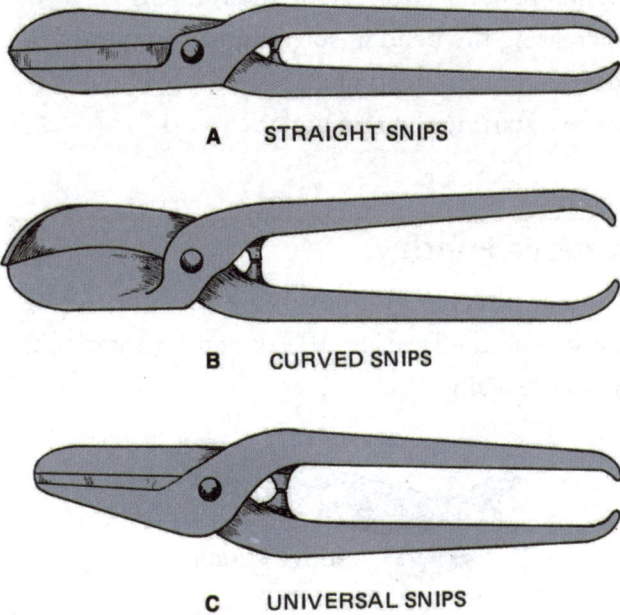

**Fig. 10.2**
Snips

There are various types of snips available. The straight snips, Fig. 10.2 A, is used for straight cuts or outside curves. The curved snips, Fig. 10.2(B), is used for cutting curves, especially inside curves. The universal snips, Fig. 10.2 C, is used for straight cuts as well as inside and outside curves.

## Bench Shears

The bench shears, Fig. 10.3, is used for cutting sheet metal, plates and bars. A large bench shears can cut mild steel plates up to 3mm thick and round bars up to 12mm in diameter. The blades are made from high carbon steel. There must be no gap between the blades. The bottom one can be adjusted, by means of screws, to take up wear. The upper blade has a hole in it for cutting round or square bars. When the shears is not in use,

a bolt should be fitted through this hole or the lever removed, if possible, to prevent the shears being closed accidentally and causing accidents. The bench shears should not be used for cutting high carbon steel, as this would damage its cutting edges.

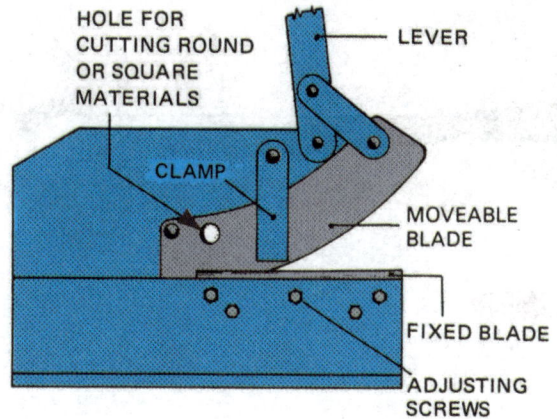

**Fig. 10.3**
Bench shears

## Mallets

Mallets are used for bending and shaping materials without damaging the surfaces of the materials. Boxwood headed mallets are commonly used in the school workshops, but they are also available with plastic heads. The handles are made from cane or ash.

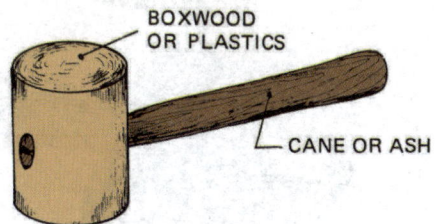

**Fig. 10.4**
Mallet

## Paning Hammers

A paning hammer, Fig. 10.5, has a narrow striking edge. It is used for folding down metal edges in restricted places, e.g. tucking in the edge of the sheet metal when forming a wired edge, Fig. 10.5 B.

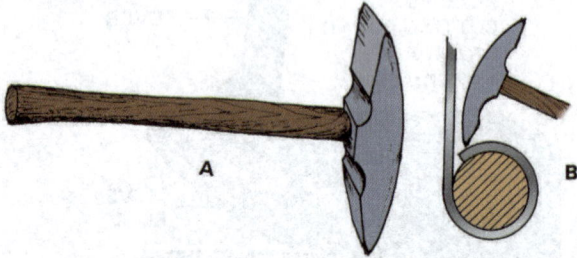

**Fig. 10.5**
Paning hammer

## Folding Bars

The folding bars, Fig. 10.6, are used for bending sheet metal. They are held in the vice, and when the vice is tightened, the bars grip the material. The bend line on the material is kept level with the edge of the folding bars.

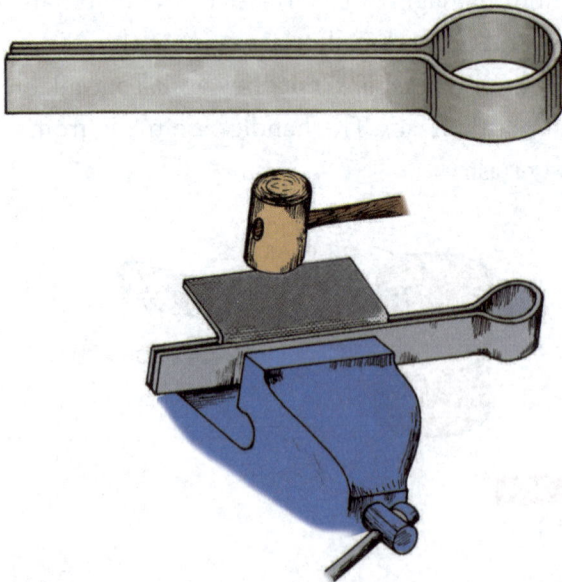

**Fig. 10.6**
Folding bars

The material is either struck with a mallet or a small block of hard wood is held against it and this is struck with a hammer. Bends in weak materials can be started with the thumbs.

When bending, work along the full length, increasing the bend in stages until complete. Do not attempt to bend one portion the whole way before starting the remainder.

## Groove Punch

Groove punches or groovers are used for closing down wired edges, Fig. 10.7 B and for interlocking grooved seams.

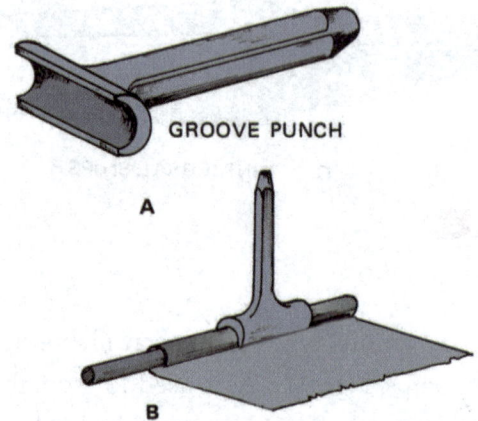

GROOVE PUNCH

**Fig. 10.7**

## Stakes

There is a wide range of stakes available for shaping sheet metal. They are held by fitting their shanks into special sockets or by gripping them in the vice. If gripping in the vice, clamps should be used; otherwise, their shanks will become rough and uncomfortable to handle.

## Hatchet Stake

The hatchet stake, Fig. 10.8, is used for forming acute angled bends.

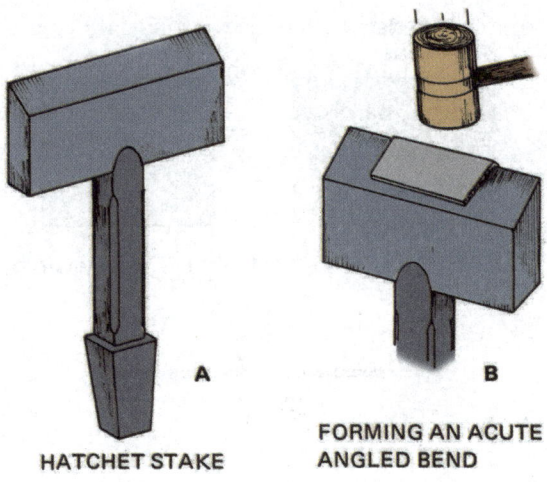

HATCHET STAKE

FORMING AN ACUTE ANGLED BEND

## Half-Moon Stake

The half-moon stake, Fig. 10.9, is used for bending up the edges of curved materials.

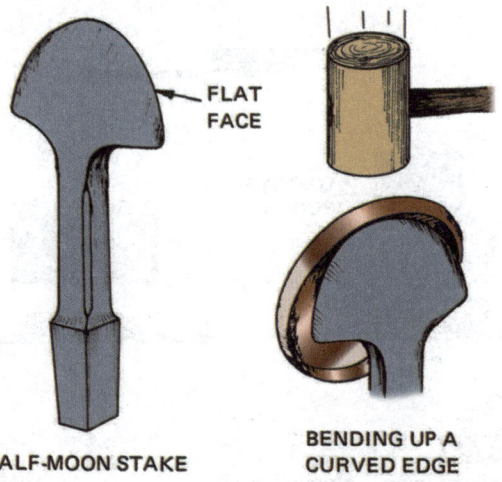

FLAT FACE

HALF-MOON STAKE

BENDING UP A CURVED EDGE

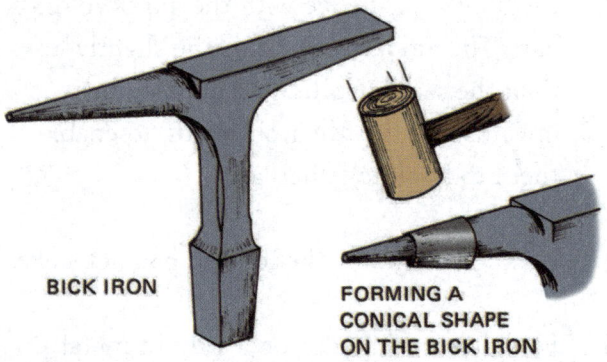

BICK IRON

FORMING A CONICAL SHAPE ON THE BICK IRON

## Bick Iron

The bick iron, Fig. 10.10, is used for forming conical and cylindrical shapes and for truing up rings. The flat part is used for flattening purposes and for forming corners.

## Funnel Stake

The funnel stake, Fig. 10.11, is also for conical and cylindrical work — for items larger than those formed on the bick iron.

FUNNEL STAKE

USING THE FUNNEL STAKE FOR CONICAL WORK

## Creasing Iron

The creasing iron, Fig. 10.12, has a series of grooves of various sizes. It is used for grooving sheet metal and for closing down sheet metal edges when forming wired edges.

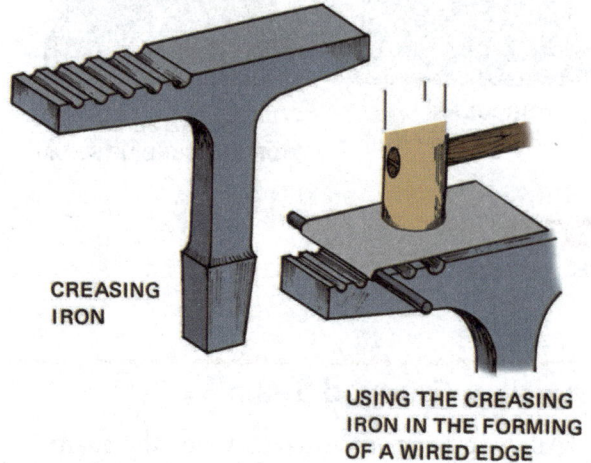

CREASING IRON

USING THE CREASING IRON IN THE FORMING OF A WIRED EDGE

## Joints

Common sheet metal joints are shown in Fig. 10.13.

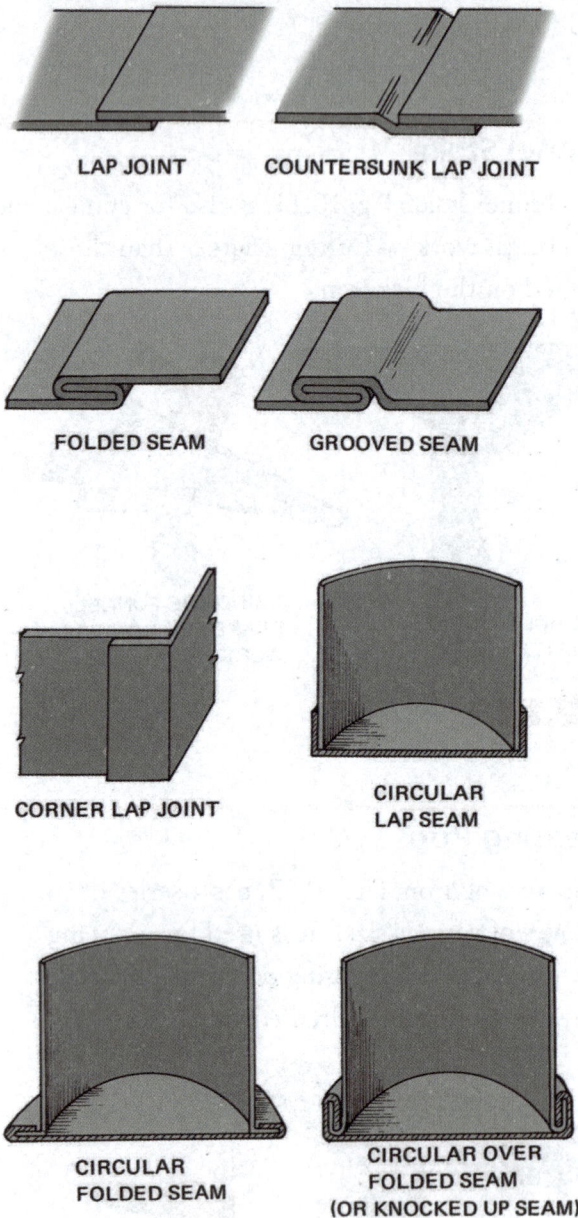

LAP JOINT  COUNTERSUNK LAP JOINT

FOLDED SEAM  GROOVED SEAM

CORNER LAP JOINT  CIRCULAR LAP SEAM

CIRCULAR FOLDED SEAM  CIRCULAR OVER FOLDED SEAM (OR KNOCKED UP SEAM)

**Fig. 10.13**
Sheet metal joints

## Forming a Grooved Seam

1. Allow an amount equal to twice the seam width on one side of the joint and an amount equal to the seam width on the other side.

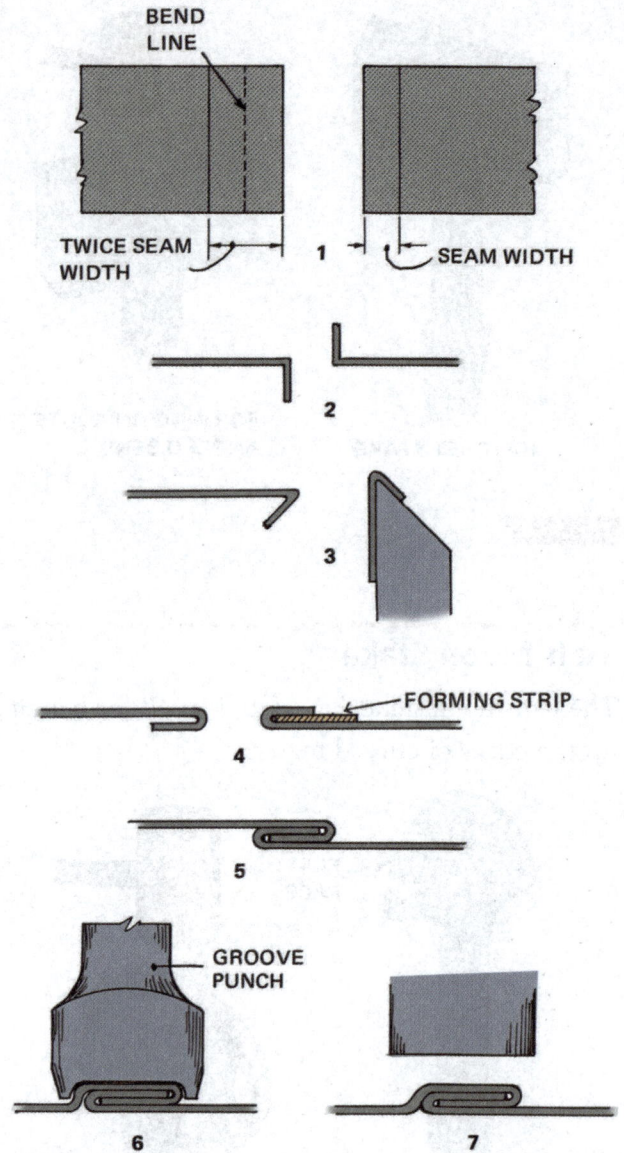

BEND LINE

TWICE SEAM WIDTH  1  SEAM WIDTH

2

3

FORMING STRIP

4

5

GROOVE PUNCH

6  7

**Fig. 10.14**
Stages in forming a grooved seam

2. Bend over each edge with the aid of folding bars. The amount bent must be slightly less than the seam width. One must be bent inwards and the other outwards, to enable them to hook together later.

3. Bend the edges further on the hatchet stake.

4. Fold down each edge on a strip of metal slightly thicker than the sheet metal.

5. Hook the folded edges together.

6. Use a groove punch to bring the surfaces into alignment and to interlock the seam.

7. Finally, tap down the seam with a mallet.

## Edges

Beaded edges and wired edges are formed on sheet metal articles to strengthen them and also to make them safe.

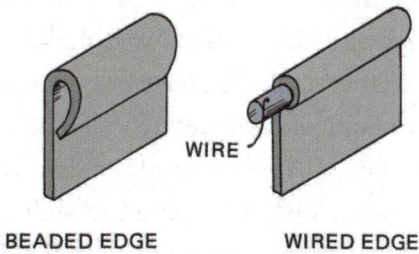

BEADED EDGE          WIRE          WIRED EDGE

Fig. 10.15

## Forming a Beaded Edge

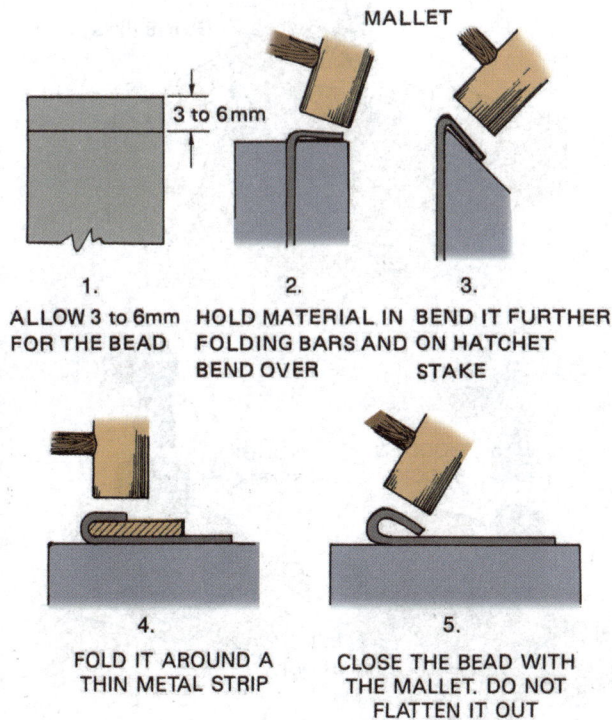

MALLET

3 to 6mm

1.
ALLOW 3 to 6mm
FOR THE BEAD

2.
HOLD MATERIAL IN
FOLDING BARS AND
BEND OVER

3.
BEND IT FURTHER
ON HATCHET
STAKE

4.
FOLD IT AROUND A
THIN METAL STRIP

5.
CLOSE THE BEAD WITH
THE MALLET. DO NOT
FLATTEN IT OUT

Fig. 10.16
Stages in forming a beaded edge

## Forming a Wired Edge

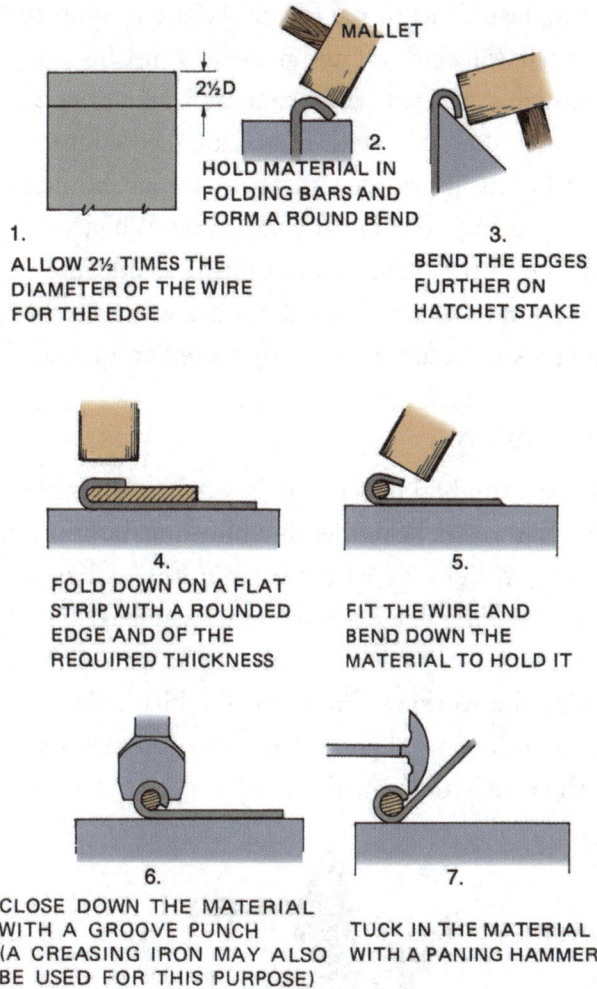

MALLET

2½D

2.
HOLD MATERIAL IN
FOLDING BARS AND
FORM A ROUND BEND

1.
ALLOW 2½ TIMES THE
DIAMETER OF THE WIRE
FOR THE EDGE

3.
BEND THE EDGES
FURTHER ON
HATCHET STAKE

4.
FOLD DOWN ON A FLAT
STRIP WITH A ROUNDED
EDGE AND OF THE
REQUIRED THICKNESS

5.
FIT THE WIRE AND
BEND DOWN THE
MATERIAL TO HOLD IT

6.
CLOSE DOWN THE MATERIAL
WITH A GROOVE PUNCH
(A CREASING IRON MAY ALSO
BE USED FOR THIS PURPOSE)

7.
TUCK IN THE MATERIAL
WITH A PANING HAMMER

Fig. 10.17
Stages in forming a wired edge

## Beaten Metalwork

This work involves the shaping of sheet metals by the use of a hammer or a mallet. Hollowing, sinking and raising are common beaten metalwork operations. The metals used must be malleable and ductile. The ones most commonly used in school workshops are copper, aluminium and brass. They must be annealed beforehand (see Chapter 11, page 128). Copper and brass need to be cleaned after heating, to remove oxides. This is done by immersing them in dilute sulphuric acid. This dilute sulphuric acid is known as 'pickle' and is made up of one part acid to about ten of water. A copper or brass tongs should be used to dip the material. On removal, the material must be thoroughly washed under running water. Special care must be taken with the pickle (see safety precautions in Chapter 4). The material should be dipped gently to avoid any splashing. When making up the pickle, do not forget to **add the acid to the water** and not the other way round. The pickle should be properly stored and labelled.

## Hollowing

This is a method of forming bowl-shaped articles. The material is beaten with a blocking hammer or bossing mallet over a depression in the end grain of a wooden block or on a leather sandbag. The diameter of the material will not change much during the working. Therefore, the blank disc needs to be only slightly larger than the diameter of the article to be made.

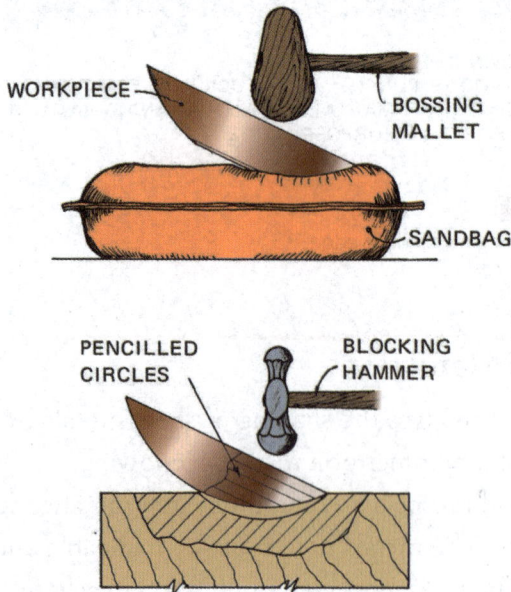

**Fig. 10.18**
Hollowing

Draw concentric circles, about 12mm apart, on the disc using pencil compasses. These circles can be used as guides for the beating. Start with the outer

circle and work in decreasing circles towards the centre. Avoid waves and wrinkles as much as possible. Any ones that do form should be dressed down after each course of blows. Continue the beating until the required depth is reached. The shape can be checked with a template. The material will become work-hardened as a result of the beating and must be annealed (see Chapter 11, page 130) from time to time.

## Sinking

This is a method of forming hollow flat rimmed articles such as small trays. As with hollowing, the diameter of the blank disc does not change much during the shaping. A shaped wooden block with guide pins, Fig. 10.19 A, is used for this work. The guide pins assist in keeping the width of the rim constant. The disc is kept against the pins and rotated as it is being beaten. After each rotation,

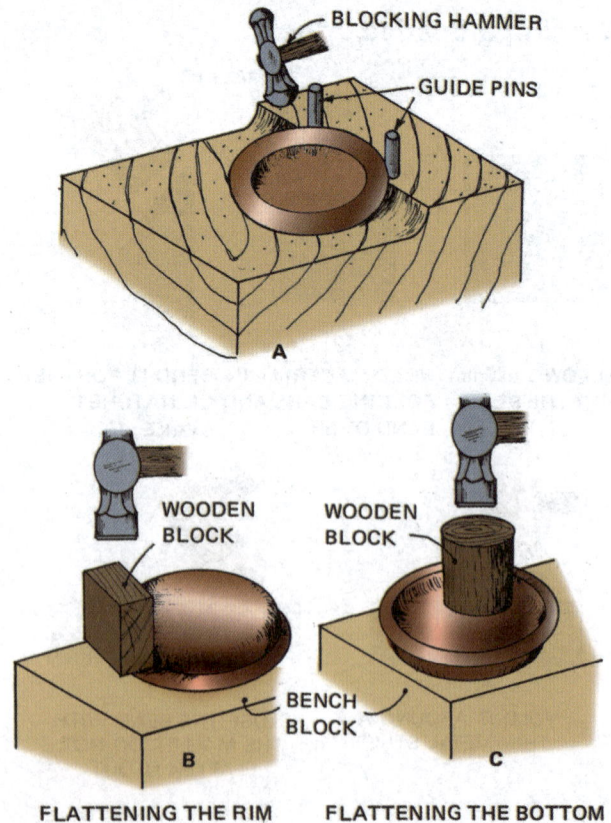

**Fig. 10.19**
Sinking

the material should be turned over on a bench block to flatten the rim with a small block of wood and a hammer, Fig. 10.19 B. The bottom of the material must also be trued, Fig. 10.19 C.

## Planishing

Articles formed by processes such as hollowing and sinking are planished to remove marks and small irregularities and to work-harden the material. Planishing involves lightly hammering the surface of the article while it is supported on a stake. The hammer and stake must suit the shape being worked.

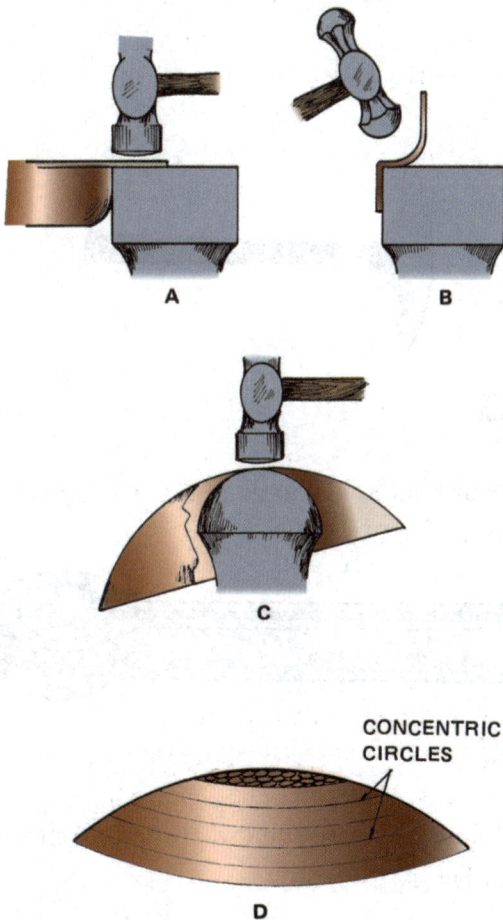

A            B

C

CONCENTRIC
CIRCLES

D

**Fig. 10.20**
Planishing

Different hammers and stakes may be required for different parts of the workpiece, Fig. 10.20 A, B and C. Both the stake and the striking face of the

hammer must be smooth and highly polished to produce a good finish. The workpiece itself must be cleaned and annealed before planishing. Concentric circles are drawn on bowl-shaped articles, Fig. 10.20 D, as guides for the beating. The article must be in contact with the stake at the point where it is being struck, and the planishing marks should touch or slightly overlap. The workpiece is often polished after planishing.

## Bending

Folding bars should only be used for bending sheet metal. Vice clamps and formers can be used for other cold bending operations.

When using round formers, Fig. 10.21, the workpiece should be gripped at the line where the bend is to start.

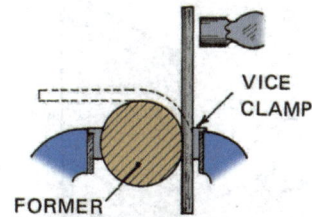

VICE
CLAMP

FORMER

**Fig. 10.21**

## Twisting

Twisting is mainly done for decorative purposes. Square bars, up to about 10mm, can be twisted cold. One end of the bar is held in the vice, while the other is turned by means of a lever with a hole in it. The length to be twisted may be marked on the bar or a tube of the required length placed down over it and the lever rested on this. The finished twist will be slightly less than the original dimension marked on the bar. If a definite length of twist is required, a tube of this length should be used. A tube also helps to keep the lever square with the bar. To estimate the amount of turning, one side of the bar can be marked with chalk and its position noted at the beginning.

If heating a bar, it is important to have it at an even temperature throughout the portion being twisted. Otherwise the twist will be irregular, since most of the twisting will occur at the hottest regions.

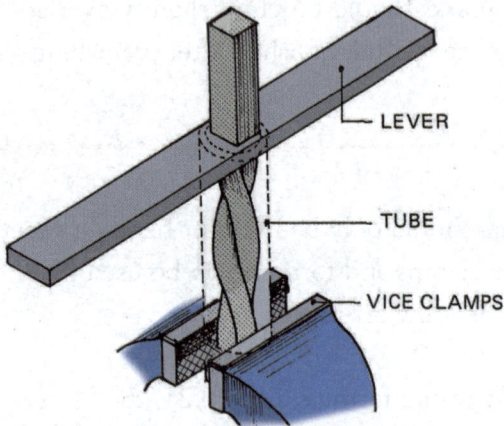

Twisting a bar with a lever

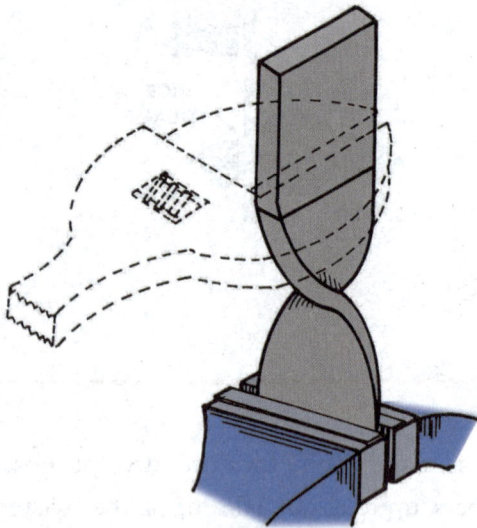

Flat light section bars can be twisted with an adjustable spanner, Fig. 10.23. Two lines are drawn to indicate the position of the twist, and it is held in the vice with one line level with the edge of the clamp. The adjustable spanner is then fitted to the bar with the lower edge of its jaw on the other line. It can now be twisted the required amount.

## Exercises

1. How is the thickness of sheet metals measured?
2. Why is a pencil often used for marking out on non-ferrous sheet metal and on tinplate?
3. Why is it bad practice to close snips fully when making a long cut in sheet metal?
4. Why is it wrong to cut wire with a snips?
5. Name three types of snips and give the uses of two of them.
6. State the uses of a bench shears.
7. How is a bench shears prevented from being closed accidentally when not in use?
8. What materials are mallet heads made from?
9. Name the hammer shown in Fig. 10.24 below.

10. Name the tool shown in Fig. 10.25 below and state its use.

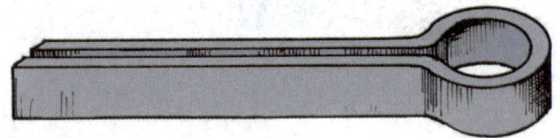

11. Name and state the use of the tool shown in Fig. 10.26 below.

12. Sketch and name four types of stake used for sheet metalwork. Give the use of each one.

13. Name the sheet metal joints A, B and C in Fig. 10.27.

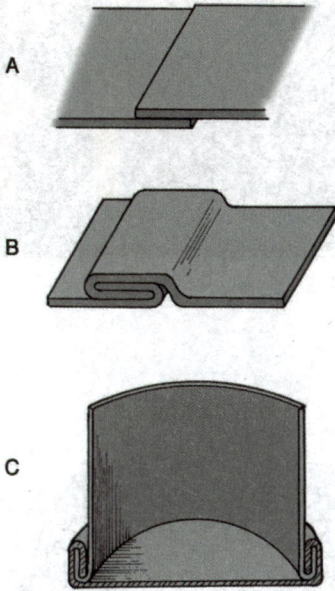

Fig. 10.27

14. (a) Name the sheet metal edges A and B shown in Fig. 10.28.
    (b) Describe, with the aid of sketches, the various stages in forming edge A.
    (c) Describe, with the aid of sketches, the various stages in forming edge B.

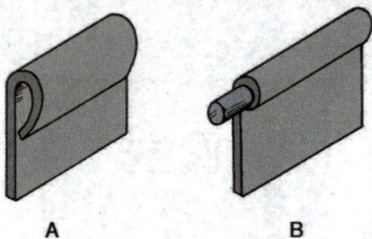

Fig. 10.28

15. What properties must a metal have to make it suitable for beaten metalwork?

16. Explain briefly what is meant by each of the following terms as applied to beaten metalwork: hollowing, sinking and planishing.

17. Describe, with the aid of sketches, how you would make a bowl from a copper disc by a beaten metalwork process. Name the process involved and list the equipment required.

18. Describe, with the aid of sketches, the making of a small tray of the shape shown in Fig. 10.29 below by sinking. List the equipment required and suggest a suitable metal for the small tray.

Fig. 10.29

19. A tube is sometimes placed over a bar when forming an ornamental twist. What is the purpose of this?

20. Describe one method of estimating the amount of twist applied to a bar.

# Hot Forming of Metals and Heat Treatments

## 11

## Forgework

In forgework, metal is heated until plastic and then shaped as required. A forged article has the advantage that the metal grain follows its shape, Fig. 11.1, thereby giving it extra strength.

In schools, forgework helps to develop a student's ability to judge size and shape and also improves hand and eye co-ordination.

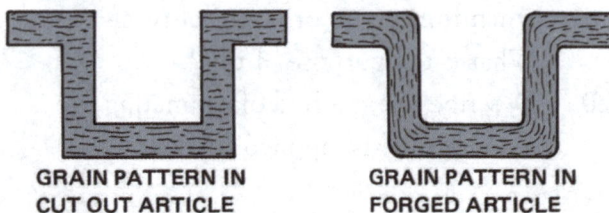

GRAIN PATTERN IN CUT OUT ARTICLE

GRAIN PATTERN IN FORGED ARTICLE

Fig. 11.1

## The Forge

The metal is heated in a forge, sometimes called a hearth. There are two main types of forge — coal or coke fired and gas fired.

Ceramic chip forges are fuelled by gas and are very suitable for school workshops. They are easier to light and do not have the same smoke, dirt, fumes and clinker formation associated with coke fired forges.

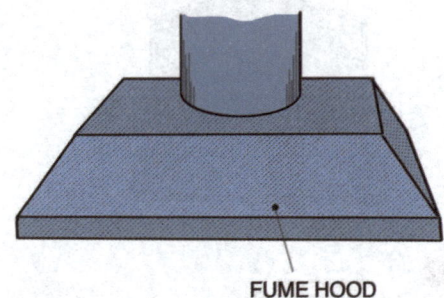

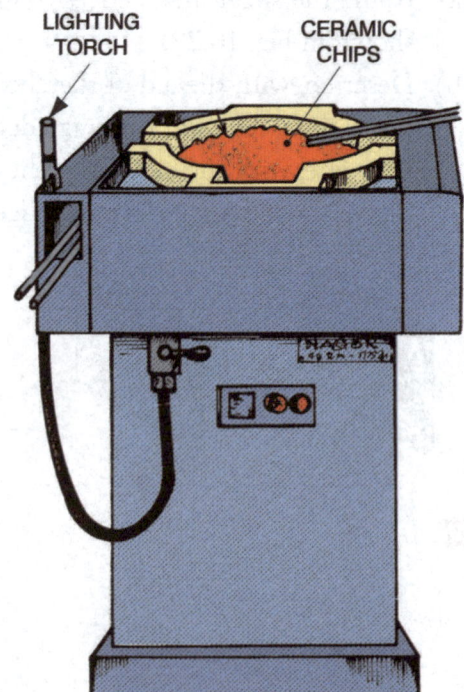

FUME HOOD

LIGHTING TORCH

CERAMIC CHIPS

Fig. 11.2
Ceramic chip gas forge

## The Anvil

The anvil is used to support hot metal being forged. Anvils are made from high carbon steel. The main working face is hardened, but the cutting table is left unhardened and is used for chiselling operations. Chiselling should not be carried out on the hardened working face, because it could lead to damage to both the surface and the chisel edge. Part of one edge, near the cutting table, is rounded and is used for bending purposes. The hardie hole is used for holding tools with square shanks, such as the hardie, the bottom swage and the bottom fuller. The punching hole allows the punch right through when making holes in hot metals. Eyes and various types of bends are formed on the bick. The anvil is mounted on a cast iron stand or on a wooden block to bring it to a suitable working height. Anvils are available in various weights.

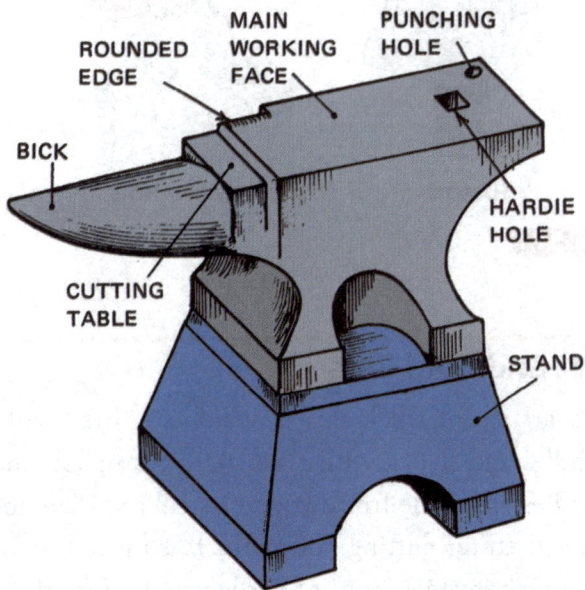

**Fig. 11.3**
The anvil

## The Leg Vice

The leg vice can withstand the hammering and bending of metals and is therefore suitable for forge work. It is bolted to the bench and the leg fits into a socket in the floor, giving it extra support. Since the moveable jaw is pivoted, there is only one position where the jaws are parallel. This affects its gripping power, Fig. 11.4.

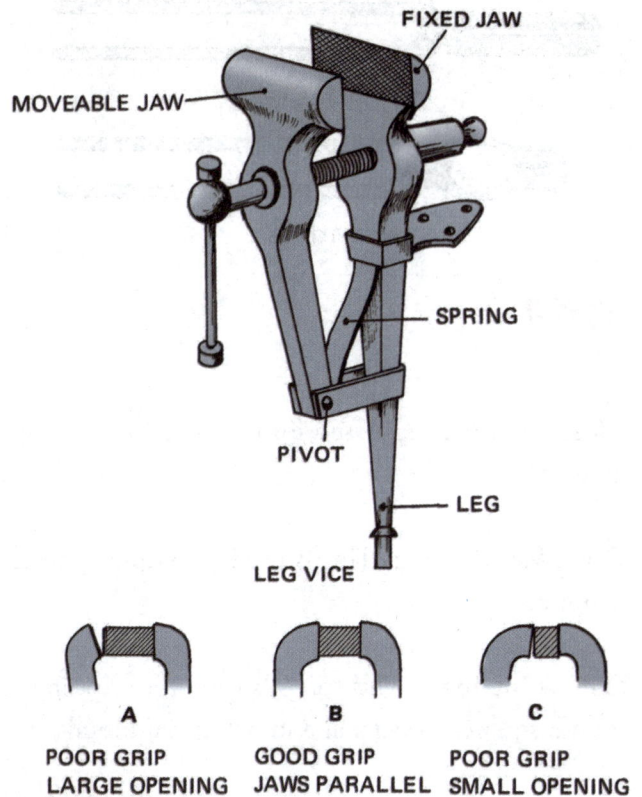

**Fig. 11.4**

## Tongs

Tongs are used for gripping hot metals while they are being forged. The tongs selected should be a good fit and grip the metal securely. If the length of the work permits, it is better to hold the cold end in the hand.

A clamping ring is sometimes used to hold the tongs closed and to relieve the pressure on the hand. There is a variety of types available. Some common examples are shown in Fig. 11.5 and their uses are given below:

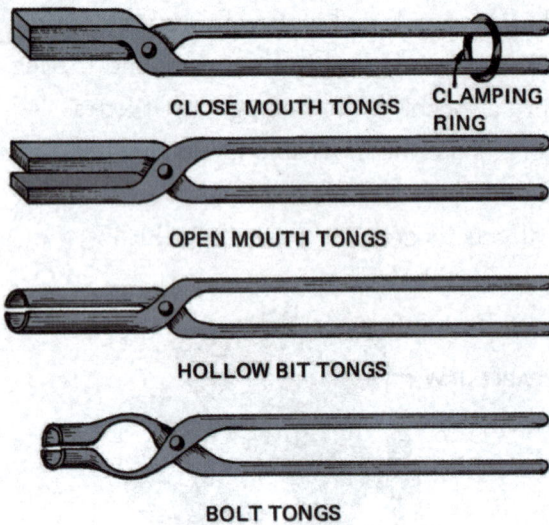

CLOSE MOUTH TONGS    CLAMPING RING

OPEN MOUTH TONGS

HOLLOW BIT TONGS

BOLT TONGS

**Fig. 11.5**
Tongs

**Close Mouth Tongs** Used for gripping thin materials.

**Open Mouth Tongs** This is used for gripping thick materials.

**Hollow Bit Tongs** This tongs is used for gripping round, square, hexagonal and octagonal metals.

**Bolt Tongs** This is used for gripping articles with large ends.

## The Sledge Hammer

This is used by a smith's assistant or striker. It can be used for striking the work directly or for striking other forging tools. Sledge hammers are available in different shapes and weights. They can be double-faced, Fig. 11.6, cross pein, straight pein or ball pein. Double-faced ones of about 4kg are commonly used.

DOUBLE-FACED SLEDGE HAMMER

**Fig. 11.6**

## The Hardie

A hardie is used for cutting metal. It has a square shank which fits into the hardie hole in the anvil, Fig. 11.7.

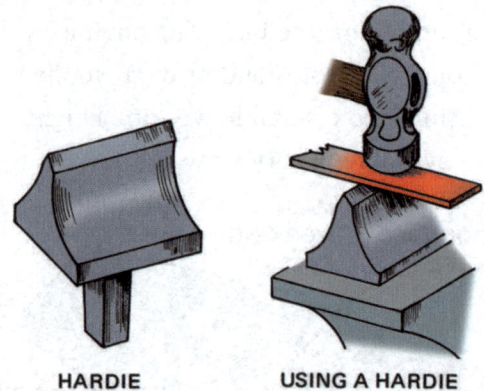

HARDIE          USING A HARDIE

**Fig. 11.7**

## Hot and Cold Sets

Sets are strong thick chisels, which are fitted with handles and struck with a sledge to cut metal. The handles are made from wood or steel rod. The hot set is used for cutting hot metal. It is made from high carbon steel, but not hardened, because the heat from the hot metal would re-soften it. The cutting edge is ground to about 30°. The cold set is used for cutting cold metal. It is made from high carbon steel with the cutting end hardened and tempered. It has a cutting edge of about 60°. Hot and cold sets can be used in conjunction with the hardie, or the metal can be supported on the anvil cutting table, Fig. 11.8.

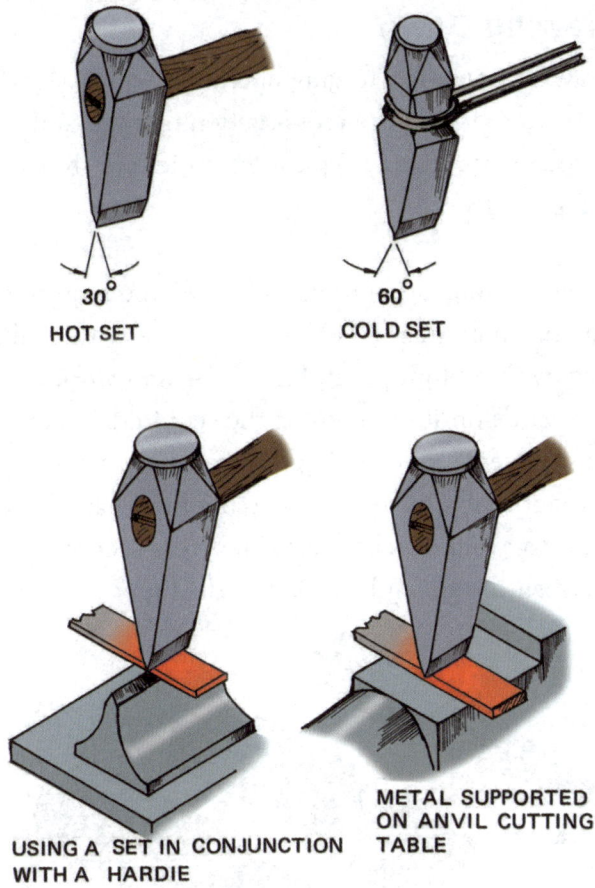

HOT SET 30°   COLD SET 60°

USING A SET IN CONJUNCTION WITH A HARDIE

METAL SUPPORTED ON ANVIL CUTTING TABLE

Fig. 11.8

## Punches

These are used for punching holes in hot metal. Punches can be round or square or any other required shape. The metal is held over the punching hole in the anvil and the punch is struck with the sledge hammer, Fig.11.9.

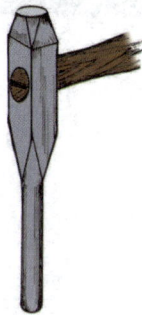

Fig. 11.9

Smith's punch

## The Flatter

This is used for finishing off flat surfaces smoothly after they have been roughly shaped by other forging operations. It is struck with the sledge.

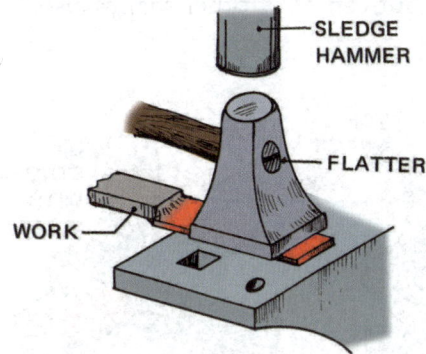

SLEDGE HAMMER

FLATTER

WORK

Fig. 11.10

## Top and Bottom Fullers

These are used for making grooves in hot metal. They are often used for drawing down operations in thick metals, but since they leave a series of ridges, the surfaces must be finished off with the flatter. The top fuller is fitted with a handle and is struck with a sledge. The bottom fuller fits into the anvil hardie hole.

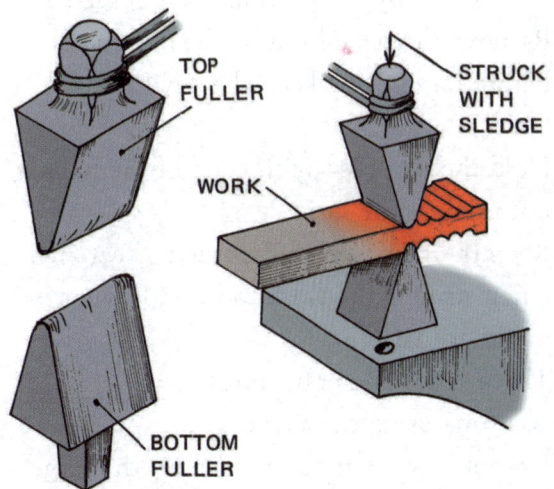

TOP FULLER

STRUCK WITH SLEDGE

WORK

BOTTOM FULLER

Fig. 11.11

## Top and Bottom Swages

These are used for reducing the sections of metals and for producing smooth finishes. The groove in each part is usually semicircular for producing round forms but can be of other shapes also.

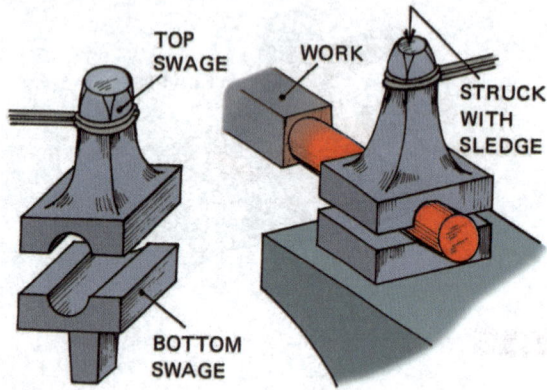

Fig. 11.12

## Hints on Forging

1. Ensure that the metal is at the correct temperature for forging. If it is at too low a temperature, it may split. If overheated, it may burn. Mild steel should be bright red and high carbon steel should be medium to dull red. Heat only the portion being forged.
2. Remove the scale from the heated metal before forging and keep the anvil face free of scale.
3. Hold the hammer by the end of the handle, not up near the head.
4. Keep the hammer head at the correct angle when striking the work to avoid leaving hammer marks.
5. There should be only one student at a time using the anvil.
6. Do not leave items strewn about the forge vicinity, especially hot tools or hot pieces of metal. Cool all tools before storing away.

## Drawing Down

Drawing down is a forging operation which involves reducing the cross-section of a bar and increasing its length. Typical examples are shown in Fig. 11.13.

When forming a point, Fig. 11.13 A, the required length can be marked on the anvil face with chalk. Start with a blunt point, Fig. 11.14, and work backwards until the point is the required length. This prevents 'piping', Fig. 11.16, which is the formation of a hollow in the end of the bar. It also helps to avoid over-reducing the cross-section between the tip and the end of the taper.

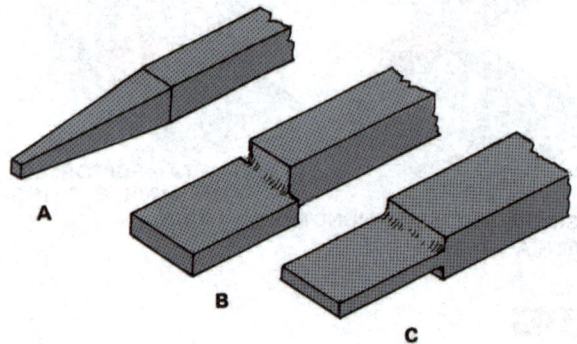

Fig. 11.13
Examples of drawing down operations

Fig. 11.14

Fig. 11.15

PIPING

Fig. 11.16

In order to keep the point central, the bar must be held at an angle to the anvil face. The correct angle is half the point angle, Fig. 11.15.

When forming a square point, the bar must be turned through 90° from time to time to keep the section square. If a round point is required, first forge a square point, then an octagonal point, and finally forge a round point by lightly hammering the corners.

Shoulders can be formed on the edge of the anvil, Fig. 11.17.

Fig. 11.17
Forming a shoulder

## Upsetting

This involves increasing the cross-section of a bar and reducing its length. Upsetting can be done at the end of a bar or anywhere along its length. The section being upset is brought to the forging temperature and any heated portion beyond this is cooled off before commencing. Two methods of upsetting a bar are illustrated in Fig. 11.18.

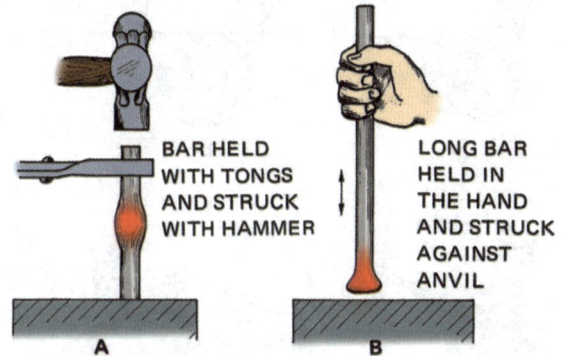

BAR HELD WITH TONGS AND STRUCK WITH HAMMER

LONG BAR HELD IN THE HAND AND STRUCK AGAINST ANVIL

A          B

Fig. 11.18
Upsetting

## Forming an Eye

The length of material required for the eye must first be calculated (see below). Mark this length on the bar, measuring from its end. Heat the material and make a right angle bend at the mark, Fig. 11.19 A.

Reheat the bent end and form the eye on the bick of the anvil, or on a former of the required diameter. Start with the end of the bar and work back to the right angle. When the eye is complete, heat it again, place flat on the anvil face and level it out, Fig. 11.19 F.

The various stages in forming an eye are illustrated in Fig. 11.19 (next page).

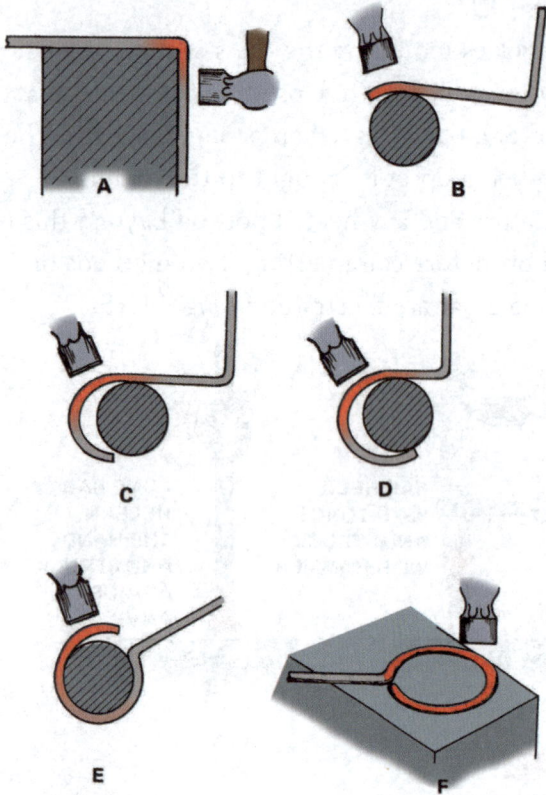

Fig. 11.19
Stages in forming an eye

During the bending, the bar must be struck at a point slightly beyond where it is in contact with the anvil or former, Fig. 11.20 A. If struck over where it is making contact, the bar will be flattened rather than bent, Fig. 11.20 B.

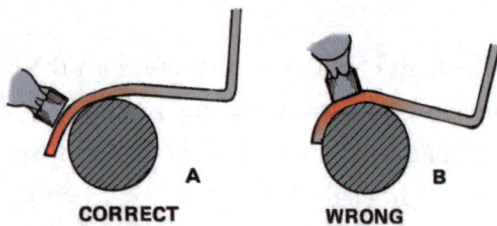

CORRECT    WRONG

Fig. 11.20

## Forming a U-Bend

This is also formed on the bick of the anvil or on a former. The various forging stages are illustrated in Fig. 11.21. First, mark the position of the beginning of the bend on the material. Start the bending with this mark in contact with the former and continue until both legs are parallel. Reheat the bent portion, place flat on the anvil and level it out.

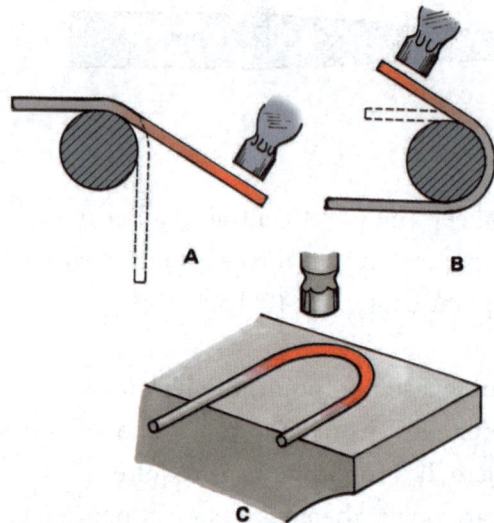

Fig. 11.21
Stages in forming a U-Bend

## Lengths of Materials for Eyes and Bends

When calculating the lengths of material required to form circular eyes and bends, the thickness of the material must be taken into account. This is done by using the mean diameter of the eye for the calculations.

If the bend forms part of a circle, first calculate the length required to form a complete circle, then calculate the length required to form the portion involved. For example, if the bend forms a semi-circle, calculate the length required to form a complete circle and divide it by two. If it forms a quadrant of a circle, divide by four.

**Example 1** Calculate the length of bar required to form the circular eye shown in Fig. 11.22.

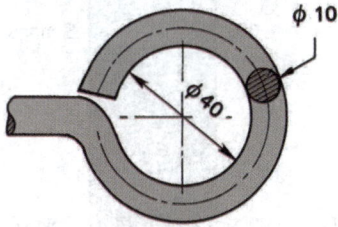

**Fig. 11.22**

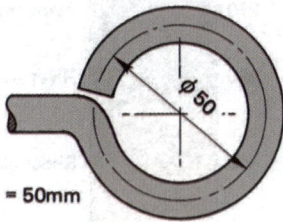

MEAN DIAMETER = 50mm

**Fig. 11.23**

Mean Diameter

$$= \frac{\text{Internal diameter + external diameter}}{2}$$

$$= \frac{40 + 60}{2}$$

$$= 50\text{mm}$$

Length of material required = π x mean diameter

$$= \frac{22}{7} \times 50\text{mm}$$

$$= 157\text{mm}$$

to nearest mm

## Scrolls

It takes some practice to become proficient at making scrolls, but they add a lot to the appearance of ornamental work. If both ends of the material are being worked, the required length must first be estimated.

This can be done by drawing the shape of the scroll on a flat surface with chalk or on paper with a pencil. A string can then be laid around it to measure the length. Flaring the end of the material improves the appearance of the scroll considerably.

Since it would be difficult to begin the bending on a jig, it is better to start on the rounded edge of the anvil, with the material red hot. Continue the bending on the face of the anvil and finish on a jig or scroll tool, Fig. 11.24 E. Finally, level out the scroll on the face of the anvil. A scroll jig can be made up of two pins held in a steel block. Scrolls are usually 'S' or 'C' shaped, Fig. 11.24 F.

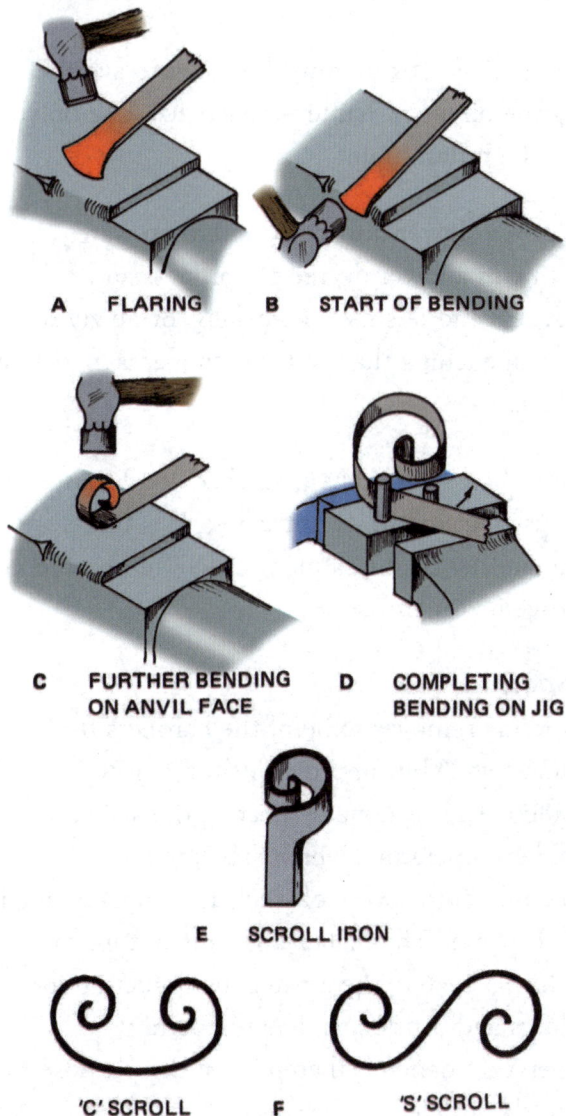

A    FLARING      B    START OF BENDING

C    FURTHER BENDING ON ANVIL FACE      D    COMPLETING BENDING ON JIG

E    SCROLL IRON

'C' SCROLL      F    'S' SCROLL

**Fig. 11.24**
Stages of making scrolls

## Heat Treatment

### Hardening

If a piece of high carbon steel is heated to cherry red and then cooled rapidly or 'quenched,' it becomes very hard and brittle. At the cherry red temperature, the steel will have just undergone structural changes and the rapid cooling does not allow it to revert to its normal condition. The exact hardening temperature depends on the carbon content of the steel and is usually about 750°C. Water, different types of oils and brine (salt water) are used as quenching media.

If using oil, great care must be taken to avoid firing the oil (see Chapter 4, page 40). Use only oil with a high flash point.

Oils give a slower quenching rate than water, resulting in a lower degree of hardness and brittleness and less risk of cracking. Brine gives fiercer quenching than water with a greater risk of cracking.

High carbon steel in the quenched condition is of little use because of its brittleness. It is therefore given another heat treatment called 'tempering' to improve its toughness.

### Tempering

Tempering removes some of the hardness from hardened steel but improves its toughness considerably. It is done by heating the article to a suitable temperature, which is below the reddening temperature of steel, and then cooling it in oil or water. The higher the temperature to which it is heated, the greater the reduction in hardness and brittleness. The tempering temperature depends therefore on the purpose for which the article is to be used.

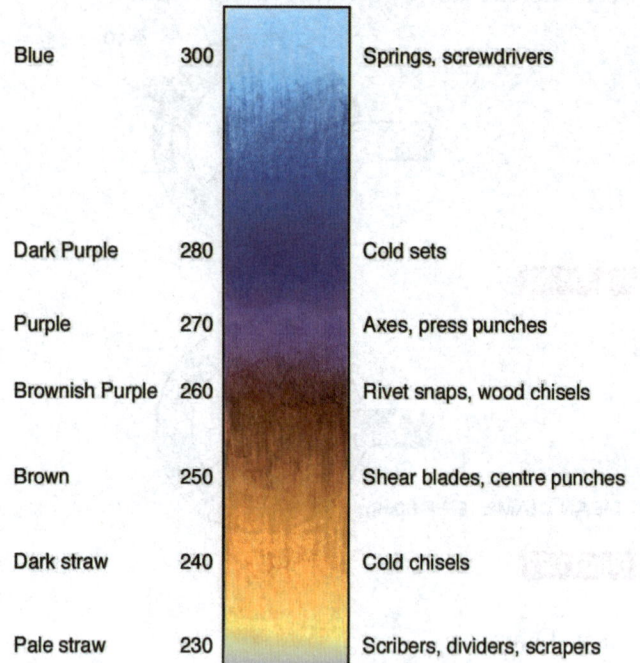

**Fig. 11.25**

Tempering colours and temperatures for a range of articles

| Temperature °C | | Articles |
|---|---|---|
| Blue | 300 | Springs, screwdrivers |
| Dark Purple | 280 | Cold sets |
| Purple | 270 | Axes, press punches |
| Brownish Purple | 260 | Rivet snaps, wood chisels |
| Brown | 250 | Shear blades, centre punches |
| Dark straw | 240 | Cold chisels |
| Pale straw | 230 | Scribers, dividers, scrapers |

In the school workshop, this temperature is gauged by the colour of the oxide film appearing on the polished surface of the heated steel. If a piece of bright steel is gradually heated with a blow torch, different colours will appear on its surface at different temperatures.

### Annealing

Annealing is done to soften metal and to relieve internal stresses. Steel is annealed by heating it to a cherry red, as for hardening, and allowing it to cool very slowly. The slow cooling can be carried out in the furnace by switching it off when the article has reached the correct temperature. Another method is to place the heated article in lime.

Copper is annealed by heating it to a dull red and either cooling it in water or leaving it to cool in air.

Brass is annealed by heating it to a dull red and allowing it to cool in air. Overheating can cause a reduction in ductility. Some types of brass become brittle if cooled rapidly.

Care must be taken when heating aluminium because it can suddenly melt without having reached an apparent change in colour. Its annealing temperature can be gauged by rubbing soap on its surface. When the soap turns brown, it will have reached the correct temperature and can then be cooled in water.

## Normalising

Normalising is carried out to refine the structure of steel and to remove internal stresses caused by cold working, e.g. hammering, rolling and bending. It is similar to the annealing of steel, except that the cooling rate is much faster, resulting in the steel being harder. The steel is heated to cherry red and allowed to cool naturally in still air. This improves its ductility and toughness.

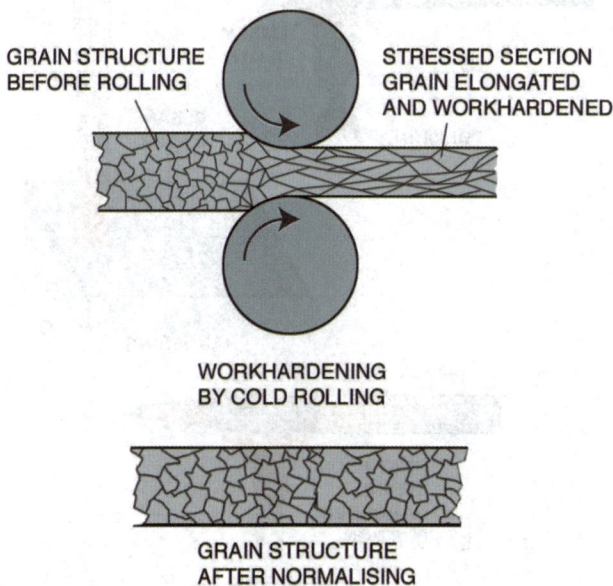

GRAIN STRUCTURE BEFORE ROLLING

STRESSED SECTION GRAIN ELONGATED AND WORKHARDENED

WORKHARDENING BY COLD ROLLING

GRAIN STRUCTURE AFTER NORMALISING

**Fig. 11.26**
Workhardening and normalising

## Case Hardening

Mild steel does not contain sufficient carbon to enable it to be hardened in the same way as high carbon steel. It is possible, however, to increase the carbon content at its surface and this skin or case can then be hardened. This is called case hardening. The hard surface enables an article to resist wear, while the tough core will enable it to resist breakage. School workshop articles that are case hardened include vee blocks, stocks of try squares and spindles.

Case hardening is done in two stages:
1.  Carburising, or raising the carbon content of the case.
2.  Heat treatment.

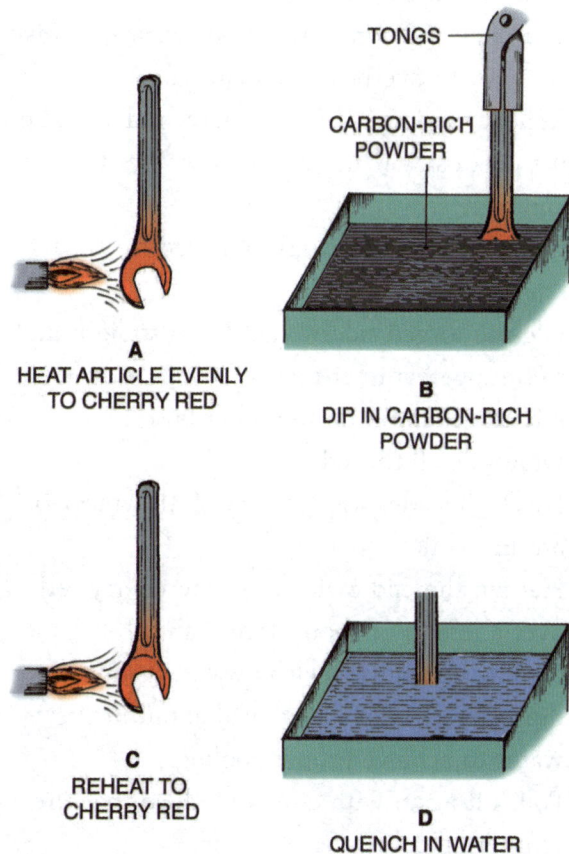

TONGS

CARBON-RICH POWDER

**A**
HEAT ARTICLE EVENLY TO CHERRY RED

**B**
DIP IN CARBON-RICH POWDER

**C**
REHEAT TO CHERRY RED

**D**
QUENCH IN WATER

**Fig. 11.27**
Case hardening

A number of methods are used and depths of up to 1.5mm are possible but will take several hours to achieve.

A simple method of producing a thin hard case is to heat the article to cherry red and then dip it in carbon–rich powder (Fig. 11.27). This is repeated two or three times to increase the depth of the casing. It is finally heated again to cherry red and quenched in water to harden the case.

## Forming and Heat Treating a Cold Chisel

1. Cut off a suitable length of material from a high carbon steel bar. It is better to leave it long enough to hold by hand if possible.
2. Heat the end of the material to medium red and draw it down to the required shape. Take care not to overheat the material.
3. Reheat the forged end to cherry red and allow it to cool slowly beside the forge fire to anneal it.
4. Cut off the exact length required for the chisel.
5. File the forged sides to get them straight and to remove hammer marks.
6. File the chamfer on the other end.
7. Draw-file all the sides.
8. Polish the sides using emery cloth wrapped around a file.
9. Harden the end by heating it to cherry red over a length of about 25mm and then by cooling it rapidly in clean water. It must be dipped vertically and moved about in the water to achieve proper cooling.
10. Polish it again with emery cloth so that the tempering colours can appear.
11. To temper, heat slowly from behind the hardened portion, allowing the heat to travel gradually to the point. The tempering colours will appear as the temperature rises. When a dark straw colour reaches the point, cool it in oil.
12. The cutting edge must now be ground to an angle of 60°. This should be done by your teacher for safety reasons. It should then be tested on mild steel.

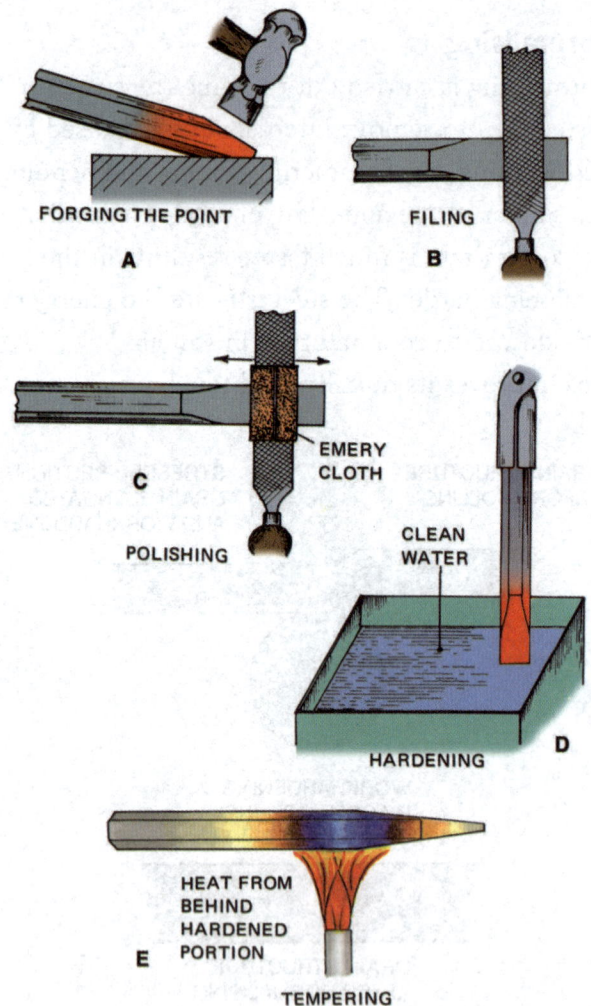

FORGING THE POINT

A

FILING

B

POLISHING

EMERY CLOTH

C

CLEAN WATER

HARDENING

D

HEAT FROM BEHIND HARDENED PORTION

E

TEMPERING

**Fig. 11.28**
Stages in the marking of a chisel

## Exercises

1. What advantage has a forged article over one cut out from blank material?

2. An anvil is shown in Fig. 11.29 below.
   (a) Name and state the function of each part A, B, C, D and E.
   (b) Why is the cutting table of the anvil left unhardened?
   (c) What material is the anvil made from?

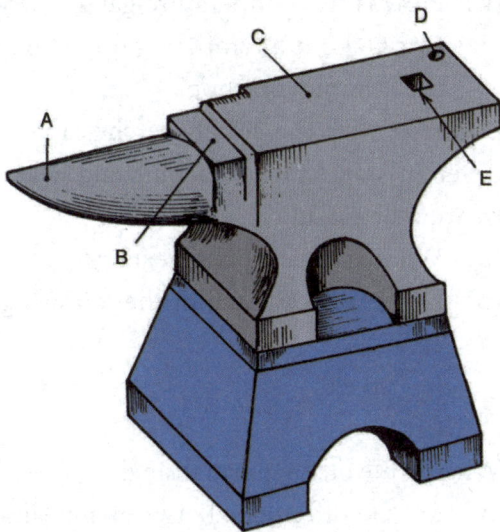

Fig. 11.29

3. Why is a leg vice used for forgework?
4. State one drawback of a leg vice.
5. Four types of tongs A, B, C and D are shown in Fig. 11.30. Name and state the use of each one.

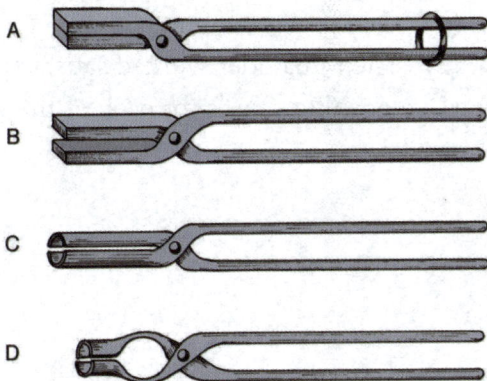

Fig. 11.30

6. What is a hardie used for?
7. State the use of:
   (a) A hot set.
   (b) A cold set.
8. What are the main differences between a hot set and a cold set?
9. What is a smith's punch used for?
10. Name and state the use of the tool shown in Fig. 11.31 below.

Fig. 11.31

11. Name and state the use of the tools shown in Fig. 11.32 below.

Fig. 11.32

12. Name and state the use of the tools shown in Fig. 11.33 below.

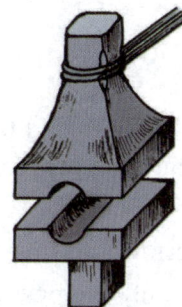

Fig. 11.33

13. What would happen to a bar of steel if it was left too long in the forge fire?

14. Name the forging operations shown in Fig. 11.34, A and B.

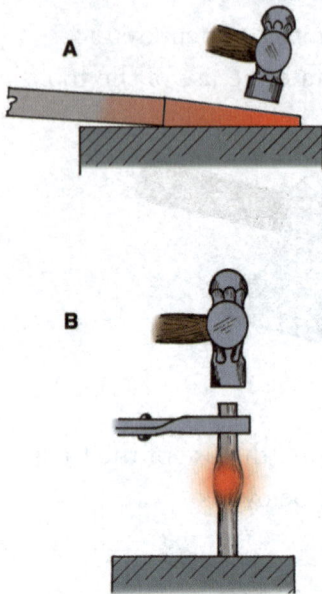

Fig. 11.34

15. Describe, with the aid of sketches, how you would forge the eye shown in Fig. 11.35.

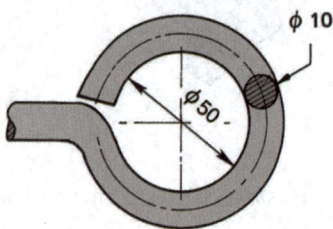

Fig. 11.35

16. (a) What is meant by 'piping'?
    (b) How can it be prevented when forging a point?

17. When performing an upsetting operation, why should only the portion being upset be at the forging temperature?

18. Why should the material be struck slightly beyond where it is in contact with the anvil bick or former when forging an eye?

19. If a piece of high carbon steel is heated to cherry red and cooled rapidly in water, what effects will this have on its mechanical properties?

20. (a) Describe the process of tempering high carbon steel, which has been hardened.
    (b) How is the temperature gauged when carrying out a tempering operation in the school workshop?

21. Describe, with the aid of sketches, the different stages in the shaping and heat treating of a cold chisel.

22. (a) What is meant by annealing?
    (b) Describe how each of the following is annealed:
        (i) Steel,
        (ii) Copper.

23. What is meant by normalising?

24. What is the difference between annealing and normalising as applied to steel?

25. (a) What is case hardening?
    (b) Describe one method of case hardening mild steel.

26. On testing centre punches made in the school workshop, the following were the results:
    (a) The point broke off one.
    (b) One became blunt.
    (c) The remainder worked satisfactorily.
    Give possible causes for each of the faulty results.

## Polishing

Hand polishing is done with a soft cloth. There are various types of metal polishes available to suit different materials. They give quite good results and are easy to use. However, certain precautions have to be taken with some of them, and manufacturers' instructions should be carefully followed.

Mops in the form of wheels are also used for polishing. They are fitted to polishing machines, Fig. 12.1 A. A polishing compound must also be used. This is applied to the mop as it revolves. There are various types of mops and compounds available to suit different applications.

Polishing machines should not be used by pupils unless the teacher is satisfied that they can do so without risk. They must have received adequate instruction and have experience in the use of machines. The work must be gripped firmly and pressed against the wheel slightly below its horizontal centre line, Fig. 12.1 B. An edge should not be pressed directly into the mop because this could cause the work to be snatched violently from the hands. If the work becomes too hot to hold, it should be allowed to cool. It should not be held with a piece of cloth or apron as these could easily get picked up by the mop.

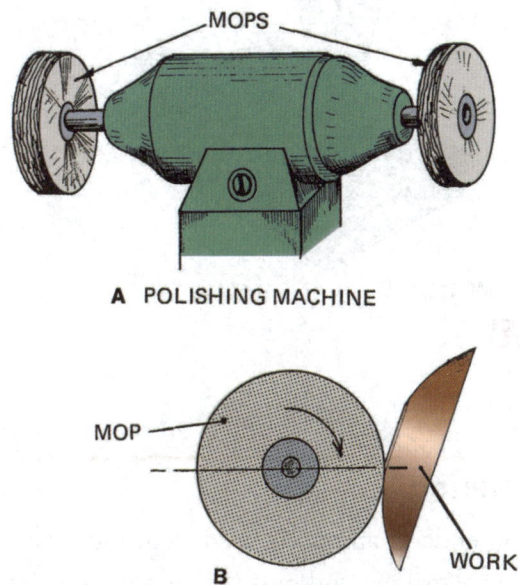

**A POLISHING MACHINE**

**Fig. 12.1**
Polishing

If a mop becomes clogged with compound, it should be cleaned. This can be done by holding a mop dresser against its periphery as it rotates.

Any deep scratches must be removed from the workpiece before polishing. The polishing would only make them more noticeable.

## Mottling

A wooden dowel about 8mm in diameter and carborundum paste is used for a mottled finish. The dowel is gripped in the drilling machine chuck and its end is coated with the paste. As the dowel rotates, it is pressed against the work, producing polished circles on its surface.

By keeping these circles in rows and allowing them to overlap, a decorative pattern can be produced.

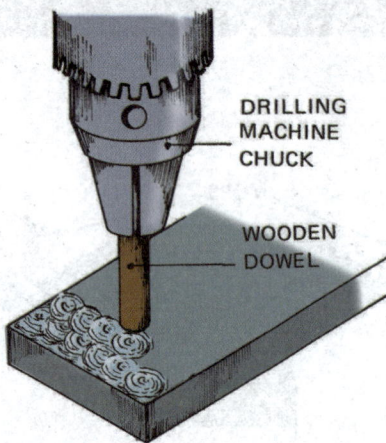

DRILLING MACHINE CHUCK

WOODEN DOWEL

MOTTLING

**Fig. 12.2**
Mottling

## Hammering

A round ended hammer is used to produce this finish. The striking end must be smooth and free from marks. The work must be firmly supported during the hammering. The indentations should be in an irregular pattern and close together. When the hammering is completed, the work must be trued up.

Mild steel articles are often coated with a flat black paint after hammering. The indentations can be made more conspicuous by draw-filing the surface when the paint is dry. The paint will remain in the indentations, but the article must be coated with a clear varnish to protect it against rusting. Another method of colouring the

indentations is to draw-file the surface and then polish it with an emery cloth before the hammering. After hammering, it can be heated until it turns blue and then cooled in oil.

The article can then be repolished using emery cloth wrapped around a file, allowing the colour to remain in the indentations.

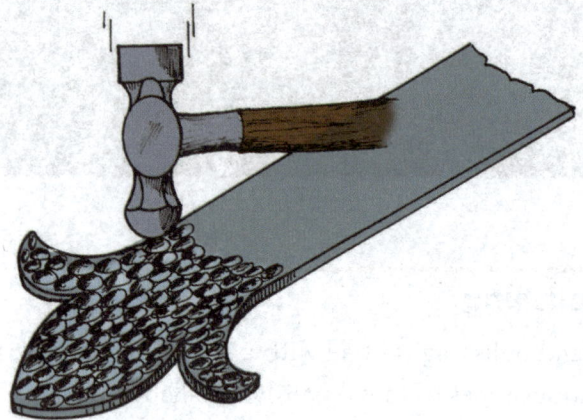

**Fig. 12.3**
Hammering

## Punching

Various shaped punches, Fig. 12.4, are used for this work. By using different combinations of punches, a great variety of designs can be produced. Thin material should be supported on lead or pitch.

EXAMPLES OF SHAPES OF PUNCHES

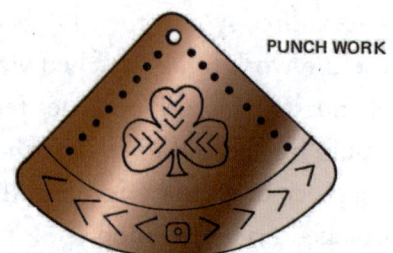

PUNCH WORK

**Fig. 12.4**
Punching

## Repoussé

In this process, raised designs are formed on the work, almost entirely from the back, while it is set in prepared pitch. Shaped punches and a repoussé hammer are used for the forming. Before embedding in the pitch, the metal should be lightly greased to aid the removal of pitch afterwards. The surface of the pitch is heated and the annealed metal pressed into it until the pitch just comes over its edges. The pitch is then allowed to cool.

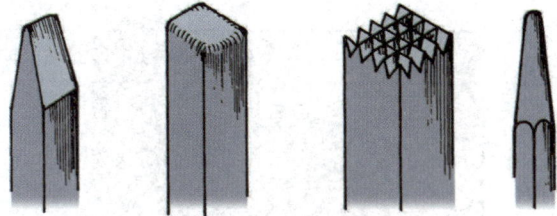

The metal is first set in the pitch face upwards to trace the design on it. Carbon paper can be used for this and the lines scribed afterwards. These lines are then lightly punched with a tracing punch so that they will show up on the other side when the work is turned over. The tracing punch should be tilted so that it moves towards the operator as it is being struck, leaving shallow continuous grooves. When all the lines are punched, the work is heated and removed from the pitch. It is then cleaned and reset in the pitch, this time face downwards. The required parts are now punched down using suitably shaped punches. The work may again be set in the pitch face upwards, to sharpen up the design from the front.

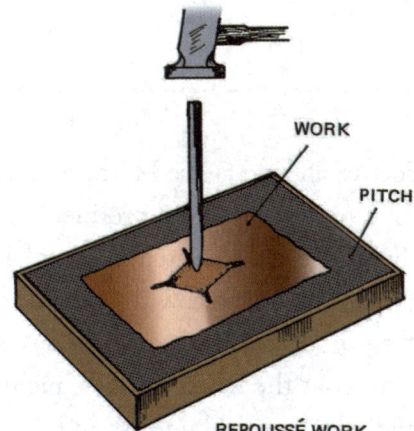

**Fig. 12.5**
Repoussé work

## Engraving

In engraving, designs are cut into metal surfaces with sharp tools. There are different shaped tools available, but the square graver is the most common type used. A fine oil stone should be used for sharpening gravers. The design must first be drawn on the metal surface. The graver is then pushed carefully along the lines, taking a light first cut. Curves are usually best cut by turning the work rather than the graver. The lines can be deepened as required by taking further cuts.

Power tools are often used for engraving letters and numbers on ornamental objects.

SQUARE GRAVER

**Fig. 12.6**
Engraving

## Etching

In this process, an acid is used to bite away portions of a metal surface to produce a desired design. The portions to be etched must be bare and the remainder covered with an acid resist. Different methods are used to achieve this. One method is to coat the whole surface, including the bottom and edges, with the resist and then to scrape it off the portions to be etched. A scriber or other suitable instrument can be used for scraping off the resist. Carbon paper can be used to transfer designs to work surfaces.

A solution of equal amounts of water and nitric acid or a solution of ferric chloride is used for etching copper and brass. Great care must be taken when using acid and you must ensure that it does not get on your skin or in your eyes. The work is completely immersed in the solution, or if in bowl form, the solution can be poured into it. Any bubbles which form should be brushed away from time to time with a feather. When the etching is deep enough, the work is taken from the solution and washed under running water. The acid resist is then removed.

A COATING THE WORKPIECE WITH AN ACID RESIST

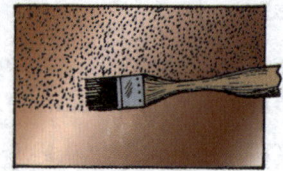

B REMOVING THE ACID RESIST FROM THE PORTIONS TO BE ETCHED

C WORKPIECE IMMERSED IN AN ACID SOLUTION

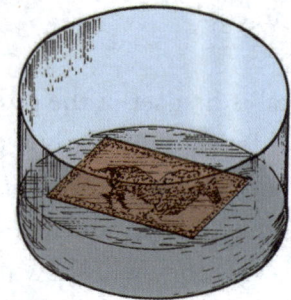

D WASH UNDER A TAP

**Fig. 12.7**
Etching

## Enamelling

This involves fusing enamel, which is basically glass, onto metal surfaces. The enamel is mostly applied in powder form and then fired. The firing can be done with a blow torch but a kiln is more suitable. Enamel is available in a wide range of colours and can be transparent, translucent or opaque. The enamelling can be confined to certain areas of the surface if desired. A number of metals can be enamelled, e.g. copper, silver, gold and steel. Copper is probably the most suitable for school work.

There are various methods used for enamelling articles. The following is a simple method for producing a design with two colours:

1. Clean the surface of the blank thoroughly, ensuring that it is free of grease or scale.
2. Place the blank on a sheet of paper and sprinkle powdered enamel over it, to a depth of about 1mm, using a small sieve. Allow a little extra at the edges. Any enamel that falls on the paper can be returned to the container.
3. Place the workpiece on panning mesh, and with the aid of a firing fork, put the mesh into the hot kiln, Fig. 12.8 B. Remember to wear a face shield or goggles when using the kiln. The firing should be done at a temperature of about 850°C and will take between one and three minutes.
4. When the enamel has melted and has a smooth glossy appearance, remove the workpiece from the kiln and allow it to cool.
5. Cut out a pattern from a sheet of paper, Fig. 12.8 C.
6. Position the pattern on the workpiece and sprinkle enamel of a different colour on the exposed area of the surface.
7. Lift the pattern carefully using a tweezers.
8. Fire as before.

**Note:** Ensure that nothing moist or wet is put into a hot kiln as this could cause an explosion. Never attempt to light a torch from a kiln as this could also cause an explosion.

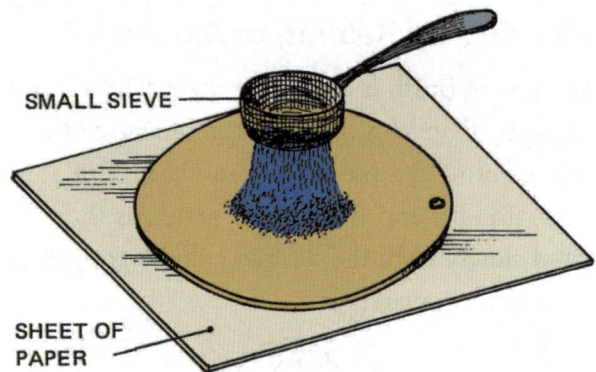

A  SPRINKLING ON POWDERED ENAMEL

SMALL SIEVE

SHEET OF PAPER

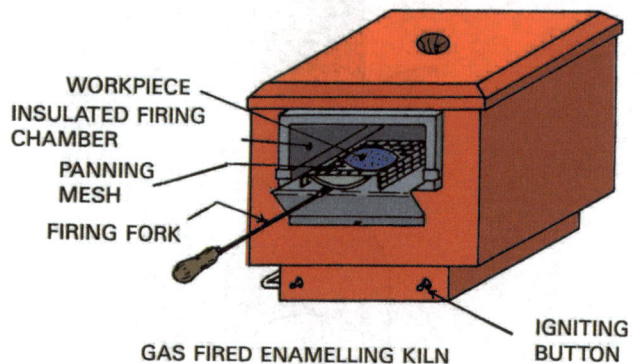

WORKPIECE
INSULATED FIRING CHAMBER
PANNING MESH
FIRING FORK
IGNITING BUTTON

GAS FIRED ENAMELLING KILN

B  FIRING

PAPER PATTERN

C  POSITIONING THE PATTERN

WORKPIECE
PAPER PATTERN
SHEET OF PAPER

D  SPRINKLING ENAMEL OF A DIFFERENT COLOUR ON THE EXPOSED AREA

Fig. 12.8
Enamelling

## Colouring by Heating or Blueing

This type of finish is applied to steel. The surface is draw-filed and finished with an emery cloth wrapped around a file beforehand to ensure a bright, smooth appearance. The article is then heated slowly until the desired colours appear and then cooled in water.

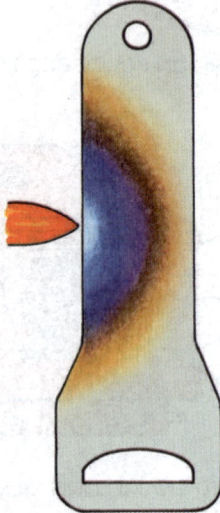

**Fig. 12.9**
Colouring by heating or blueing

## Lacquering

Lacquers or varnishes are applied to metals to preserve their surface finish. They can be used on both ferrous and non-ferrous metals and are available colourless or tinted. They are applied by brushing, dipping or spraying. The surface of the work must be perfectly clean.

## Painting

Painting can greatly improve the appearance of ferrous metal articles and give protection against corrosion. Surfaces to be painted must be free of rust, oil and grease. Best results are usually obtained by applying a number of coats, i.e. a primer, undercoat and finish. If using an aerosol can, the spraying must be done in a well-ventilated area. The nozzle must be cleaned when finished to prevent it getting clogged by solidified paint. To do this, turn the can upside down and press the top until the spray becomes clear. When the can is empty, it must be disposed of safely.

## Plastic Coating
### — Fluidised Bed Method

This is a process by which a plastic coating is applied to metal articles. The coating gives an attractive appearance as well as good resistance to corrosion. Common applications include dish drainers, refrigerator shelves, wire baskets and coat hangers. A number of plastic powders are used, e.g. polyethylene, PVC and nylon. They are available in a variety of colours.

The following equipment is required: a fluidising unit, Fig. 12.10 B, an air supplying unit and a heating appliance. A means of regulating the air flow must also be provided. The fluidising unit has two compartments, which are separated from each other by a porous material.

The upper compartment contains the plastic powder and the air supply is connected to the lower one. Air passes up through the porous material and causes the plastics powder to act like a fluid. This allows the heated article to sink into the powder and to receive an even coating all over.

The article to be coated must be free of loose scale, oil or grease. A fine wire can be attached to it for dipping and for hanging it up afterwards to cool. It must be heated to enable the plastic powder to fuse onto it. A temperature of about 180°C is suitable for low density polyethylene. The heating is best done in a kiln. Even heating is difficult if using a torch. The heated article is dipped into the fluidised powder and held there for a few seconds. It is then removed and surplus powder shaken off. Unless the article is of thin construction, its residual heat will be sufficient to completely fuse the powder that has stuck onto it. Thin articles must be reheated in an oven. When all the powder has fused, the article is allowed to cool. The wire can then be cut off.

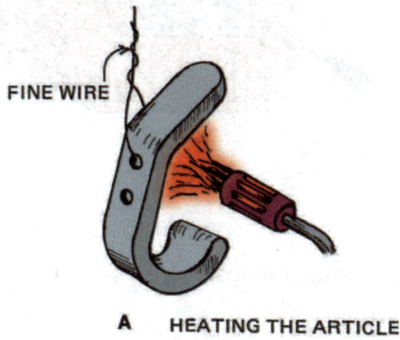

A    HEATING THE ARTICLE

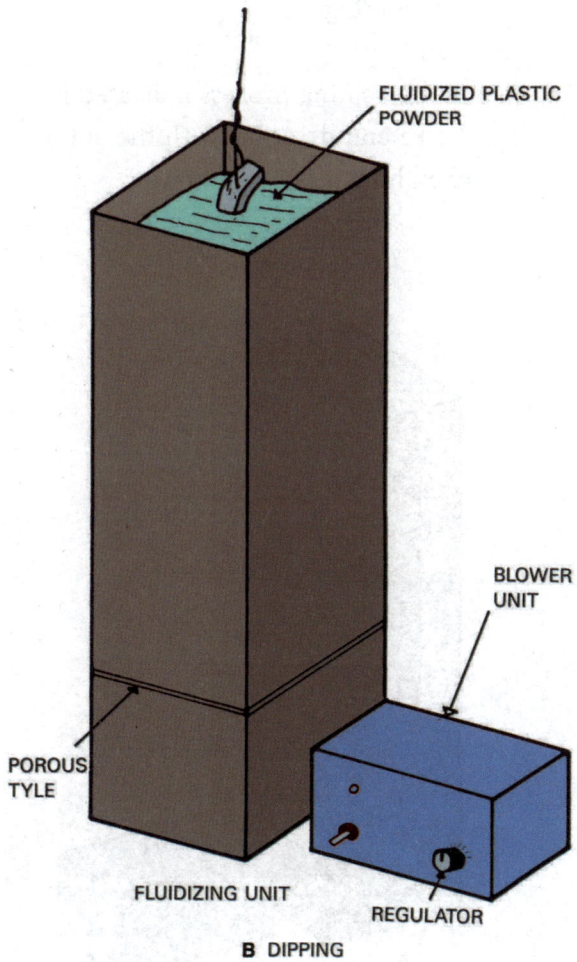

B    DIPPING

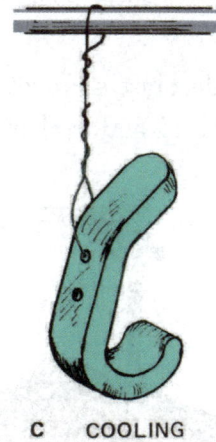

C    COOLING

**Fig. 12.10**
Plastic coating

## Exercises

1. Describe, with the aid of sketches, how an article is polished using a polishing machine. Include in your answer the safety precautions that must be observed.

2. Name the decorative finish shown in Fig. 12.11 and explain how it is carried out.

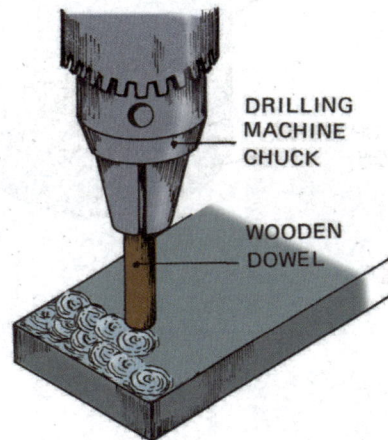

**Fig. 12.11**

3. Describe how a hammered finish is applied to an article.

4. Describe how a surface can be decorated by punching.
5. Name the decorative process being carried out in Fig 12.12 and explain how it is done.

Fig. 12.12

6. Explain how surfaces are engraved.
7. Name the decorative process being carried out in Fig. 12.13 and explain, with the aid of diagrams, the various steps involved.

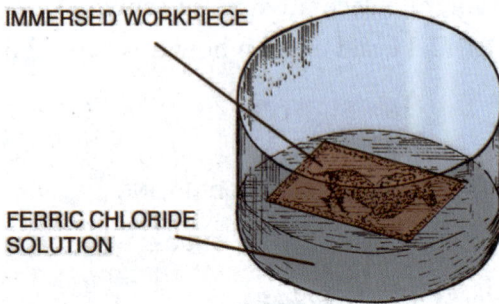

IMMERSED WORKPIECE

FERRIC CHLORIDE SOLUTION

Fig. 12.13

8. Name the decorative process being carried out in Fig. 12.14 and describe, with the aid of sketches, the various steps involved.

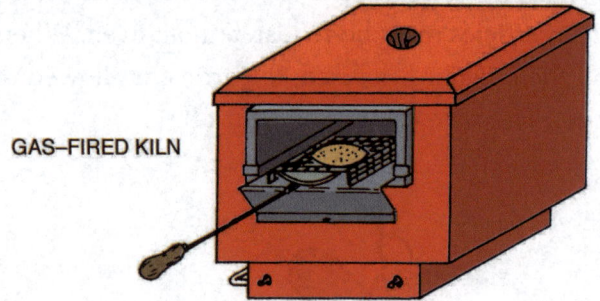

GAS–FIRED KILN

Fig. 12.14

9. What is the purpose of each of the following?
   (a) Lacquering.
   (b) Painting.
10. Name the coating process indicated in Fig. 12.15 and describe, with the aid of sketches, how it is carried out.

Fig. 12.15

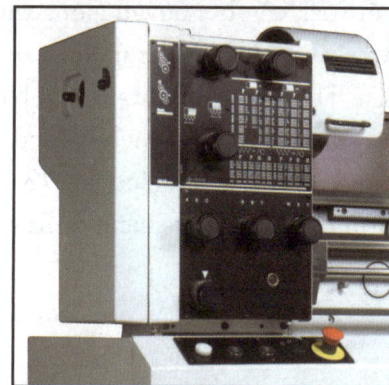

## The Centre Lathe

The lathe is a very important machine tool and one of the most widely used in engineering. In lathework, the workpiece is rotated against a cutting tool. The cutting tool is moved along a certain path to produce the required shape. Lathework is normally referred to as turning. The main parts of a centre lathe are shown in Fig. 13.1.

## The Lathe Bed

This is a rigid, cast iron member which is mounted on the lathe stand. Accurately machined slideways are formed on the top of the bed. These guide the carriage and tailstock as they move along it. The headstock is mounted on the left-hand end of the bed. Some beds have a gap just in front of the headstock to accommodate large diameter work.

## Headstock

This houses the lathe spindle and also contains gears to provide a range of spindle speeds. A chuck, a face plate or a driving plate can be mounted on the nose of the spindle to rotate the work. The spindle is hollow to allow long bars to pass through it, and the inside of its nose end has a Morse taper to take a lathe centre.

## Tailstock

The tailstock can be moved along the bed slideways and may be clamped in any desired position. The bore of the tailstock barrel is tapered to take a lathe centre, which is used to support the outer end of long work (see Fig. 13.5). It can also take drill chucks, taper shank drills and reamers.

## Carriage

This is moved along the lathe bed between the headstock and the tailstock. The part which lies across the lathe is called the saddle, and the part which hangs down the front is called the apron.

## Cross Slide

This is mounted on the saddle. It moves the tool at right angles to the lathe bed, as for facing operations.

## Top Slide or Compound Slide

This is fitted to the top of the cross slide and carries the toolpost and tool. It can be rotated to any required angle and is used for turning tapers.

## Feed Shaft

The feed shaft is used to traverse the carriage or cross slide automatically.

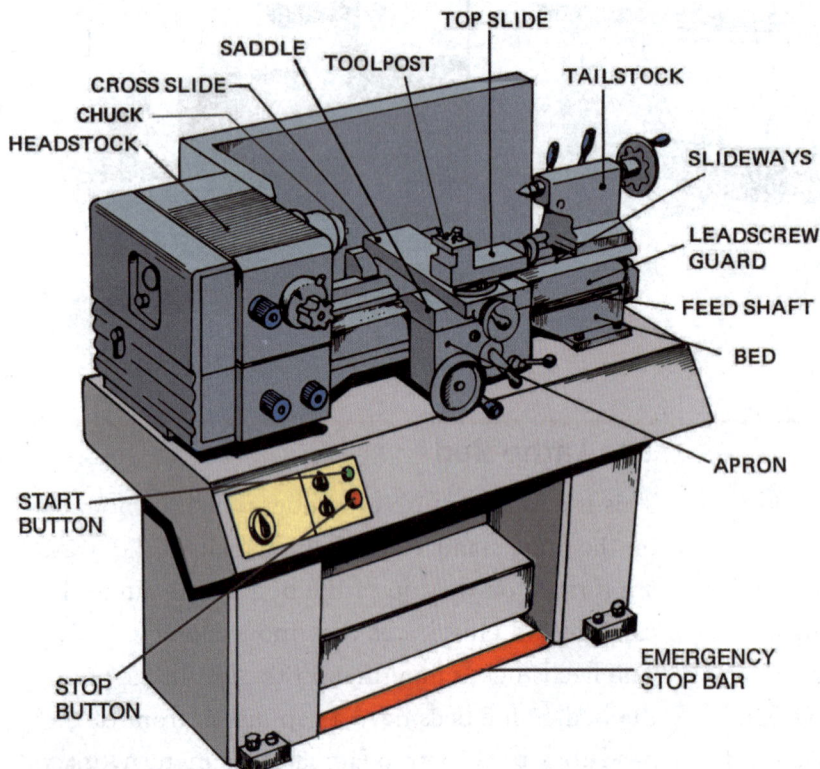

**Fig. 13.1**
A centre lathe

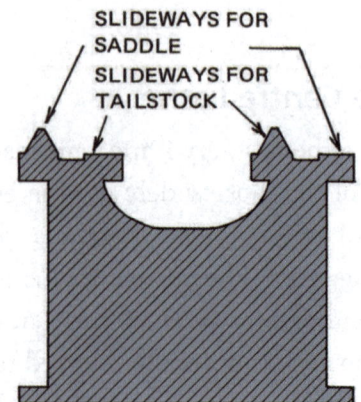

**Fig. 13.2**
An example of a lathe bed cross-section

## Leadscrew

This is used for screwcutting on the lathe.

## Three-Jaw Self-Centring Chuck

This is used for holding round or hexagonal work. The jaws are located on a scroll, so that all three move together when the scroll is rotated. The work is therefore centred automatically within reasonable accuracy. A chuck key is used to open and close the chuck.

Two sets of jaws are supplied with these chucks. One set is used for gripping small diameter work, Fig. 13.3 A. The other set is used for gripping large diameter work, Fig. 13.3 B. The jaws of each set are stamped 1, 2 and 3 and corresponding numbers are stamped beside each slot on the chuck body. This is to ensure that each jaw is returned to its proper slot after removal.

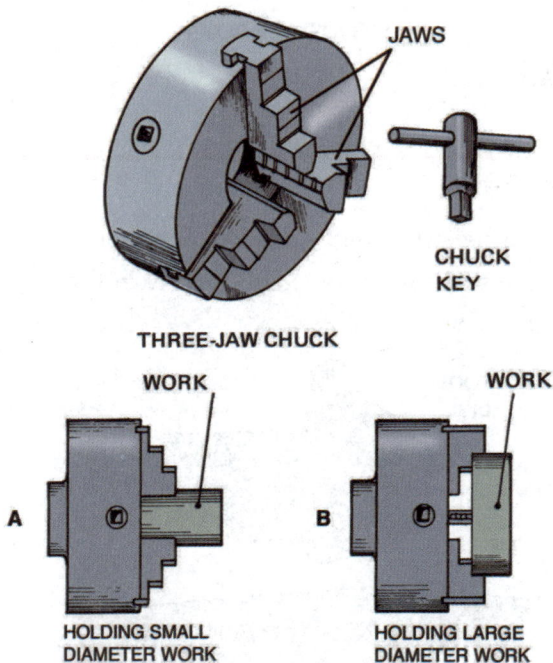

THREE-JAW CHUCK

A HOLDING SMALL DIAMETER WORK

B HOLDING LARGE DIAMETER WORK

Fig. 13.3

## Four-Jaw Independent Chuck

The jaws in this chuck can be moved independently of one another, each being actuated by its own screw. They are also reversible so only one set is required. The four-jaw independent chuck is used for eccentric turning and for gripping square, round, rectangular and irregular shapes. The work can be centred more accurately in this chuck than in the self-centring one, but it takes longer. The concentric circles on the face of the chuck serve as a guide when positioning the work.

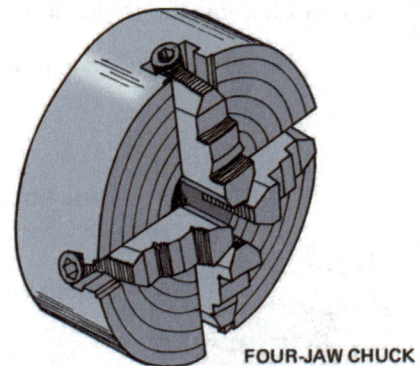

FOUR-JAW CHUCK

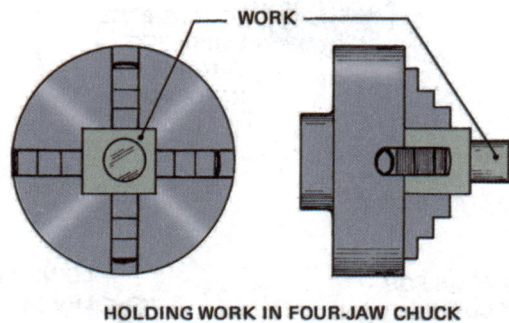

HOLDING WORK IN FOUR-JAW CHUCK

Fig. 13.4

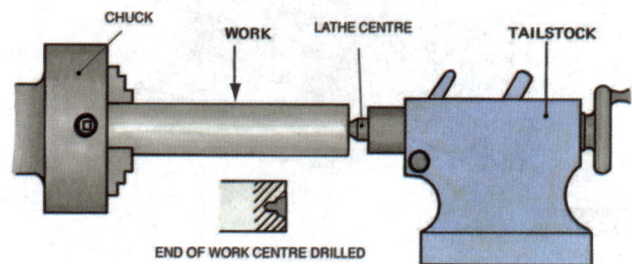

END OF WORK CENTRE DRILLED

Fig. 13.5

Long work supported on a lathe centre in the tailstock

## Toolposts

The toolpost is mounted on the top slide and carries the tool or a tool holder.

The American type, Fig. 13.6, is suitable for light work. The tool holder rests on a segmental rocker in the toolpost. When the locking screw is loosened, the tool holder can be rocked and the tool height adjusted quickly. This has the disadvantage, however, that as the tool holder rocks, the clearance and rake angles of the tool change. One screw locks both the tool holder and the toolpost in position.

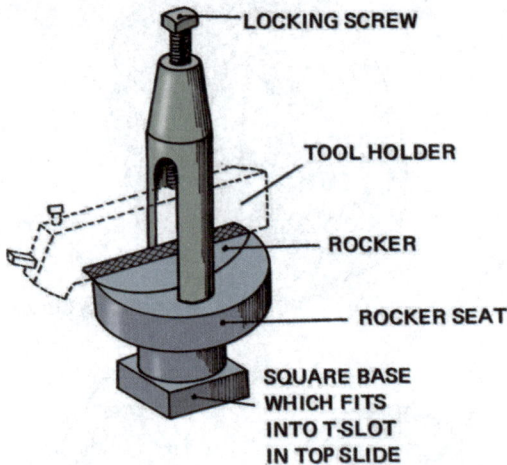

**Fig. 13.6**
American type toolpost

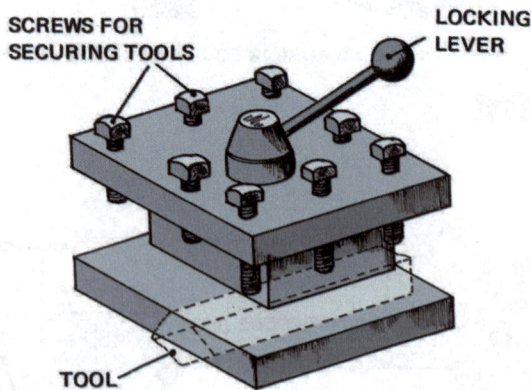

**Fig. 13.7**
Four-way toolpost

The four-way toolpost, Fig. 13.7, can hold four tools simultaneously. It is very suitable for work requiring different types of tools, especially when a number of similar components are being produced. The required tool is brought into position by releasing the locking lever and rotating the toolpost. Packing pieces are placed under the tool to bring it to the correct height.

## Tool Holders

These are used for holding tool bits. There are three types available: right-hand, left-hand and straight.

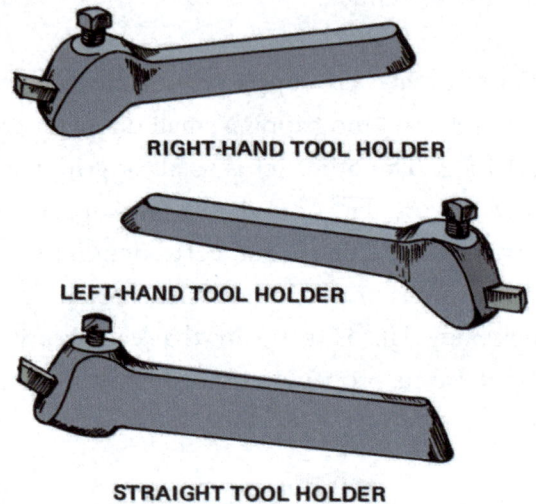

**Fig. 13.8**
Tool holders

## Lathe Tools

These can be either high speed steel bits held in tool holders or solid tools held directly in the toolpost.

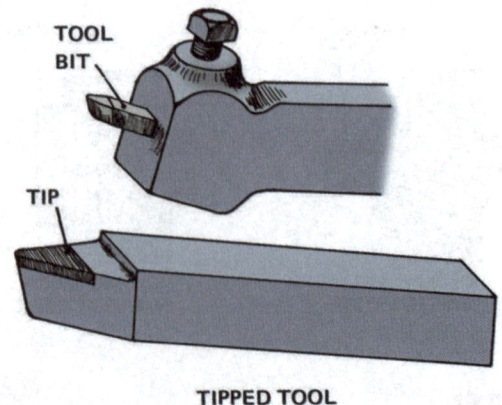

**Fig. 13.9**
Lathe tools

Tipped tools are widely used nowadays. They consist of a shank to which a tip of very hard material, such as tungsten carbide, is brazed or clamped.

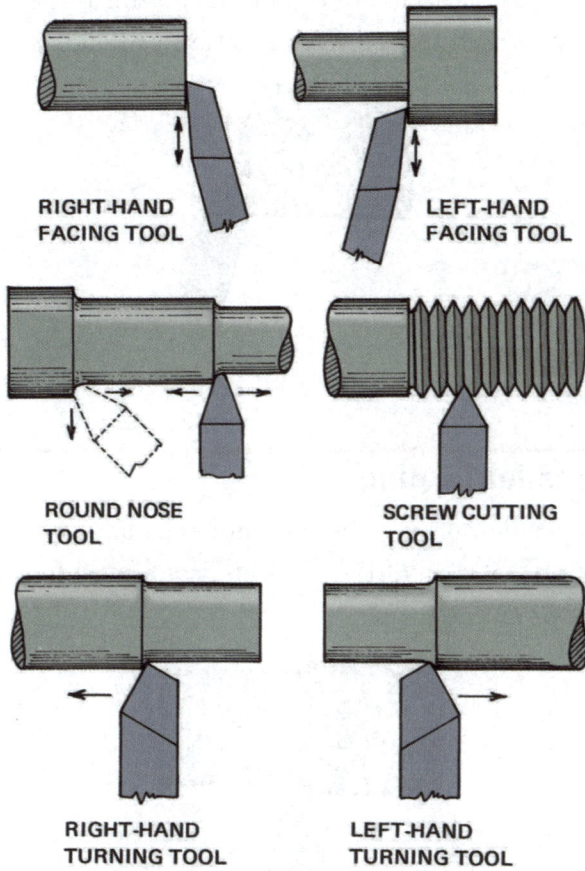

RIGHT-HAND FACING TOOL

LEFT-HAND FACING TOOL

ROUND NOSE TOOL

SCREW CUTTING TOOL

RIGHT-HAND TURNING TOOL

LEFT-HAND TURNING TOOL

**Fig. 13.10**
Common lathe tool shapes

## Lathe Tool Angles

**Clearance:** This ensures that only the cutting edge of the tool comes into contact with the work. Without clearance, the tool would just rub against the work without cutting. Excessive clearance weakens the tool and causes chatter.

**Rake:** The rake facilitates the removal of the chip being cut. Increasing the rake reduces the amount of power consumed in cutting and also the amount of heat generated. However, excess rake can lead to tool breakage, digging in or chattering.

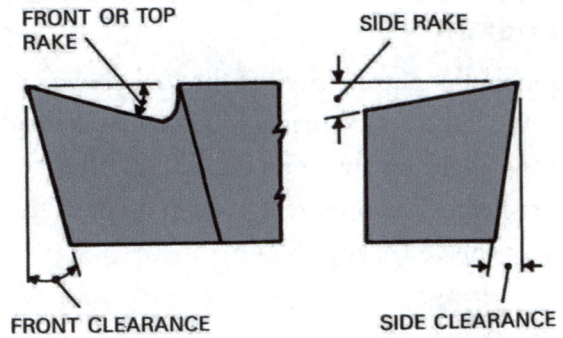

FRONT OR TOP RAKE

SIDE RAKE

FRONT CLEARANCE

SIDE CLEARANCE

**Fig. 13.11**
Lathe tool angles

In general, large rake angles are required for soft, ductile materials and small rake angles for hard, brittle materials.

Tool bits are held in tool holders at an angle of about 15°, Fig. 13.12. This provides some rake but reduces clearance. It must therefore be taken into account when grinding tool bits.

15°

**Fig. 13.12**

The table below gives a guide as to the required rake and clearance angles for cutting some common metals:

| Metal | Front rake | Side rake | Front and side clearance |
|---|---|---|---|
| Mild Steel | 20° | 15° | |
| High Carbon Steel | 10° | 5° | 5° to 10° |
| Cast Iron | 10° | 10° | For All |
| Aluminium | 30° | 15° | |
| Brass | 0 | 5° | |

## Tool Height

Positioning the cutting edge of the tool above or below the lathe centre height affects the rake and clearance angles, as shown in Fig. 13.13. Also, if the tool height is not correct, it cannot cut at the centre of the work, Fig. 13.14.

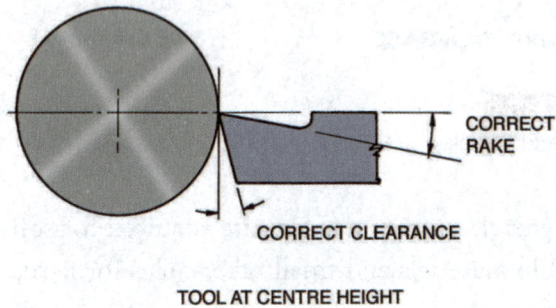

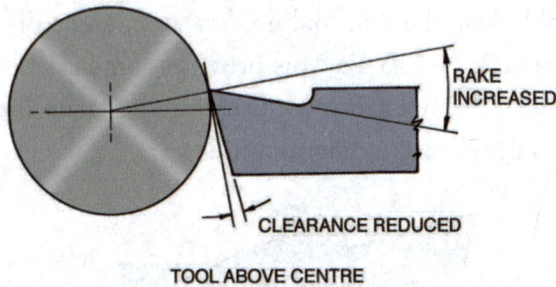

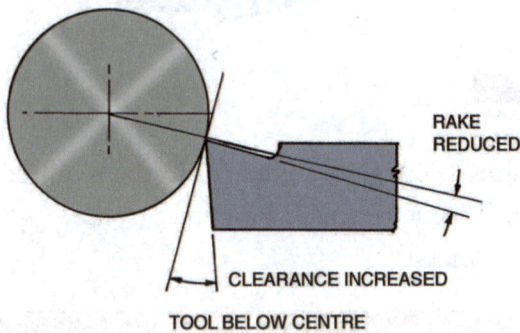

CORRECT RAKE

CORRECT CLEARANCE

**TOOL AT CENTRE HEIGHT**

RAKE INCREASED

CLEARANCE REDUCED

**TOOL ABOVE CENTRE**

RAKE REDUCED

CLEARANCE INCREASED

**TOOL BELOW CENTRE**

**Fig. 13.13**
Effect of tool height on rake and clearance angles

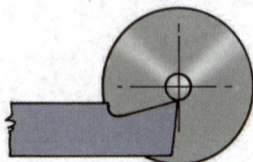

**Fig. 13.14**
If tool is not at correct height, it cannot cut at centre

## Facing

In facing, the tool is moved at right angles to the axis of rotation of the work by means of the cross slide. Flat surfaces are produced and this is the process used to face work and finish shoulders.

**Fig. 13.15**
Facing

## Parallel Turning

In parallel turning, the tool moves parallel to the axis of rotation of the work and cylindrical forms are produced.

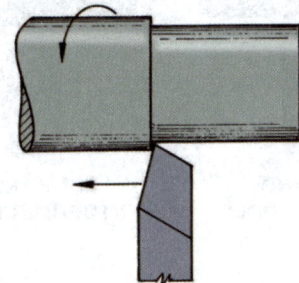

**Fig. 13.16**
Parallel turning

## Taper Turning

A number of methods are used for cutting tapers on a lathe. The top slide is used for cutting short tapers. It must be set to half the included angle of the taper, Fig. 13.18. Its base, or the surface on which it rests, is graduated in degrees for setting it to the required angle. There is a nut on each side for locking it in position. The tool is fed by hand, using the top slide feed handle. The length of taper that can be cut is governed by the length of travel of the top slide.

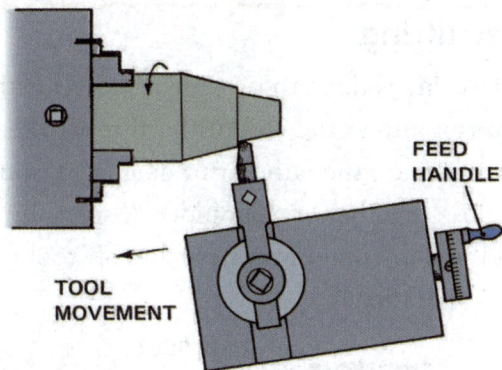

Fig. 13.17
Taper turning using the compound slide

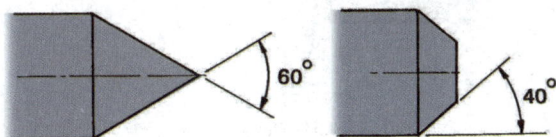

INCLUDED ANGLE = 60°
SET TOP SLIDE TO 30°

SET TOP SLIDE
AT 40°

Fig. 13.18
Setting top slide

## Centre Drill

The centre drill is used for drilling countersunk holes to accommodate lathe centres, see Fig. 13.19, and also for starting the holes when drilling on the lathe. The countersink is drilled to an angle of 60° to match the lathe centre. The small hole inside the countersink provides clearance for the point of the lathe centre and also a reservoir for a lubricant. The centre drill is held in a chuck, which in turn is held in the tailstock.

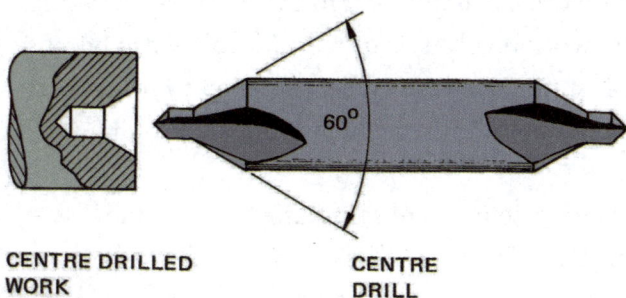

CENTRE DRILLED
WORK

CENTRE
DRILL

Fig. 13.19

## Drilling on the Lathe

When drilling on the lathe, the work revolves and the drill is fed into it by turning the tailstock handwheel. Parallel shank drills are held in a chuck. The chuck is fitted to a tapered arbor, which fits into the tailstock barrel. Taper shank drills are fitted into the tailstock barrel either directly or by means of a Morse taper sleeve. A centre drill is used at the beginning to ensure that the hole starts on centre. During the drilling, the drill must be withdrawn from time to time to remove swarf from its flutes and to apply cutting fluid.

Cutting fluid should be fed into the hole also. The hole depth can be checked by means of the graduations on the tailstock barrel.

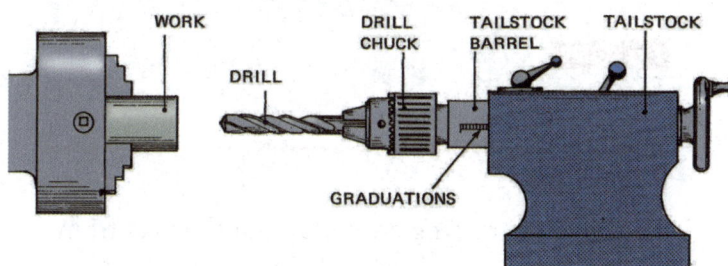

Fig. 13.20
Drilling on the lathe

## Knurling

Knurling is the operation of impressing serrations on articles to enable them to be gripped securely by hand. It can be of diamond or straight pattern.

There are a number of types of knurling tools used. In knurling, the work is rotated at a slow speed and a pair of wheels is pressed against it.

The wheels rotate with the work. If the work is of steel, it must be kept well oiled.

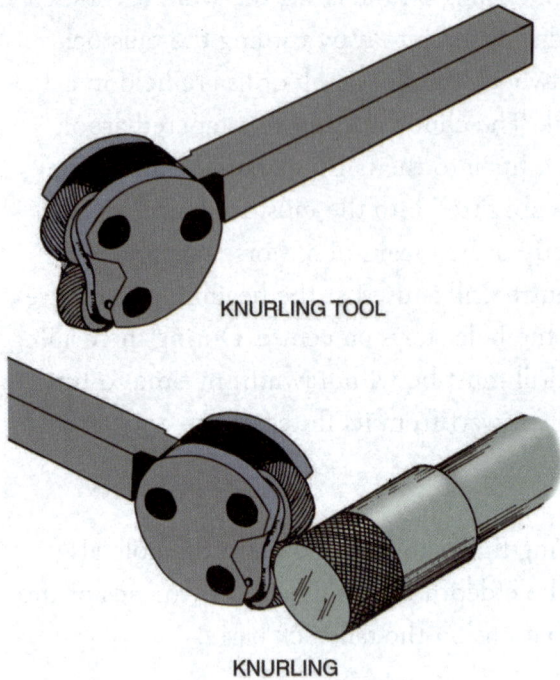

KNURLING TOOL

KNURLING

## Parting Off

This involves cutting off parts from the bars from which they were turned and cutting off lengths of waste on the lathe. The tool used is called a parting off tool. It may be a thin blade and holder as shown in Fig. 13.22 or a specially shaped solid tool.

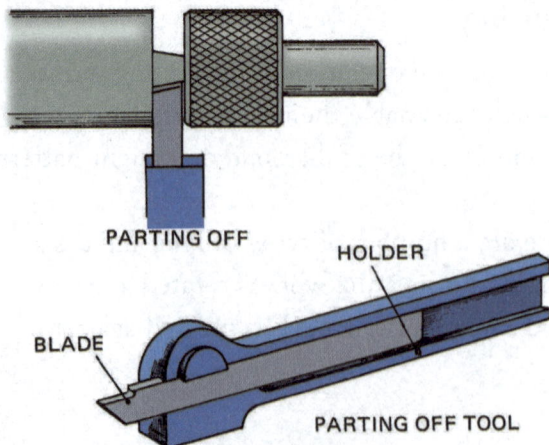

PARTING OFF

HOLDER

BLADE

PARTING OFF TOOL

## Undercutting

Undercutting is done to provide a space for the tool to run into at the end of the thread when screwcutting on the lathe or to enable components to fit close together at a shoulder. A specially ground tool or sometimes a parting off tool is used for this operation.

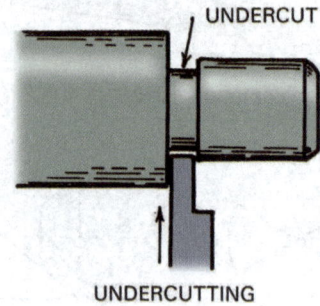

UNDERCUT

UNDERCUTTING

Undercutting

## Lathe Centres

A lathe centre is used for supporting the end of long work on the lathe. One end of a bar can be held in a chuck and the other supported on a tailstock centre (see Fig 13.5, page 143) or it can be mounted between a headstock centre and a tailstock centre. Centres have Morse taper shanks and their points are usually finished to an angle of 60°.  They are made from high carbon or high-speed steel. The headstock centre rotates with the work and is called a 'live' centre. It need not be hardened, since there is no rubbing between it and the work. A centre held in the tailstock, on which the work revolves, is called a 'dead' centre because it is stationary. It must be hardened to resist wear and its point must be kept lubricated during use.

Rotating centres are sometimes used in the tailstock. These have bearings that allow their points to rotate with the work.

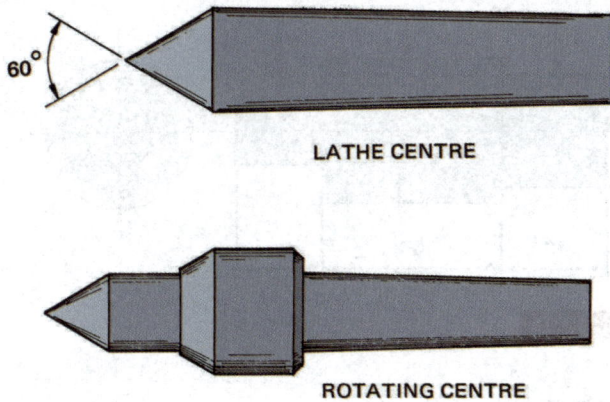

**LATHE CENTRE**

**ROTATING CENTRE**

60°

## Lathe Spindle Speeds and Cutting Speeds

Lathe spindle speeds are given in revolutions per minute (rev/min). The work will, of course, have the same rotational speed as the lathe spindle. When selecting the spindle speed, the following factors must be taken into account:

(a) **The diameter of the work** Small diameter work must have a higher rotational speed than large diameter work for them both to have the same cutting speed.

(b) **The material being turned** Hard, tough materials require lower speeds than soft, ductile ones.

(c) **The type of tool** Higher speeds can be used with tungsten carbide tipped tools than with high-speed steel tools.

(d) **The type of operation**, e.g. a light finishing cut can be taken at a higher speed than a heavy roughing cut.

(e) **Use of coolant** Higher speeds are possible when using a coolant.

(f) **Method of holding the work** Some types of work can be supported better than others and can be run at higher speeds. No operation should be carried out without the work being safely secured.

Cutting speeds for tools are given in metres per minute. In turning, the cutting speed is the surface speed of the work.

To calculate the speed (rotational) at which a lathe should be run for a particular operation, the following formula is used:

$$N = \frac{S \times 1000}{\pi \times D}$$

where N = rotational speed in rev/min
S = cutting speed in metres/min
D = diameter of the workpiece in mm

It is usually sufficiently accurate to use $\pi = 3$ for these calculations.

**Example:** Calculate the lathe speed required to turn a 25mm round mild steel bar at a cutting speed of 30m/min.

$$N = \frac{S \times 1000}{\pi \times D}$$

S = 30m/min
D = 25mm

$$\therefore N = \frac{30 \times 1000}{3 \times 25} \text{ rev/min}$$

$$= 400 \text{ rev/min}$$

A table of cutting speeds for high speed steel tools is given below. These can only be used as a guide because of the number of factors involved:

| Material | Cutting Speed Metres / Min |
|---|---|
| High Carbon Steel | 12 – 18 |
| Cast Iron | 18 – 24 |
| Mild Steel | 24 – 30 |
| Brass | 45 – 120 |
| Aluminium | 120 – 300 |

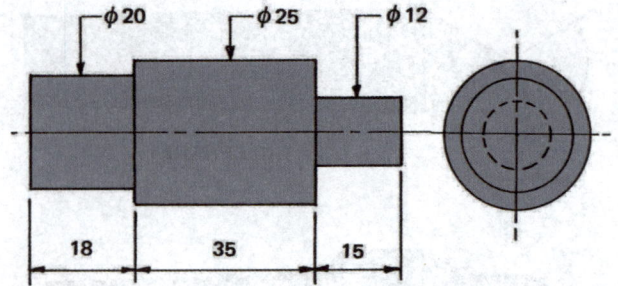

**Fig. 13.25**

## Operating the Lathe

(a) Do not carry out any work on the lathe until you have received proper instruction and are competent at using it.

(b) Do not wear any loose clothing.

(c) Wear protective goggles.

(d) Ensure that both the work and tool are securely held.

(e) Ensure that the work and all other parts which are to revolve can do so without striking anything.

(f) Do not leave the chuck key in the chuck.

(g) Keep the tool away from the work when starting the lathe.

(h) Always stop the lathe when checking the work.

(i) Do not handle the swarf.

(j) Keep the lathe clean and tidy, but make sure it is switched off before cleaning it down.

## Exercise involving Facing and Parallel Turning

To turn the component shown in Fig. 13.25 from 25mm diameter by 80mm long, bright mild steel shafting.

## Stages

1. Grip the material in the chuck, leaving about 30mm protruding.

2. Face the end.

3. Set the odd-leg callipers to 18mm and scribe a line at this distance from the end.

4. Set the outside callipers to 21mm on the end of the rule.

5. Reduce a length of about 3mm at the end of the material to this size, Fig. 13.26 A. Should the diameter of this portion be reduced under 20mm, it can be cut off and a fresh start made.

6. Using the reduced portion as a guide, turn the material to the same diameter almost to the scribed line, Fig 13.26 B.

7. Set the outside callipers to 20mm using an accurate bar such as a ground silver steel one.

8. Take a light cut for a length of about 3mm, stop the lathe and check the diameter, Fig. 13.26 C. If it is 20mm or over, continue with the cut to the shoulder. Take successive cuts as required until the callipers can just slide down over the work under its own weight. Feed the tool at a slow and regular pace to obtain a good finish. Take care not to alter the callipers setting during the checking.

9. Finish the shoulder to the line.

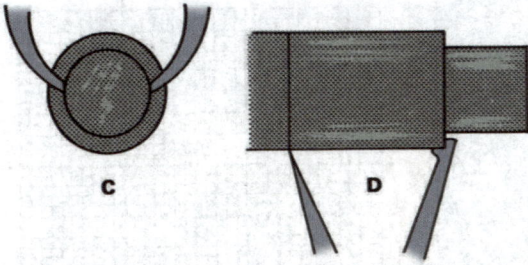

10. Re-grip the work with its finished shoulder about 40mm away from the chuck. Set the odd-leg callipers to 35mm, place its leg on the finished shoulder and scribe a line for the other shoulder, Fig. 13.26 D.
11. Reverse the work in the chuck, keeping the scribed line about 10mm away from the chuck.
12. Face this end.
13. Reduce this end to 12mm diameter and finish the shoulder in the same manner as the other end was turned.
14. Mark a distance of 15mm from this shoulder. Set the odd-leg callipers to the mark and scribe a line as shown in Fig. 13.26 E. If the amount of waste is insufficient for this method, the line can be scribed as shown in Fig. 13.26 F.

15. Face off the work to the scribed line.

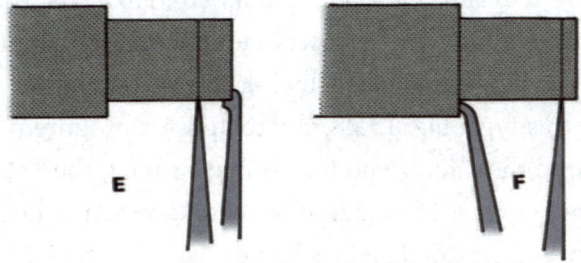

**Fig. 13.26**
Stages in turning the component shown in Fig. 13.25

## CNC Lathework

CNC stands for Computer-Numerical-Control. CNC machines are controlled by a set of instructions based on numbers. On conventional lathes, the slides are moved mechanically, but on CNC lathes they are moved by special electric motors called stepper motors (Fig. 13.27). When making a component or part on a conventional lathe, you continually make decisions and carry out various operations until the part is finished. On a CNC lathe you write a computer program and this controls the lathe in making the part. Once the program is written, you can make as many identical parts as you wish from it.

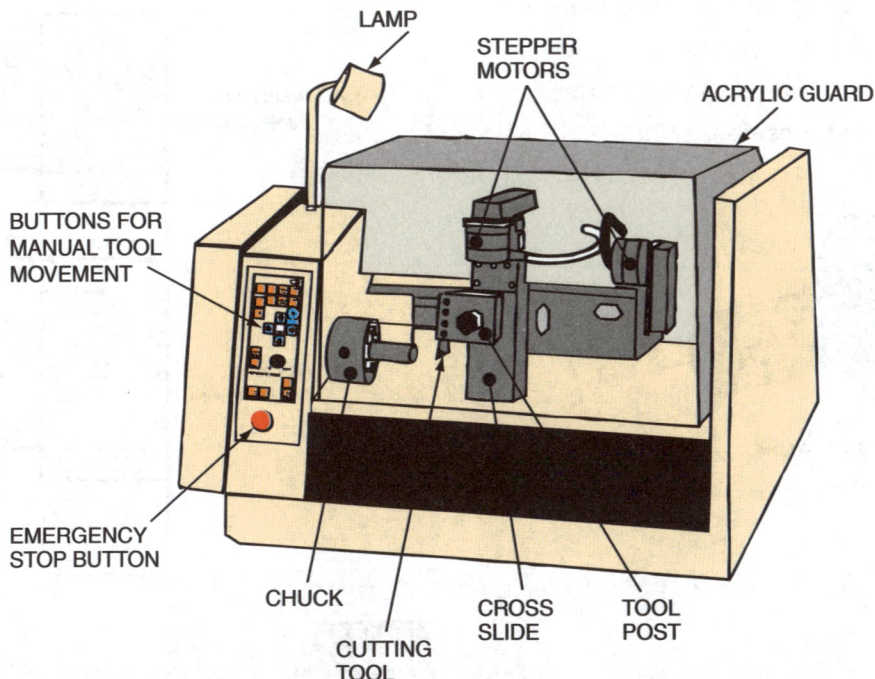

**Fig. 13.27**
CNC Lathe

LAMP
STEPPER MOTORS
ACRYLIC GUARD
BUTTONS FOR MANUAL TOOL MOVEMENT
EMERGENCY STOP BUTTON
CHUCK
CUTTING TOOL
CROSS SLIDE
TOOL POST

Traditional lathes have horizontal beds, and CNC lathes may also have horizontal beds. However, the programming which we will be undertaking here is for the 'Boxford TCL', which is a slant bed lathe. On this type, Fig. 13.28, the toolpost is mounted behind the chuck, and for normal turning, the spindle moves in an anti-clockwise direction when viewed from the headstock end.

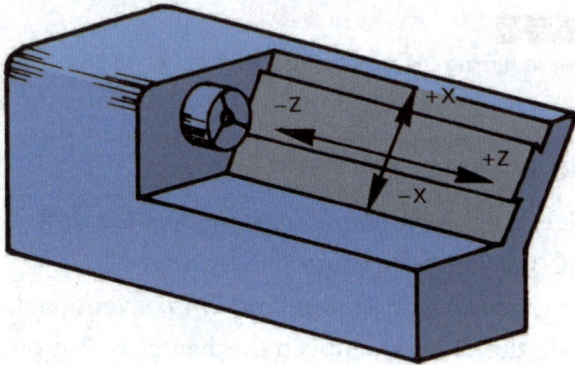

**Fig. 13.28**

X and Z axes on a slant bed lathe

A CNC program contains co-ordinates for defining the positions that the tool must move to during the various operations, commands for controlling the tool movement and commands for controlling the spindle (chuck). Positions are defined by 'X' and 'Z' co-ordinates. Distances perpendicular to the lathe centre line are given as X co-ordinates and distances parallel to the centre line are given as Z co-ordinates. The X co-ordinates are the diameters at the various positions.

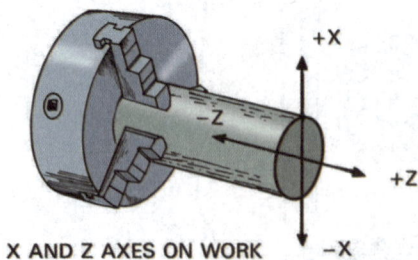

X AND Z AXES ON WORK

**Fig. 13.29**

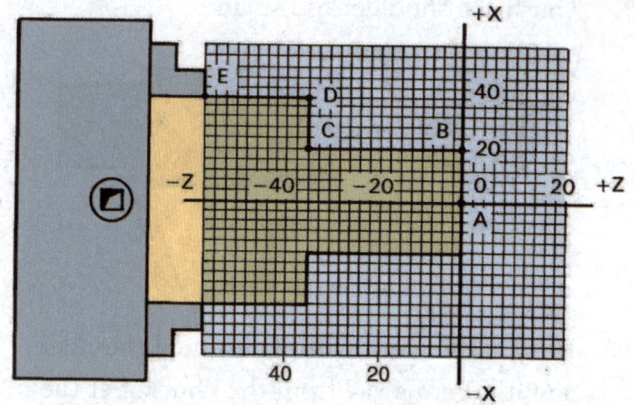

The X and Z co-ordinates for the various points A to E are given in the table below.

| Point | A | B | C | D | E |
|-------|---|----|-----|-----|-----|
| X | 0 | 20 | 20 | 40 | 40 |
| Z | 0 | 0 | -30 | -30 | -50 |

**Fig. 13.30**

Co-ordinates of points

## Dimensioning

There are two methods for giving the dimensions or co-ordinates in computer programming:

(i) Incremental — each section is dimensioned, Fig. 13.31 A.

(ii) Absolute — all dimensions are taken from a datum point or line, Fig. 13.31 B.

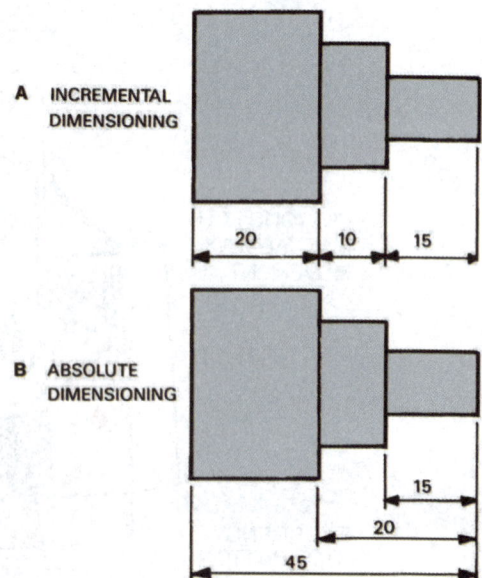

A INCREMENTAL DIMENSIONING

20  10  15

B ABSOLUTE DIMENSIONING

15

20

45

**Fig. 13.31**

Dimensioning

## Jog Keys

These are used to move the tool by hand in the X and Z axes in the directions indicated on the keys. This is required for taking trial cuts and positioning the tool for executing a program. They are also used for setting tool offsets. To operate the keys, the lathe must be set in the manual mode. The speed of movement of the tool is set by adjusting the feed override knob. If, however, the 'rapid' key is also pressed, this setting is overridden and the tool moves rapidly.

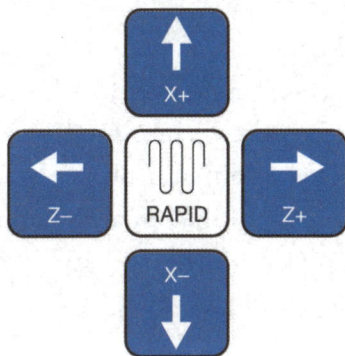

## G Codes and M Codes

'G' codes are used for controlling the tool movement. For instance, a G00 code moves the tool rapidly to a designated position and G01 code moves the tool in a straight line at the feed rate selected.

Canned cycles are used when a series of tool movements is required to perform a specific operation, e.g. G81 is the code for a canned parallel turning cycle.

'M' codes are used for miscellaneous commands, e.g. to turn on the spindle, to turn it off, to stop the spindle for a tool change.

## A Summary of Standardised G and M Codes

| | |
|---|---|
| G00 | Rapid traverse positioning. |
| G01 | Linear interpolation. |
| G02 | Circular interpolation C.W. |
| G03 | Circular interpolation C.C.W. |
| G04 | Time Dwell. |
| G70 | Programmable imperial dimensions. |
| G71 | Programmable metric dimensions. |
| G90 | Absolute data input. |
| G91 | Incremental data input. |
| G94 | Feed/min. |
| G95 | Feed/rev. |
| G96 | Constant surface speed (C.S.S.). |
| G97 | Constant rev/min. |

Note  c.w.   = clockwise
c.c.w.  = counter clockwise

### Examples of Canned Cycles

| | |
|---|---|
| G80 | Canned cycle — cancel. |
| G81 | Canned cycle — parallel turning. |
| G82 | Canned cycle — facing or grooving. |
| G83 | Canned cycle — deep hole (peck drilling). |
| G84 | Canned cycle — thread cutting. |

### M Codes

| | |
|---|---|
| M02 | Marks the end of the program. |
| M03 | Starts spindle forward. Enter spindle speed S. |
| M04 | Starts spindle reverse. Enter spindle speed S. |
| M05 | Stops spindle. |
| M06 | Tool change. Enter: |

I  = tool type number.

K = tool turret number (when fitted).

S = speed range (1R — 4R).

| | |
|---|---|
| M39 | Closes automatic chuck (if fitted). |
| M40 | Opens automatic chuck (if fitted). |
| M97 | Continuous manufacture. |
| M99 | Continuation code. Entering M99 into a partially written program causes the program to be saved to disc. Recall of the program is simulated on the screen up to the break off point and then the prompt to 'continue writing' is made. |

## CNC Lathe Tools

A selection of CNC lathe tools is shown in Fig. 13.33.

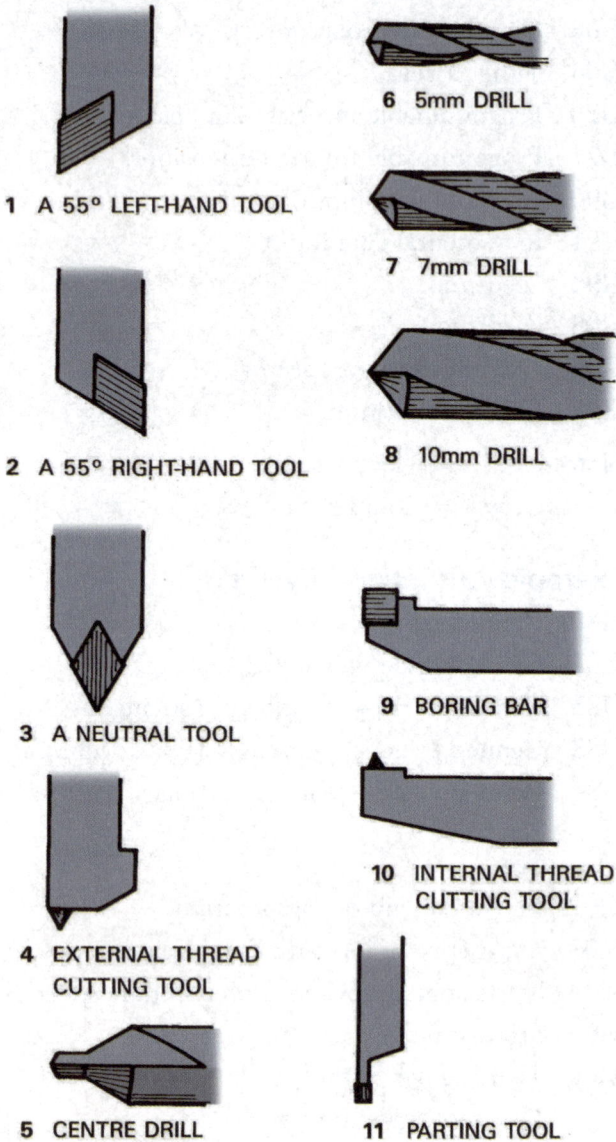

**1  A 55° LEFT-HAND TOOL**

**2  A 55° RIGHT-HAND TOOL**

**3  A NEUTRAL TOOL**

**4  EXTERNAL THREAD CUTTING TOOL**

**5  CENTRE DRILL**

**6  5mm DRILL**

**7  7mm DRILL**

**8  10mm DRILL**

**9  BORING BAR**

**10  INTERNAL THREAD CUTTING TOOL**

**11  PARTING TOOL**

Fig. 13.33

## CNC Programming

A CNC program is made up of a number of lines called **blocks**. Each block contains the block number and the information required to perform a certain operation. The types of information that can be contained in a block are shown in the table below:

| N | G | M | X | Z | I | K | F | S |
|---|---|---|---|---|---|---|---|---|

| | |
|---|---|
| N | the block number |
| G | the G code |
| M | the M code |
| X | the X co-ordinate (mm) |
| Z | the Z co-ordinate (mm) |
| I | additional information as required |
| K | additional information as required |
| F | feed rate (mm/min) |
| S | spindle speed (rev/min) |

When writing a program, it is very helpful to first list the operations involved. A special **operations sheet** is very useful for this. The exercises that follow will give you plenty of practice in writing CNC programs.

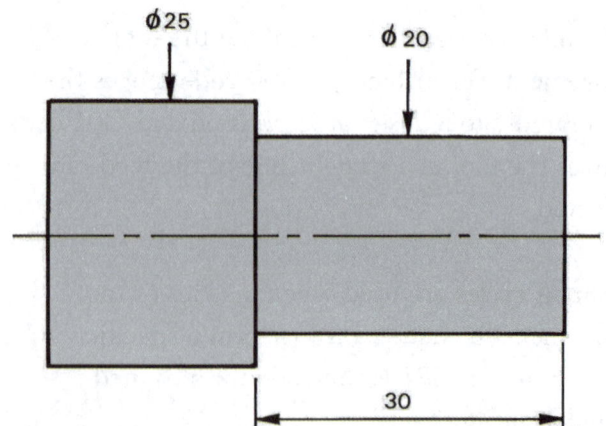

$\phi 25$   $\phi 20$

30

Fig. 13.34

## Exercise 1

Write a CNC program to machine portion of a ø25 aluminium bar as shown in Fig. 13.34.

## Operations Sheet

| No. | Operation | Spindle Speed | Tool Feed | Tool Req. |
|---|---|---|---|---|
| 1 | Face | 2500 | 75 | 1 |
| 2 | Turn ø23 x 30 | 2500 | 75 | 1 |
| 3 | Turn ø21 x 30 | 2500 | 75 | 1 |
| 4 | Turn ø20 x 30 | 2500 | 75 | 1 |
| 5 | Tool park position | | Rapid | |
| 6 | End program | | | |

**Note:** O. Dia = Outside Diameter, i.e. diameter of material

I. Dia = Inside Diameter. This will be zero, unless the material has a bore.

Stickout = The length of material protruding beyond the chuck jaws.

Always start your program with the first three blocks as follows:
10 — type of measurement (G90 or G91).
20 — type of unit (G70 or G71).
30 — park position and tool number.

## Programming Sheet

**Title: CNC 1      Material: Aluminium      O. Dia: 25      I. Dia: 0      Stickout: 35**

| Notes | N | G | M | X | Z | I | K | F | S |
|---|---|---|---|---|---|---|---|---|---|
| Absolute programming | 10 | 90 | | | | | | | |
| Metric dimensions | 20 | 71 | | | | | | | |
| Tool park positions/Select tool 1 | 30 | | | 30 | 10 | 1 | | | |
| Start spindle in reverse | 40 | 97 | 04 | | | | | | 2500 |
| Rapid to start position | 50 | 00 | | 26 | 0 | | | | |
| Face end | 60 | 01 | | -1 | | | | 75 | |
| Clear work | 70 | 00 | | | 1 | | | | |
| Rapid position for first cut | 80 | 00 | | 23 | | | | | |
| Turn ø23 x 30 | 90 | 01 | | | -30 | | | 75 | |
| Rapid clear of work | 100 | 00 | | 24 | 1 | | | | |
| Position for next cut | 110 | 00 | | 21 | | | | | |
| Turn ø21 x 30 | 120 | 01 | | | -30 | | | 75 | |
| Rapid clear of work | 130 | 00 | | 22 | 1 | | | | |
| Position for next cut | 140 | 00 | | 20 | | | | | |
| Turn ø20 x 30 | 150 | 01 | | | -30 | | | 75 | |
| Clear work | 160 | 00 | | 26 | | | | | |
| Tool park position/stop spindle | 170 | 00 | 05 | 30 | 10 | | | | |
| End program | 180 | | 02 | | | | | | |

## Exercise 2

Write a CNC program to machine the shape shown in Fig. 13.35 from ø25 aluminium. When there is a chamfer to be machined, a scale drawing of the chamfer section on square grid paper, Fig. 13.36, will enable us to find the lengths of the various cuts.

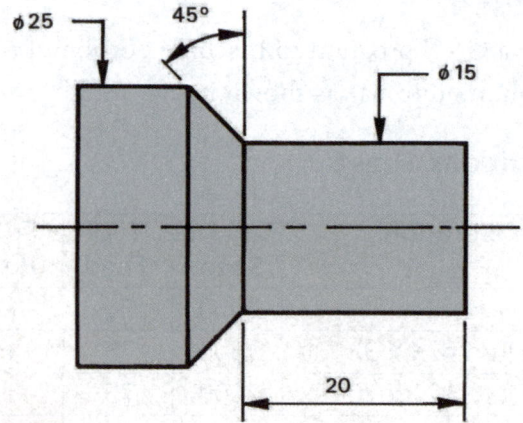

Fig. 13.35

## Programming Sheet

Title: CNC 2     Material: Aluminium     O. Dia: 25     I. Dia: 0     Stickout: 30

| Notes | N | G | M | X | Z | I | K | F | S |
|---|---|---|---|---|---|---|---|---|---|
| Absolute programming | 10 | 90 | | | | | | | |
| Metric dimensions | 20 | 71 | | | | | | | |
| Tool park position | 30 | | | 30 | 10 | 1 | | | |
| Start spindle in reverse | 40 | 97 | 04 | | | | | | 2500 |
| Rapid to start position | 50 | 00 | | 26 | 0 | | | | |
| Face end | 60 | 01 | | -1 | | | | 75 | |
| Clear work | 70 | 00 | | | 1 | | | | |
| Position for first cut | 80 | 00 | | 23 | | | | | |
| Turn ø23 x 24 | 90 | 01 | | | -24 | | | 75 | |
| Clear work | 100 | 00 | | 24 | 1 | | | | |
| Position tool for next cut | 110 | 00 | | 21 | | | | | |
| Turn ø21 x 23 | 120 | 01 | | | -23 | | | 75 | |
| Clear work | 130 | 00 | | 22 | 1 | | | | |
| Position tool for next cut | 140 | 00 | | 19 | | | | | |
| Turn ø19 x 22 | 150 | 01 | | | -22 | | | 75 | |
| Clear work | 160 | 00 | | 20 | 1 | | | | |
| Position tool for next cut | 170 | 00 | | 17 | | | | | |
| Turn ø17 x 21 | 180 | 01 | | | -21 | | | 75 | |
| Clear work | 190 | 00 | | 18 | 1 | | | | |
| Position tool for next cut | 200 | 00 | | 15 | | | | | |
| Turn ø15 x 20mm | 210 | 01 | | | -20 | | | 75 | |
| Turn 5 x 45° chamfer | 220 | 01 | | 25 | -25 | | | 75 | |
| Tool park position/stop spindle | 230 | 00 | 05 | 30 | 10 | | | | |
| End program | 240 | | 02 | | | | | | |

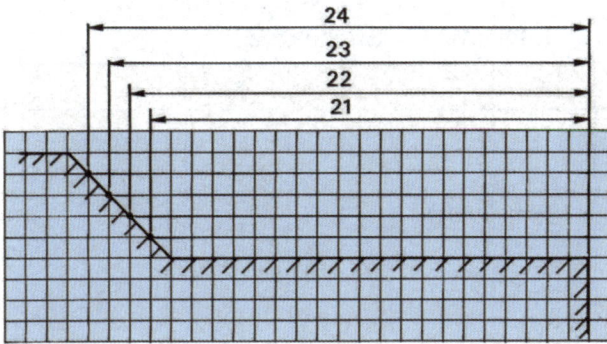

**Fig. 13.36**

Finding the lengths of cuts for a chamfer

## Operations Sheet

| No. | Operation | Spindle Speed | Tool Feed | Tool Req. |
|-----|-----------|---------------|-----------|-----------|
| 1 | Face | 2500 | 75 | 1 |
| 2 | Turn ø23 x 24 | 2500 | 75 | |
| 3 | Turn ø21 x 23 | 2500 | 75 | |
| 4 | Turn ø19 x 22 | 2500 | 75 | |
| 5 | Turn ø17 x 21 | 2500 | 75 | |
| 6 | Turn ø15 x 20 | 2500 | 75 | |
| 7 | Turn 5 x 45° chamfer | 2500 | 75 | |
| 8 | Tool park position | | Rapid | |
| 9 | End program | | | |

## Exercise 3

Write a CNC program to produce the shape shown in Fig. 13.37 from ø30 aluminium.

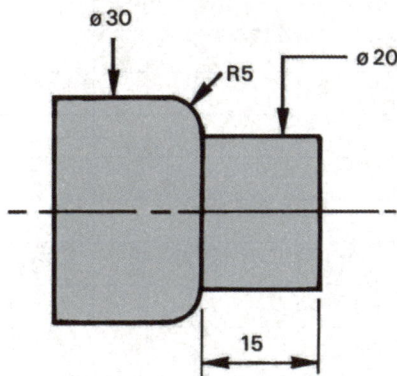

**Fig. 13.37**

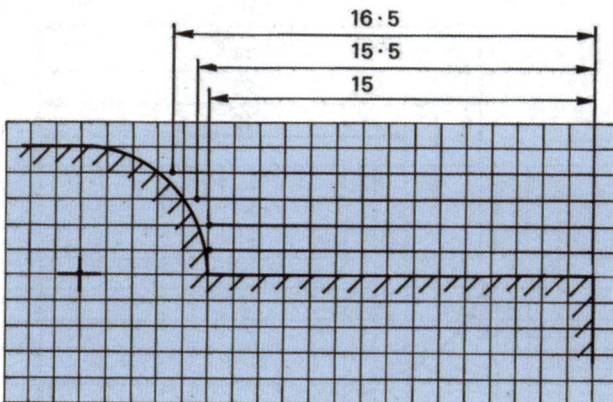

I VALUE = 0    K VALUE = 5

**Fig. 13.38**

Finding the lengths of cuts to points close to the curve and also I and K values

When machining curves, we need to make a scale drawing of the curved section, to find:

(i) the lengths of the parallel turning cuts which will be close enough to the curve to avoid exceeding the maximum depth of cut allowable when machining the curve.

(ii) the 'I' and 'K' values required when machining the curve.

The I value is the distance from the curve centre to the tool position at the start of the cut, **along the X axis**. The K value is the distance from the curve centre to the tool position at the start of the cut, **along the Z axis**. Both values are incremental.

## Operations Sheet

| No. | Operation | Spindle Speed | Tool Feed | Tool Req. |
|-----|-----------|---------------|-----------|-----------|
| 1 | Face | 2500 | 75 | 1 |
| 2 | Turn ø28 x 16.5 | 2500 | 75 | |
| 3 | Turn ø26 x 15.5 | 2500 | 75 | |
| 4 | Turn ø24 x 15 | 2500 | 75 | |
| 5 | Turn ø22 x 15 | 2500 | 75 | |
| 6 | Turn ø20 x 15 | 2500 | 75 | |
| 7 | Turn C.C.W. curve to ø30 | 2500 | 75 | |
| 8 | Tool park position | | Rapid | |
| 9 | End program | | | |

## Programming Sheet

Title: CNC 3    Material: Aluminium    O. Dia: 30    I. Dia: 0    Stickout: 25

| Notes | N | G | M | X | Z | I | K | F | S |
|---|---|---|---|---|---|---|---|---|---|
| Absolute programming | 10 | 90 | | | | | | | |
| Metric dimensions | 20 | 71 | | | | | | | |
| Tool park position | 30 | | | 35 | 10 | 1 | | | |
| Start spindle in reverse | 40 | 97 | 04 | | | | | | 2500 |
| Rapid to start position | 50 | 00 | | 31 | 0 | | | | |
| Face | 60 | 01 | | -1 | | | | 75 | |
| Clear work | 70 | 00 | | | 1 | | | | |
| Position for first cut | 80 | 00 | | 28 | | | | | |
| Turn ø28 x 16.5 | 90 | 01 | | | -16.5 | | | 75 | |
| Clear work | 100 | 00 | | 29 | 1 | | | | |
| Position next cut | 110 | 00 | | 26 | | | | | |
| Turn ø26 x 15.5 | 120 | 01 | | | -15.5 | | | 75 | |
| Clear work | 130 | 00 | | 27 | 1 | | | | |
| Position for next cut | 140 | 00 | | 24 | | | | | |
| Turn ø24 x 15 | 150 | 01 | | | -15 | | | 75 | |
| Clear work | 160 | 00 | | 25 | 1 | | | | |
| Position for next cut | 170 | 00 | | 22 | | | | | |
| Turn ø22 x 15 | 180 | 01 | | | -15 | | | 75 | |
| Clear work | 190 | 00 | | 23 | 1 | | | | |
| Position for next cut | 200 | 00 | | 20 | | | | | |
| Turn ø20 x 15 | 210 | 01 | | | -15 | | | 75 | |
| Turn C.C.W. curve to ø30 | 220 | 03 | | 30 | -20 | 0 | 5 | 75 | |
| Tool park position/stop spindle | 230 | 00 | 05 | 35 | 10 | | | | |
| End program | 240 | | 02 | | | | | | |

## Exercise 4

Write a CNC program to produce the component shown in Fig. 13.39 from ø30 aluminium.

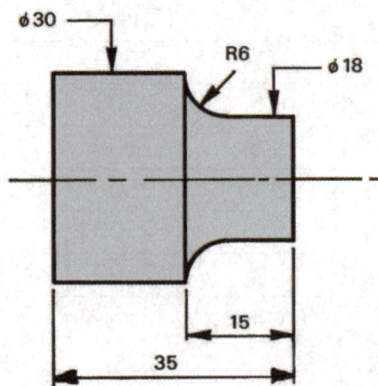

Fig. 13.39

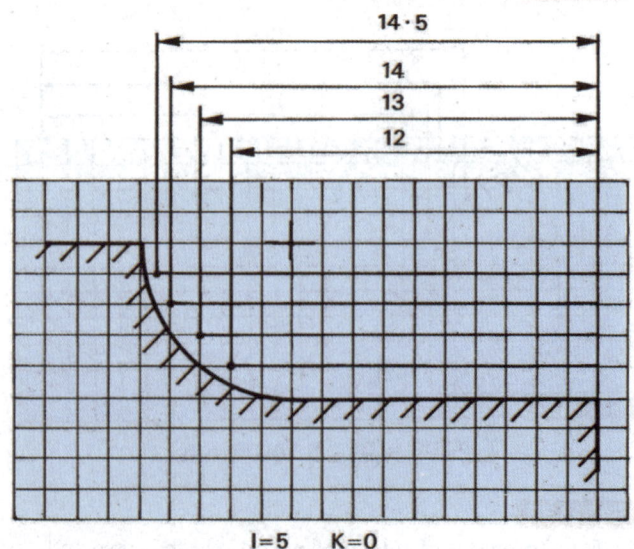

Fig. 13.40

**Note:** This exercise involves parting off. When writing the program, the tool thickness, 1.6mm, must be taken into account, i.e. the Z co-ordinate for parting off to 35mm will be: $-(35 + 1.6) = -36.6$mm.

## Operations Sheet

| No. | Operation | Spindle Speed | Tool Feed | Tool Req. |
|-----|-----------|---------------|-----------|-----------|
| 1 | Face | 2500 | 75 | 1 |
| 2 | Turn ø28 x 14.5 | 2500 | 75 | |
| 3 | Turn ø26 x 14 | 2500 | 75 | |
| 4 | Turn ø24 x 13 | 2500 | 75 | |
| 5 | Turn ø22 x 12 | 2500 | 75 | |
| 6 | Turn ø20 x 10 | 2500 | 75 | |
| 7 | Turn curve, radius 5, to ø30 | 2500 | 75 | |
| 8 | Tool park position | | Rapid | |
| 9 | Change tool | | | 11 |
| 10 | Part off to length | 2000 | 35 | |
| 11 | End program | | | |

## Programming Sheet

**Title: CNC 4**  **Material: Aluminium**  **O. Dia: 30**  **I. Dia: 0**  **Stickout: 40**

| Notes | N | G | M | X | Z | I | K | F | S |
|-------|---|---|---|---|---|---|---|---|---|
| Absolute programming | 10 | 90 | | | | | | | |
| Metric dimensions | 20 | 71 | | | | | | | |
| Tool park position | 30 | | | 35 | 10 | 1 | | | |
| Start spindle in reverse | 40 | 97 | 04 | | | | | | 2500 |
| Position for facing | 50 | | | 31 | 0 | | | | |
| Face | 60 | 01 | | −1 | | | | 75 | |
| Clear work | 70 | 00 | | | 1 | | | | |
| Position for first diameter cut | 80 | 00 | | 28 | | | | | |
| Turn ø28 x 14.5 | 90 | 01 | | | −14.5 | | | 75 | |
| Clear work | 100 | 00 | | 29 | 1 | | | | |
| Position for next cut | 110 | 00 | | 26 | | | | | |
| Turn ø26 x 14 | 120 | 01 | | | −14 | | | 75 | |
| Clear work | 130 | 00 | | 27 | 1 | | | | |
| Position for next cut | 140 | 00 | | 24 | | | | | |
| Turn ø24 x 13 | 150 | 01 | | | −13 | | | 75 | |
| Clear work | 160 | 00 | | 25 | 1 | | | | |
| Position for next cut | 170 | 00 | | 22 | | | | | |
| Turn ø22 x 12 | 180 | 01 | | | −12 | | | 75 | |
| Clear work | 190 | 00 | | 23 | 1 | | | | |
| Position for next cut | 200 | 00 | | 20 | | | | | |
| Turn ø20 x 10 | 210 | 01 | | | −10 | | | 75 | |
| Turn C.W. arc to ø30 | 220 | 02 | | 30 | −15 | 5 | 0 | 75 | |
| Tool park position/stop spindle | 230 | 00 | 05 | 35 | 10 | | | | |

159

| Notes | N | G | M | X | Z | I | K | F | S |
|---|---|---|---|---|---|---|---|---|---|
| Tool change | 240 | | 06 | | | 11 | | | |
| Start spindle/position for parting | 250 | 97 | 04 | 31 | −36.6* | | | | 2000 |
| Part off to 35 | 260 | 01 | | −1 | | | | 35 | |
| Clear work | 270 | 00 | | 31 | | | | | |
| Tool park position/stop spindle | 280 | 00 | | 35 | 10 | | | | |
| End program | 290 | | 02 | | | | | | |

*Z co-ordinate = component length + tool thickness = −(35 + 1.6) = −36.6

## Exercise 5

Write a CNC program to shorten the length of a ø25 x 35mm aluminium bar by 10mm with 15 cuts using a canned cycle.

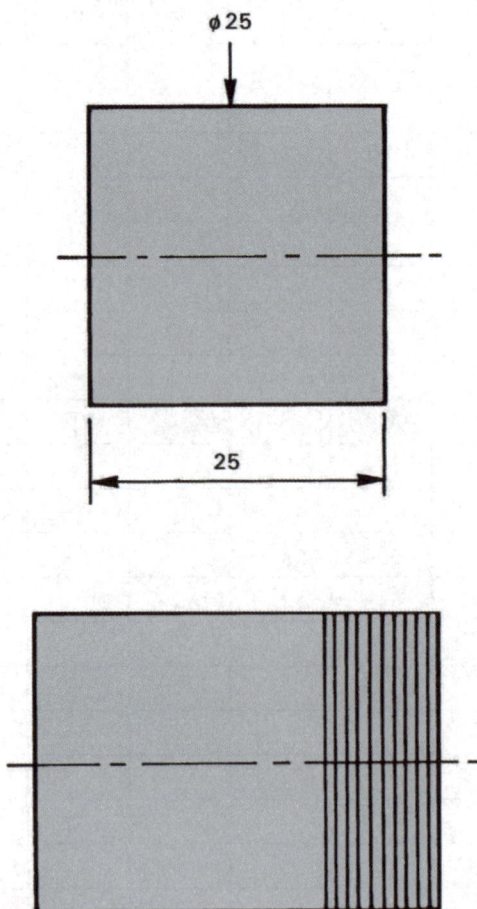

A canned facing, G82, exercise

## Canned Cycles

The object of this exercise is to examine the canned facing cycle, G82.

A canned cycle enables a number of repetitive operations to be carried out by a single block of a program. For example, if reducing a diameter, the G81 canned cycle can replace a series of G00 and G01 blocks, provided the Z co-ordinates remain the same. This makes a program simpler and shorter.

When using canned cycles, the tool must be positioned at the starting point of the cycle by the previous block. This point, which must be clear of work, is called **'the stand off point'**.

For parallel turning (G81), facing (G82) and thread cutting (G84), the stand off point is 2mm clear of the work on both the X and Z co-ordinates. For peck drilling (G83), the stand off point is 2mm clear on the Z axis only (X = 0). All information within a canned cycle is incremental.

For exercise 5, the co-ordinates of the stand off point will be:

X = 25 + 2 = 27 (work diameter + 2 mm)

Z = 2

The canned cycle block will contain the following information:

G82     = canned facing cycle

X value = 28 (total cut depth, i.e. stand off plus 1mm to go past work centre)

Z value = −10 (total cut width, exclude stand off)

I       = 15 (number of cuts)

F       = 75 (feed rate)

## Operations Sheet

| No. | Operation | Spindle Speed | Tool Feed | Tool Req. |
|-----|-----------|---------------|-----------|-----------|
| 1 | Tool park position | 2500 | Rapid | 1 |
| 2 | Stand off position | 2500 | Rapid | |
| 3 | Face off to 25mm, with 15 cuts, using a canned cycle | 2500 | 75 | |
| 4 | Tool park position | | Rapid | |
| 5 | End program | | | |

## Programming Sheet

Title: CNC 5     Material: Aluminium     O. Dia: 25     I. Dia: 0     Stickout: 24

| Notes | N | G | M | X | Z | I | K | F | S |
|-------|---|---|---|---|---|---|---|---|---|
| Absolute programming | 10 | 90 | | | | | | | |
| Metric dimensions | 20 | 71 | | | | | | | |
| Tool park position | 30 | | | 30 | 10 | 1 | | | |
| Start spindle in reverse | 40 | 97 | 04 | | | | | | 2500 |
| Stand off position | 50 | | | 27 | 2 | | | | |
| Canned facing | 60 | 82 | | 28 | −10 | 15 | | 75 | |
| Tool park position/stop spindle | 70 | | 05 | 30 | 10 | | | | |
| End program | 80 | | 02 | | | | | | |

## Exercise 6

Reduce a portion of a ø25 aluminium bar, as shown in Fig. 13.42, with 5 cuts, using a canned cycle.

In this exercise, we make use of the G81, canned parallel turning cycle.

Stand off position: X = 27, Z = 2

Information in canned cycle block:

| | | |
|---|---|---|
| G81 | = | canned cycle |
| X value | = | 10 (total cut depth, i.e. difference between original diameter and final diameter, exclude stand off) |
| Z value | = | −17 (total length of travel in Z axis i.e. cut length plus stand off) |
| I | = | 5 (number of cuts) |
| F | = | 75 (feed rate) |

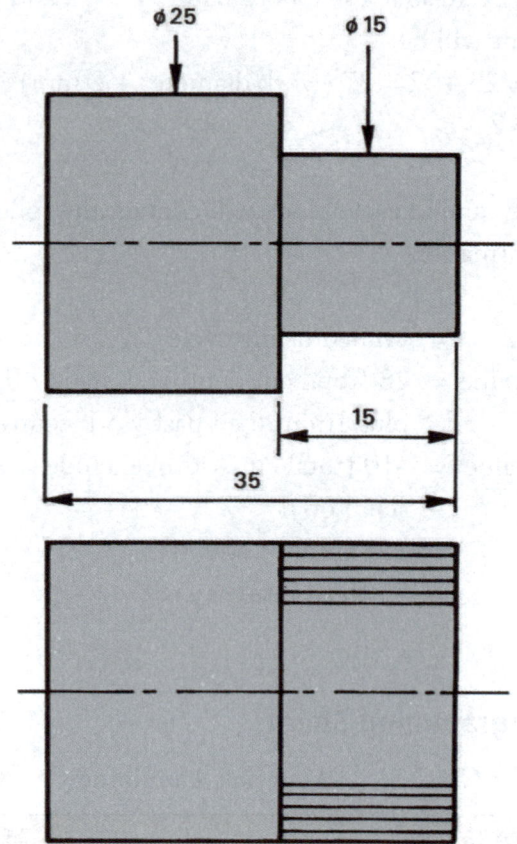

Fig. 13.42
A canned parallel turning, G81, exercise

## Operations Sheet

| No. | Operation | Spindle Speed | Tool Feed | Tool Req. |
|---|---|---|---|---|
| 1 | Tool park position | 2500 | Rapid | 1 |
| 2 | Stand off position | 2500 | Rapid | |
| 3 | Turn ø15 x 15 with 5 cuts, using a canned cycle | 2500 | 75 | |
| 4 | Tool park position | | Rapid | |
| 5 | End program | | | |

## Programming Sheet

Title: CNC 6      Metal: Aluminium      O.Dia: 25      I.Dia: 0      Stickout: 24

| Notes | N | G | M | X | Z | I | K | F | S |
|---|---|---|---|---|---|---|---|---|---|
| Absolute programming | 10 | 90 | | | | | | | |
| Metric dimensions | 20 | 71 | | | | | | | |
| Tool park position | 30 | | | 30 | 10 | 1 | | | |
| Start spindle in reverse | 40 | 97 | 04 | | | | | | 2500 |
| Stand off position | 50 | | | 27 | 2 | | | | |
| Turn ø15 x 15 using a canned cycle | 60 | 81 | | 10 | −17 | 5 | | 75 | |
| Tool park position/stop spindle | 70 | | 05 | 30 | 10 | | | | |
| End program | 80 | | 02 | | | | | | |

## Exercise 7

Write a CNC program to machine the component shown in Fig. 13.43, from a ø30 aluminium bar.

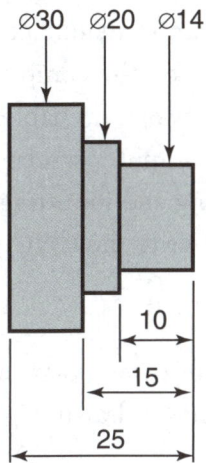

**Fig. 13.43**

## Operations Sheet

| No. | Operation | Spindle Speed | Tool Feed | Tool Req. |
|-----|-----------|---------------|-----------|-----------|
| 1 | Face | 2000 | 75 | 1 |
| 2 | Tool park position | 2000 | Rapid | |
| 3 | Stand off position 1 | 2000 | Rapid | |
| 4 | Turn ø20 x 15 | 2000 | 70 | |
| 5 | Stand off position 2 | 2000 | Rapid | |
| 6 | Turn ø14 x 10 | 2000 | 70 | |
| 7 | Tool park position | | Rapid | |
| 8 | Change tool | | | 11 |
| 9 | Part off to length | 2000 | 35 | |
| 10 | Tool park position | | | |
| 11 | End program | | | |

## Programming Sheet

Title: CNC 7    Material: Aluminium    O. Dia: 30    I. Dia: 0    Stickout: 50

| Notes | N | G | M | X | Z | I | K | F | S |
|-------|---|---|---|---|---|---|---|---|---|
| Absolute programming | 10 | 90 | | | | | | | |
| Metric dimensions | 20 | 71 | | | | | | | |
| Tool park position | 30 | | | 35 | 10 | 1 | | | |
| Start spindle in reverse | 40 | 97 | 04 | | | | | | 2000 |
| Position for facing | 50 | | | 31 | 0 | | | | |
| Face | 60 | 01 | 1 | | | | 70 | | |
| Clear | 70 | | | | 1 | | | | |
| Stand off position 1 | 80 | | | 32 | 2 | | | | |
| Turn ø20 x 15 by canned cycle | 90 | 81 | | 10 | −17 | 5 | | 70 | |
| Stand off position 2 | 100 | | | 22 | 2 | | | | |
| Turn ø14 x 10 by canned cycle | 110 | 81 | | 10 | −12 | 5 | | 70 | |
| Tool park position/stop spindle | 120 | | 05 | 35 | 10 | | | | |
| Change tool | 130 | | 06 | | | 11 | | | |
| Start spindle/position for parting | 140 | 97 | 04 | 31 | −26.6 | | | | 2000 |
| Part off to 25 | 150 | 01 | | −1 | | | | 35 | |
| Clear work | 160 | | | 31 | | | | | |
| Tool park position | 170 | | 05 | 35 | 10 | | | | |
| End program/Repeat | 180 | | 30 | | | | | | |

## Test Run

This is a means of checking the CNC program. It enables the machining of the component to be simulated on the computer screen. It can detect program errors, which can be corrected, thereby avoiding lathe damage and waste of material. It cannot, however, detect mechanical errors such as using a wrong tool or a tool being off centre.

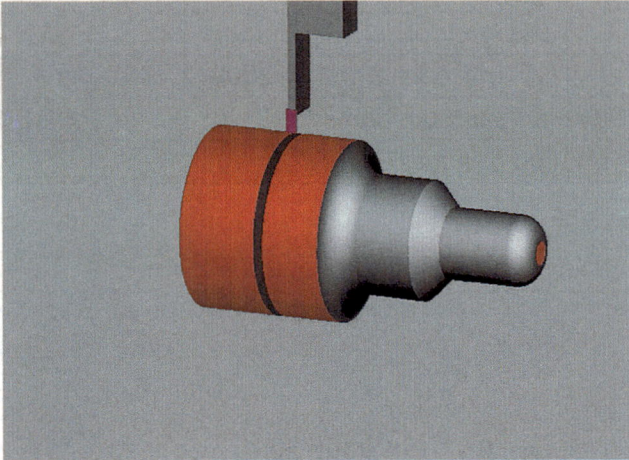

Test run of a program

## Tool Offsets

When machining a component, a number of tools may be used. The positions of the tips of these tools vary in relation to one another and this must be taken into account when controlling the CNC lathe.

The position of the first tool used in the program is taken as the datum and given values of X = 0, Z = 0. The positions of the tips of the other tools used are expressed as variations (+ or –) to this position.

## CAD/CAM

CAD/CAM stand for Computer-Aided-Design and Computer-Aided-Manufacture, respectively. Instead of designing a part on paper and then writing the program to manufacture it, the two stages can be done on the computer with the aid of CAD/CAM software. It enables the part to be designed on the computer screen with the aid of a mouse. By selecting and inputting a command, the software will write the CNC program to produce the part.

Since the shapes of turned parts are symmetrical, only half the profile is drawn, Fig. 13.45.

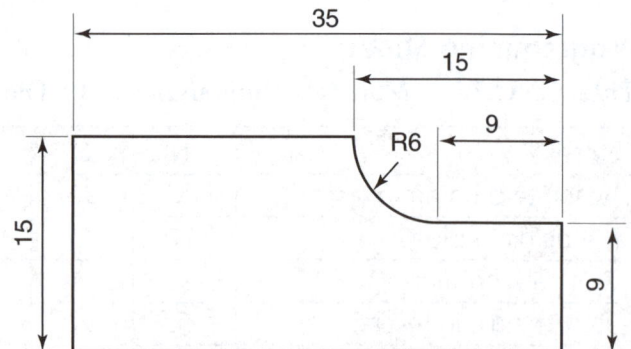

The half-profile to be drawn by CAD/CAM to produce the program to manufacture Exercise 4 Page 158. The full profile is automatically completed.

If a printer or plotter is available, 2-D or 3-D engineering drawing can also be produced from the screen. 2-D stands for 'two-dimensional' and 3-D stands for 'three-dimensional', Fig. 13.46.

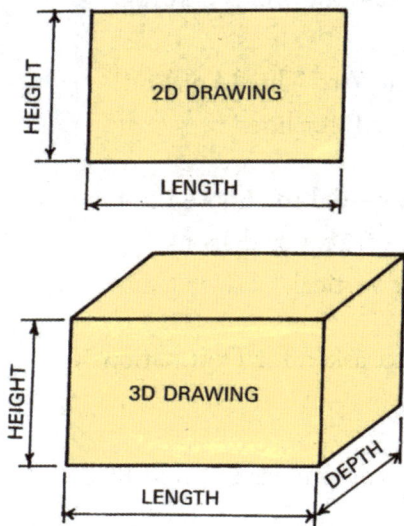

Fig. 13.46

CAD/CAM software is often used as a quick method of producing a CNC program to machine a component already designed. The half profile of the component is drawn on the screen and the processing command is entered to produce the program.

The Boxford CAM software provides a quick and simple method of producing CNC programs. Although prior experience of CNC programming is not essential, it is recommended because it makes the use of CNC more relevant and enables modifications to be carried out easily.

A drawing of the component is required to obtain the X and Z co-ordinates of the various points on the profile. The half profile of the component is drawn on the screen using the **path** commands, Line, Arc and Thread to move from point to point and entering the required details for each type of path. By pressing the Return key, the software will translate the data into a CNC program. It will select the G and M codes, the tools, speeds and feeds required.

## Exercise 8

Use CAM software to produce the CNC program to machine the component shown in Fig. 13.47 from ø25 aluminium bar.

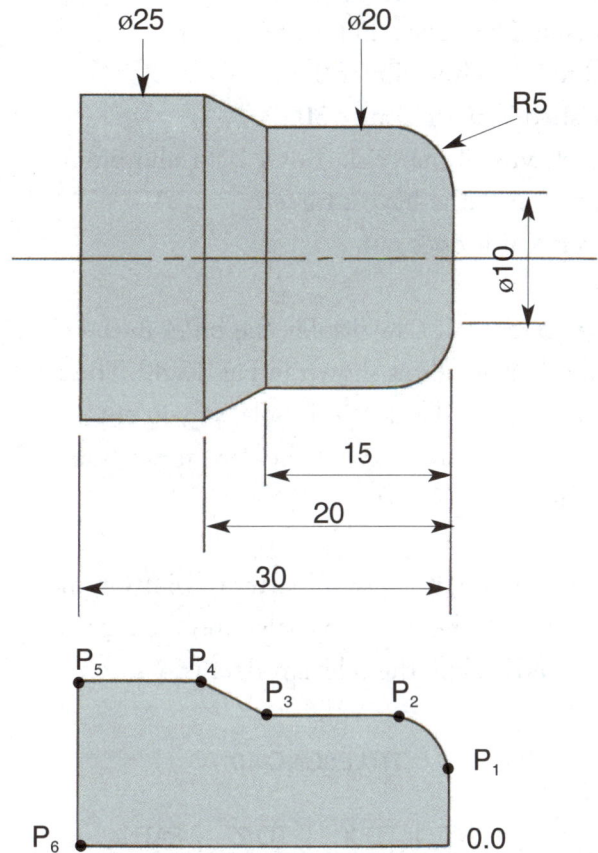

Fig. 13.47

The profile to be entered to produce the program

| Point | X co-ordinate | Z co-ordinate |
|-------|---------------|---------------|
| $P_1$ | 10 | 0 |
| $P_2$ | 20 | −5 |
| $P_3$ | 20 | −15 |
| $P_4$ | 25 | −20 |
| $P_5$ | 25 | −30 |
| $P_6$ | 0 | −30 |

Fig. 13.48

The X and Z co-ordinates for the points on the profile. Note that the X co-ordinates are diameters.

Select **Define a Profile** from the main menu.
The following information will be requested:

Title:   Enter **CNC 8**.
Metric or Imperial:  Enter **M** (for metric units).
Outside Diameter:  Enter **25**.
Inside Diameter:  Enter **0**.
Finished Length:  Enter **30**.
Select type of material:  Enter **2** for aluminium.
Does your lathe have a turret?:
Enter **N** if it does not.

The screen will now display the billet in the chuck and other details as shown in Fig. 13.49. The first prompt is for the depth of hole, so you enter 0. The curser will remain at the datum position, that is, X = 0, Z = 0.

From here on, it is just a matter of plotting the profile with the cursor by selecting the type of path and adding the relevant details.

TITLE: CNC 10

| POINT | TO X | TO Z | PATH |
|-------|------|------|------|

ENTER HOLE DEPTH ■

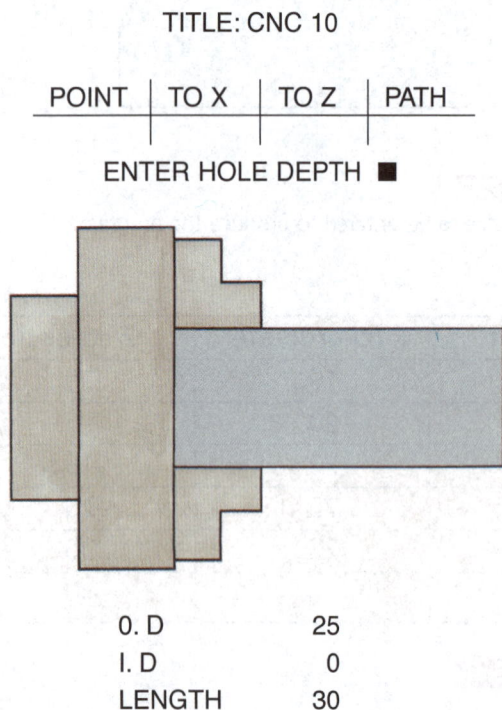

| O. D | 25 |
|------|----|
| I. D | 0 |
| LENGTH | 30 |

To get to point $P_1$, proceed as follows:

Path = (Line, Arc, Thread or End)
    Enter **L** for line.

You are requested to choose the type of line – horizontal, vertical or diagonal.
Enter **V** for vertical.

You are next asked for Destination X.
Enter **10**.

The cursor now moves to point $P_1$.
Complete the profile to point $P_6$ in this manner.

The details to get to each point are as follows:

$P_1$   Enter L for line, V for vertical and 10 for destination.

$P_2$   Enter A for arc, 5 for arc radius, A for anticlockwise arc, 20 for X destination and -5 for Z destination.

$P_3$   Enter L for line, H for horizontal and -15 for Z destination.

$P_4$   Enter L for line, D for diagonal (taper), 25 for X destination and -20 for Z destination.

$P_5$   Enter L for line, H for horizontal and -30 for Z destination.

$P_6$   Enter L for line, V for vertical and 0 for X destination.

The software now recognises that the profile has been completed.

**End of Shape** is displayed on the screen. On pressing the Return key, the minimum length of billet will appear (allowing for parting off).

When the Return key is again pressed, the profile will be translated into a CNC program.

## Programming Sheet

Title: CNC 8        O Dia: 25        I Dia: 0        Length: 34

| line | G | M | X | Z | I | K | F | S |
|------|-----|-----|-------|--------|------|------|------|-----|
| N10 | 90 | | | | | | | |
| N20 | 71 | | | | | | | |
| N30 | | | 45 | 10 | 1 | | | |
| N40 | 95 | | | | | | | |
| N50 | 96 | 04 | | 1 | | | | 150 |
| N60 | | | 27 | | | | | |
| N70 | 81 | | 4 | -15.50 | 2 | | 0.08 | |
| N80 | | | 23 | | | | | |
| N90 | 81 | | 10 | -1 | 3 | | 0.08 | |
| N100 | | | | 0.75 | | | | |
| N110 | | | 16.25 | | | | | |
| N120 | 03 | | 21 | -2.37 | 2.46 | 4.34 | 0.08 | |
| N130 | | | | 0.75 | | | | |
| N140 | | | 11.50 | | | | | |
| N150 | 03 | | 21 | -4.50 | 0.23 | 4.98 | 0.08 | |
| N160 | 96 | 04 | | 0 | | | | 200 |
| N170 | 01 | | -1 | | | | 0.04 | |
| N180 | | | | 0.50 | | | | |
| N190 | | | 10 | | | | | |
| N200 | 01 | | | 0 | | | 0.04 | |
| N210 | 03 | | 20 | -5 | 0 | 5 | 0.04 | |
| N220 | 01 | | | -15 | | | 0.04 | |
| N230 | 01 | | 25 | -20 | | | 0.04 | |
| N240 | 01 | | | -32 | | | 0.04 | |
| N250 | | 05 | 45 | | | | | |
| N260 | | | | 10 | | | | |
| N270 | | 06 | | | 11 | | | |
| N280 | 96 | 04 | | -31.60 | | | | 150 |
| N290 | | | 27 | | | | | |
| N300 | 01 | | -1 | | | | 0.05 | |
| N310 | | | 45 | | | | | |
| N320 | | 05 | | | | | | |
| N330 | | | | 10 | | | | |
| N340 | | 30 | | | | | | |

The CNC program produced by CAM software (Define a profile) to machine component shown in Fig. 13.47.

Note that the software has selected the following:

1. Feed per revolution, G95, rather than feed per minute.
2. Constant surface speeds, G96, rather than constant rotational speeds.
3. A canned cycle to reduce the diameter.
4. A finishing cut to produce a smooth surface.

167

## Use of computers in technology

Computers are widely used in technology, e.g. CNC turning.

Other applications include:

- Controlling machines
- Controlling robots
- Designing articles
- Producing drawings
- Producing printed reports
- Accessing information
- Simulation (to represent an operation, situation or system)

## Hardware and Software

The physical parts that make up a computer are called hardware, and the programs, languages and procedures used in computer systems are called software.

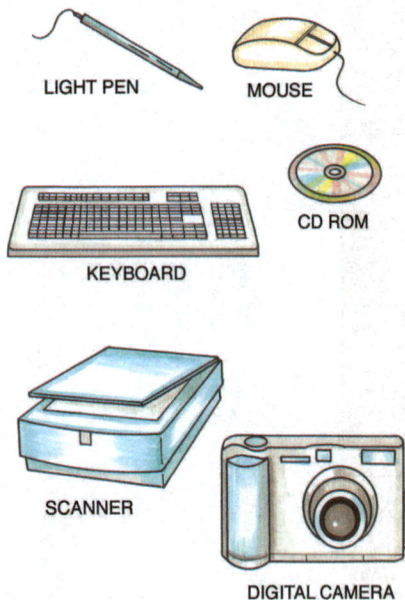

LIGHT PEN
MOUSE
CD ROM
KEYBOARD
SCANNER
DIGITAL CAMERA

**Fig. 13.50**
Common input devices

As with other electronic systems, the hardware consists of three types of device – input, process and output. Some input and output devices, together with the central processing unit, are shown in Fig. 13.50, 13.51 and 13.52.

**Fig. 13.51**
Central Processing Unit (CPU)

CPU

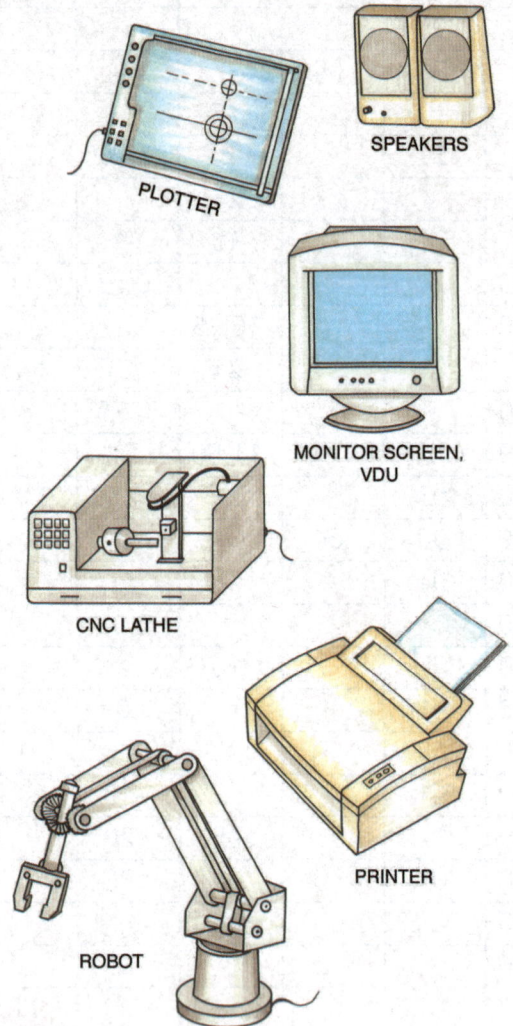

PLOTTER
SPEAKERS
MONITOR SCREEN, VDU
CNC LATHE
ROBOT
PRINTER

**Fig. 13.52**
Common output devices

## Central Processing Unit (CPU)

The CPU contains the main electronic chips that run the computer. It could be regarded as the 'brain' of the computer. It performs all the calculations within the computer, carries out instructions and transfers data to and from all the computer components.

## Common Input Devices

**Keyboard** This is the most common type of input device. It is used for entering instructions and data.

**Mouse** By moving a mouse along a pad, a cursor can be moved over the screen to select items and initiate actions.

**CD-ROM** This stands for compact disk-read only memory. It can store a lot of data which can be inputted quickly.

**Scanner** This is used to input photographs, drawings and typed material into the computer. The material can then be altered and printed as required.

## Common Output Devices

**Monitor** This has a screen that displays information such as instructions being sent to the computer and information and results being sent back.

**Printer** A printer produces a printed copy of material from the computer.

**Plotter** This enables drawings from the computer to be produced on paper.

**Machines** A wide range of machines can be controlled by computers.

**Robots** These can be programmed to carry out operations automatically, e.g. assembly work, welding and painting. They are particularly useful for single action, monotonous work, activities being carried out in hazardous environments and the handling of dangerous materials (e.g. hot materials, radioactive materials).

## Input and Output Devices

Some devices can be used to both enter data and extract data and can therefore be classified as input and output devices.

A **touch screen** enables the computer to be controlled by a finger touching the screen.

A **modem** is a piece of hardware that connects a computer to telephone lines to send and receive information.

Removable input and output devices include floppy disks, data cartridges, compact disks (CDs) and USB sticks.

## Storage Devices

**Hard disk** This is enclosed in the computer system box. It has a large storage capacity and is used to store operating systems, application programs (e.g. word processor) and other data.

**Floppy disk or diskette** This has far less storage capacity than a hard disk. Floppy disks are used for supplying software, to back–up (copy) data from the hard disk and to transfer files from one computer to another. They are now being superseded by larger capacity devices such as CDs and DVDs.

**CD (Compact Disk)** This can store large amounts of data.

**CD-R (Compact Disk Recordable)** This can be recorded, or written, on once and read many times.

**CD-RW (Compact Disk Re-Writeable)** This can be recorded on many times.

**CD-ROM (Compact Disk Read Only Memory)** This is a pre-recorded compact disk that cannot be recorded on.

**DVD (Digital Versatile Disk)** This is a development of the CD-ROM disc. It can store a great amount of data. It has many uses and can, for example, store a complete feature film. A recordable version **(DVD-R)** is now also available.

## Some Common Computer Terms

**Memory** The electronic holding place for programs and data required by the computer.

**ROM (Read-Only Memory)** This is memory that can be read but not changed because it is fixed in the hardware. It is retained after the computer is shut down.

**RAM (Random Access Memory)** This memory is used to temporarily store programs and files while working on them. The information in RAM is lost when the computer is shut down.

**Bit** Computers store data digitally – in terms of binary numbers. A bit is a binary digit with a value of 0 or 1 and is the smallest unit of computer data.

**Byte** A collection of eight bits is called a byte. The storage capacity of a computer is given in bytes. A kilobyte is $2^{10}$ bytes (1024 bytes), a megabyte is $2^{20}$ bytes and a gigabyte is one billion bytes.

**Operating system** This is basic software required to run the computer. DOS (disk operating system) and Windows are examples of operating systems.

**Menu** A list of options displayed on the screen.

**File** A collection of information that has been given a name and stored.

**Virus** A computer program that can damage the system. It can pass from program to program or disk to disk.

**WWW** This stands for World Wide Web. It is a facility that uses the internet to provide a huge library of information.

## Exercises

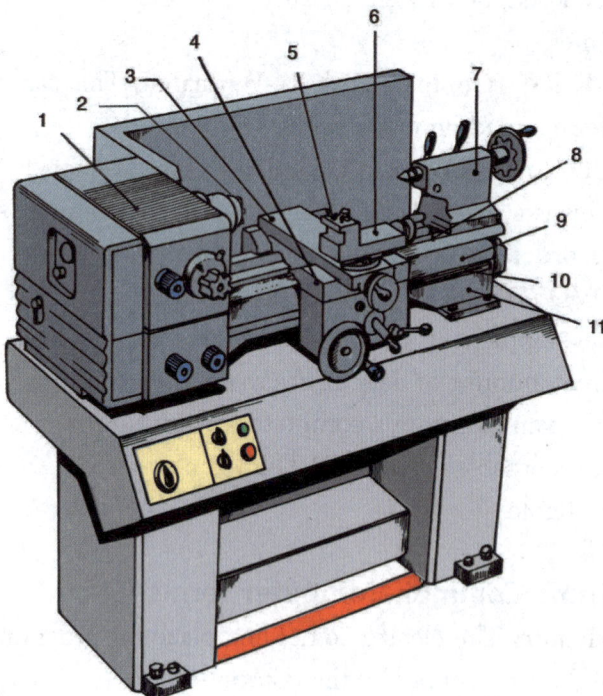

Fig.13.53

1.  A lathe is shown in Fig. 13.53.
    (a) Name the lathe parts 1 to 11.
    (b) What is the purpose of the slideways on the lathe bed?
    (c) What is the purpose of the gap in some lathe beds?
    (d) Why are lathe spindles hollow?
    (e) State two uses for the tailstock.

2.  (a) What is the cross slide used for?
    (b) What is the top slide used for?
    (c) What is the feed shaft used for?
    (d) What is the leadscrew used for?
    (e) What shapes of material can be gripped in the three-jaw chuck?
    (f) Give two uses for a four-jaw chuck.

3. Name the toolposts shown in Fig. 13.54 below and describe how the tool is set to the correct height in each one.

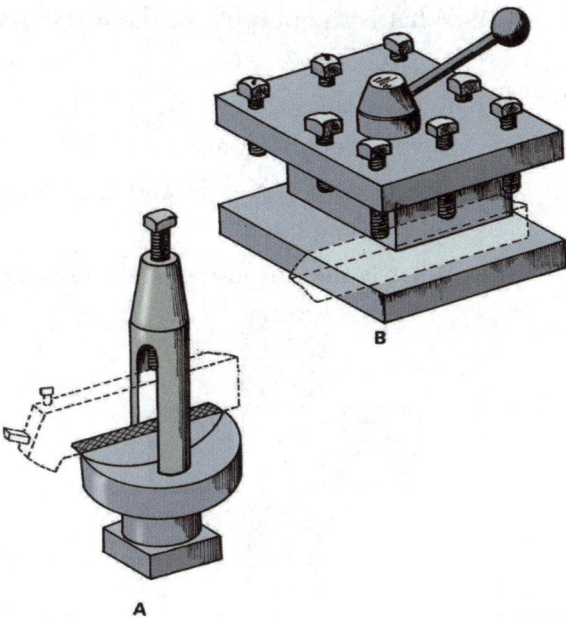

Fig. 13.54

4. Name three types of tool holder.
5. Explain the difference between a tool bit and a solid tool.
6. What is a tipped tool?
7. Name the tool angles A, B, C and D indicated in Fig. 13.55 below.

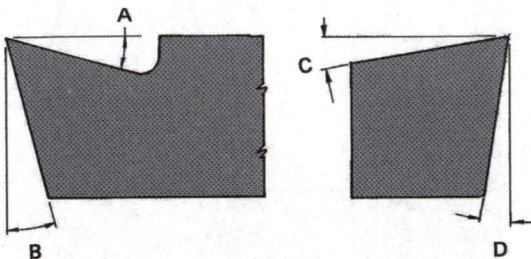

Fig. 13.55

8. What is the purpose of (i) clearance (ii) rake on a cutting tool?
9. What would be the effect on the clearance and rake angles if a lathe tool was set:
   (i) above the lathe centre height?
   (ii) below the lathe centre height?
   Assume that the tool shank is horizontal in both cases.

10. Why is it important to have the tool set at centre height when facing?
11. A 20mm diameter mild steel bar is to be turned on the lathe. If the surface cutting speed is 33m/min. calculate the lathe speed in rev/min (RPM).
12. List five factors that must be taken into account when selecting the lathe spindle speed.
13. List six safety precautions that must be observed when using the lathe.
14. (a) Name each of the turning operations A and B shown in Fig. 13.56.
    (b) Explain each operation.

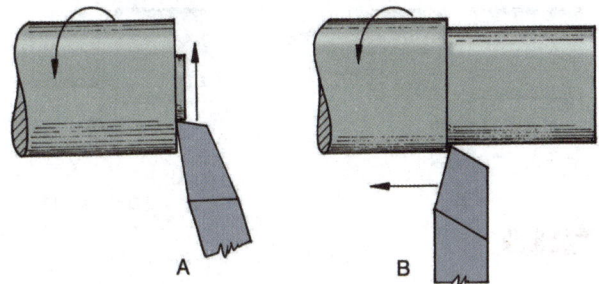

Fig. 13.56

15. By how much will the diameter of the work be reduced if the depth of a parallel cut is 1mm?
16. At what angles should the top slide be set, to turn the tapers shown in
    (i) Fig. 13.57 A,
    (ii) Fig. 13.57 B.

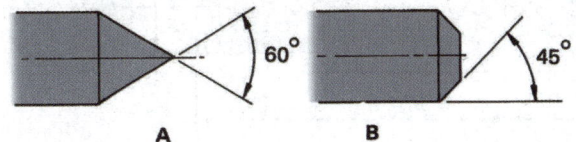

Fig. 13.57

17. Sketch a centre drill and give two uses for it.
18. How are (i) parallel shank, (ii) taper shank drills held in a lathe?
19. How could you check the depth to which a hole has been drilled on the lathe?

**20.** Name, explain and state the purpose of the lathe operation shown in Fig. 13.58.

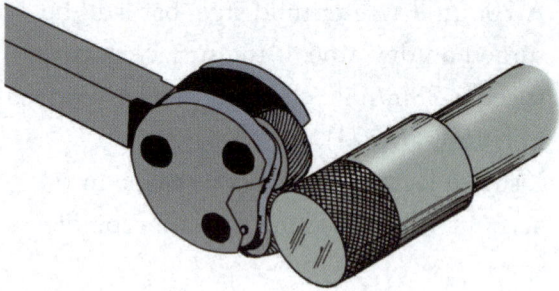

Fig 13.58

**21.** Name, explain and state the purpose of the lathe operation shown in Fig. 13.59.

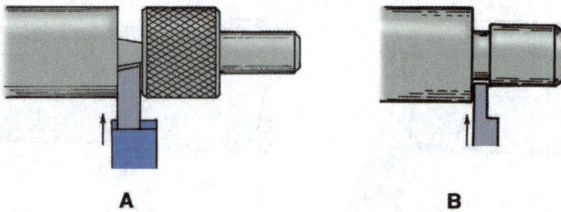

A                    B

Fig 13.59

**22.** Sketch and state the use of a lathe centre.

**23.** Describe, with the aid of sketches, the various stages in the turning of the component shown in Fig. 13.60 below, using 25mm diameter by 85mm long, bright, mild steel shafting.

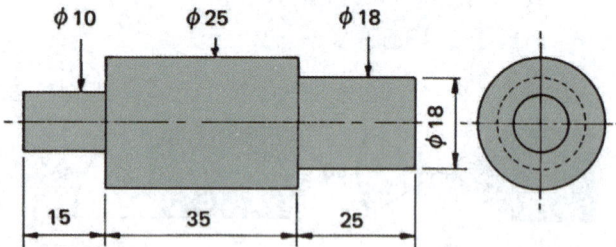

Fig 13.60

**24.** Give two advantages of a CNC lathe over a conventional lathe.

**25.** Explain, with the aid of a diagram, the difference between incremental dimensioning and absolute dimensioning.

**26.** Explain, with the aid of a diagram, how tool positions are defined in a CNC program.

**27.** (a) What is the purpose of the jog keys on a CNC lathe?
(b) Redraw the jog keys, Fig. 13.61, in your copybook and label the directions X+, X–, Z+ and Z– on the appropriate keys.
(c) What is the purpose of the centre key?

Fig 13.61

**28.** What are the functions of the G codes: G00, G01, G71 and G91?

**29.** What are the functions of the following M codes: M02, M03, M04, M05 and M06?

**30.** Write a CNC program to machine the shape shown in Fig. 13.62 below from a 25mm diameter bar.

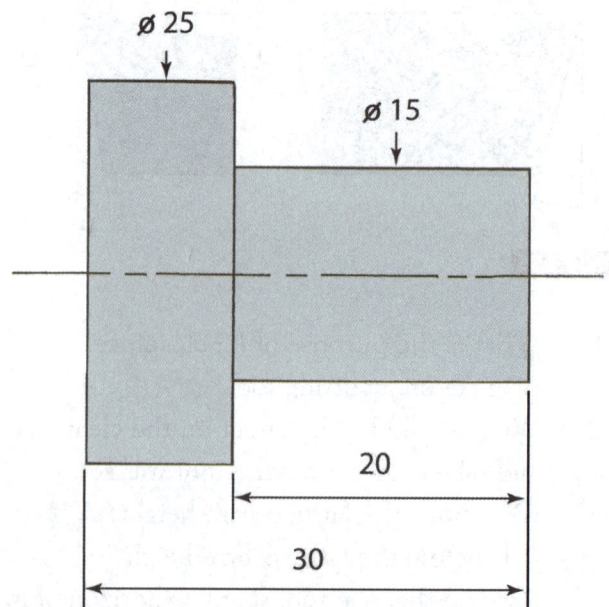

Fig. 13.62

**31.** Describe the steps taken to produce the CNC program to machine the component shown in Fig. 13.63 using CAM software (define a profile option).

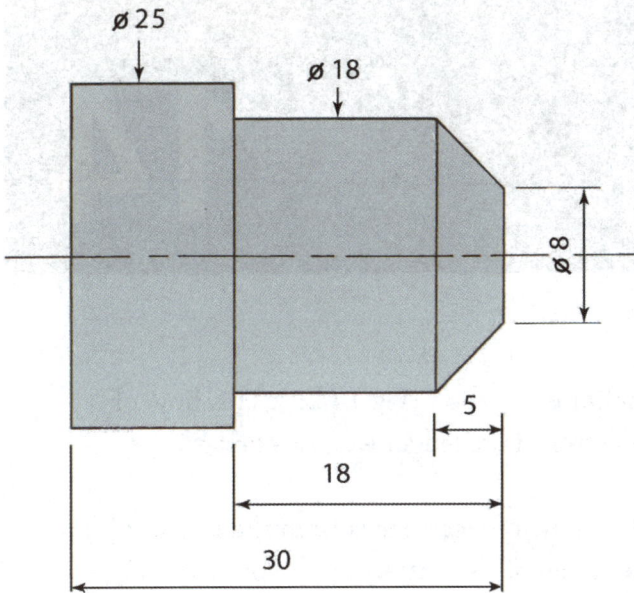

Ø 25
Ø 18
Ø 8
5
18
30

Fig. 13.63

**32.** What is meant by **Test Run** in CNC machining?

**33.** What is meant by tool offsets in CNC machining?

**34.** What is meant by CAD?

**35.** What is meant by CAM?

**36.** Give three examples of the use of computers in technology.

**37.** Name and state the function of four computer input devices.

**38.** Name and state the function of four computer output devices.

**39.** Explain each of the following computer abbreviations and terms:

(a) ROM      (b) RAM
(c) Byte      (d) Operating system
(e) Menu      (f) WWW
(g) Virus

# Electricity and Electronics

## 14

## Electric Current

Matter is made up of atoms. An atom consists of a nucleus of protons and neutrons with electrons orbiting it (Fig. 14.1). Each electron has a negative electric charge and each proton has a positive charge of equal magnitude.

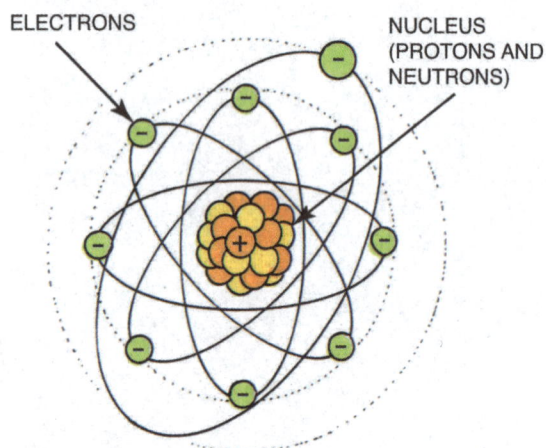

In metals, some of the outer electrons are free to move haphazardly through the atomic structure, Fig. 14.2 A. If, however, a piece of metal is made part of a circuit and an electrical 'pressure' or voltage applied to it (e.g. if connected to terminals of a battery), the free electron will flow in a

definite direction (Fig 14.2B). This flow of electrons is called an **electric current**.

The flow of electrons is from the negative(–) terminal of the battery to the positive (+) terminal.

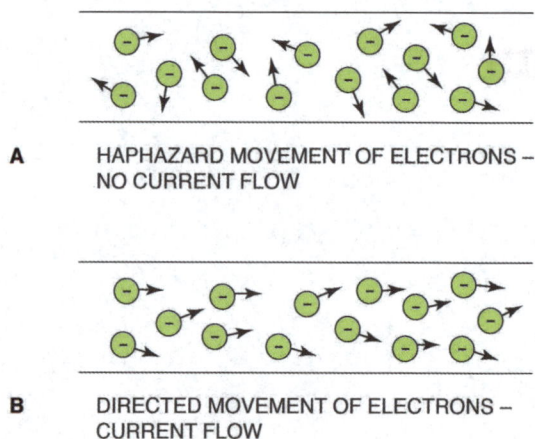

A    HAPHAZARD MOVEMENT OF ELECTRONS – NO CURRENT FLOW

B    DIRECTED MOVEMENT OF ELECTRONS – CURRENT FLOW

**Fig. 14.2**

Before the discovery of the electron, it was thought that current consisted of positive charges moving from the + terminal of a battery to its – terminal. This choice of direction has been retained. Therefore, the direction of **conventional current** is from + to – and is the opposite to the direction of electron flow in metals.

## Conductors

Materials that allow current to flow freely through them are called conductors. Metals are good conductors.

## Insulators

These are materials that do not allow current to flow through them. Examples of insulators are PVC, acrylic (perspex), phenol formaldehyde (Bakelite), wood, mica and rubber.

## Power Sources

A power source is required to supply the electrical 'pressure' to drive the electrons around a circuit. The electrical pressure is called electromotive force (e.m.f.) and is measured in volts (V).
A battery is made up of a number of cells joined together. There are different types of cells. The carbon/zinc cell is a common type and gives an e.m.f. of 1.5V. A 4.5V battery consists of three cells connected together. The current supplied by a battery is called direct current (d.c.). This means that it flows in the same direction all the time.

The current supplied by the ESB is called alternating current (a.c.). It flows in one direction for one instant and in the opposite direction for the next. The beginning of flow in one direction to the end of flow in the opposite direction is called a cycle. The ESB supplies current at 50 cycles per second and at 220V.

Low voltage sources are used for school course work. These can be batteries or special units which transform the mains supply to ranges of about 0 – 25V. These units have rectifiers to supply d.c. current. They are also capable of supplying low voltage a.c. current. The 220V mains supply should never be used directly for school course work, because it could cause fatal accidents or damage equipment.

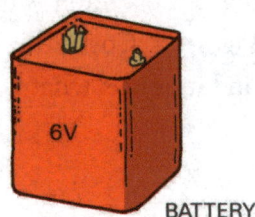

BATTERY

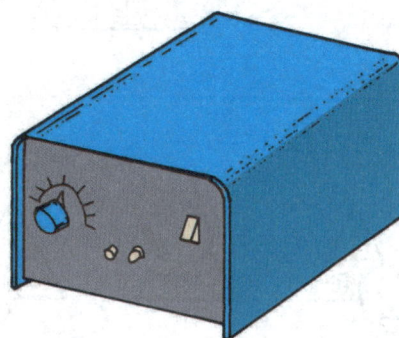

LOW VOLTAGE POWER UNIT

**Fig. 14.3**
Power sources

**Voltage, Current and Resistance**

Resistance (R) is another electrical property. It is the ability of a conductor to resist the flow of current. Conductors especially made to have particular resistances are called resistors. They are used to control the flow of current in a circuit. In addition to resistors with fixed resistances, there are also variable resistors, or rheostats available.

The unit of resistance is the ohm ($\Omega$) and the unit of current is the ampere (A) or amp. Current is denoted by the letter 'I'.

There is a definite relationship between voltage, current and resistance in a circuit and it is known as **Ohm's Law**. This law states that the current flowing through a conductor is proportional to the 'potential difference' (p.d.) across it, provided the temperature remains constant. This can be stated as $V/I$ = constant. The constant is the resistance. Therefore, the equation can be written as $V/I = R$, $V = IR$ or $V/R = I$ (where V is volts, I is amps and R is ohms).

An easy way of remembering this equation is to use a triangle as shown in Fig. 14.4. Cover the quantity you want to find and it equals what is left visible.

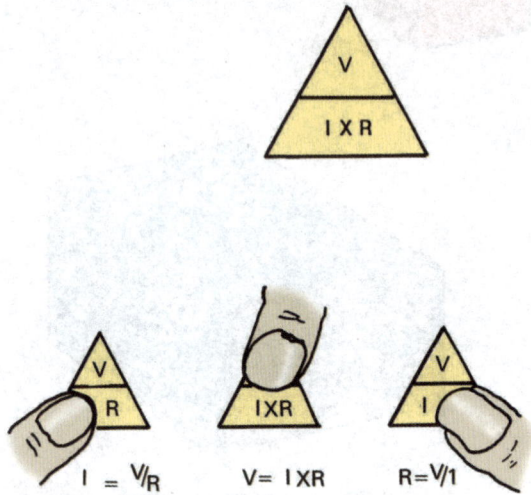

**Fig. 14.4**
Ohm's Law

**Example:** If the voltage across a conductor is 6V and the current flowing through it is 3 amps, what is its resistance?

$$R = \frac{V}{I} = \frac{6}{3} = 2\Omega$$

## Measuring Current, Voltage and Resistance

**Current** The instrument used to measure current is called an **ammeter**. The units commonly used for school work are the amp (A), the milliamp (mA), which is 1/1000 amp and the microamp (μA), which is 1/1000,000 amp.

An ammeter must be connected directly into a circuit in series, Fig. 14.5.

Its positive terminal must be connected to the positive side of the circuit and the negative terminal to the negative side.

Overloading an ammeter can burn it out. Therefore, always ensure that an ammeter of the correct range is being used.

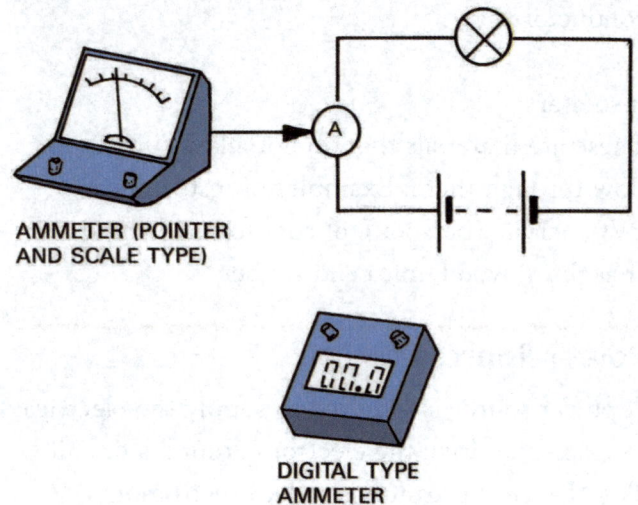

AMMETER (POINTER AND SCALE TYPE)

DIGITAL TYPE AMMETER

**Fig. 14.5**
An ammeter must be connected in series in a circuit

**Voltage** A **voltmeter** is used to measure voltage. It measures the potential difference (p.d.) between two points in a circuit, e.g. between the terminals of a lamp or battery or between the ends of a resistor. There would be a voltage drop across a lamp or resistor and a voltage rise across a battery.

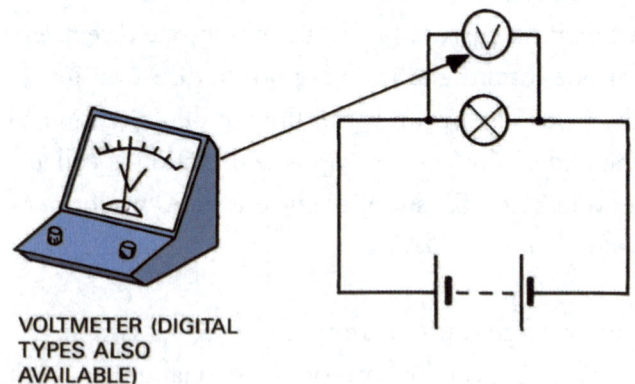

VOLTMETER (DIGITAL TYPES ALSO AVAILABLE)

**Fig. 14.6**
A voltmeter must be connected in parallel with a component

**Note:** p.d.s and e.m.f.s are usually called voltages, as both are measured in volts.

A voltmeter must be connected in parallel with the component or part of a circuit in which the p.d. is being measured, and a voltmeter capable of measuring the maximum voltage expected must be used.

**Resistance** The resistance of a component can be calculated from $R = V/I$ if the magnitude of the current flowing through it and the voltage drop across it are known.

Two circuits for finding the current and voltage drop are shown in Fig. 14.7. In Fig. 14.7 A the ammeter reading can be taken as the current through the component R if the resistance of R is low compared to that of the voltmeter. If not, the voltmeter should be connected as shown in Fig. 14.7 B. Here the ammeter gives the exact current through R and the voltmeter reading is almost equal to the voltage drop across R if the resistance of R is much greater than that of the ammeter.

Other circuits are also used for finding the resistance of components.

Resistance can be measured directly with a **multimeter**, Fig. 14.8. A multimeter can also be used to measure current and voltage. To use it as an **ohmmeter** (a meter to measure resistance), you select the resistance range and read the ohm scale. This scale reads from right to left with a zero mark on the right and the infinite resistance mark on the left. Before using the meter, the zero ohm's mark should be checked and adjusted if necessary. Probes or crocodile clips are used to make contact with the component. When the probes are touched off one another, the pointer should move across the scale to the zero mark. For ease of reading, multimeters can be set to a range of multiplier resistance values such as Rx1, Rx100 and Rx1000.

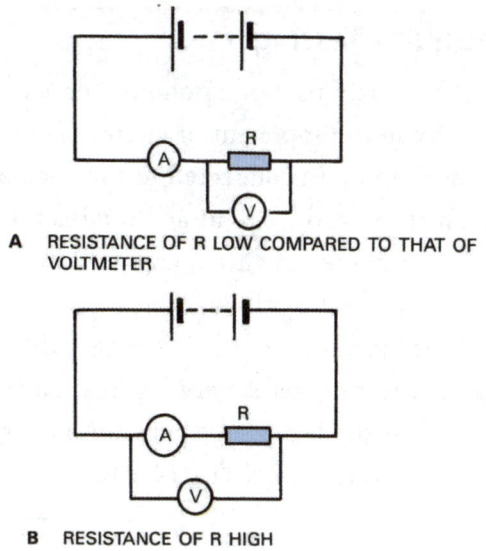

**A** RESISTANCE OF R LOW COMPARED TO THAT OF VOLTMETER

**B** RESISTANCE OF R HIGH

**Fig. 14.7**

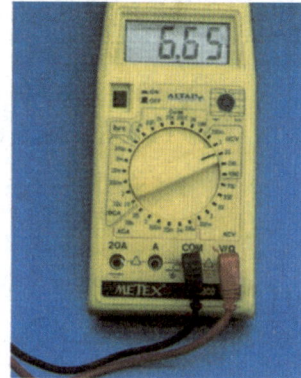

A digital multimeter

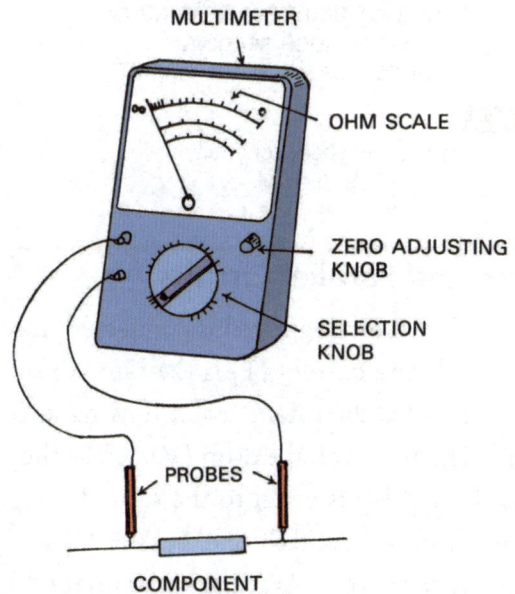

MULTIMETER

OHM SCALE

ZERO ADJUSTING KNOB

SELECTION KNOB

PROBES

COMPONENT

**Fig. 14.8**
Measuring resistance

## Continuity Testing

One of the main uses of an ohmmeter is to test for continuity in a component or circuit. To do this, the meter leads are connected to the ends of the component or into a circuit and the reading is noted. An infinitely high reading indicates a break in the component or circuit. For instance, to check if a fuse is blown, Fig. 14.9 A, connect the ohmmeter to its ends. A very low resistance would indicate that the fuse is not blown. An example of another test is shown in Fig. 14.9 B.

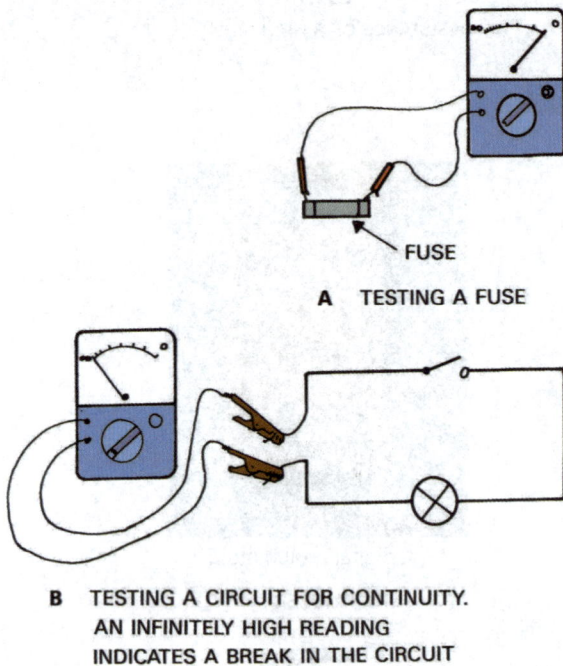

**A    TESTING A FUSE**

**B    TESTING A CIRCUIT FOR CONTINUITY. AN INFINITELY HIGH READING INDICATES A BREAK IN THE CIRCUIT**

**Fig. 14.9**
Using a multimeter to check continuity

**A    BULBS CONNECTED IN SERIES**

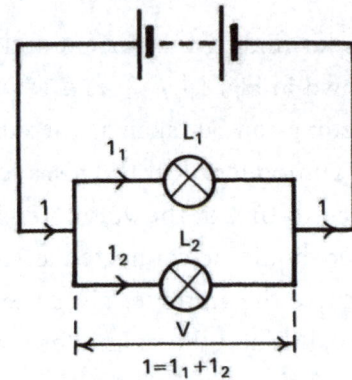

**B    BULBS CONNECTED IN PARALLEL**

**Fig. 14.10**

In Fig. 14.10 B the bulbs are connected in parallel, side by side. The total current divides between the two branches, $1 = 1_1 + 1_2$. If the resistance of $L_1$ is greater than that of $L_2$, then $1_1$ will be less than $1_2$ and vice versa. The voltage drop across each bulb is equal to the voltage drop across both, $V = V_1 = V_2$.

## Series and Parallel Circuits

Fig. 14.50 A shows light bulbs connected in series, end to end. The current (1) is the same through each one and is the total current flowing in the circuit. The total voltage drop (V) across the two bulbs ($L_1$ and $L_2$) is equal to the sum of the voltage drops across each one, i.e. $V = V_1 + V_2$. If the resistance of $L_1$ is greater than that of $L_2$, then $V_1$ will be greater than $V_2$ and vice versa.

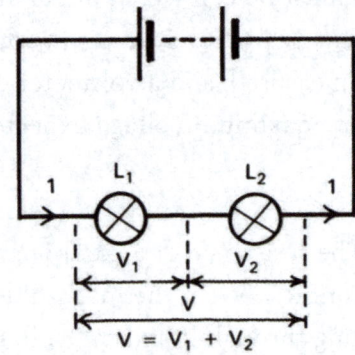

## Some Simple Circuits

**Circuit diagrams** are used to show how electrical components are joined together. Internationally agreed symbols are used to denote the components (see page 183).

Fig. 14.11 A shows a battery, a switch and a bulb connected together to form a circuit. Fig. 14.11 B shows the appropriate circuit diagram.

When the circuit is completed, the current flows and the bulb lights. A break anywhere in the circuit prevents the bulb lighting. The switch is used to make or break the circuit. Turning on the switch completes the circuit and turning it off breaks the circuit.

A practical application of this circuit is the torch, Fig. 14.11 C.

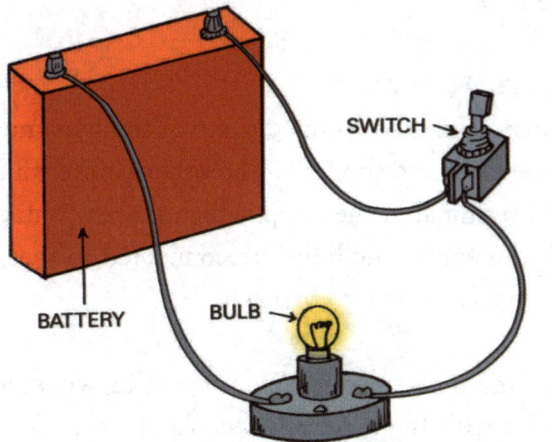

**A   DEXTERITY GAME**

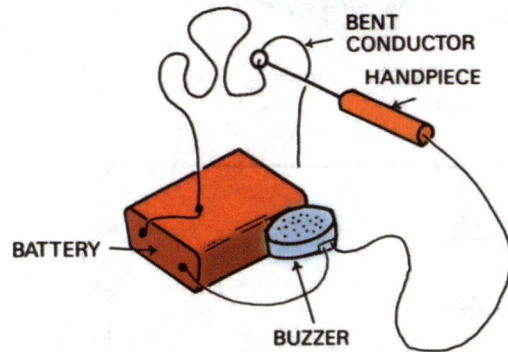

**A   COMPONENTS CONNECTED TO FORM A CIRCUIT**

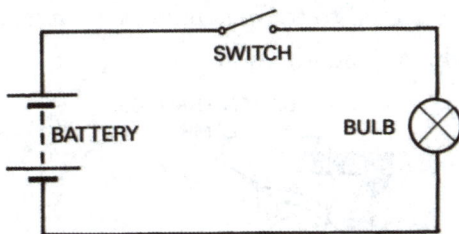

**B   CIRCUIT DIAGRAM**

**B   COMPONENTS**

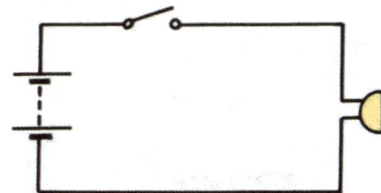

**C   CIRCUIT DIAGRAM WITH EYE AND CONDUCTOR SHOWN AS A SWITCH**

Fig. 14.12

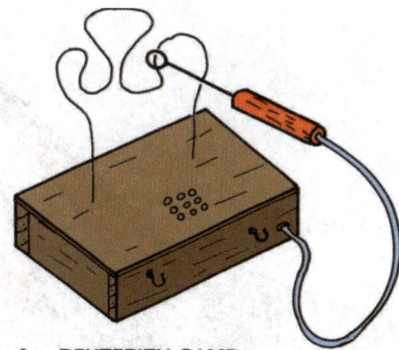

**(C)   ELECTRIC TORCH**

Fig. 14.11

## Dexterity Game

The challenge here is to get the eye piece around the bent conductor without touching it. If the eye touches the conductor, the circuit is completed and the buzzer sounds.

## Model Crane

The circuit for operating the motor of the model crane in just one direction is shown in Fig. 14.12 B. By changing the polarity of the supply to the motor, we can reverse its direction of rotation to raise and lower the crane hook. To enable us to change the direction of rotation as required, we must use another type of switch called a double pole double throw (D.P.D.T.) switch. This circuit is shown in Fig. 14.12 C.

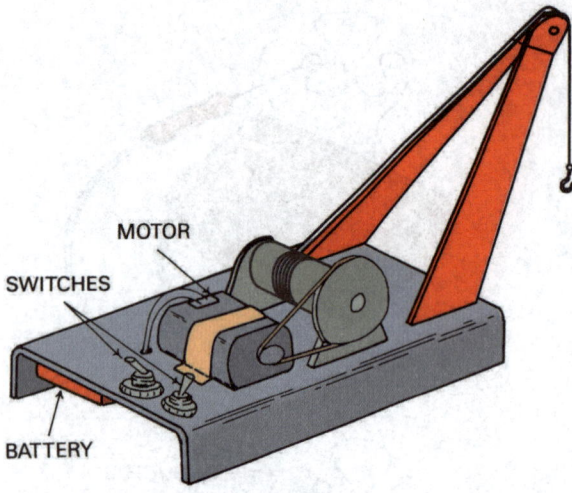

MOTOR

SWITCHES

BATTERY

**A  MODEL CRANE**

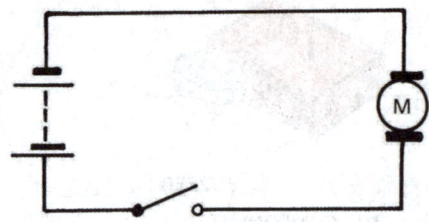

**B  CIRCUIT FOR OPERATING THE MOTOR IN JUST ONE DIRECTION**

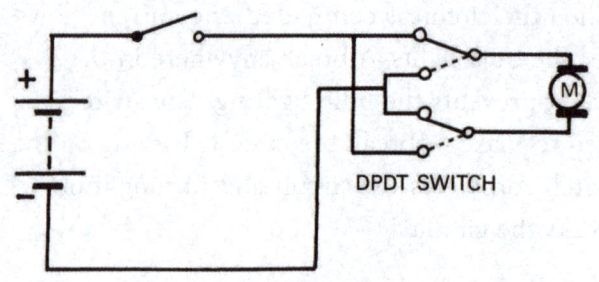

DPDT SWITCH

**C  CIRCUIT WHICH ENABLES DIRECTION OF ROTATION OF MOTOR TO BE CHANGED**

**Fig. 14.13**
Model crane

## Bicycle Dynamo

An insulated cable connects one of the dynamo coil terminals to the bulb. The other coil terminal and a terminal in the lamp, which makes contact with the end of the bulb, are connected to the bicycle frame via two brackets.

The dynamo is operated by bringing its wheel into contact with the bicycle wheel. As the bicycle wheel rotates, it turns the dynamo wheel and the magnet connected to it. This induces a current in the coil which lights the bulb.

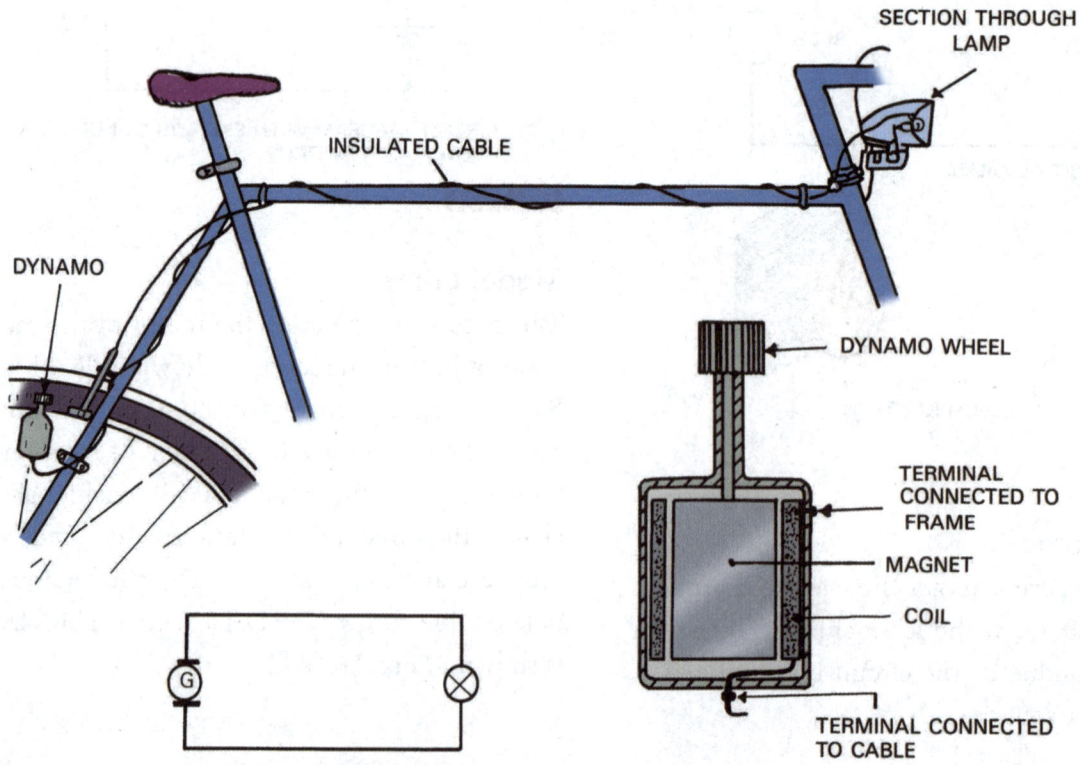

SECTION THROUGH LAMP

INSULATED CABLE

DYNAMO

DYNAMO WHEEL

TERMINAL CONNECTED TO FRAME

MAGNET

COIL

TERMINAL CONNECTED TO CABLE

CIRCUIT DIAGRAM

SECTION THROUGH DYNAMO

**Fig. 14.14**
Bicycle dynamo

## Domestic Light Switch (rocker switch)

The input cable is clamped in a brass socket which is joined to terminal A of the switch, Fig. 14.15 A. The output cable is clamped in another brass socket which is joined to terminal B. The function of the switch is to connect or disconnect terminals A and B in a safe manner, thereby making or breaking the circuit as required.

The end of terminal B is bent upwards and acts as a pivot for the bridge piece C. The bridge piece is kept in contact with the end of terminal B at all times by the pressure exerted by the two springs under the plastics operating rocker.

The casing of this type of switch is made from urea formaldehyde.

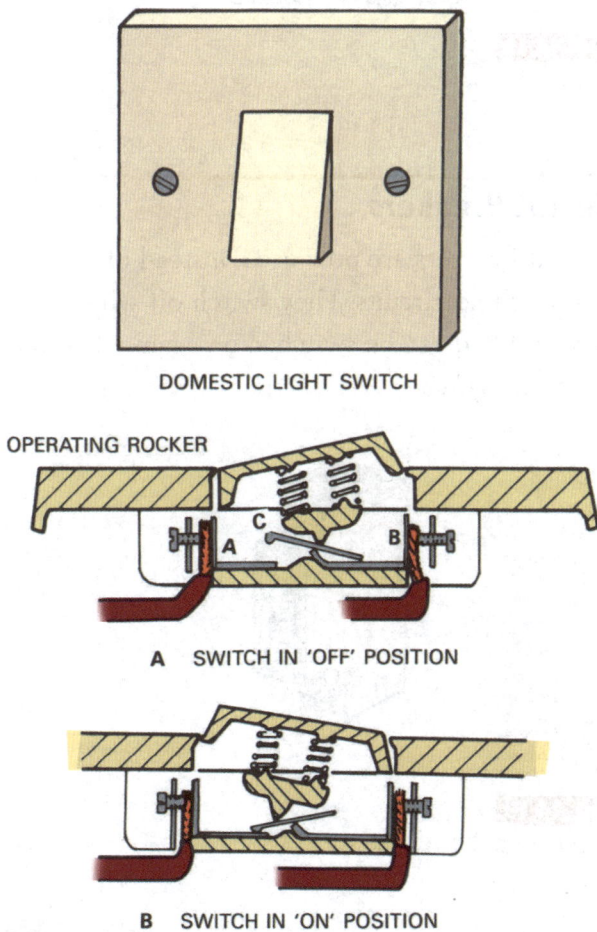

DOMESTIC LIGHT SWITCH

OPERATING ROCKER

**A    SWITCH IN 'OFF' POSITION**

**B    SWITCH IN 'ON' POSITION**

**Fig. 14.15**
Domestic light switch

## Three-pin Plug

The wiring of a three-pin plug is shown in Fig. 14.16. The live and neutral pins are necessary to complete the circuit for the appliance. The **earth** pin is connected to the metal case of the appliance by means of one of the wires in its lead.

The earth socket of a power point is connected to a metal rod which is fixed into the ground. Therefore, when the appliance is plugged in, its metal case is earthed; it is joined to earth by a path of almost zero resistance. If a fault develops, causing the metal case to become 'live', a large current can flow to earth and the fuse will blow and cut off the supply. Without the earth, a person touching the case would get an electric shock which could be fatal.

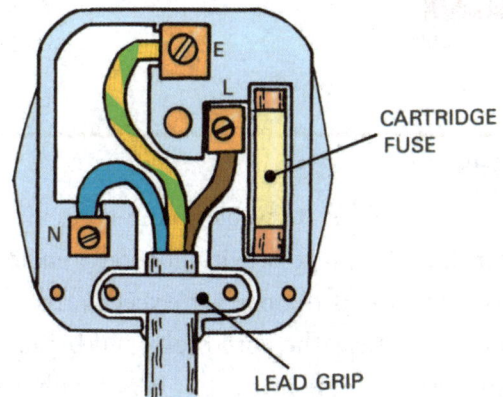

CARTRIDGE FUSE

LEAD GRIP

E = EARTH → YELLOW, GREEN

L = LIVE → BROWN

N = NEUTRAL → BLUE

**Fig. 14.16**
A three-pin plug

## Filament Bulbs

The light is produced by heating a tungsten coil (filament) white hot by passing a current through it. Tungsten has a high melting point and can withstand the high temperature. The glass bulb also contains inert gases (nitrogen and argon).

If the bulb contained air, the filament would oxidise. The gases also reduce evaporation of the filament.

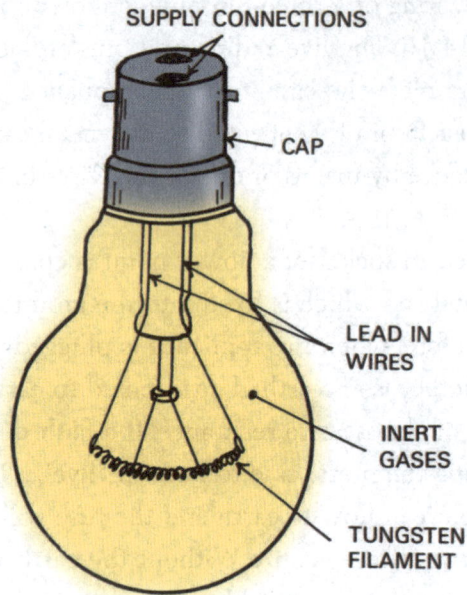

SUPPLY CONNECTIONS

CAP

LEAD IN WIRES

INERT GASES

TUNGSTEN FILAMENT

**Fig. 14.17**
Filament bulb

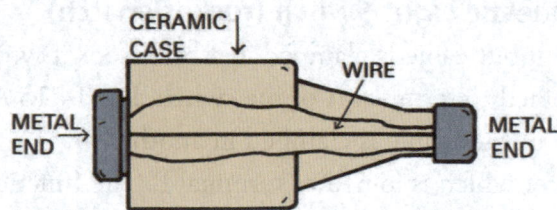

CERAMIC CASE

WIRE

METAL END

METAL END

**A   FUSE BOARD TYPE**

13 A

**B   CERAMIC CARTRIDGE TYPES FITTED IN PLUG**

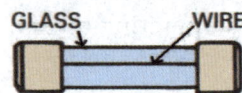

GLASS          WIRE

**C   GLASS CARTRIDGE TYPE WIRE CAN BE SEEN ENABLING FUSE TO BE EASILY CHECKED**

**Fig. 14.18**
Fuses

## Fuses

A fuse is a deliberate weak link in a circuit. It consists of a piece of wire generally enclosed in a ceramic case. If the current exceeds the rated value of the fuse, the wire melts and breaks the circuit. An increase in current is normally caused by a fault which could lead to a fire or damage to an appliance. Fuses are available with different ratings, e.g. 6A, 10A, 16A.

A fuse does not prevent a person getting an electric shock; the normal current in a household circuit could kill. A fuse of the correct rating should always be fitted and should never be replaced with a piece of ordinary wire or tinfoil.

Fuses and switches must be fitted in the 'live' side of a circuit. If fitted in the neutral side, lights and sockets would be 'live' even with switches turned off or fuses 'blown'.

## Circuit Breakers

Circuit breakers are now used, instead of fuses, in household circuits. They switch off when there is a fault and can be switched on again when the fault is repaired.

**Fig. 14.19**
Circuit breaker

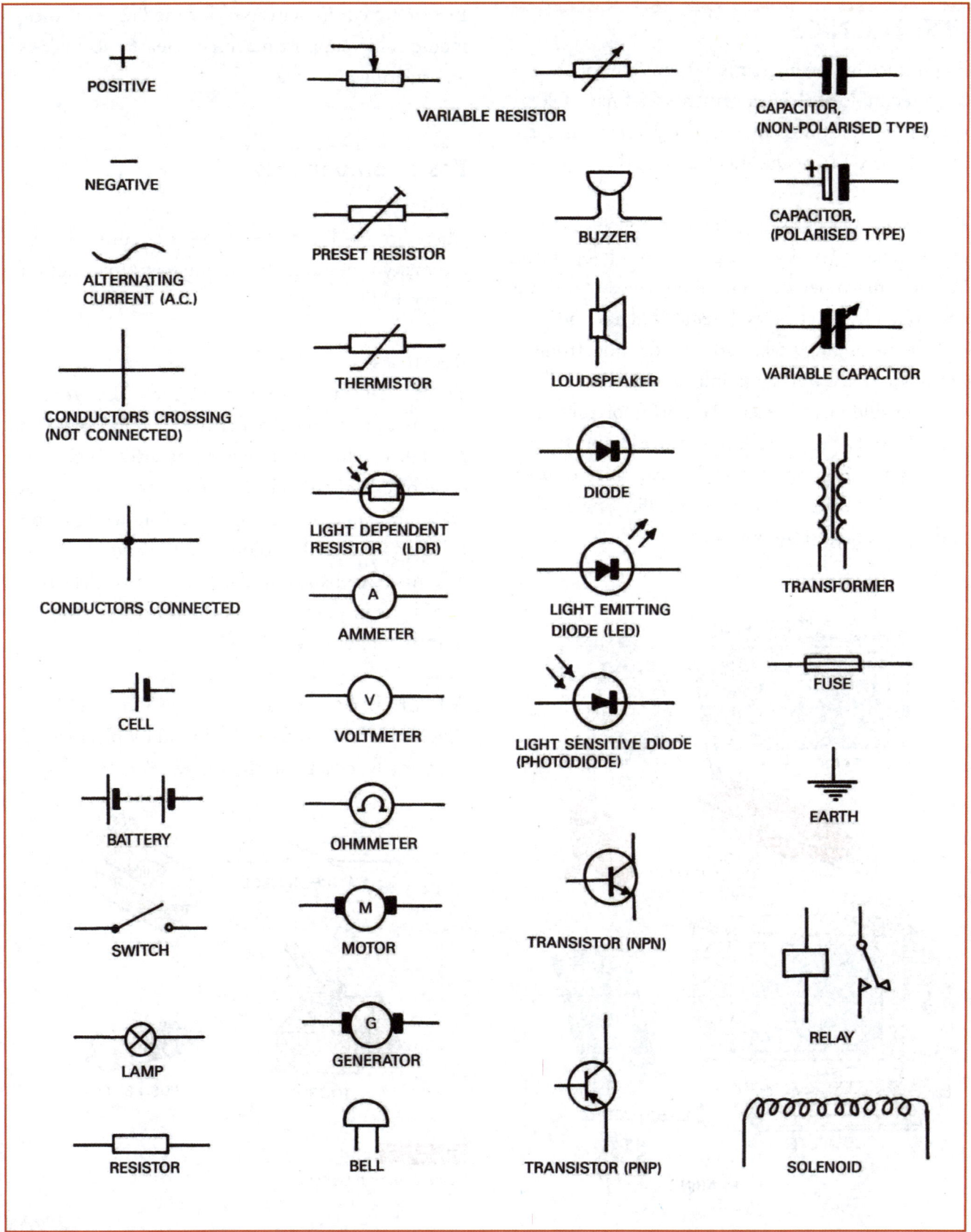

POSITIVE

NEGATIVE

ALTERNATING
CURRENT (A.C.)

CONDUCTORS CROSSING
(NOT CONNECTED)

CONDUCTORS CONNECTED

CELL

BATTERY

SWITCH

LAMP

RESISTOR

VARIABLE RESISTOR

PRESET RESISTOR

THERMISTOR

LIGHT DEPENDENT
RESISTOR    (LDR)

AMMETER

VOLTMETER

OHMMETER

MOTOR

GENERATOR

BELL

BUZZER

LOUDSPEAKER

DIODE

LIGHT EMITTING
DIODE (LED)

LIGHT SENSITIVE DIODE
(PHOTODIODE)

TRANSISTOR (NPN)

TRANSISTOR (PNP)

CAPACITOR,
(NON-POLARISED TYPE)

CAPACITOR,
(POLARISED TYPE)

VARIABLE CAPACITOR

TRANSFORMER

FUSE

EARTH

RELAY

SOLENOID

Fig. 14.20

Electric and electronic symbols

183

# ELECTRONICS

Electronics has been greatly responsible for the huge technological advancements that have taken place in recent times. Indeed, the present time is often referred to as the 'electronic age'.

Electronic devices used in the home include radios, dvds, televisions, cd players and telephones. Washing machines and central heating systems are controlled by electronics. Digital watches and calculators are now taken for granted. Electronics has made space travel possible and aviation safer. It has enabled us to receive television pictures, not alone from the other side of the world, but from outer space. Computers have a great range of uses from storing information to controlling machines and connecting to the Internet.

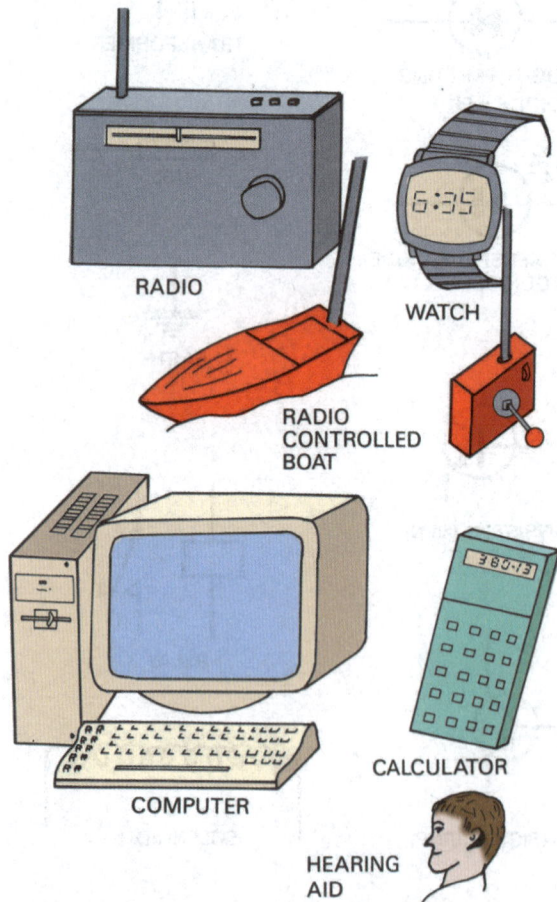

RADIO

WATCH

RADIO CONTROLLED BOAT

COMPUTER

CALCULATOR

HEARING AID

**Fig. 14.21**
Applications of electronics

Electronic equipment used for medical purposes includes life-support machines, heart pacemakers and hearing aids.

## Basic Components
### Switches
These are used to make or break circuits. There are many types available. Some common ones are shown in Fig. 14.22.

### Resistors
These reduce the current in circuits. The greater their resistance, the smaller the current flow. Their resistance values are indicated by either a colour code or a printed code. In the printed code, letters and numbers indicate the value. A range of colour bands is used in the colour code to give the value. The first two bands on the resistor give the first two digits in the value and the third gives the number of zeros which follow.

A fourth band gives the tolerance and is gold or silver. The first band can be found by placing the gold or silver band on the right.

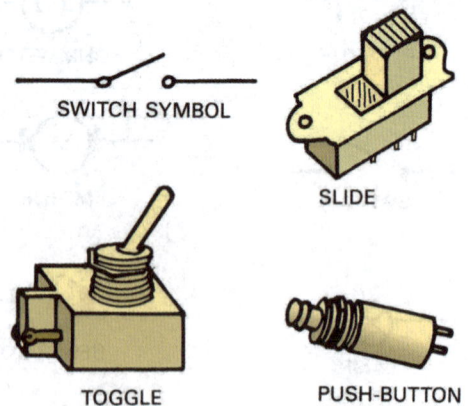

SWITCH SYMBOL

SLIDE

TOGGLE

PUSH-BUTTON

**Fig. 14.22**
Some common switches

**RESISTOR SYMBOL**

1ST DIGIT
2ND DIGIT

TOLERANCE
NUMBER OF O'S

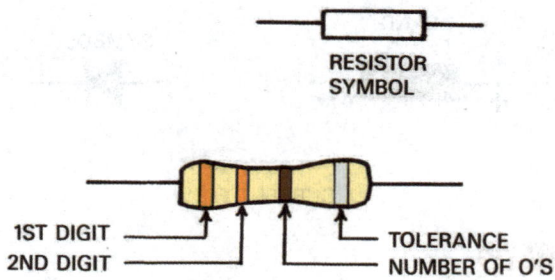

| COLOUR | NUMBER |
|--------|--------|
| BLACK | 0 |
| BROWN | 1 |
| RED | 2 |
| ORANGE | 3 |
| YELLOW | 4 |
| GREEN | 5 |
| BLUE | 6 |
| VIOLET | 7 |
| GREY | 8 |
| WHITE | 9 |

**Fig. 14.23**
Resistors

**Example 1**

GREEN 5
BLUE 6
BROWN 1

i.e. 560$\Omega$

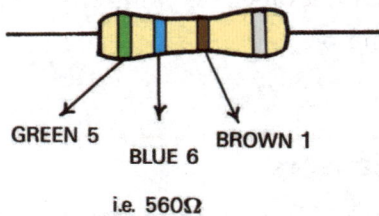

**Example 2**    First three colour bands: red, red and orange. Red = 2, orange = 3.
Value = 22,000 $\Omega$.

This can be written as 22 k$\Omega$ (1000$\Omega$ = 1K$\Omega$).

## Variable Resistors

The resistance between the centre terminal and the end terminals of a variable resistor can be changed by turning the spindle. It can be set at any resistance between zero and the value marked on its case. The preset type, Fig. 14.24 B, is small and can be adjusted with a small screwdriver. Only two of the three terminals are used. A variable resistor can be used as a potentiometer (see page 190). For this all three terminals are used.

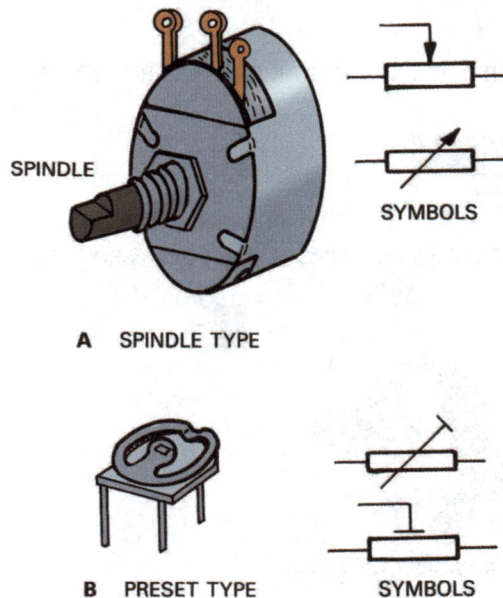

SPINDLE

SYMBOLS

**A    SPINDLE TYPE**

**B    PRESET TYPE**          SYMBOLS

**Fig. 14.24**
Variable resistors (or potentiometers)

## Capacitors

Capacitors store electric charge. Their 'capacitance' or charge-storing ability is measured in microfarads or μF. This is sometimes marked on capacitors as 'mfd'. Another value of importance that is often marked on capacitors is their 'working voltage'. This is the maximum voltage they can withstand.

Non-polarised types can be connected either way in a circuit. Polarised types must be connected the right way round, i.e. their positive terminal must be connected to the positive side of the circuit. Variable capacitors, Fig. 14.25, are used for tuning radios.

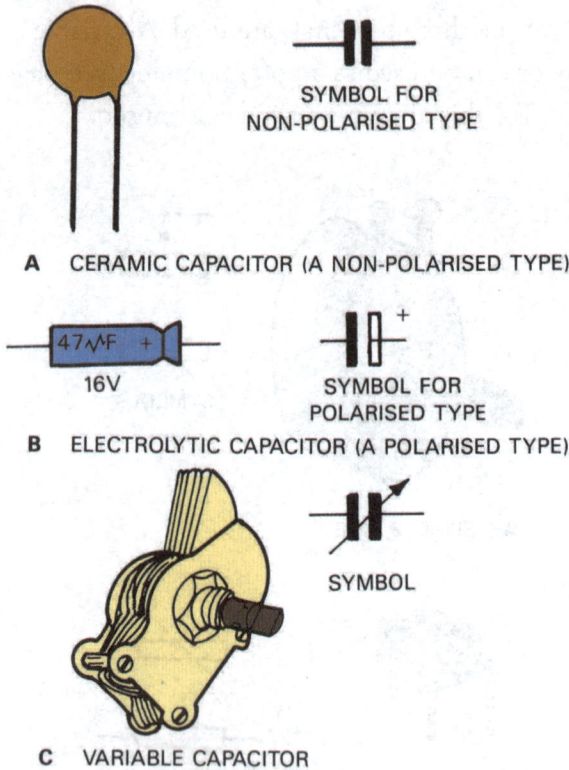

**A** CERAMIC CAPACITOR (A NON-POLARISED TYPE)

SYMBOL FOR NON-POLARISED TYPE

**B** ELECTROLYTIC CAPACITOR (A POLARISED TYPE)

SYMBOL FOR POLARISED TYPE

**C** VARIABLE CAPACITOR

SYMBOL

Capacitors

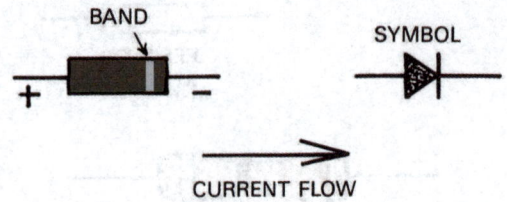

BAND

SYMBOL

CURRENT FLOW

**Fig. 14.26**
Diode

## Diodes

The purpose of a diode is to allow current to flow in one direction only. It is often used to protect other components in a circuit. A coloured band, or tapered end, on the diode and the arrow of its symbol indicate the direction of current flow.

## Electronic Systems

Electronic systems are made up of three main parts — input, process and output. A system can, therefore, be represented by a block diagram as shown in Fig. 14.27.

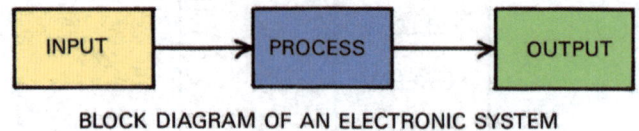

INPUT → PROCESS → OUTPUT

BLOCK DIAGRAM OF AN ELECTRONIC SYSTEM

**Fig. 14.27**

**Input Sensors** respond to changes in their surroundings. They include temperature sensors, light sensors and moisture sensors.

**Process Units** react to changes in input sensors and then operate output devices accordingly.

**Output Devices** include bulbs, bells, buzzers and electric motors.

## Input Sensors

**Thermistors** These are temperature dependent sensors. They are really resistors whose resistance changes when their temperature changes. The most common types are those whose resistance decreases as their temperature increases.

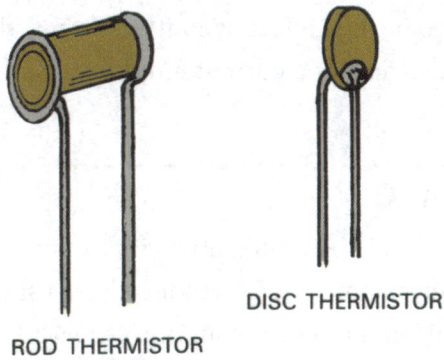

**ROD THERMISTOR**

**DISC THERMISTOR**

**Fig. 14.28**

**Light Dependent Resistors (LDRs)** The resistance of an LDR drops as the light falling on it increases. It has a high resistance in the dark and a low resistance in daylight.

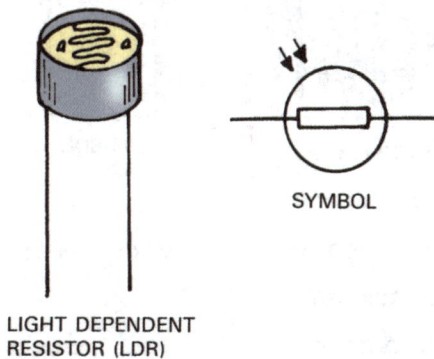

SYMBOL

**LIGHT DEPENDENT RESISTOR (LDR)**

**Fig. 14.29**

**Moisture Sensors** These can easily be made up. Water is an electrical conductor so it can be used to complete a circuit. Bared cables or a small printed circuit board can be used, see Fig. 14.30.

## Process Units

**Transistors** These small devices have revolutionised electronics. They are used as high-speed switches and as current, voltage and power amplifiers. Two types, n – p – n and p – n – p, are shown in Fig. 14.31. They have three terminals: **collector c, base b** and **emitter e**. They must be connected the right way round in a circuit.

On the n – p – n transistor shown in Fig. 14.31 A, the emitter terminal is the one nearest the tag and the collector is the one connected to the metal case.

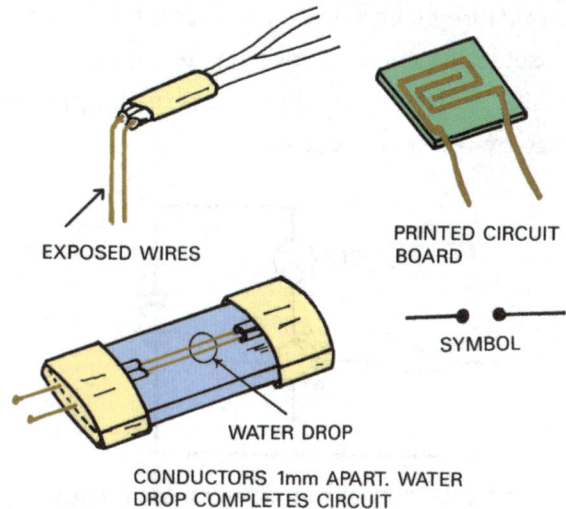

**EXPOSED WIRES**

**PRINTED CIRCUIT BOARD**

SYMBOL

**WATER DROP**

**CONDUCTORS 1mm APART. WATER DROP COMPLETES CIRCUIT**

**Fig. 14.30**
Moisture sensors

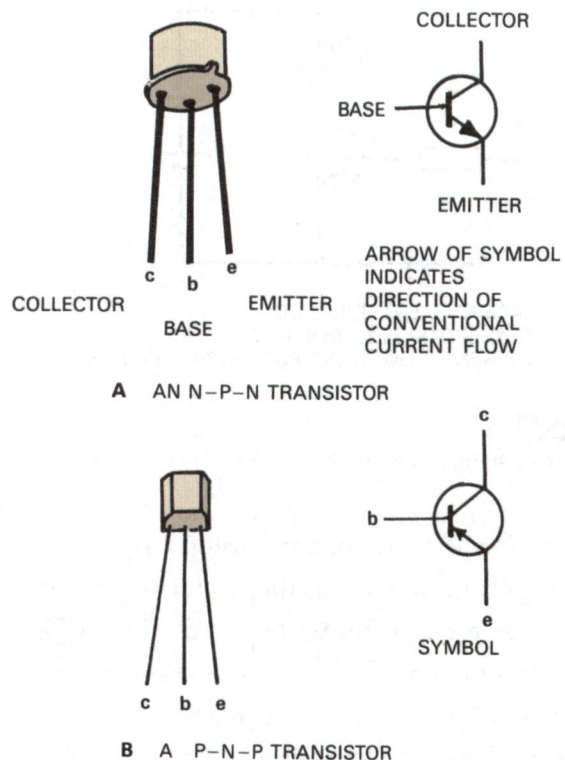

COLLECTOR

BASE

EMITTER

ARROW OF SYMBOL INDICATES DIRECTION OF CONVENTIONAL CURRENT FLOW

COLLECTOR

BASE

EMITTER

c  b  e

**A   AN N–P–N TRANSISTOR**

c

b

e

SYMBOL

c  b  e

**B   A  P–N–P TRANSISTOR**

**Fig. 14.31**
Transistors

For n – p – n types, the collector and base must be positive with respect to the emitter.

For p – n – p types, they must be negative.

Care must be taken not to overheat a transistor when soldering connections to its terminals. A resistor is often connected to its base to prevent damage by too high a current.

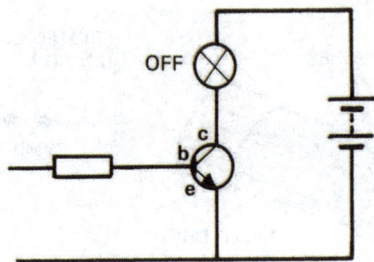

**A**  NO BASE CURRENT. TRANSISTOR RESISTANCE HIGH. LAMP OFF.

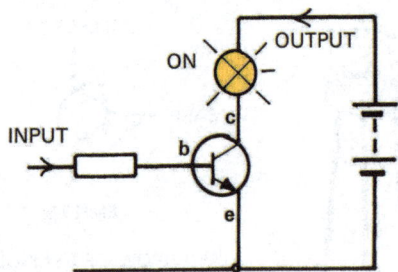

**B**  BASE CURRENT SUPPLIED. TRANSISTOR RESISTANCE LOW. CURRENT FLOW IN OUTPUT CIRCUIT. LAMP ON.

**Fig. 14.32**

Transistor operating as a switch

When acting as a switch, a transistor turns 'on' and 'off' the current flowing in the circuit connected to the collector and emitter terminals, Fig. 14.32. If no current enters the base, the resistance across the collector/emitter is very high and practically no current flows; the transistor is 'off' [Fig. 14.32 A]. If a voltage of about 0.6V (for a silicon transistor) is applied to the base/emitter, a current enters the base and the resistance across the collector/emitter becomes low and current can now flow; the transistor is 'on' [Fig. 14.32 B].

Since a small change in the base current causes a large change in the collector/emitter circuit, the transistor also acts as a current amplifier.

## 555 Timer IC

**Integrated circuit**  An integrated circuit is a miniature electronic circuit produced on a small 'chip' of silicon, no more than 5mm square. It contains transistors and usually diodes, resistors and capacitors. The chip is enclosed in a plastic or ceramic case and connected to pins in the side of the case. These pins are used to connect it into a circuit. An integrated circuit is commonly known as a 'chip' or an IC.

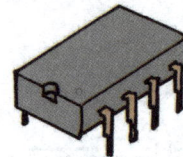
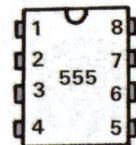

555 TIMER IC                SYMBOL

PINS

1  0V (CONNECTED TO –VE OF SUPPLY)

2  TRIGGER

3  OUTPUT

4  RESET

5  CONTROL

6  THRESHOLD

7  DISCHARGE

8  VC (CONNECTED TO +VE OF SUPPLY)

**Fig. 14.33**

An eight-pin 555 chip is shown in Fig. 14.33. The pins are numbered one to eight. They are not marked on the case but are arranged as shown on the symbol.

The 555 timer can be used in either of two ways — monostable or astable. A monostable circuit has one stable state. It can be used to switch an output, e.g. a LED, 'on' or 'off' for a fixed length of time. An astable circuit has no stable state. It can be used to switch an output 'on' and 'off' continuously, e.g. to make lights come on and off at definite intervals. The intervals depend on the values of resistors and capacitors used in conjunction with the chip.

## Output Devices

**Bulbs**  Bulbs produce light and heat when a current passes through their filament, i.e. they convert electrical energy into light and heat energy. They can be connected either way round in circuits.

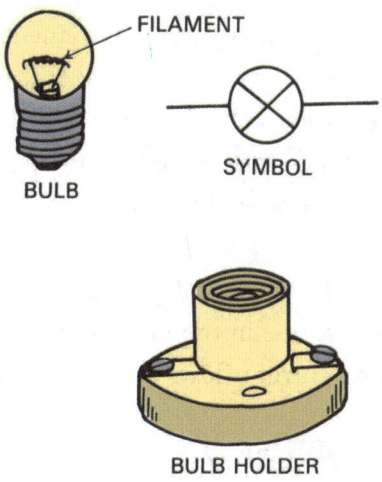

**Fig. 14.34**

**Electric Bells**  Electric bells make use of electromagnets to make the hammers strike the gongs in order to produce sound. They convert electrical energy into sound energy.

**Buzzers**  Buzzers give a continuous sound but not as loud as electric bells. They also convert electrical energy into sound energy.

**Loudspeakers**  These are used to produce continuous sounds, notes or speech. They too convert electrical energy into sound energy.

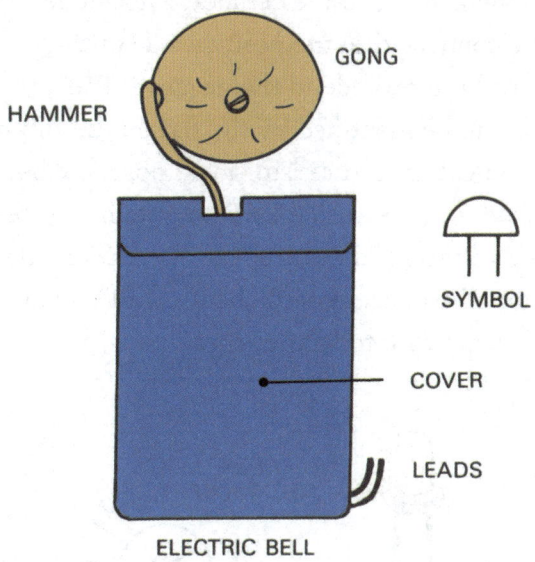

**Fig. 14.35**

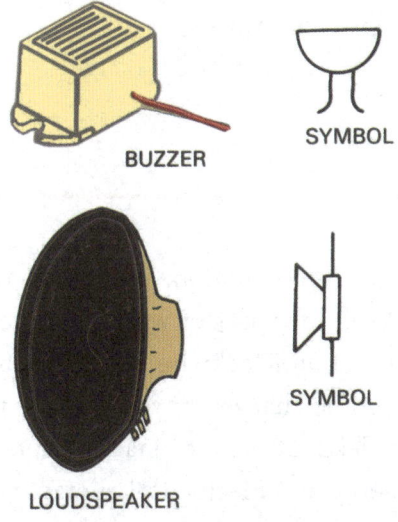

**Fig. 14.36**

## Light Emitting Diodes (LEDs)

LEDs produce light and are available in red, green and amber colours. They are often used to indicate that a circuit is functioning. LEDs give off very little heat, use far less power than a bulb, have a long life and are relatively cheap. Like all diodes, a current can only pass through them in one direction; they must, therefore, be connected the right way round in a circuit. The diode has two leads – the anode and the cathode. The anode must be connected to the positive side of the circuit and the cathode to the negative. The cathode can be identified by the flat on the rim of the LED next to it. A resistor must normally be connected in series with a LED to obtain a correct working voltage. If the current to the LED is too great, it will damage it permanently. LEDs convert electrical energy into light energy.

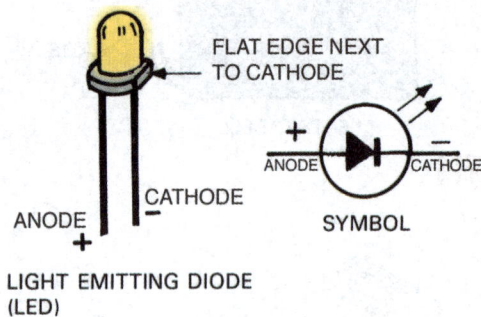

FLAT EDGE NEXT TO CATHODE

ANODE      CATHODE

SYMBOL

ANODE
+

CATHODE
−

LIGHT EMITTING DIODE (LED)

Fig. 14.37

## Motors

These produce rotary motion, and low voltage d.c. motors are useful for project work. They can be run clockwise or anticlockwise and their direction of rotation can be changed by altering the positive and negative leads at the terminals. Motors convert electrical energy into mechanical energy.

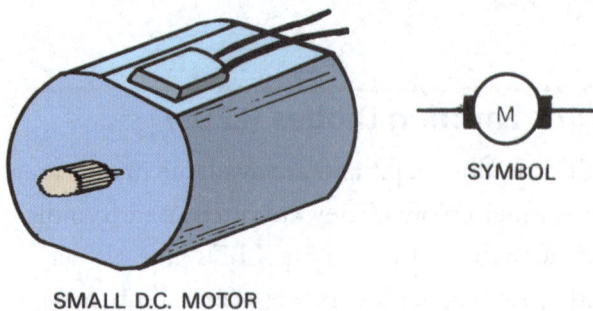

SYMBOL

SMALL D.C. MOTOR

Fig. 14.38

**Stepper Motors**  These are special motors whose movement can be controlled to a fraction of a revolution. They are driven by electrical pulses. It would take 36 pulses to turn a 36 step motor one revolution (10° per step). They are used where controlled movement is required, e.g. the movement of cutting tools on CNC lathes. They are operated by driver circuits or computers.

## Designing Circuits

**Potential Dividers**  These are used to divide supply voltages in order to obtain voltages of desired values.

If two resistors of equal value are connected in series to an input of, for example, 6V [Fig. 14.39 A], there will be a total voltage drop of 6V across the two resistors. Since they are equal, the voltage drop across each one will be 3V.

If unequal resistors are used [Fig. 14.39 B], the voltage drops will be in the ratio of their values, since the same current flows through each.

Voltage drop across 2K resistor = 6 x $\frac{2}{3}$ = 4V.
Voltage drop across 1K resistor = 6 x $\frac{1}{3}$ = 2V.
The voltage drop between X and Y will be 2V.

A variable resistor can be used as a potential divider or potentiometer by using its three connections, see Fig. 14.40. The resistance between connections 1 and 2 represents one resistor and that between 2 and 3 represents the other. The ratio of the two resistances can be changed by turning the spindle of the potentiometer. Therefore, voltages from zero to V (supply voltage) can be obtained between X and Y.

A 6V
1KΩ 3V
1KΩ 3V

B 6V
2KΩ 4V
1KΩ 2V
X
Y

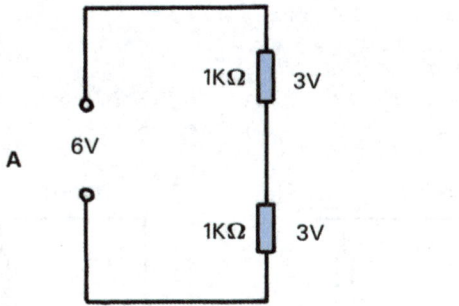

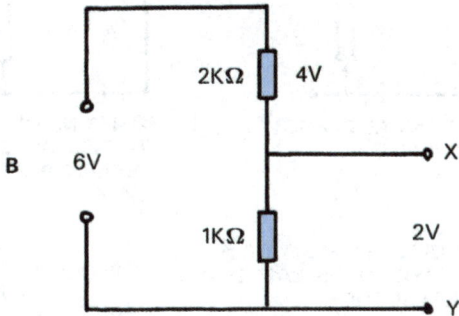

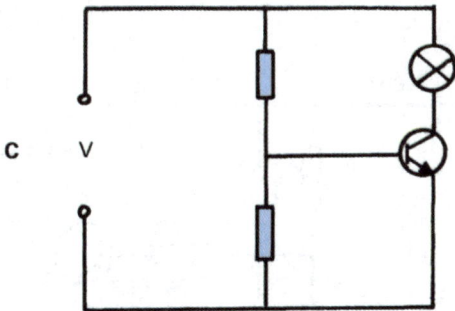

C V
POTENTIAL DIVIDER BEING USED TO
PROVIDE THE BASE VOLTAGE FOR A
TRANSISTOR

Fig. 14.39

POTENTIOMETER
1
2
V
X
3
Y

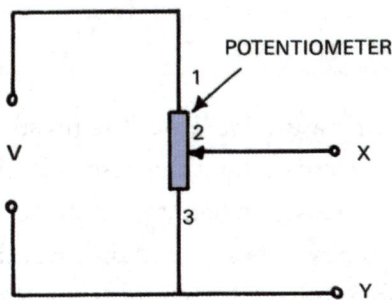

POTENTIOMETER BEING USED TO DIVIDE A
VOLTAGE

Fig. 14.40

Driving a current through another circuit 'loads' the potential divider and the output voltage becomes less than the calculated value. Therefore, to keep the difference small, the load resistance, RL in Fig. 14.41, should be at least ten times greater than that of the resistor ($R_2$) across which it is connected.

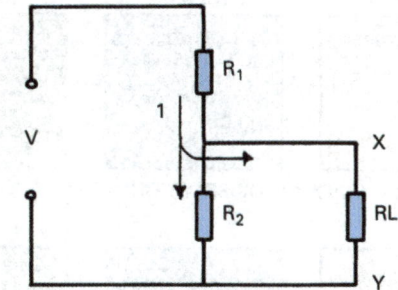

$R_1$ SHOULD BE AT LEAST TEN TIMES
THE VALUE OF $R_2$

Fig. 14.41

## Some Simple Circuits

As mentioned on page 186, we can use a block diagram to represent an electronic circuit.
The basic blocks are: **input, process** and **output**. We can, therefore, use a block diagram to design a circuit.

**Task** Design a circuit which will sound an alarm when conditions get hot.

**Input** We can use the thermistor and the variable resistor to form a potential divider for operating the transistor. We have to decide where to place each one.

We need the voltage to the transistor to increase as the temperature rises. If the resistance of $R_1$ [Fig. 14.42 E] falls, this will happen (the voltage drop across it will decrease).

191

The resistance of the thermistor decreases as the temperature increases. We must, therefore, use the thermistor as $R_1$. By using the variable resistor as $R_2$, we can vary the voltage drop across $R_1$ (by altering the ratio of the resistances).

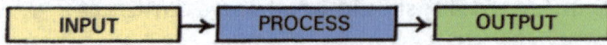

**A   BLOCK DIAGRAM OF ELECTRONIC CIRCUIT**

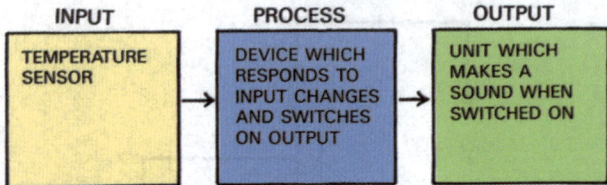

INPUT → PROCESS → OUTPUT

**B   BLOCK DIAGRAM OF SOLUTION**

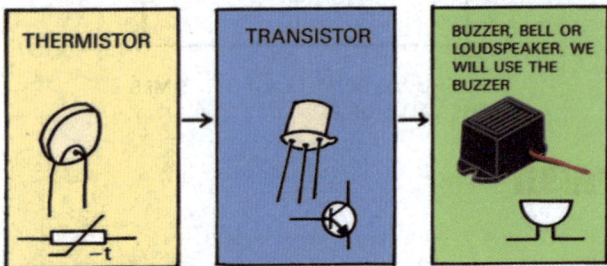

| INPUT | PROCESS | OUTPUT |
|---|---|---|
| TEMPERATURE SENSOR | DEVICE WHICH RESPONDS TO INPUT CHANGES AND SWITCHES ON OUTPUT | UNIT WHICH MAKES A SOUND WHEN SWITCHED ON |

**C   SELECTING COMPONENTS**

| THERMISTOR | TRANSISTOR | BUZZER, BELL OR LOUDSPEAKER. WE WILL USE THE BUZZER |
|---|---|---|

GENERAL COMPONENTS NEEDED

1   A BATTERY TO SUPPLY THE ENERGY

2   A RESISTOR TO PROTECT THE TRANSISTOR

3   A VARIABLE RESISTOR TO ENABLE THE ALARM TO BE SET FOR DIFFERENT TEMPERATURES

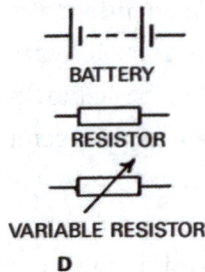

BATTERY

RESISTOR

VARIABLE RESISTOR

**D**

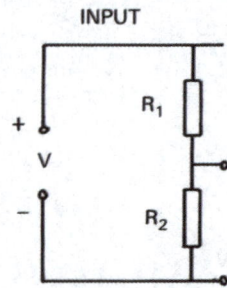

**E   POTENTIAL DIVIDER AS INPUT**

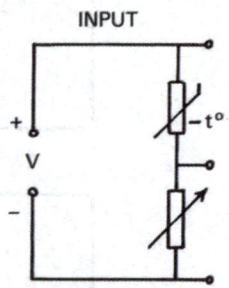

INPUT

$R_1$

$+$

$V$

$-$

$R_2$

**F   POSITIONS OF THERMISTOR AND VARIABLE RESISTOR IN INPUT**

INPUT

$+$

$V$

$-$

$-t°$

THE PROTECTIVE RESISTOR IS CONNECTED TO THE BASE LEAD OF THE TRANSISTOR

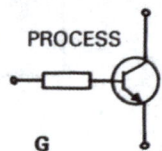

PROCESS

**G**

| INPUT | PROCESS | OUTPUT |
|---|---|---|

9V

$-t^{ol}$

2.2KΩ

2N3053 or BFY 51

0V

10KΩ

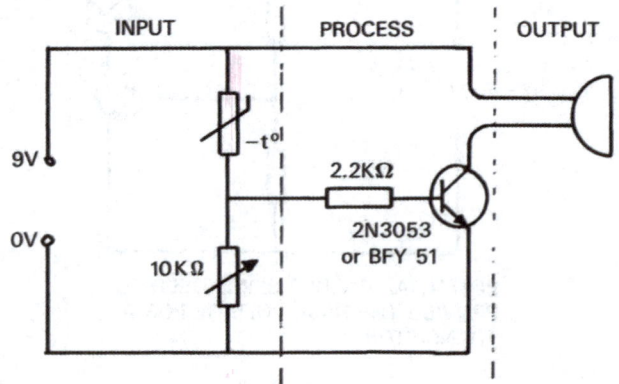

**H   COMPLETE CIRCUIT TO SWITCH ON A BUZZER WHEN CONDITIONS GET HOT**

Fig. 14.42

The circuit diagram can now be drawn by connecting the blocks, see Fig. 14.42 H.

**How it works** When conditions are cold, the resistance of the thermistor is much higher than that of the variable resistor. Therefore, the voltage drop across the variable resistor is low and the voltage to the transistor is also low.

As the temperature increases, the resistance of the thermistor decreases and the base voltage of the transistor increases. When it goes above 0.6V, the transistor switches on and operates the buzzer. The variable resistor enables us to set the temperature at which the buzzer comes on.

**Task** Design a circuit which will sound an alarm when conditions get cold.

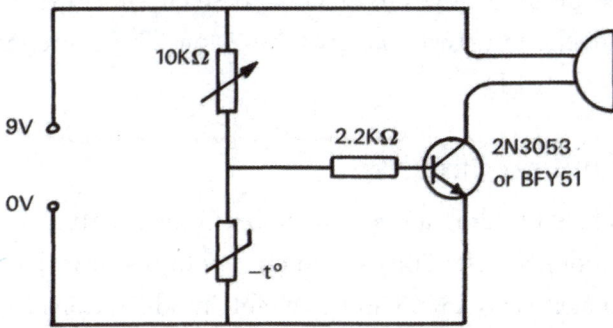

CIRCUIT TO SWITCH ON A BUZZER WHEN IT GETS COLD

Fig. 14.43

By changing the positions of the thermistor and the variable resistor in Fig. 14.43, we have a circuit that will switch on an output when it gets cold. Can you explain why?

**Task** Design a circuit which switches on a light when it gets dark.

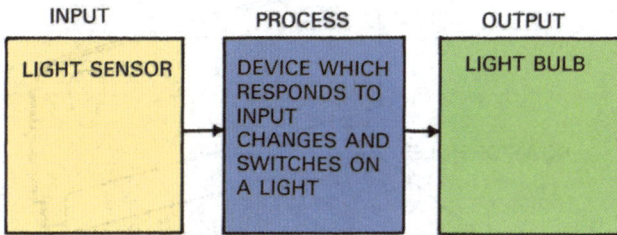

A   BLOCK DIAGRAM OF SOLUTION

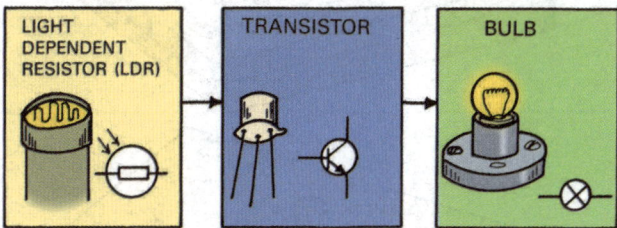

B   SELECTING COMPONENTS

**Input** We will again use a potential divider as the input. In this case, the resistance of the sensor, i.e. the LDR, increases as the light fades. We must, therefore, make it the bottom resistor in the potential divider, Fig.14.44 C.

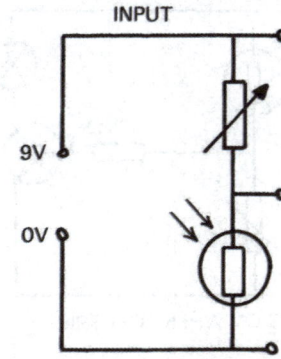

C   POSITIONS OF LDR AND VARIABLE RESISTOR IN INPUT

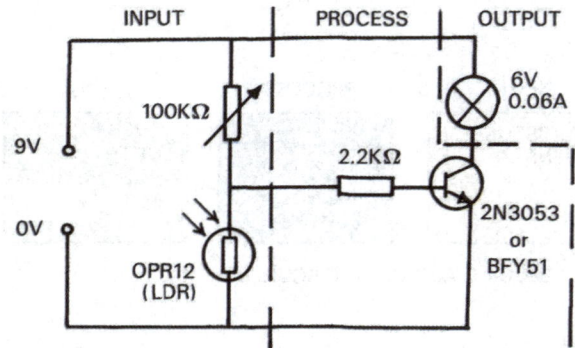

D   BULB COMES ON WHEN IT GETS DARK

Fig. 14.44

**How it works** As it gets dark the resistance of the LDR increases and the voltage drop across it also increases, thereby increasing the voltage to the transistor. When the voltage to the transistor goes above 0.6V, it switches on, thereby switching on the bulb. The variable resistor enables the transistor circuit to be set for different levels of darkness.

By changing the positions of the LDR and the variable resistance, we can reverse the action of the circuit as shown in Fig. 14.45. In this case, we need a variable resistor of a different value. The bulb will come 'on' when a light is shone on the LDR and it will go 'off' if the LDR is covered.

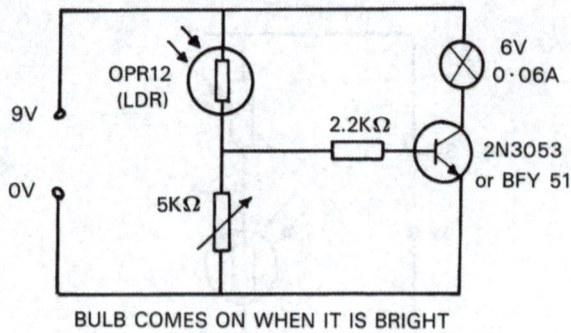

BULB COMES ON WHEN IT IS BRIGHT

**Fig. 14.45**

**Task** Design a rain alarm circuit. See Fig. 14.45 for solution.

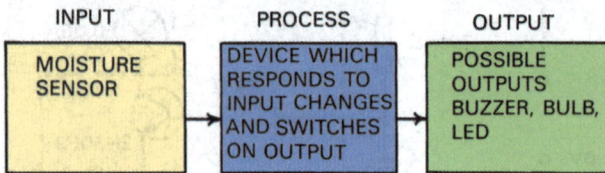

A    BLOCK DIAGRAM OF CIRCUIT

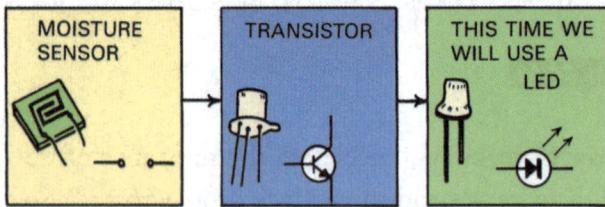

B    SELECTING COMPONENTS

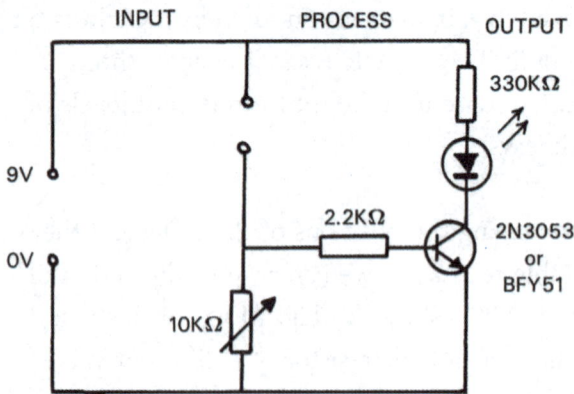

C    RAIN ALARM CIRCUIT

**Fig. 14.46**

**How it works** With the sensor dry there is no base current for the transistor. If a raindrop falls on the sensor and bridges its tracks, a base circuit flows into the transistor and switches it on. This switches on the LED.

## Building Circuits

Before building a permanent circuit, it is better to 'model' it first. This is a quick way to test if it does what it is meant to and to enable modifications to be made if necessary.

Different types of modelling boards are used, e.g. S —DeC, Loctronics and Soft Board with screws and cup washers.

**S—DeC** This board is in two sections with seven rows of holes in each section. There are five holes in each row. There is a metal contact strip under each row of holes and this connects wires pushed into any of the holes in the row.

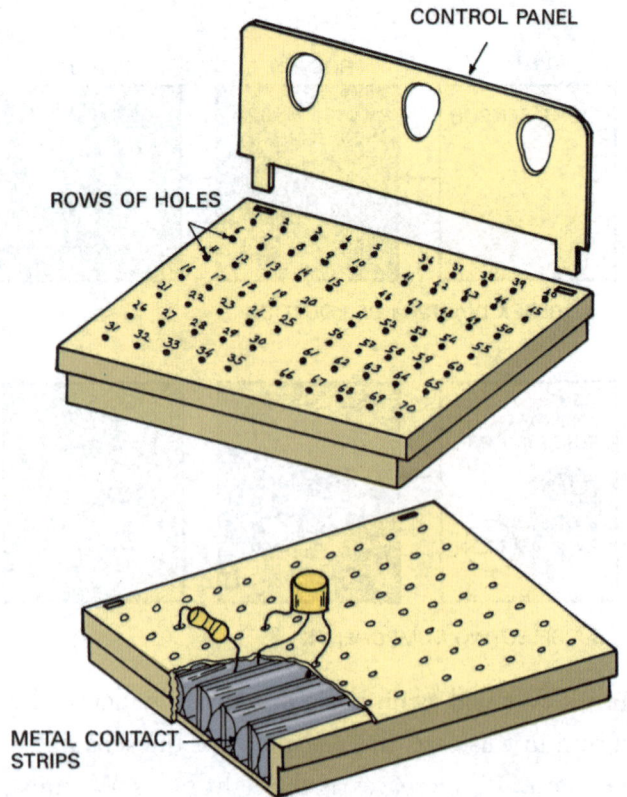

**Fig. 14.47**
S—DeC

**Loctronics**  Specially formed components and connecting links are used in this system. Circuits are built by plugging the components and links into sockets on a baseboard. The circuit layout is easily followed.

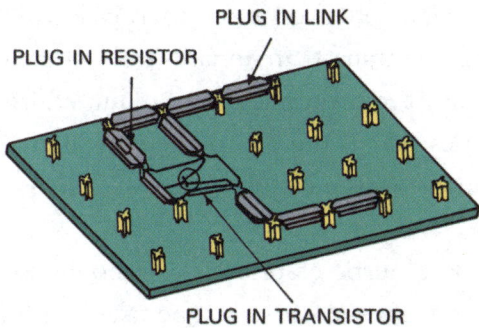

PLUG IN LINK
PLUG IN RESISTOR
PLUG IN TRANSISTOR

Loctronics system

**Soft Board**  Screws and cup washers are used to make the connections. The circuit is built on a piece of softwood.

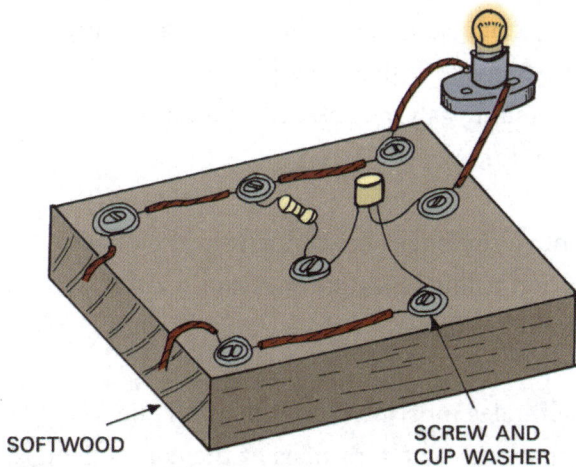

SOFTWOOD
SCREW AND CUP WASHER

Fig. 14.49
Soft board

**Permanent Circuits**  These have components soldered together. There are several types of boards used for this, e.g. matrix board, strip-board and printed circuit board (PCB).

**Matrix Board**  This is a plastic board with rows of holes. Circuits are built by pushing terminal pins into the holes and soldering the components on to them.

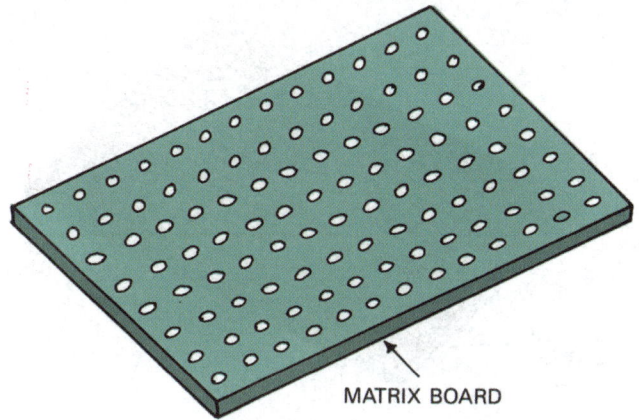

MATRIX BOARD

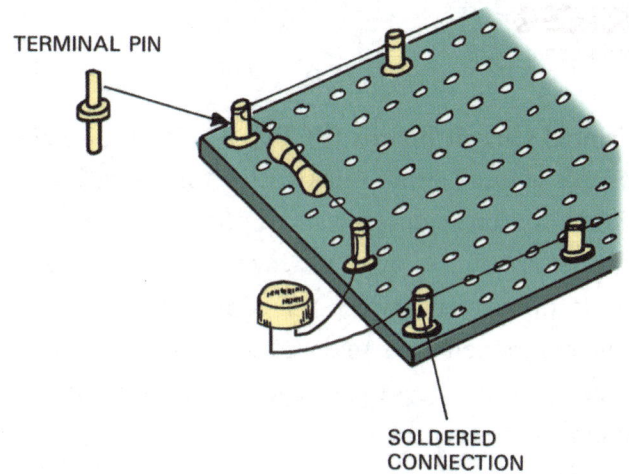

TERMINAL PIN
SOLDERED CONNECTION

Fig. 14.50
Matrix board

**Strip Board**  This is made up of pierced copper strips bonded to a baseboard. The strips form the connections between the components. The component terminals are pushed in from the far side and soldered to the strips.

A break can be made in a strip by enlarging a hole with a special hand tool until it comes through the edges.

Matrix boards and strip boards are useful for building permanent circuits if etching facilities are not available. However, the best type of permanent circuit is the printed circuit.

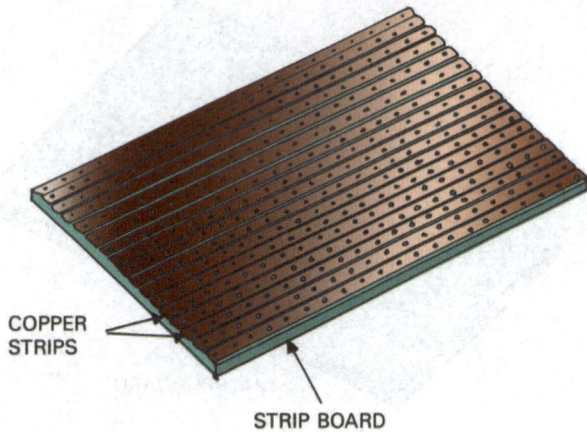

COPPER STRIPS

STRIP BOARD

**Fig. 14.51**
Strip board

**Printed Circuit Boards (PCBs)** These are plastic boards about 1.5mm thick with a thin layer of copper on one side. Unwanted portions of the copper are etched away to leave strips which form the connections between the components. The components are soldered to these strips, thereby connecting them together and attaching them to the board.

Before making a printed circuit, it must first be designed and its layout on the board planned.

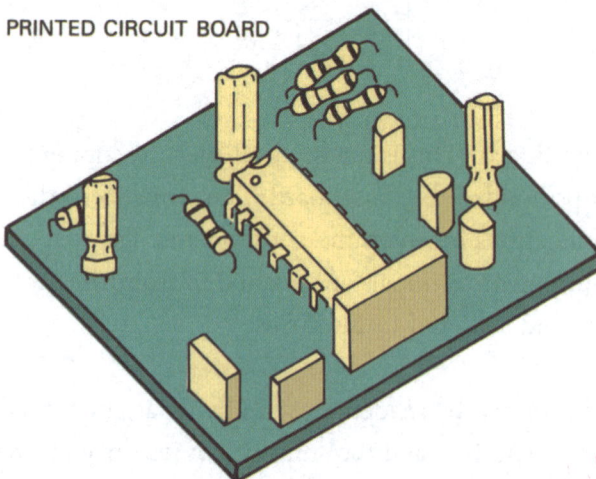

PRINTED CIRCUIT BOARD

**Fig. 14.52**

A rain alarm circuit is shown in Fig. 14.53 A. It is better to make a model first on a modelling board, Fig. 14.53 B.

Now draw the circuit on the copper side of the board using an etch resist pen or 'rub-down' transfers. The transfer material acts as an etch resist. Since the components are mounted from the plastics side of the board, the drawing will be a mirror image of the circuit layout.

A solution of ferric chloride is commonly used for the etching. Special care must be taken with ferric chloride as it is poisonous and corrosive — protect your eyes and skin.

The etching is best done in a bubble etch tank, Fig. 14.53 D. This heats and circulates the etching solution which greatly speeds up the etching. A tray can also be used, but great care must be taken to avoid spillage or splashing. The etching can take about 20 minutes depending on conditions.

Remove the board carefully from the etching solution using a plastic tongs and wash it thoroughly under a tap.

Small holes must now be drilled for the components. The terminals of the components are pushed in from the plastics side of the board and soldered to the strips.

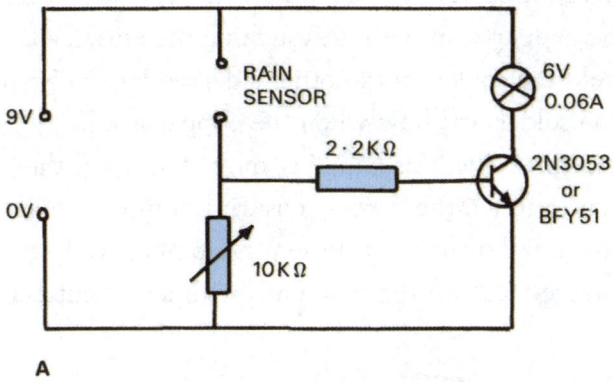

A

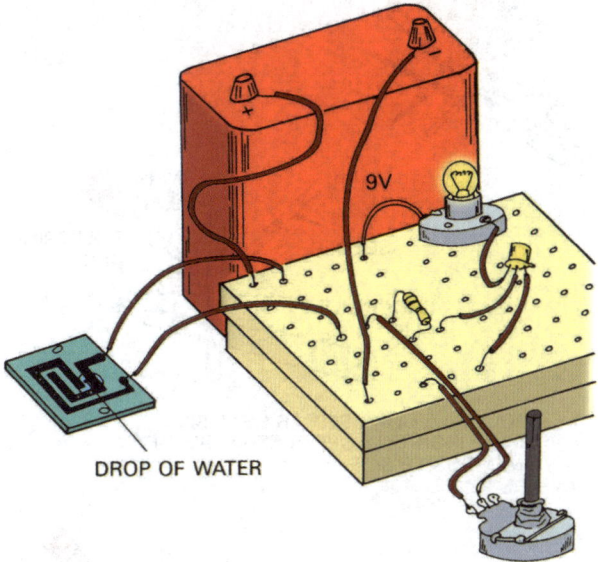

B  MODELLING A CIRCUIT ON AN S-DEC

DROP OF WATER

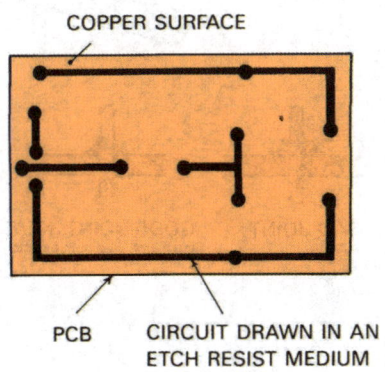

C

COPPER SURFACE

PCB

CIRCUIT DRAWN IN AN
ETCH RESIST MEDIUM

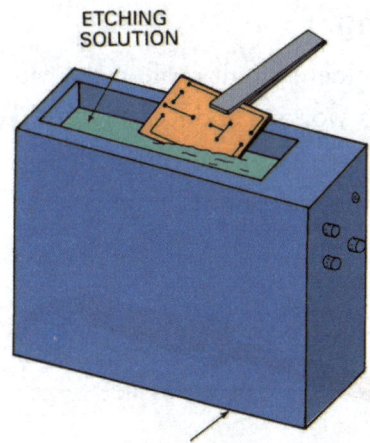

ETCHING
SOLUTION

D  BUBBLE ETCH TANK

E  WASHING THE BOARD

F  DRILLING HOLES FOR COMPONENTS

WOODEN BLOCK

**Fig. 14.53**
Making a PCB

## Soldering

A badly soldered joint is often the cause of a circuit not working and it is a fault that is difficult to trace. To ensure good connections and to avoid short circuits, care must be taken.

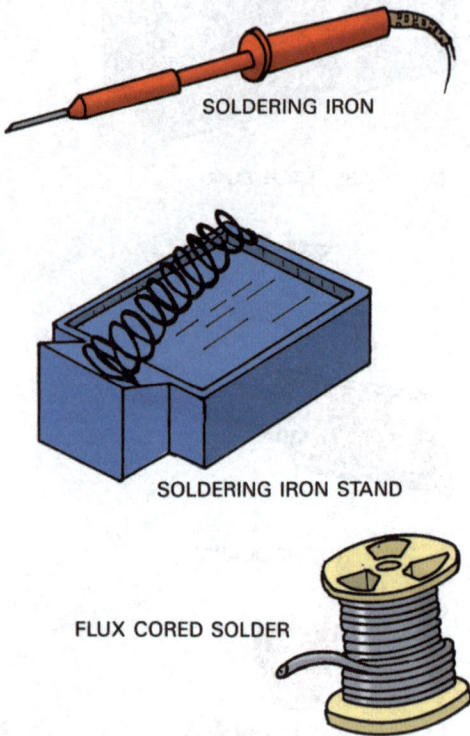

SOLDERING IRON

SOLDERING IRON STAND

FLUX CORED SOLDER

**Fig. 14.54**
Soldering equipment

A 15 watt soldering iron with 1.5mm tip is suitable for most applications. It should be kept in its stand when not in use to prevent damage to the lead or other equipment. Fluxed cored solder is used. The resin flux is non-corrosive.

Some components, such as transistors, diodes and LEDs, can be damaged by overheating. A crocodile clip or small pliers attached to the wire lead between the joint and the component acts as a heat sink, Fig. 14.55 A, by removing heat.

Heat the soldering iron and tin the tip. Place it on the copper strip without touching the wire lead. Hold the solder on the other side, see Fig. 14.55 B. The solder will flow when the copper is hot enough. When this happens, move the tip of the iron to touch the wire — ensuring complete solder flow around the joint. When the joints have been soldered, cut off the wire ends with a side cutters.

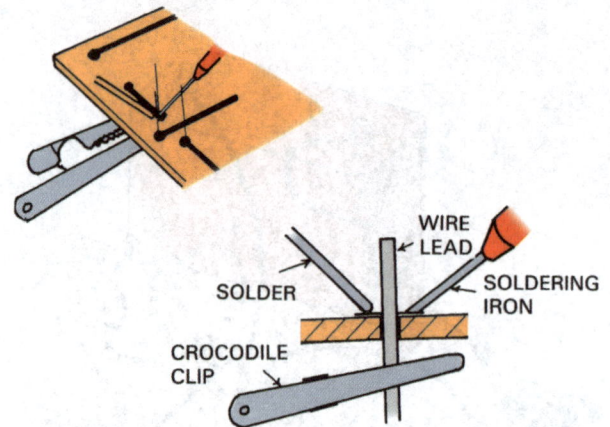

WIRE LEAD

SOLDER

SOLDERING IRON

CROCODILE CLIP

**A** CROCODILE CLIP USED AS HEAT SINK TIP OF IRON ON COPPER STRIP. SOLDER ON OPPOSITE SIDE.

**B** SOLDER MELTS WHEN COPPER IS HOT ENOUGH. THEN MOVE IRON TO TOUCH BOTH COPPER AND WIRE.

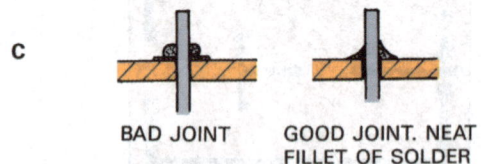

**C**

BAD JOINT

GOOD JOINT. NEAT FILLET OF SOLDER

**Fig. 14.55**
Soldering a PCB

# Case for Alarm

Having completed the soldering, a case must be made for the alarm. In designing the case, provision must be made for clear visibility of the signal light, size of components, securing components and accessibility of battery and bulb.

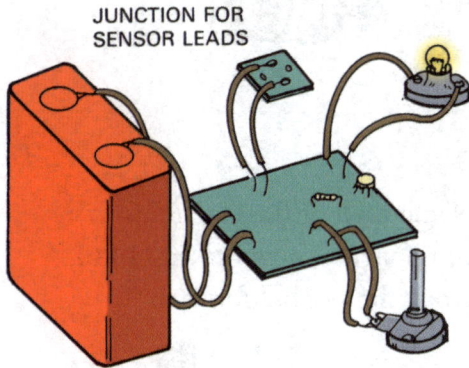

**Fig. 14.56**
Components soldered to PCB

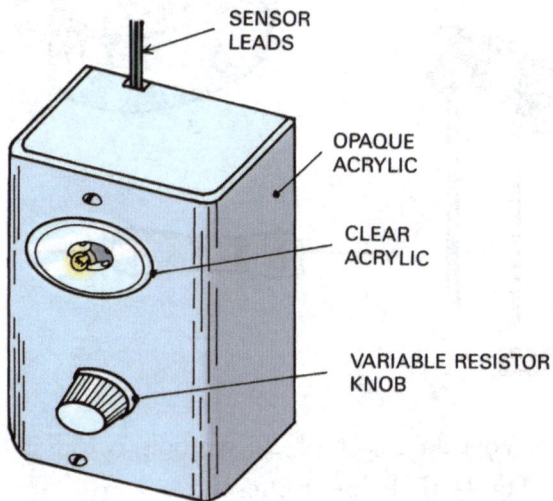

**Fig. 14.57**
An example of a case for the alarm

## Exercises

1. What is an electric current?
2. Name two types of power source used for school course work.
3. What is the name given to materials through which current can easily flow?
4. What are the electrical units of each of the following:
   (a) electromotive force (e.m.f.)
   (b) current
   (c) resistance
5. (a) State Ohm's Law.
   (b) Write Ohm's Law as a mathematical equation.
6. Name the instrument used to measure:
   (a) current
   (b) voltage
7. What is a multimeter?
8. What is a circuit diagram?
9. Name the components 1, 2 and 3 in Fig. 14.58 below.

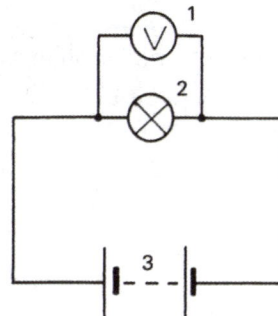

**Fig. 14.58**

10. A three-pin plug with its back removed is shown in Fig. 14.59 below.

Name the terminals 1, 2 and 3 and the components 4 and 5.

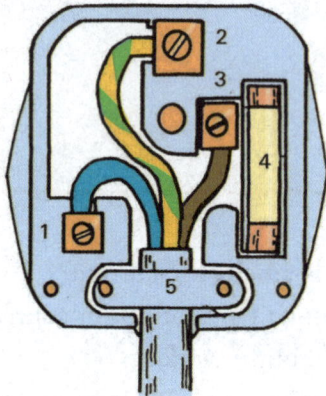

Fig. 14.59

11. What is the function of the 'earth' in an electric plug?

12. Why is tungsten used in the filament of electric bulbs?

13. Explain how a domestic light switch, Fig. 14.60 below, works.

Fig. 14.60

14. What is the function of a fuse in an electric circuit?

15. Name five electronic appliances.

16. Name each type of switch, A, B and C shown in Fig. 14.61 below.

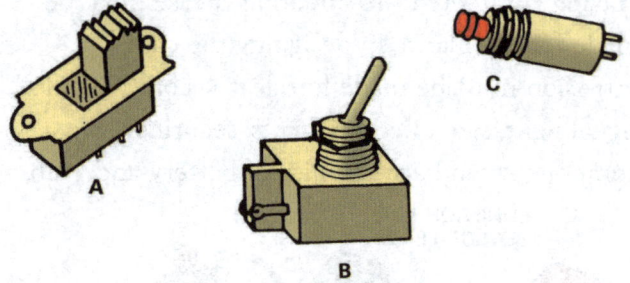

Fig. 14.61

17. (a) Name each of the electronic components shown in Fig. 14.62.
    (b) Draw the symbol for each.

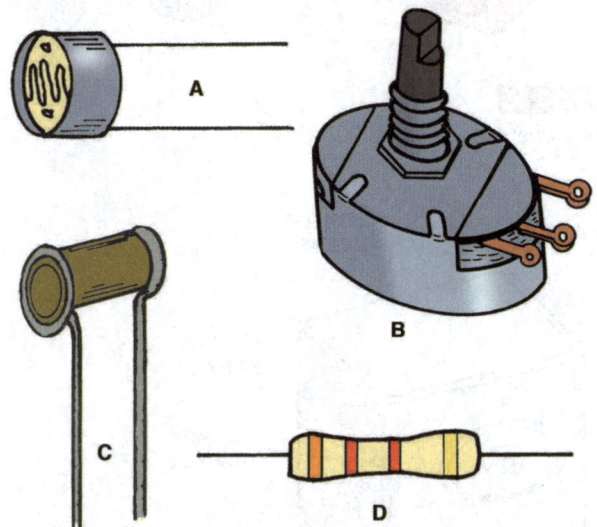

Fig. 14.62

18. What does each of the symbols, A to F in Fig. 14.63 below, represent?

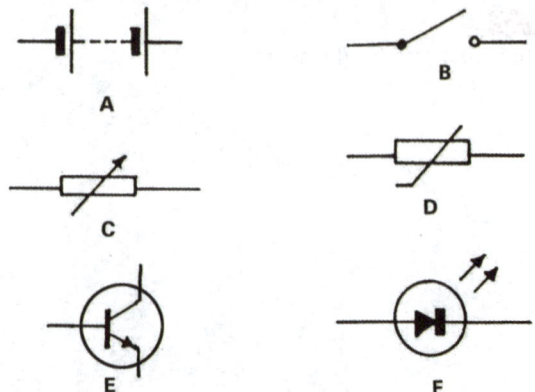

Fig. 14.63

19. Describe one method of indicating the values of resistors.

20. What is the value of each of the resistors colour-coded as follows:
    (a) brown, black, brown, gold?
    (b) red, red, red, gold?
    (c) yellow, violet, red, gold?

21. What is the function of each of the following in an electronic circuit:
    (a) a diode?
    (b) a thermistor?
    (c) a light dependent resistor (LDR)?

22. Give two uses for transistors in electronic circuits.

23. Name the component shown in Fig. 14.64 below.

 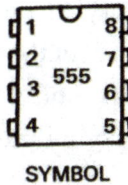

SYMBOL

24. Name four output devices used in electronics.

25. What is a stepper motor?

26. What is the function of a potential divider?

27. A circuit to switch on a buzzer when conditions get cold is shown in Fig. 14.65 below.
    (a) Name and identify by number the five electronic components shown.
    (b) Explain how the circuit works.

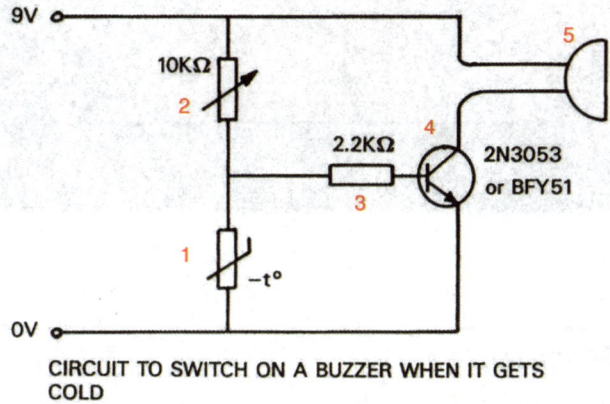

CIRCUIT TO SWITCH ON A BUZZER WHEN IT GETS COLD

28. Design a rain alarm circuit.

29. Give two examples of modelling boards used for electronic circuit designing.

30. What is a printed circuit board (PCB)?

31. What is the function of a heat sink when soldering electronic components?

# Structures and Mechanisms

# 15

## Mechanisms

A mechanism transfers an input motion and force into a desired output motion and force — it uses energy to do work. Levers, linkages, pulleys, gears, cams, screws and ratchets are basic mechanisms. Machines are made up of mechanisms and they also use energy to produce work. There is a great variety of machines, e.g. lathes, engines, hand drills, bicycles, lawn mowers, clocks and washing machines.

The operation of mechanisms involves forces and motion. There are four basic types of motion, i.e. linear, rotary, reciprocating and oscillating, Fig. 15.1. Construction kits such as 'Fischertechnik' and 'Meccano' are very useful for the investigation of mechanisms.

## Structures

Structures are used to carry loads. They must be designed so that they do not collapse under the loads. There is a great variety of structures, e.g. buildings, bridges, cranes, chairs, tables, trains and cars.

The types of force exerted by loads are compression, tension, bending, shear and torsion, Fig. 15.2. Loads are either 'static' or 'dynamic', e.g. a car stopped on a bridge subjects the bridge to a static load, but if it is moving it is a dynamic load.

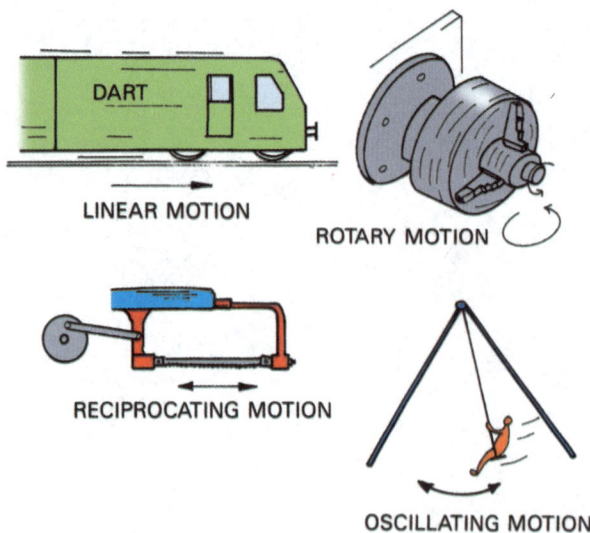

LINEAR MOTION

ROTARY MOTION

RECIPROCATING MOTION

OSCILLATING MOTION

**Fig. 15.1**

Types of motion

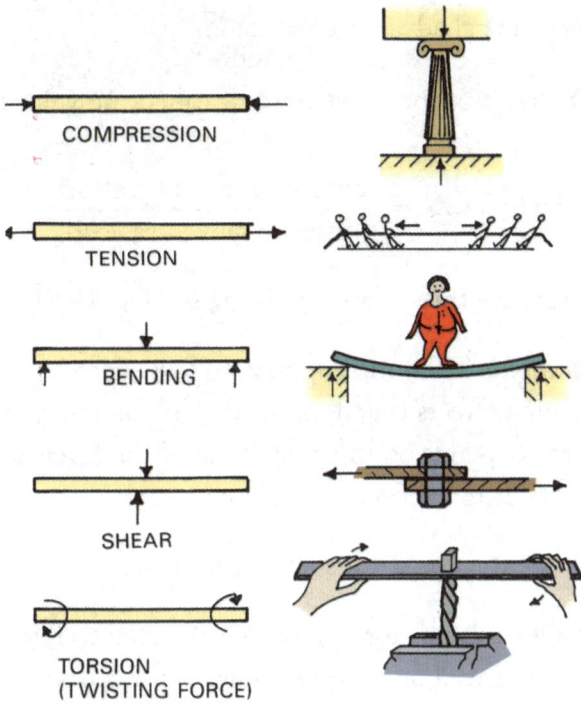

**Fig. 15.2**
Forces on structures

COMPRESSION

TENSION

BENDING

SHEAR

TORSION
(TWISTING FORCE)

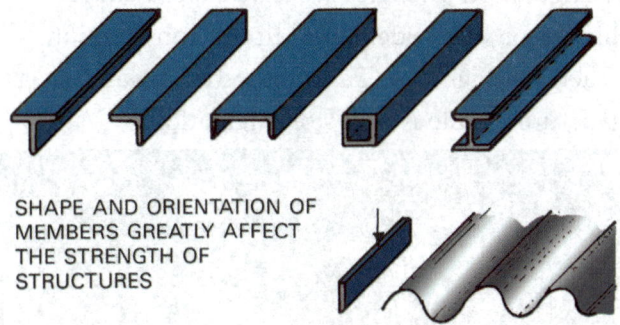

SHAPE AND ORIENTATION OF MEMBERS GREATLY AFFECT THE STRENGTH OF STRUCTURES

**Fig. 15.3**
Shapes of members

## Shape of Structure Members

The shape and orientation of members greatly affect the strength of structures, Fig. 15.3. Hollow sections can be both rigid and light. Depth and corrugation give good resistance to bending.

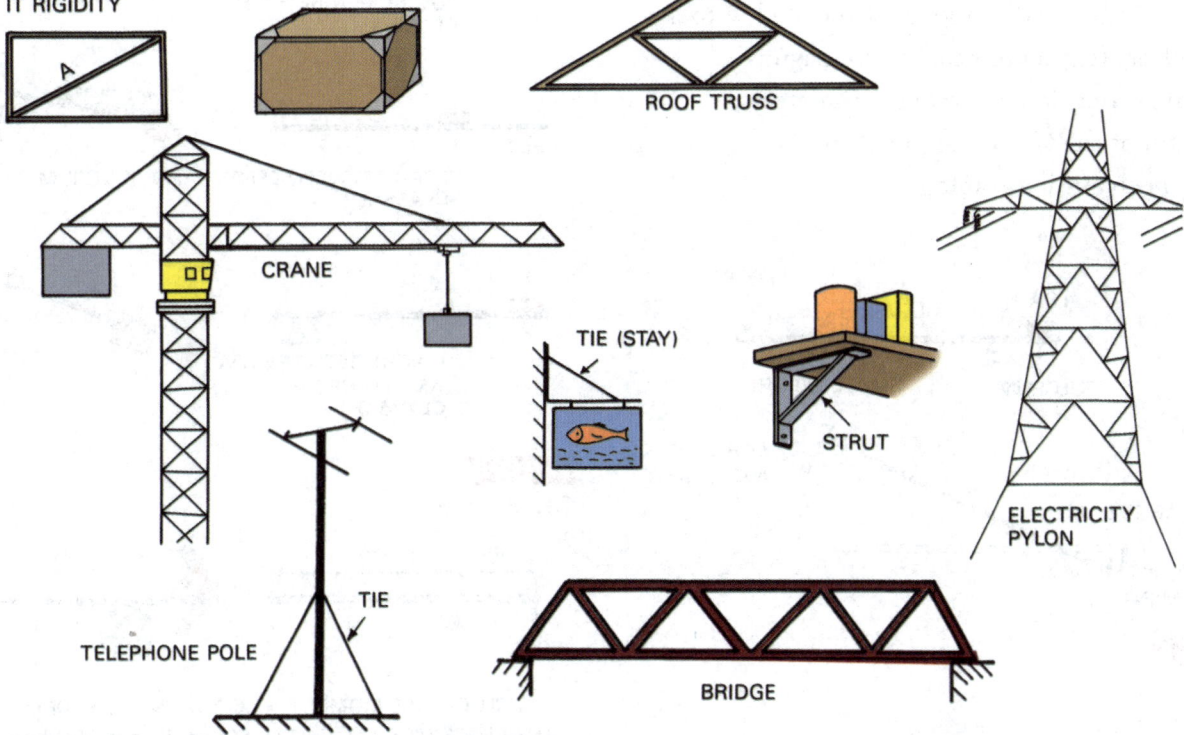

MEMBER 'A' MAKES TWO TRIANGLES OF THE STRUCTURE GIVING IT RIGIDITY

A

ROOF TRUSS

CRANE

TIE (STAY)

STRUT

ELECTRICITY PYLON

TELEPHONE POLE

TIE

BRIDGE

**Fig. 15.4**
Use of triangulation to give strength and rigidity

**Triangulation** Triangles are rigid shapes and, for this reason, are widely used in the construction of structures, Fig. 15.4. This method of making structures stable is called 'triangulation'.

Triangular shapes are widely used in the construction of structures

## Levers

A lever is basically a bar that can pivot about a fixed point called a **fulcrum**. The force used to move the lever about the fulcrum is called the **effort** and the output force is called the **load**. A lever can be used to move a large load with a small effort (e.g. a crowbar) or to magnify a movement (e.g. in an aneroid barometer). The ratio of the two forces, load and effort, is called **mechanical advantage**.

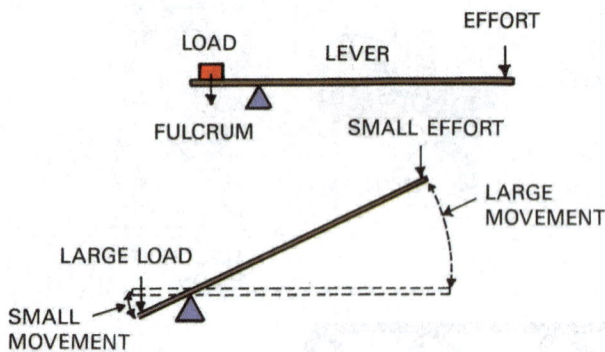

Fig. 15.5
A lever

$$\text{Mechanical advantage} = \frac{\text{load}}{\text{effort}}$$

The ratio of the movements is called the velocity ratio.

$$\text{Velocity ratio} = \frac{\text{distance moved by effort}}{\text{distance moved by load}}$$

There are three classes of lever, see Fig. 15.6.

**Moments** The forces applied to levers produce turning effects called moments. The moment of a force depends on the magnitude of the force and on its distance from the fulcrum.

Moment = force x distance from fulcrum.

If a lever is not turning while subjected to forces, it is balanced or in **equilibrium** — the clockwise moments equal the anticlockwise moments, see Fig. 15.7.

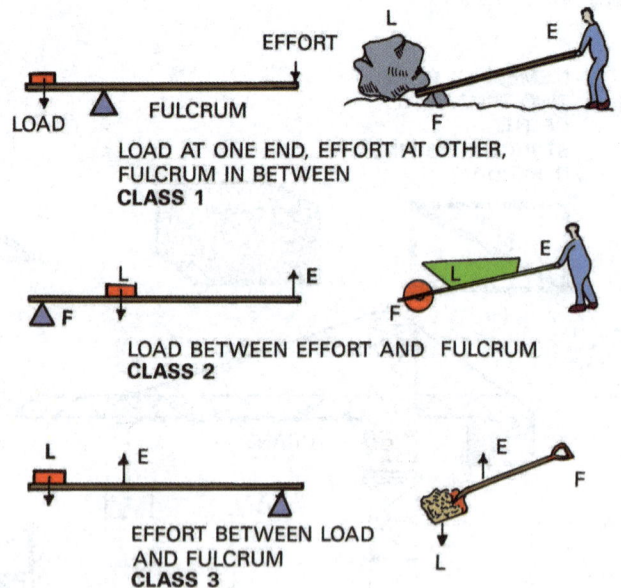

LOAD AT ONE END, EFFORT AT OTHER, FULCRUM IN BETWEEN
**CLASS 1**

LOAD BETWEEN EFFORT AND FULCRUM
**CLASS 2**

EFFORT BETWEEN LOAD AND FULCRUM
**CLASS 3**

**Fig. 15.6**
Classes of lever

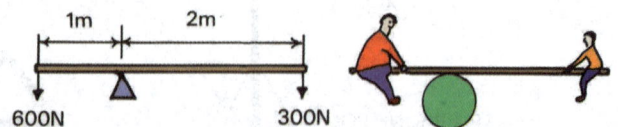

CLOCKWISE MOMENT = 300 × 2Nm = 600Nm
ANTICLOCKWISE MOMENT = 600 × 1Nm = 600Nm
CLOCKWISE MOMENT = ANTICLOCKWISE MOMENT
∴ LEVER IS IN EQUILIBRIUM

**Fig. 15.7**
Moments

REMOVING A CAN LID

CLAW HAMMER

SPANNER

HAND BRAKE

PLIERS

TWEEZERS

NUTCRACKER

EXCAVATOR ARM

TIPPER TRUCK

PINCH BAR

SNIPS

BICYCLE BRAKE LEVER

FOOT BRAKE

PNEUMATIC BRAKE RELEASE

SCALES

**Fig. 15.8**

Some common levers

**Exercise**

Study the levers in Fig. 15.8:

1.  Find the positions of the fulcrum, the load and the effort in each.
2.  Classify each lever.

# Linkages

A linkage is made up of levers. Linkages have a wide range of applications, e.g. to change the direction of an input force or motion, to produce a number of outputs from one input and to move objects parallel to one another.

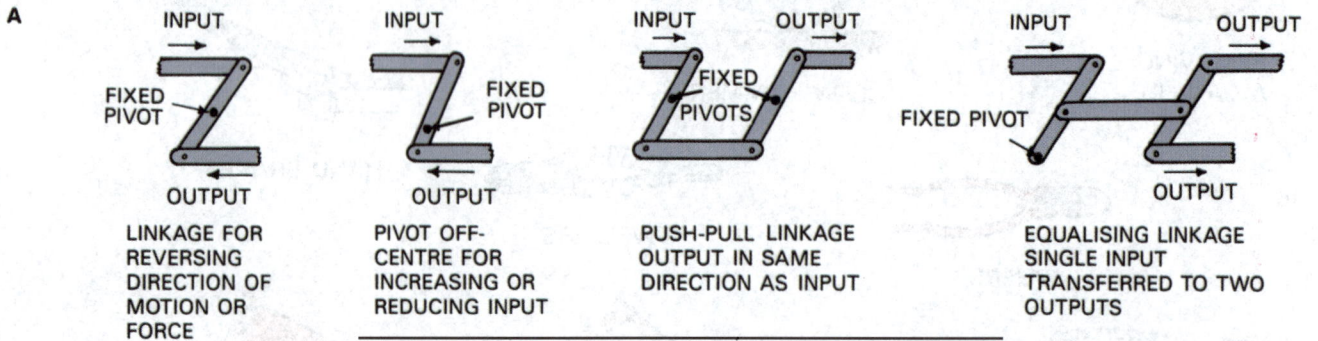

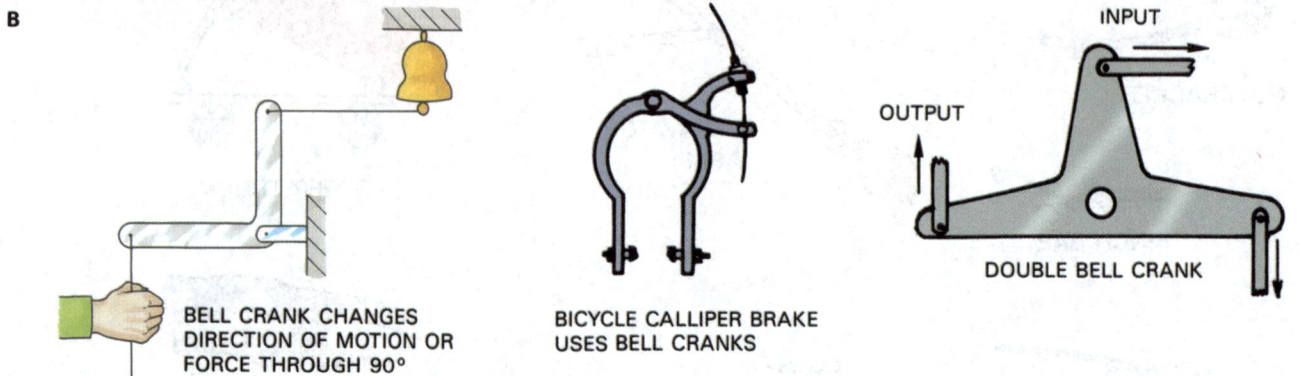

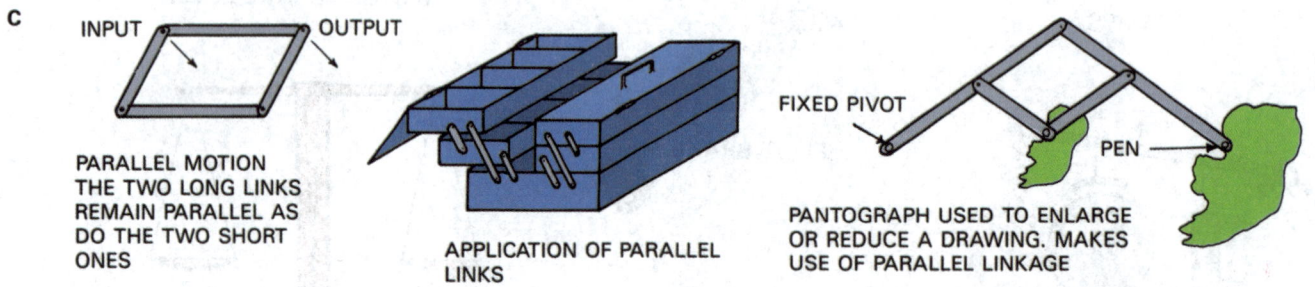

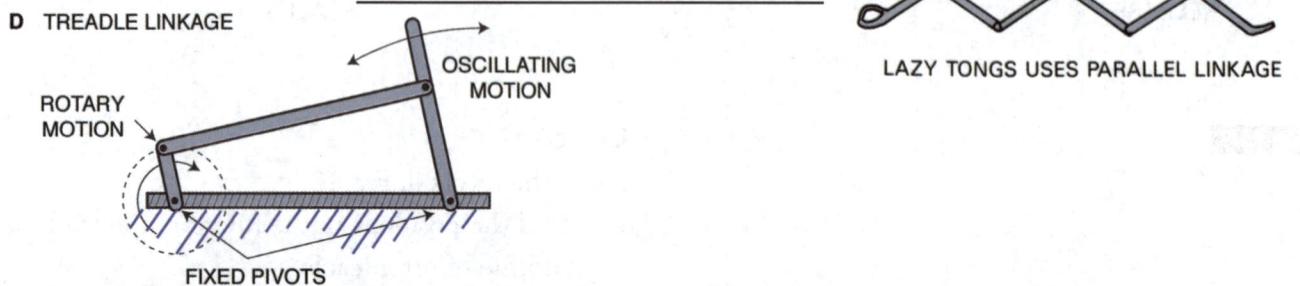

**A**

INPUT

FIXED PIVOT

OUTPUT

LINKAGE FOR REVERSING DIRECTION OF MOTION OR FORCE

INPUT

FIXED PIVOT

OUTPUT

PIVOT OFF-CENTRE FOR INCREASING OR REDUCING INPUT

INPUT    OUTPUT

FIXED PIVOTS

PUSH-PULL LINKAGE OUTPUT IN SAME DIRECTION AS INPUT

INPUT    OUTPUT

FIXED PIVOT

OUTPUT

EQUALISING LINKAGE SINGLE INPUT TRANSFERRED TO TWO OUTPUTS

**B**

BELL CRANK CHANGES DIRECTION OF MOTION OR FORCE THROUGH 90°

BICYCLE CALLIPER BRAKE USES BELL CRANKS

INPUT

OUTPUT

DOUBLE BELL CRANK

**C**

INPUT    OUTPUT

PARALLEL MOTION THE TWO LONG LINKS REMAIN PARALLEL AS DO THE TWO SHORT ONES

APPLICATION OF PARALLEL LINKS

FIXED PIVOT

PEN

PANTOGRAPH USED TO ENLARGE OR REDUCE A DRAWING. MAKES USE OF PARALLEL LINKAGE

LAZY TONGS USES PARALLEL LINKAGE

**D** TREADLE LINKAGE

OSCILLATING MOTION

ROTARY MOTION

FIXED PIVOTS

THIS CONVERTS ROTARY MOTION INTO OSCILLATING MOTION OR OSCILLATING MOTION INTO ROTARY MOTION. IT WAS USED IN THE PAST TO OPERATE SEWING MACHINES – THE TREADLE WAS DRIVEN BY FOOT.

**Fig. 15.9**
Linkages

## Toggle Mechanisms

These mechanisms are used to achieve large clamping forces. The mechanism is basically two links joined by a common pivot, Fig. 15.10. The end of one link is pivoted to a fixed surface and the end of the other is free to move. By applying a force to the common pivot, the free end is pushed downwards. The clamping force is at its greatest when the links are in a straight line. Moving the common pivot slightly further will lock the clamp in the 'on' position.

Usually one link is extended to form a handle for applying the effort, Fig. 15.10. The link then becomes a lever. Toggle clamps have a wide range of applications. In school workshops they are used for clamping plastic sheets on vacuum forming and blow moulding machines and for holding kiln doors closed. They can also be used for holding work for drilling. Toggle mechanisms are used on prams and buggies for keeping the hood up, on brake mechanisms and on vice grips.

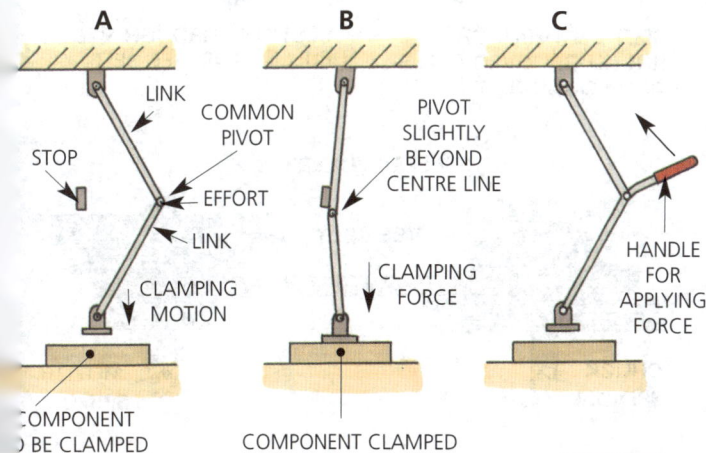

**Fig. 15.11**
The vice grips makes use of a toggle mechanism

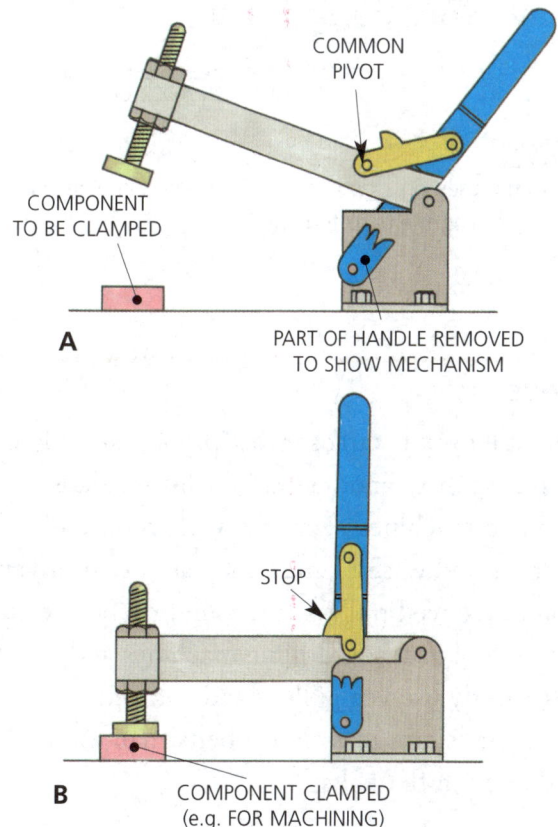

**Fig. 15.10**
Toggle mechanism

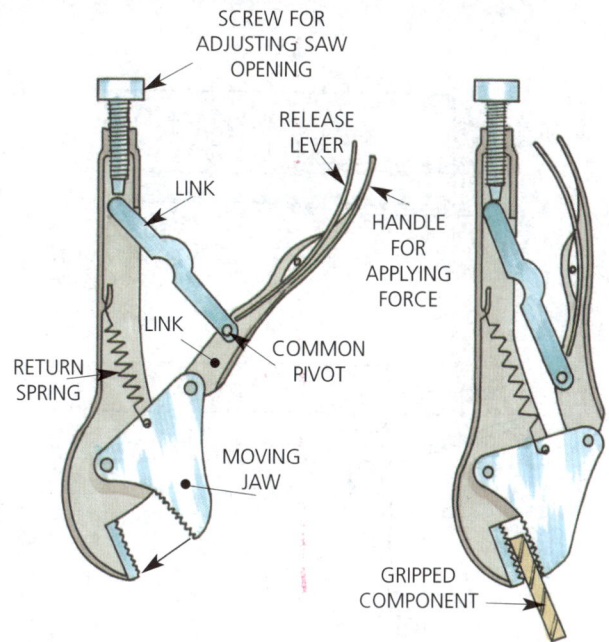

**Fig. 15.12**
A type of toggle clamp suitable for clamping work to a table or holding plastic sheets for vacuum forming

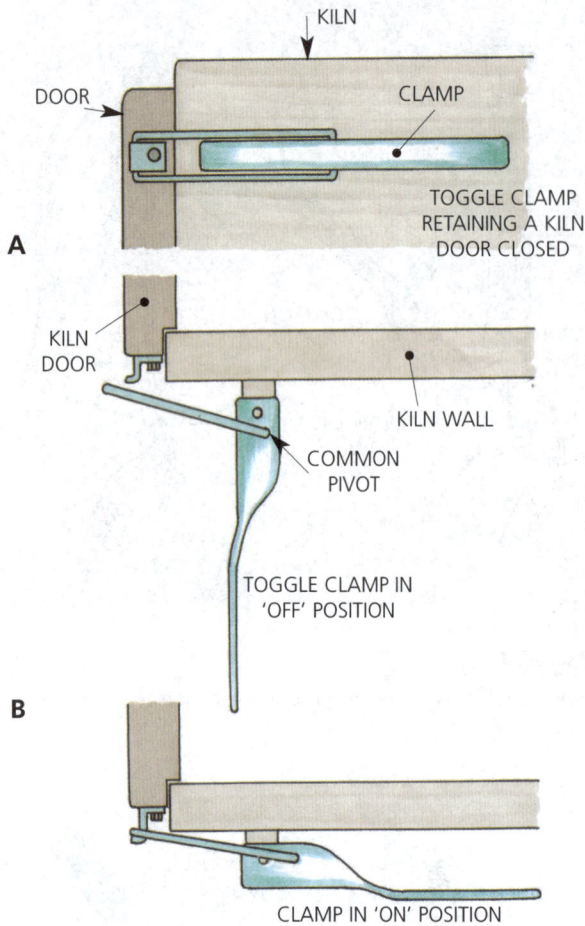

KILN

DOOR

CLAMP

TOGGLE CLAMP
RETAINING A KILN
DOOR CLOSED

A

KILN
DOOR

KILN WALL

COMMON
PIVOT

TOGGLE CLAMP IN
'OFF' POSITION

B

CLAMP IN 'ON' POSITION

**Fig. 15.13**

Toggle clamp used on a door. In this case, the clamping link is in tension (pulling the parts together).

DRIVEN PULLEY

MOTOR

DRIVER
PULLEY

CROSSED BELT REVERSES
DIRECTION

EFFORT

LOAD

LIFTING A LOAD, EFFORT
HALVED BY USING TWO
PULLEYS

ROUND
BELT

GRUB
SCREW

SHAFT

VEE BELT

KEYWAY

KEY

SECTION THROUGH
ROUND GROOVED PULLEY
AND ROUND BELT

SECTION THROUGH VEE
PULLEY AND VEE BELT

STEPPED PULLEYS

VEE BELT

CHUCK
SPINDLE

MOTOR
SPINDLE

**Fig. 15.14**

Pulleys

## Pulleys

Pulleys are used for transferring motion and force from one shaft to another and for lifting loads. Household machines, such as sewing machines, spin driers and washing machines, are often driven by round grooved pulleys and round rubber belts. Machine tools, such as drilling machines and lathes, mostly use vee pulleys and vee belts. There is less slippage with vee belts than there would be with flat belts.

The pulley on the driving shaft, e.g. a motor pulley, is called the driver pulley and the pulley on the shaft being driven is called the driven pulley.

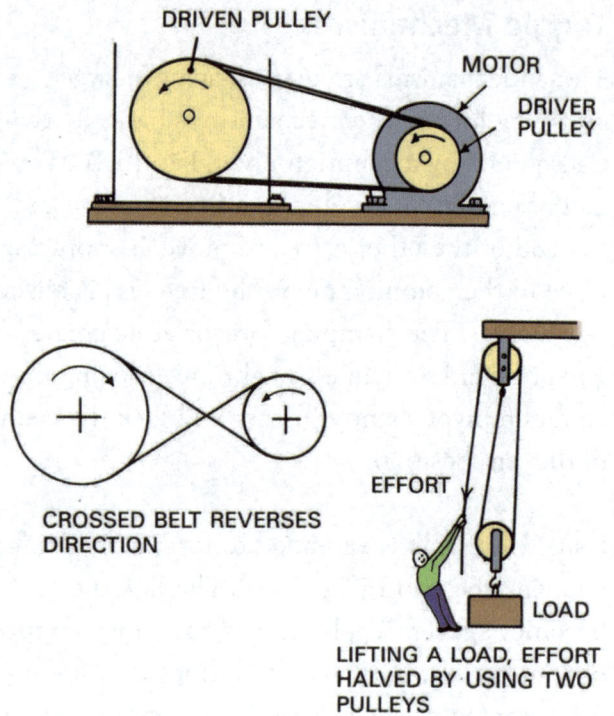

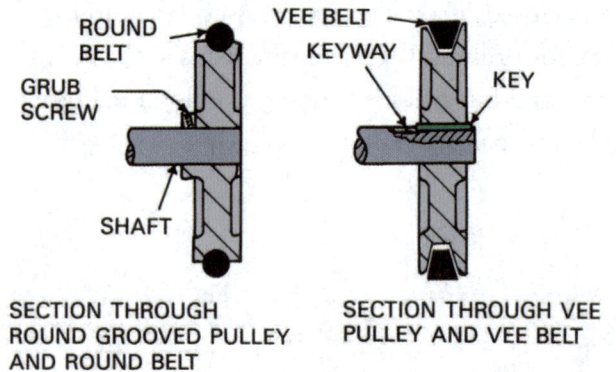

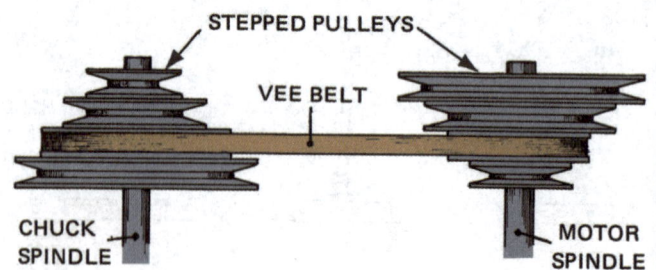

**Toothed belt** In situations where no slip between the driven and driver pulleys can be allowed, a toothed belt and toothed pulleys may be used. They provide a quiet, positive drive and are commonly used for driving the camshaft on engines.

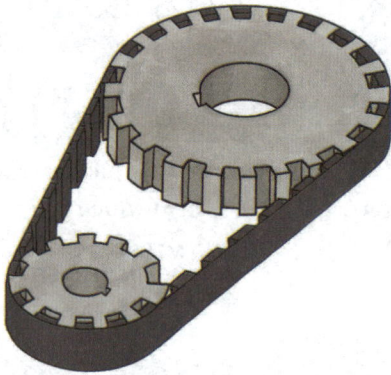

**Fig. 15.15**
Toothed belt and pulleys

The speed of rotation of a shaft depends on:
1.     The speed of the driving motor.
2.     The diameters of the pulleys.

If a small pulley is driven by a large pulley, the small pulley will revolve faster. So, a large pulley driving a small pulley gives an increase in speed and a small pulley driving a large pulley gives a decrease in speed. Suppose a 100mm diameter pulley drives a 50mm diameter pulley – for each revolution of the driver pulley, the driven pulley does two.

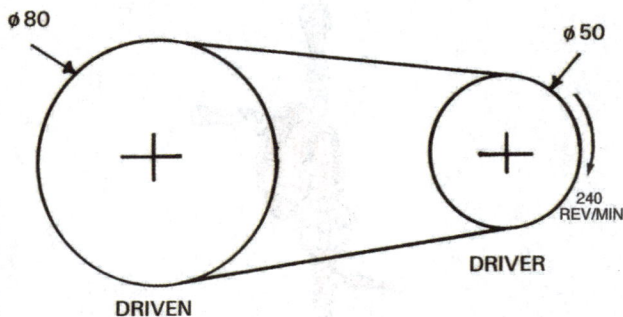

**Fig. 15.16**

**Example: Fig. 15.16**
The diameter of a motor pulley is 50mm and it revolves at 240 rev/min. The diameter of the driven pulley is 80mm. What is its rotational speed?

**Note:** The driven pulley is larger than the motor pulley, therefore it will revolve more slowly.

$$\text{Speed of driven pulley} = \frac{240 \times 50}{80} \text{ rev/min}$$

$$= 150 \text{ rev/min}$$

Some machines, such as drilling machines, need a range of speeds. This is achieved by using stepped cone pulleys. Different size pulleys are used to give different drill speeds.

## Chains and Sprockets

Chains and sprockets provide direct positive drives; there is no slippage. They are used on bicycles, motorcycles, go-karts and the camshaft drives of some engines.

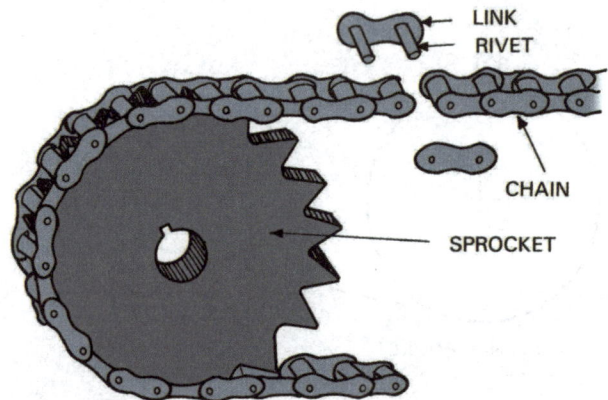

**Fig. 15.17**
Chains and sprockets

209

An output speed depends on:

1. The speed of the driving sprocket.
2. The number of teeth on each sprocket.

The pedal sprocket of a bicycle has 45 teeth and the back wheel sprocket has 15 teeth. Therefore, for each revolution of the pedal sprocket, the back wheel sprocket does three revolutions.

**Example: Fig. 15.18**
The sprocket on the engine of a go-kart has 10 teeth and the sprocket on the back axle has 80. If the engine revolves at 4,000 rev/min, what is the rotary speed of the back axle?

**Note:** The back axle sprocket is larger and therefore revolves more slowly.

$$\text{Speed of back axle} = 4{,}000 \times \frac{10}{80}$$

$$= 500 \text{ rev/min.}$$

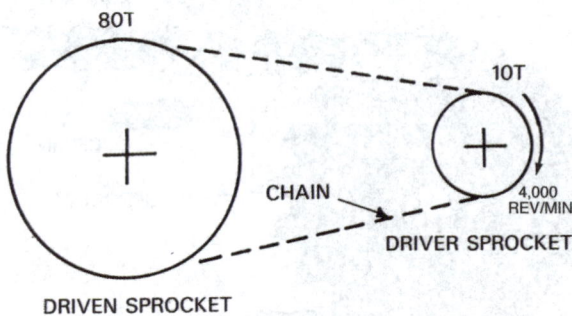

**Fig. 15.18**

## Gears

Like pulleys, gears are used to transmit motion and force. A gear is a wheel with teeth equally spaced around its rim.

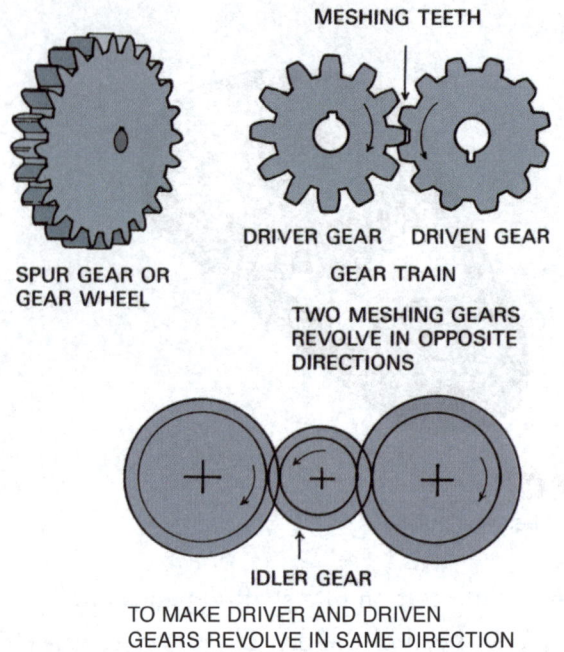

MESHING TEETH

SPUR GEAR OR GEAR WHEEL

DRIVER GEAR    DRIVEN GEAR
GEAR TRAIN

TWO MESHING GEARS REVOLVE IN OPPOSITE DIRECTIONS

IDLER GEAR

TO MAKE DRIVER AND DRIVEN GEARS REVOLVE IN SAME DIRECTION

**Fig. 15.19**
Spur gears

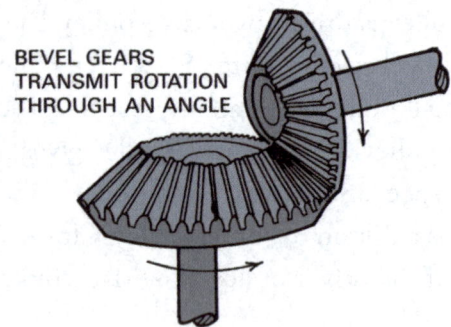

BEVEL GEARS TRANSMIT ROTATION THROUGH AN ANGLE

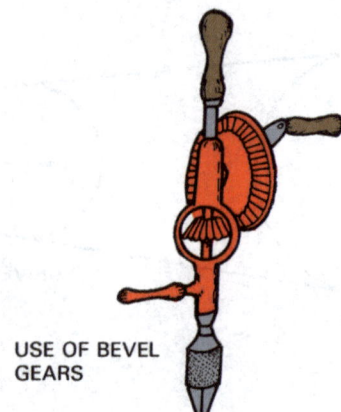

USE OF BEVEL GEARS

**Fig. 15.20**
Bevel gears

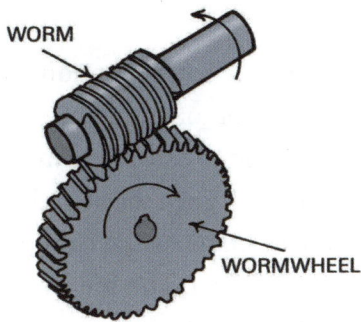

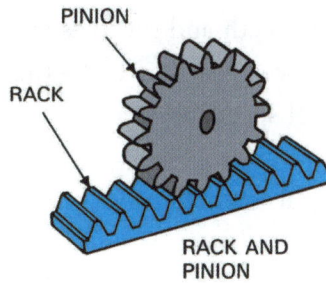

RACK AND PINION

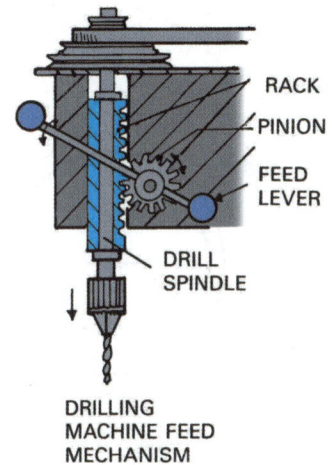

DRILLING MACHINE FEED MECHANISM

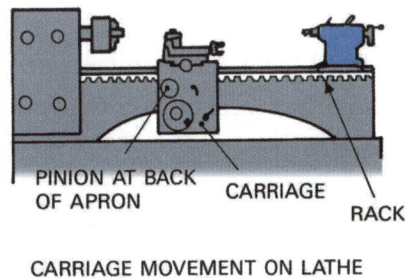

CARRIAGE MOVEMENT ON LATHE

**Fig. 15.21**

Worm and wormwheel cause a large reduction in speed

A set of interlocking or meshing gears is called a **gear train**. Two gears meshed together rotate in opposite directions. An 'idler' gear is used to make two gears revolve in the same direction. It does not change the speed ratio between the two gears.

**Bevel gears** transmit rotary motion where shafts are at an angle to one another.

A **worm** and **wormwheel** transmit rotary motion through a right angle and also give a very large gear reduction.

A **rack** and **pinion** convert rotary motion to linear motion and vice versa.

Speed is changed by using gears with different numbers of teeth. A gear with a large number of teeth driving a gear with a small number of teeth gives an increase in rotational speed and vice versa. Suppose a 100 tooth gear drives a 25 tooth gear. For each revolution of the driver gear, the driven gear does four. This relationship is called the gear ratio.

**Note:** The gear ratio =

$$\frac{\text{number of teeth on driven gear}}{\text{number of teeth on driver gear}}$$

e.g. for the above train, the gear ratio

$$= \frac{25}{100} = \frac{1}{4}$$

This is usually written as 1:4.

**Fig. 15.22**

Rack and pinion and some applications

**Example 1:    Fig. 15.23**

A motor gear has 36 teeth and revolves at 100 rev/min. The driven gear has 12 teeth. What is its rotational speed?

**Note:** The driven gear is smaller so it will revolve faster.

Speed of driven gear $= 100 \times \dfrac{36}{12} = 100 \times 3$

$= 300$ rev/min

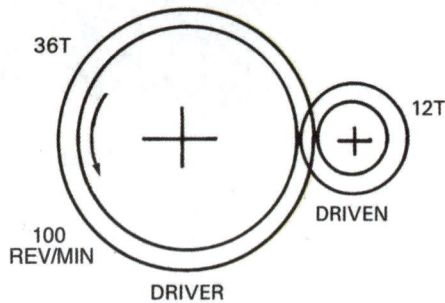

Fig. 15.23

**Example 2:    Fig. 15.24**

A motor gear has 20 teeth and revolves at 280 rev/min. The driven gear has 35 teeth. What is its rotational speed?

**Note:** The driven gear is larger so it will revolve more slowly.

Speed of driven gear $= 280 \times \dfrac{20}{35}$ rev/min

$= 160$ rev/min.

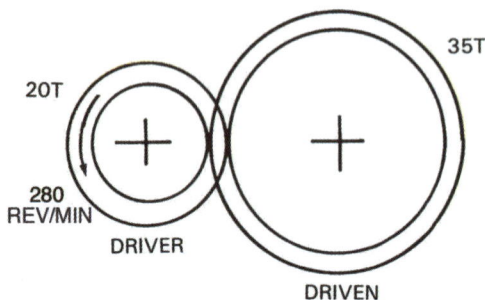

Fig. 15.24

## Cams

**Rotary cams** change rotary motion into reciprocating motion or sometimes oscillating motion. A follower in contact with the edge of the cam moves up and down, or in and out, as the cam rotates. The shape of the cam controls the motion of the follower. The follower is kept in contact with the cam by its own weight or by pressure exerted on it.

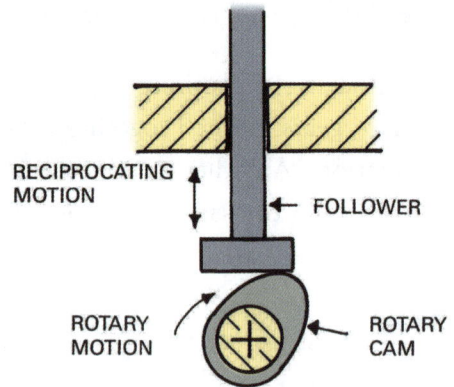

Fig. 15.25
Rotary cam and follower

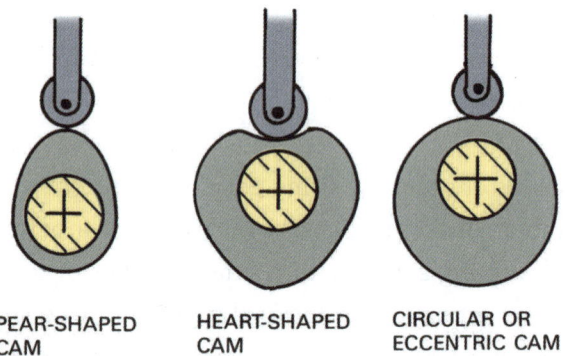

PEAR-SHAPED CAM      HEART-SHAPED CAM      CIRCULAR OR ECCENTRIC CAM

Fig. 15.26
Some common cam profiles

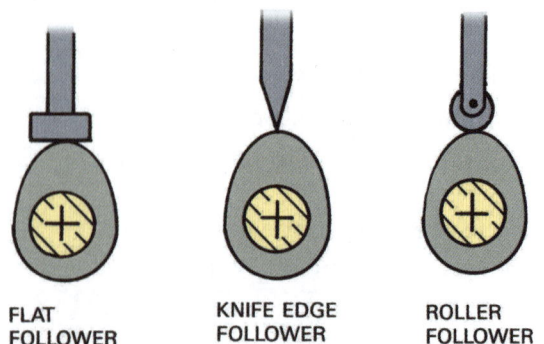

FLAT FOLLOWER      KNIFE EDGE FOLLOWER      ROLLER FOLLOWER

Fig. 15.27
Some types of cam follower

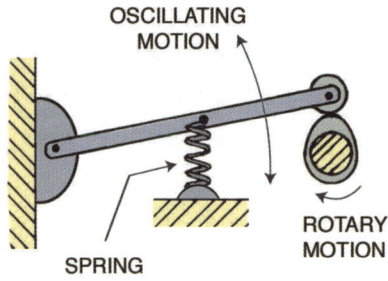

**Fig. 15.28**
Follower on pivoted arm – rotary motion to oscillating motion

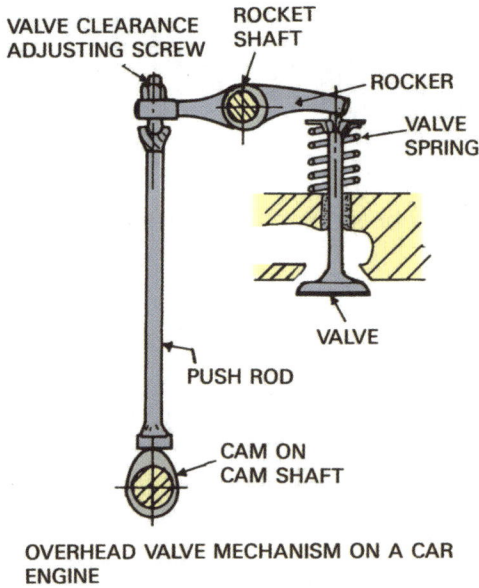

**Fig. 15.29**

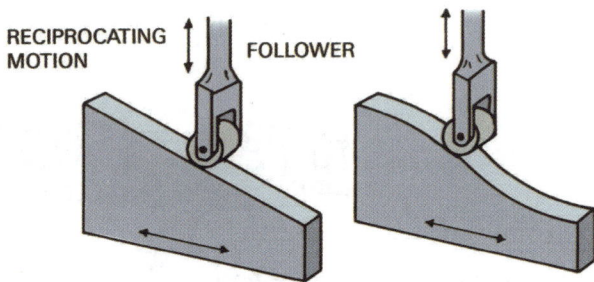

**Fig. 15.30**
Linear or flat plate cams

**Linear Cams**, or flat plate cams, change the direction of reciprocating motion. The cam and follower move with reciprocating motion but they move in different directions.

## Screw Threads

Screw threads have already been described in Chapter 8. There is a great variety of screw thread mechanisms. Some are shown in Fig. 15.31.

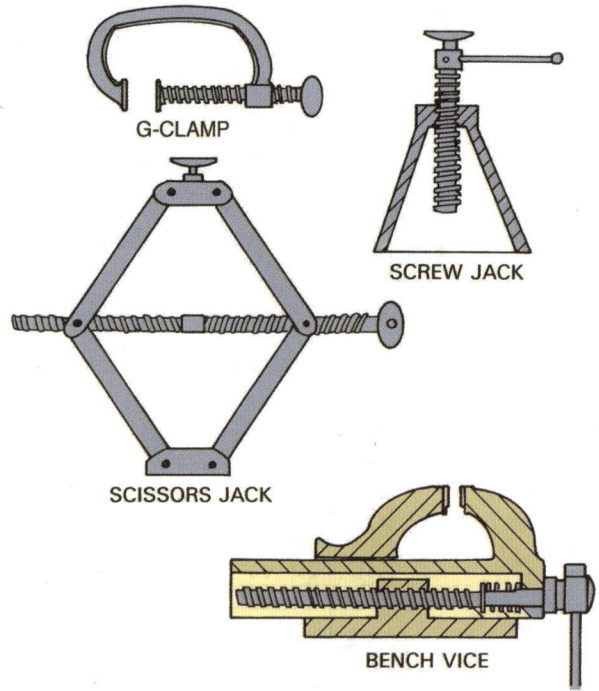

**Fig. 15.31**
Screw thread mechanisms

## Ratchets

Ratchets allow rotation in one direction only. They are used in mechanisms such as ratchet spanners, fishing reels, ratchet screwdrivers, micrometers and the winding mechanisms of watches.

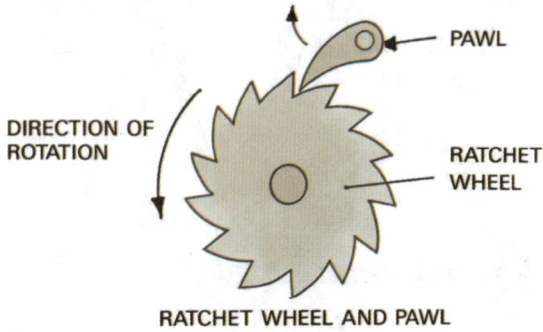

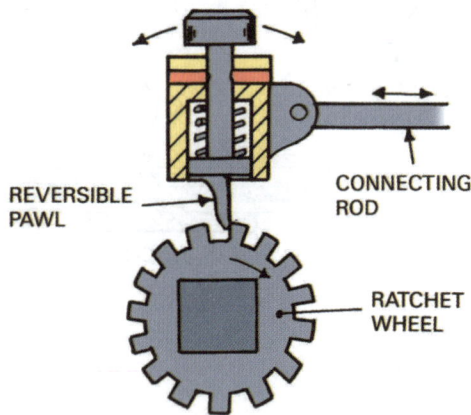

RATCHET WHEEL AND PAWL

PAWL

DIRECTION OF ROTATION

RATCHET WHEEL

REVERSIBLE PAWL

CONNECTING ROD

RATCHET WHEEL

FEED MECHANISM ON A SHAPING MACHINE

DIRECTION OF ROTARY MOTION CAN BE REVERSED BY REVERSING THE PAWL

**Fig. 15.32**
Ratchet mechanisms

## Clutches

A clutch is a mechanism which enables two shafts to be easily connected or disconnected from one another when they are being used to transmit drive from one to the other.

The two basic types are positive clutches and friction clutches. Positive clutches, e.g. claw clutches, can only be used where the shafts can be brought to rest before engagement. Friction clutches allow smooth take-up of the drive and enable engagement and disengagement while the shafts are in motion.

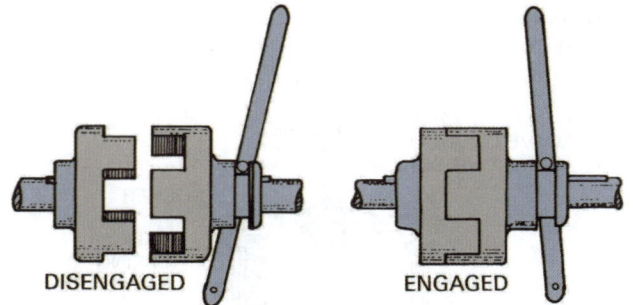

DISENGAGED    ENGAGED

A    CLAW OR DOG CLUTCH (A POSITIVE TYPE CLUTCH) SHAFTS MUST BE AT REST FOR ENGAGEMENT

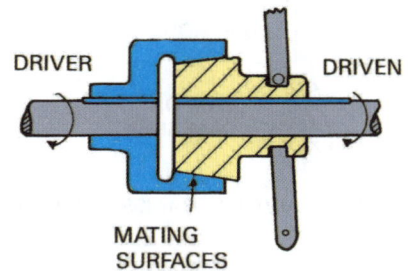

DRIVER    DRIVEN

MATING SURFACES

B    CONE CLUTCH ALLOWS SMOOTH TAKE-UP OF DRIVE

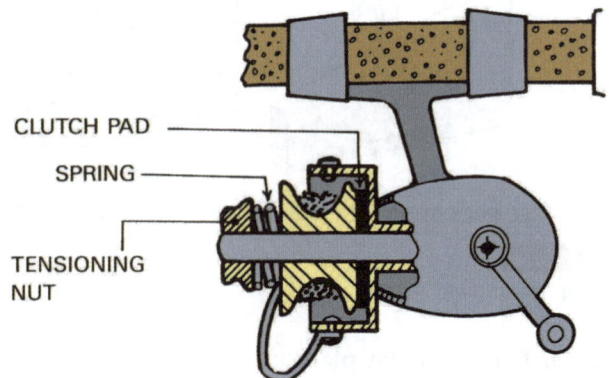

CLUTCH PAD

SPRING

TENSIONING NUT

C    FRICTION CLUTCH ON FISHING REEL

**Fig. 15.33**
Clutches

## Crank and Crank/Slider Mechanisms

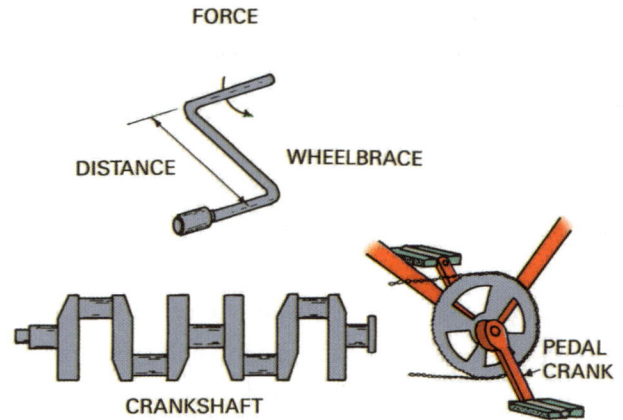

A crank is used to apply torque (turning force) to a shaft. The greater the distance of the force from the centre of the shaft, the greater the torque. A shaft with a number of cranks is called a crankshaft. A crank/slider mechanism converts rotary motion to reciprocating motion or vice versa.

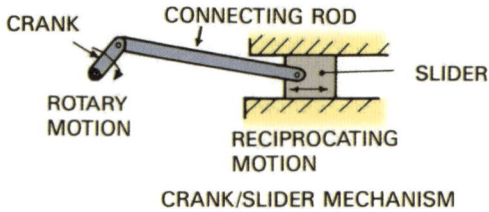

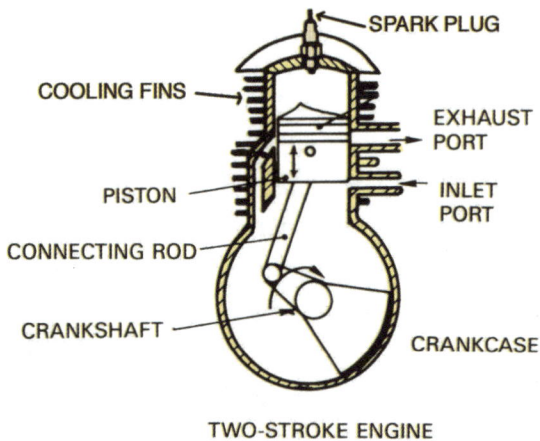

CRANK
CONNECTING ROD
SLIDER
ROTARY MOTION
RECIPROCATING MOTION
CRANK/SLIDER MECHANISM

SPARK PLUG
COOLING FINS
EXHAUST PORT
PISTON
INLET PORT
CONNECTING ROD
CRANKSHAFT
CRANKCASE
TWO-STROKE ENGINE

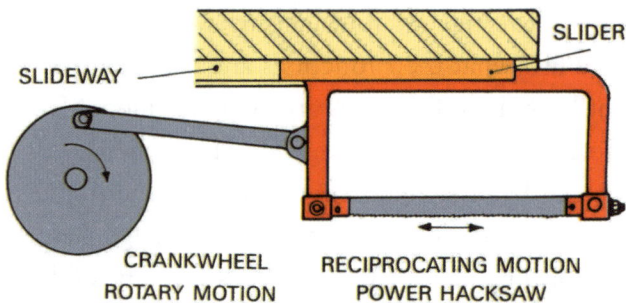

SLIDER
SLIDEWAY
CRANKWHEEL ROTARY MOTION
RECIPROCATING MOTION POWER HACKSAW

**Fig. 15.34**
Crank/Slider mechanisms

FORCE
DISTANCE
WHEELBRACE
CRANKSHAFT
PEDAL CRANK

**Fig. 15.35**
Crank mechanisms

## Bearings

A bearing guides and supports a moving part of a mechanism and allows the movement to take place freely. There are three main types — flat bearings, journal bearings and thrust bearings.

**Flat bearings, Fig. 15.36,** make use of sliding flat surfaces. They are widely used on machine tools, e.g. a lathe bed and carriage, a lathe cross slide, a lathe top slide and the ram and slides of a shaping machine. The action in a flat bearing is 'sliding' between slides and slideways. Cast iron is used for flat bearing. Two cast iron surfaces running together make an excellent bearing.

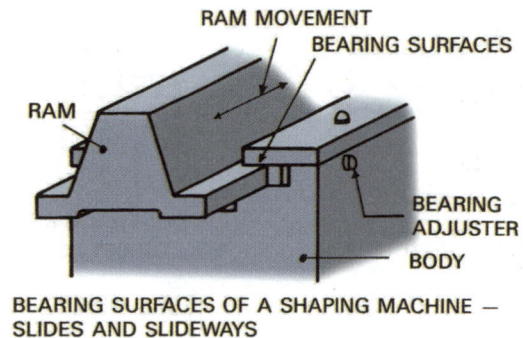

RAM MOVEMENT
BEARING SURFACES
RAM
BEARING ADJUSTER
BODY
BEARING SURFACES OF A SHAPING MACHINE —
SLIDES AND SLIDEWAYS

**Fig. 15.36**
Flat bearing

**Journal bearings, Fig. 15.37,** support round shafts. They carry radial loads only. They can be of the plain, ball or roller type.

**Thrust bearings, Fig. 15.38,** take axial loads on shafts.

**Plain bearings** are mainly used where only moderate speeds and loads are involved. Bronze and nylon are commonly used for the bushes and thrust washers of these bearings.

Shafts are usually made of steel and can be either soft or hard, depending on use.

The action in plain bearings is 'sliding' – between the shafts and bushes or thrust washers. The action in ball bearings is 'rolling' – between the balls and their races.

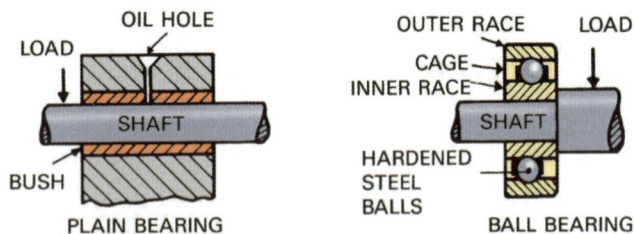

**Fig. 15.37**
Journal bearings

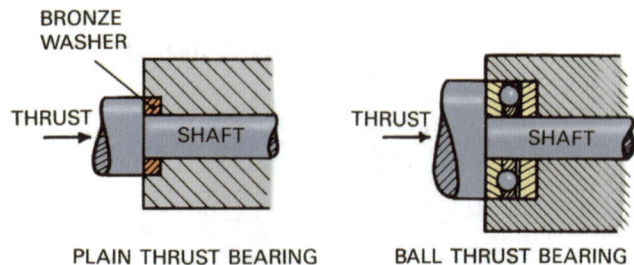

**Fig. 15.38**
Thrust bearings

## Lubrication

When two surfaces are moved over one another without a lubricant, heat and wear are produced as a result of friction. In certain circumstances, the heat could be so great as to cause the surfaces to weld together. Lubrication is the use of a lubricant between the surfaces. This separates the surfaces slightly and greatly reduces friction. Using a lubricant helps to:

1. Reduce wear.
2. Reduce the heat produced as a result of friction.
3. Reduce the power required to move the surfaces over one another.
4. Keep the surfaces cool.

## Investigation of Mechanisms

A knowledge of the design features of a variety of mechanisms is very beneficial when searching for solutions to our own design problems. Understanding the construction and operation of articles will help in their maintenance and repair. Also, when buying articles, we will be better able to compare them with others and evaluate them.

When investigating mechanisms, we should first establish what their functions are and then find out how these functions are being fulfilled. Many mechanisms can be examined without being dismantled. Beginners should dismantle only discarded articles to avoid causing damage. Before dismantling an article, find out as far as possible how it works. The sequence in which the parts are assembled should be recorded so that they can be replaced correctly.

## Can-opener

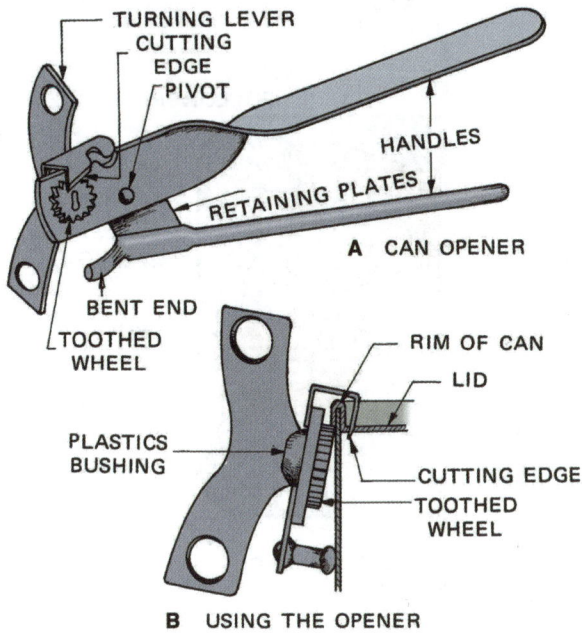

**Fig. 15.39**
Can-opener

The upper handle of the can-opener pivots on a pin in the retaining plate and the twist in the handle enables the pressure to be exerted on its flat side. A portion of the turning lever fits through a plastic bushing in the other end of the handle. The toothed wheel is fitted onto this portion which is riveted over to hold the wheel. The holes in the turning lever provide a good grip. The lower handle is riveted to the retaining plate.

The bent end of the can-opener prevents the wheel rubbing against the side of the can. The upper end of the retaining plate is bent over to provide the cutting edge.

The opener is fitted to the rim of the can as shown in Fig. 15.39 B. When the handles are pressed together, the cutting edge is forced into the lid and the toothed wheel bites into the underside of the rim. By maintaining the pressure and operating the turning lever, the opener will be driven around the rim, cutting the lid as it goes.

The toothed wheel is hard so that it resists wear and the cutting edge is also hard to enable it to cut into the lid. All the steel parts, except the retaining plate, are chromium plated.

## Surface Gauge

A surface gauge is used for scribing lines parallel to the surface of the surface plate and also for checking the parallelism of the work (see page 50).

The surface gauge must have provision for setting the scriber at any angle and also for clamping the scriber at any height on the spindle.

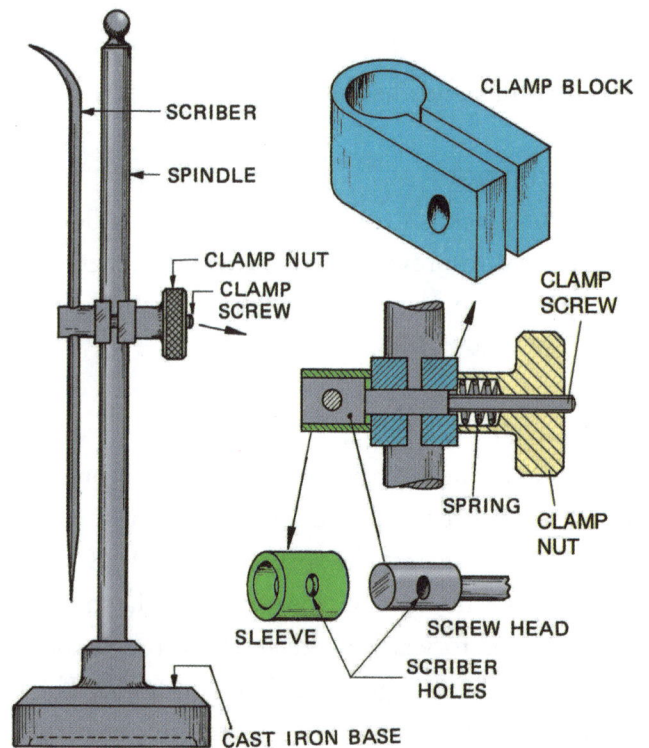

**Fig. 15.40**
Surface gauge

The clamp block has a slot cut into it so that it can be closed slightly and clamped at any height on the spindle. The clamp screw fits through the sleeve and clamp block and has a nut containing a spring screwed onto its end. The scriber fits through holes in the sleeve and screw head.

When the nut is tightened, the sleeve is brought against the clamp block. The screw head, being slightly shorter than the sleeve, will not come against the clamp block. The holes will therefore tend to pass each other, clamping the scriber in position. At the same time, the tightening of the nut closes the clamp block, clamping it on the spindle. The spring in the nut maintains a slight clamping pressure on the scriber when the nut is loosened to prevent the scriber from falling out.

The parts are generally made from mild steel, with the exception of the base, scriber and spring. The base is made from cast iron with its bottom machined. The scriber is made from high carbon steel with its ends hardened and tempered.

## Mortice Lock

A mortice lock is fitted into a mortice in a door and is used to prevent the door being opened except by using a key. It also has a latch to keep the door closed without it being locked.

## The Latch

One side of the latch is curved, and when pressed against the receiver in the doorframe, it is forced into the lock against the spring, Fig. 15.41 B. This allows the door to close fully. The latch is then pushed forward by the spring, through the receiver and into a groove in the doorframe. The other side of the latch is flat; therefore, pressure from the opposite side will not open the door. The ends of the latch holder are hooked to the follower, and a square spindle fits through the follower and into the door handles. This enables either of the door handles to turn the follower and withdraw the latch. When the handle is released, the spring returns the latch to its original position.

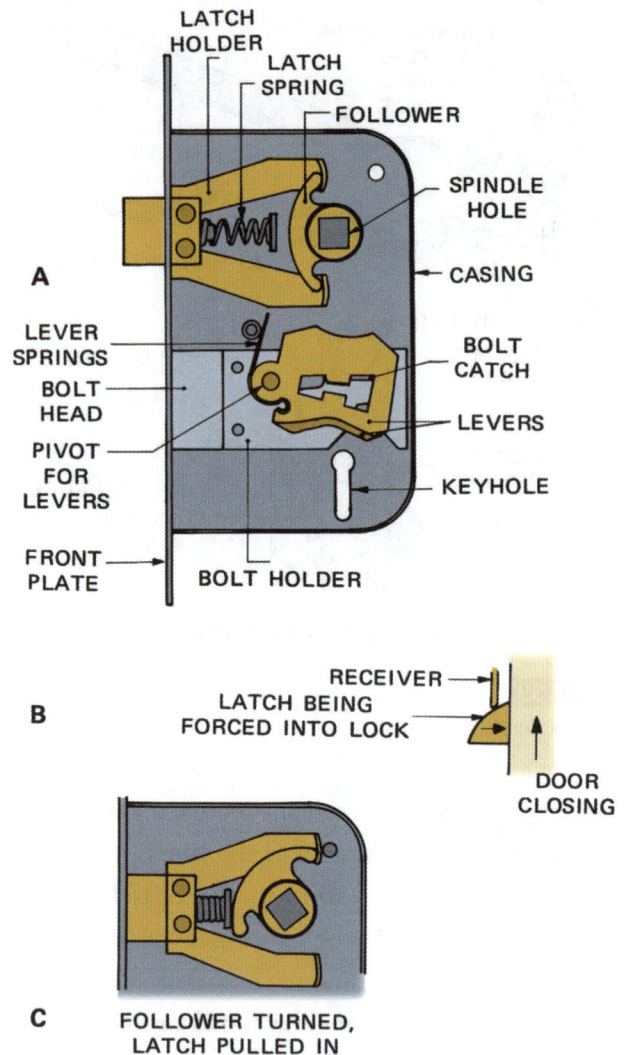

**Fig. 15.41**
Mortice lock

## The Electric Bell

The construction of an electric bell is shown in Fig. 15.42. The electromagnet, brass pillar and spring are attached to the base but insulated from it. The hammer, which strikes the gong, is attached to a soft iron bar called an armature.

The bell is operated by a direct current. Its path is from terminal A, around the limbs of the electromagnet, onto the brass pillar, through the contact screw to the spring, and back to terminal B. When the bell switch-button is pressed, the current flows and the electromagnet becomes magnetised. It then attracts the armature, causing the hammer to strike the gong. At the same time, the spring is pulled away from the contact screw, thus breaking the circuit. The current then stops flowing and the electromagnet loses its magnetism, allowing the armature and the spring to return and close the circuit again. This procedure is repeated for as long as the switch button is pressed.

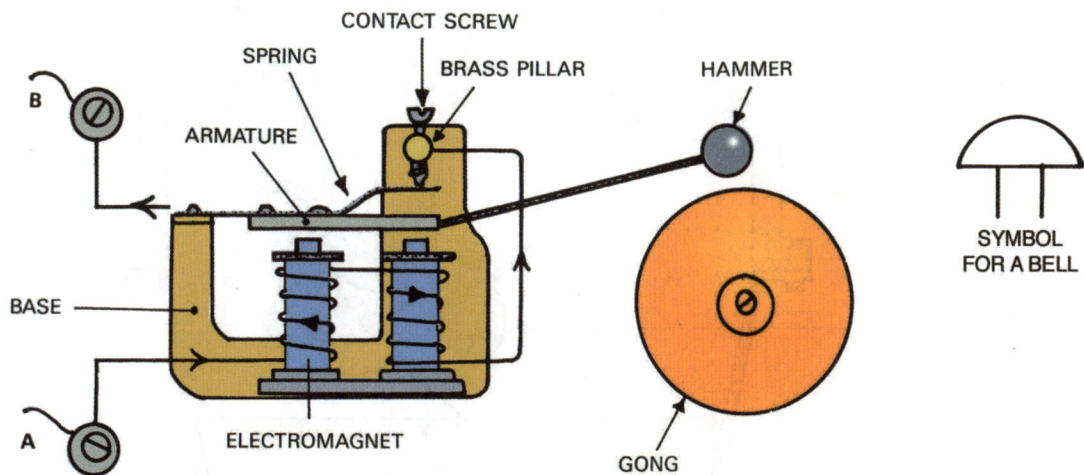

NOTE: THE NUMBER OF TURNS OF WIRE IN THE ELECTROMAGNETS IS FAR GREATER THAN SHOWN.

**Fig. 15.42**
Electric bell

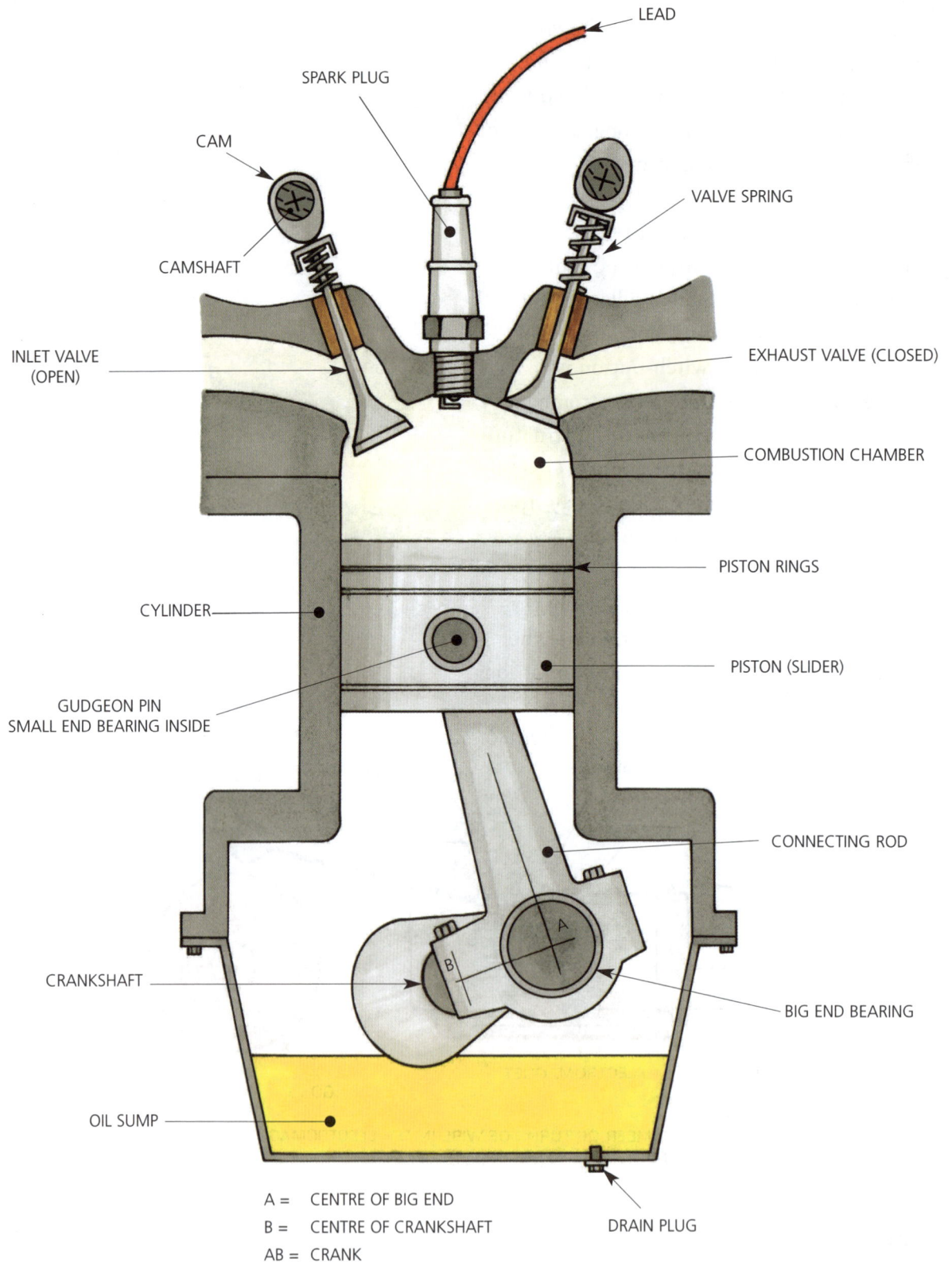

LEAD

SPARK PLUG

CAM

CAMSHAFT

VALVE SPRING

INLET VALVE
(OPEN)

EXHAUST VALVE (CLOSED)

COMBUSTION CHAMBER

PISTON RINGS

CYLINDER

PISTON (SLIDER)

GUDGEON PIN
SMALL END BEARING INSIDE

CONNECTING ROD

CRANKSHAFT

BIG END BEARING

OIL SUMP

A =    CENTRE OF BIG END

B =    CENTRE OF CRANKSHAFT

AB =  CRANK

DRAIN PLUG

**Fig. 15.43**

Main parts of a four-stroke spark-ignition engine

## The Four-Stroke Spark-Ignition Engine

This is the type of engine used in most motor cars. It makes use of a crank/slider mechanism. The main parts are shown in Fig. 15.43.

**Piston** This is the slider. It travels up and down in the cylinder with reciprocating motion.

**Combustion chamber** This is the space into which the fuel mixture is compressed by the piston. It is also here that the combustion starts which provides the power stroke.

**Cylinder** This guides the movement of the piston. It also provides part of the space for the fuel mixture intake.

**Connecting rod** It connects the piston to the crankshaft.

**Crankshaft** This converts the reciprocating motion of the piston into rotary motion.

**Gudgeon pin** It joins the connecting rod to the piston.

**Small end bearing** This allows swivel movement between the piston and the connecting rod.

**Big end bearing** It allows the crankshaft to rotate in the end of the connecting rod.

**Inlet valve** This admits the fuel mixture into the cylinder.

**Exhaust valve** This allows the burnt gases to exit from the cylinder.

**Valve spring** This returns the valve to the closed position and also keeps the valve retaining mechanism in place.

**Cam** This opens the valve.

**Camshaft** This has the cams machined on it and rotates to operate the cams.

**Spark plug** This provides the spark for igniting the compressed fuel mixture.

**Piston rings** These provide a gas seal between the piston and the cylinder and also prevent lubricating oil passing into the combustion chamber.

**Lead** This delivers the high voltage current to the spark plug.

## The Four-Stroke Cycle

The movement of the piston from its highest point in the cylinder to its lowest, or vice versa, is called a **stroke**.

The complete series of operations that occurs in a definite order in an engine is called a **cycle**.

The four-stroke engine requires four strokes of the piston, or two revolutions of the crankshaft, for each cycle. When the engine is running, the cycle is being constantly repeated. Each stroke is shown in Fig. 15.44.

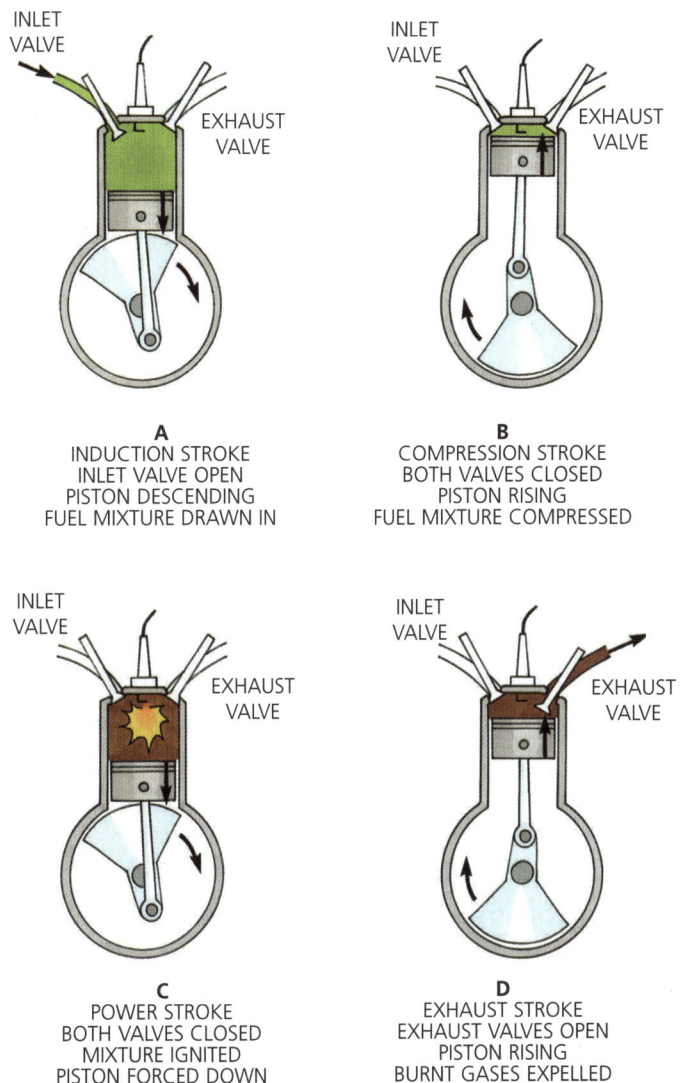

**A**
INDUCTION STROKE
INLET VALVE OPEN
PISTON DESCENDING
FUEL MIXTURE DRAWN IN

**B**
COMPRESSION STROKE
BOTH VALVES CLOSED
PISTON RISING
FUEL MIXTURE COMPRESSED

**C**
POWER STROKE
BOTH VALVES CLOSED
MIXTURE IGNITED
PISTON FORCED DOWN

**D**
EXHAUST STROKE
EXHAUST VALVES OPEN
PISTON RISING
BURNT GASES EXPELLED

**Fig. 15.44**
The four-stroke cycle

## Induction stroke

The inlet valve is open and the exhaust valve is closed. The piston is moving down the cylinder creating a partial vacuum. This causes the fuel mixture, which is air and petrol, to flow into the cylinder.

## Compression stroke

The inlet and exhaust valves are closed. The piston is rising, compressing the mixture into the combustion chamber.

## Power stroke

At the end of the compression stroke, the fuel mixture is ignited by a spark from the spark plug. The resulting rapid combustion causes a huge increase in temperature and pressure. This creates a large force on the surface of the piston, forcing it downwards. Both valves remain closed.

## Exhaust stroke

The exhaust valve is open and the inlet valve is closed. The piston is rising, driving the burnt gases out through the exhaust valve.

## The Two-Stroke Engine

This type of engine is commonly used for motor cycles and for small outboard engines for boats. It takes two strokes or one revolution of the crankshaft to complete the cycle. A number of operations take place on each stroke. Instead of valves, three ports are used. These are covered and uncovered as the piston moves up and down the cylinder. The two strokes are shown in Fig. 15.46.

## The Upward Stroke

As the piston moves upwards, the transfer and exhaust ports are covered and the inlet port uncovered. The partial vacuum created below the piston causes the fuel mixture of air and petrol to flow into the crankcase. At the same time, the charge from the previous stroke is being compressed above the piston.

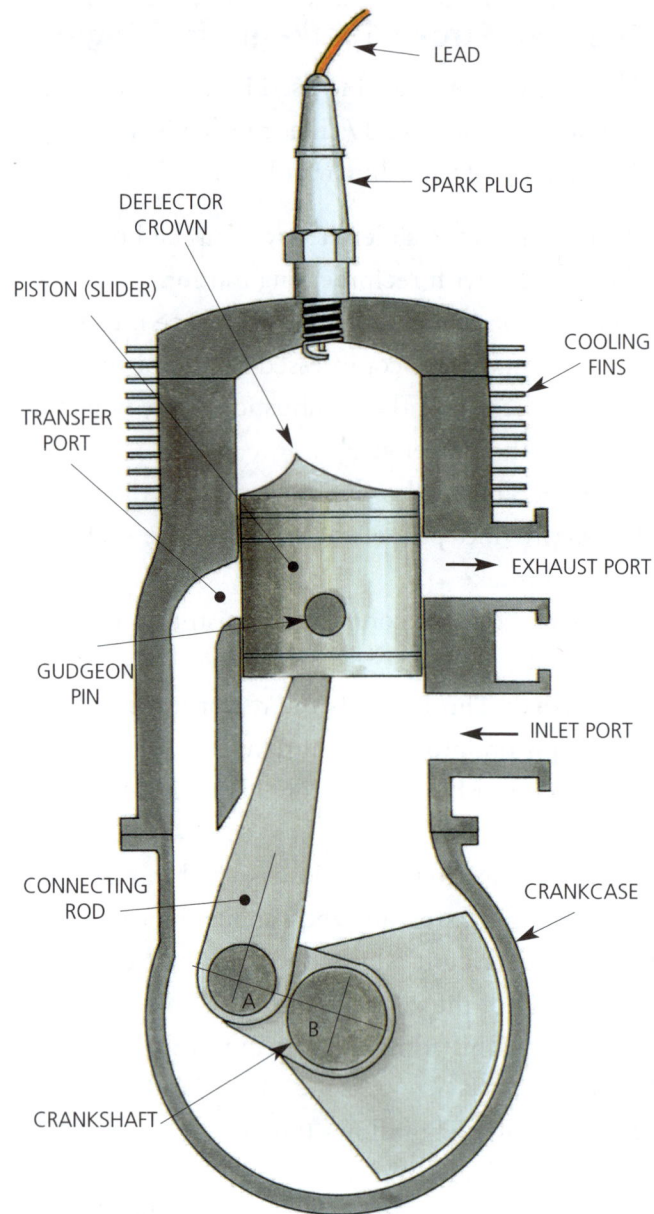

**Fig. 15.45**
Two-Stroke engine

## The Downward Stroke

At the end of the upward stroke the compressed fuel mixture is ignited by the spark plug. The rise in pressure caused by the combustion forces the piston down the cylinder. As it travels downwards, it compresses the mixture in the crankcase and uncovers the transfer and exhaust ports. This enables the compressed mixture to transfer to the top of the cylinder and the burnt gases to escape.

The cycle is continuously repeated while the engine is running.

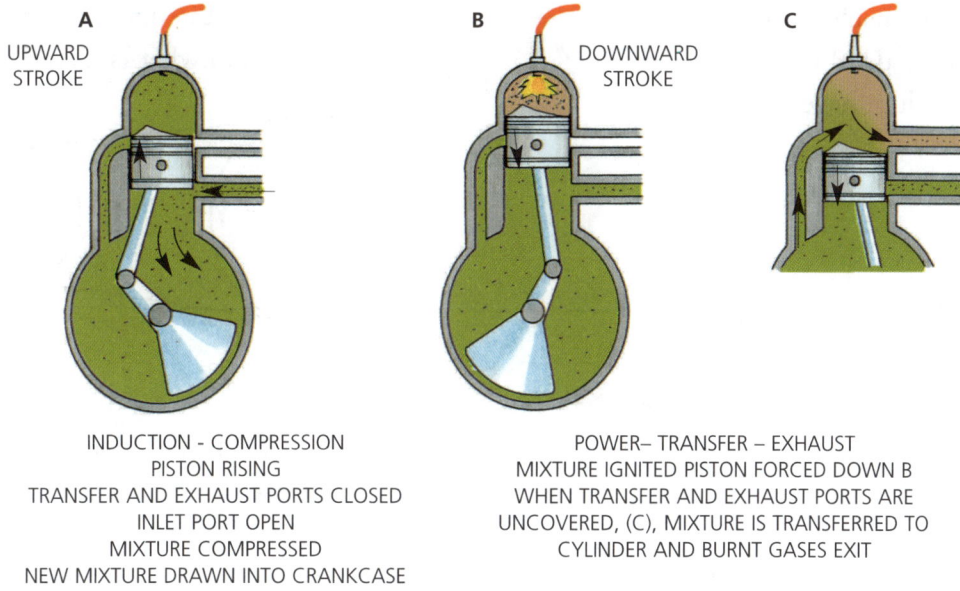

**A**
UPWARD STROKE

**B**
DOWNWARD STROKE

**C**

INDUCTION - COMPRESSION
PISTON RISING
TRANSFER AND EXHAUST PORTS CLOSED
INLET PORT OPEN
MIXTURE COMPRESSED
NEW MIXTURE DRAWN INTO CRANKCASE

POWER– TRANSFER – EXHAUST
MIXTURE IGNITED PISTON FORCED DOWN B
WHEN TRANSFER AND EXHAUST PORTS ARE
UNCOVERED, (C), MIXTURE IS TRANSFERRED TO
CYLINDER AND BURNT GASES EXIT

**Fig. 15.46**
The Two-Stroke cycle

# Exercises

1.  (a) Name the types of force indicated at A, B, C and D in Fig 15.47.
    (b) Explain the difference between a static load and a dynamic load.

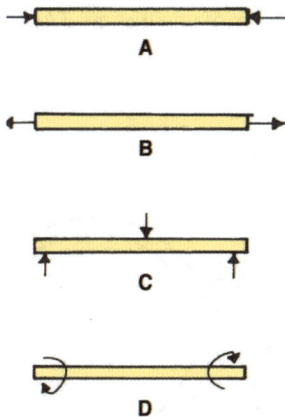

**A**

**B**

**C**

**D**

**Fig. 15.47**

2.  (a) Show where an extra member could be added to the structure in Fig 15.48 to make it more rigid.
    (b) Give four examples of the use of triangulation to increase the rigidity of structures.

**Fig. 15.48**

3.  Name six types of basic mechanisms.

4.  (a) Name the four basic types of motion.
    (b) (i) What type of motion does a sewing machine needle have?
        (ii) What type of motion does a pendulum have?

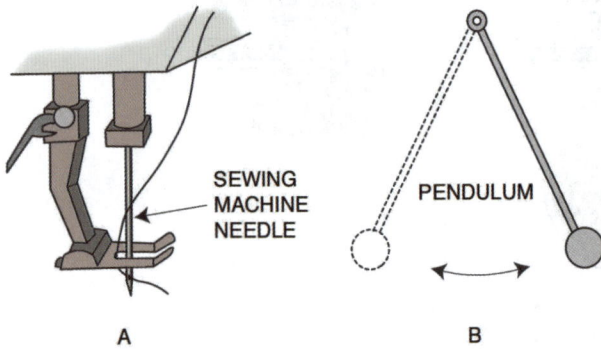

Fig. 15.49

5.  What is a lever?
6.  Describe, with the aid of diagrams, the three classes of lever.
7.  Give a practical application of each class of lever.
8.  What state is a lever in when it is in 'equilibrium'?
9.  Sketch a linkage that would reverse the direction of a linear motion.
10. Name the type of linkage used in the bicycle calliper brake, Fig. 15.50.

Fig. 15.50

11. Give two applications of a parallel linkage.
12. Give two examples of the use of the pulley drives in the school workshop.
13. Give one application of a toothed belt and toothed pulleys.

14. The diameter of a motor pulley in Fig. 15.51 below is 120mm and it rotates at 300 rev/min. If the diameter of the driven pulley is 90 mm, what is its rotary speed?

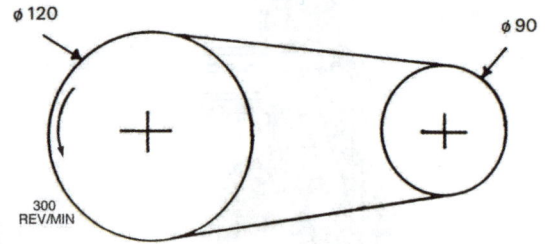

Fig. 15.51

15. Explain, with the aid of a diagram, how a driven gear could be made to rotate in the same direction as the driver gear.
16. Give one application of bevel gears.
17. Name each of the gears shown in Fig. 15.52 below.

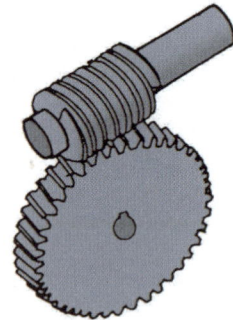

Fig. 15.52

18. Give two applications of rack and pinion gears in the school workshop.
19. An electric motor runs at 1400 rev/min. It has a 20 tooth gear on its shaft which drives a 70 tooth gear. What is the speed of the driven gear?

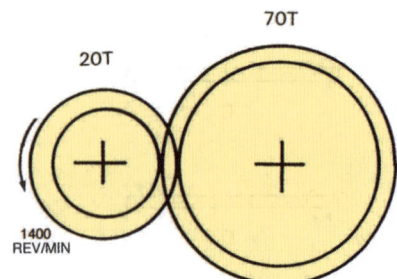

Fig. 15.53

224

20. Give two examples of chain drives.
21. The sprocket on the engine of a go-kart has 9 teeth and the back axle sprocket has 75 teeth. What is the rotary speed of the back axle when the engine is running at 4,500 rev/min?
22. Give an application of a cam in a motor car engine.
23. Sketch three types of cam profile.
24. Sketch three types of cam follower.
25. Sketch and name three types of screw mechanism.
26. Give an application of a ratchet mechanism in the school workshop.
27. What type of mechanism is used to convert the reciprocating motion of the piston of a two-stroke engine, Fig. 15.54 below, to rotary output motion?

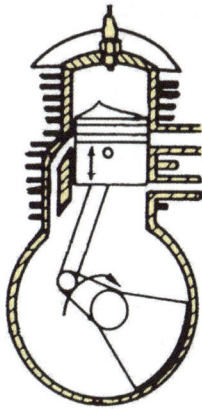

28. What is the function of a clutch?
29. Name the type of clutch shown in Fig. 15.55 below.

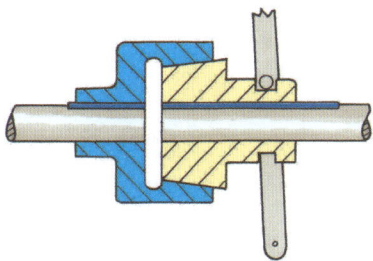

30. State three functions of a lubricant.
31. Give two functions of a bearing.
32. Name each type of bearing shown in Fig. 15.56 below.

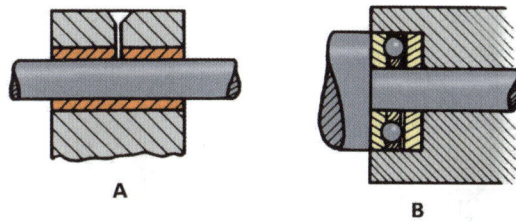

A          B

33. The main parts, A to M, of a four-stroke spark-ignition engine are shown in Fig. 15.57. Name each part and state its function.

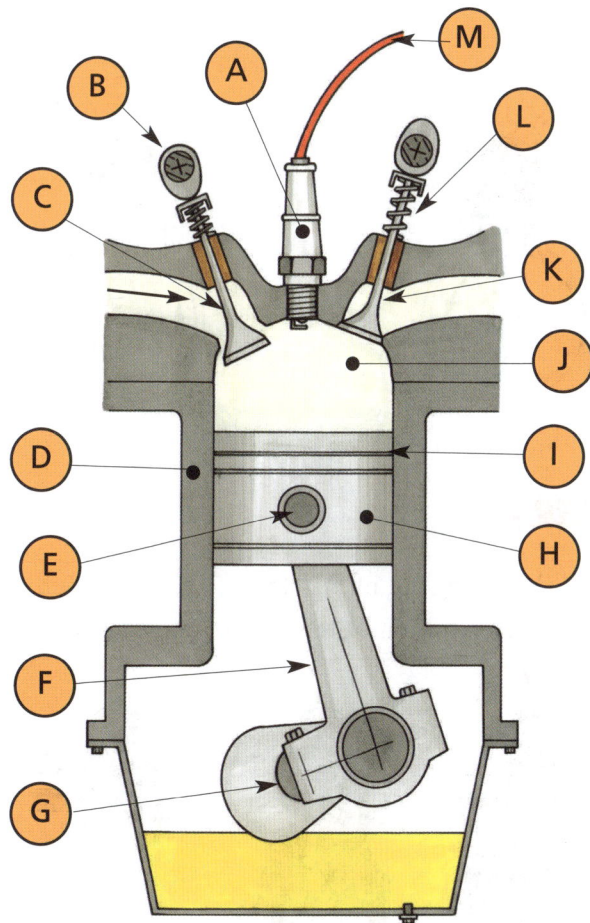

**34.** The four strokes of a four-stroke engine are illustrated in Fig. 15.58. Name each stroke and describe briefly what occurs during each stroke.

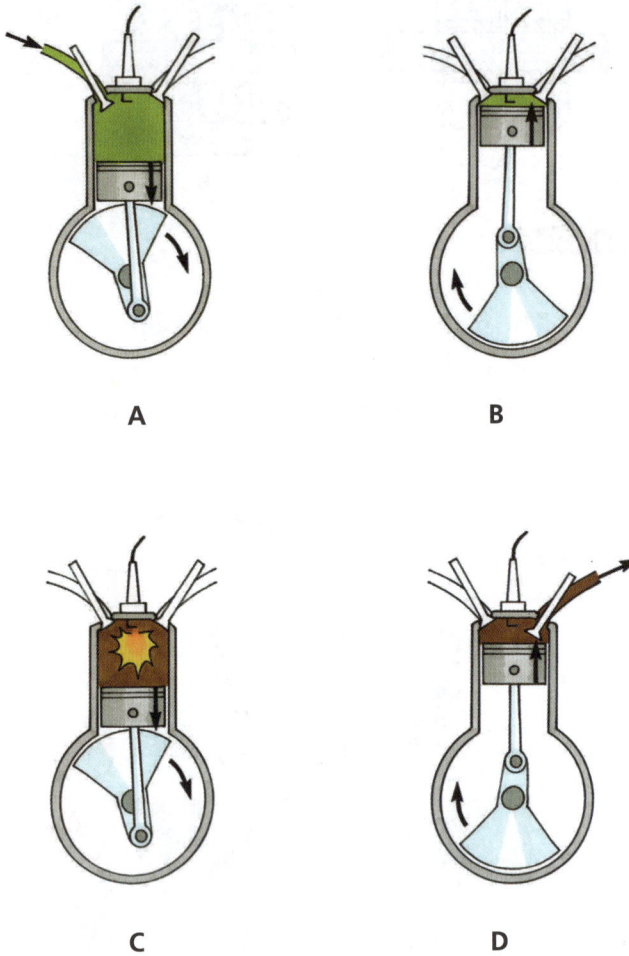

A

B

C

D

Fig. 15.58

**35.** With the aid of Fig. 15.59, describe briefly the operation of the two-stroke engine.

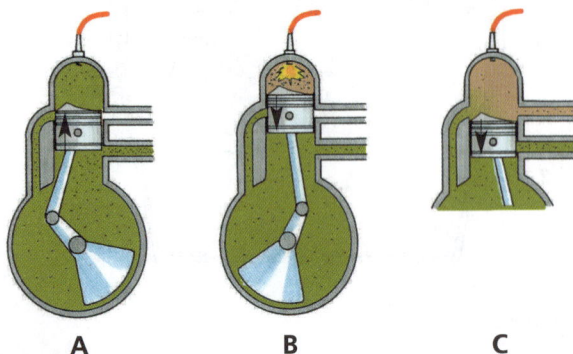

A

B

C

Fig. 15.59

**36.** The main parts of a two-stroke spark-ignition engine are shown in Fig. 15.60. Name each part and state its function.

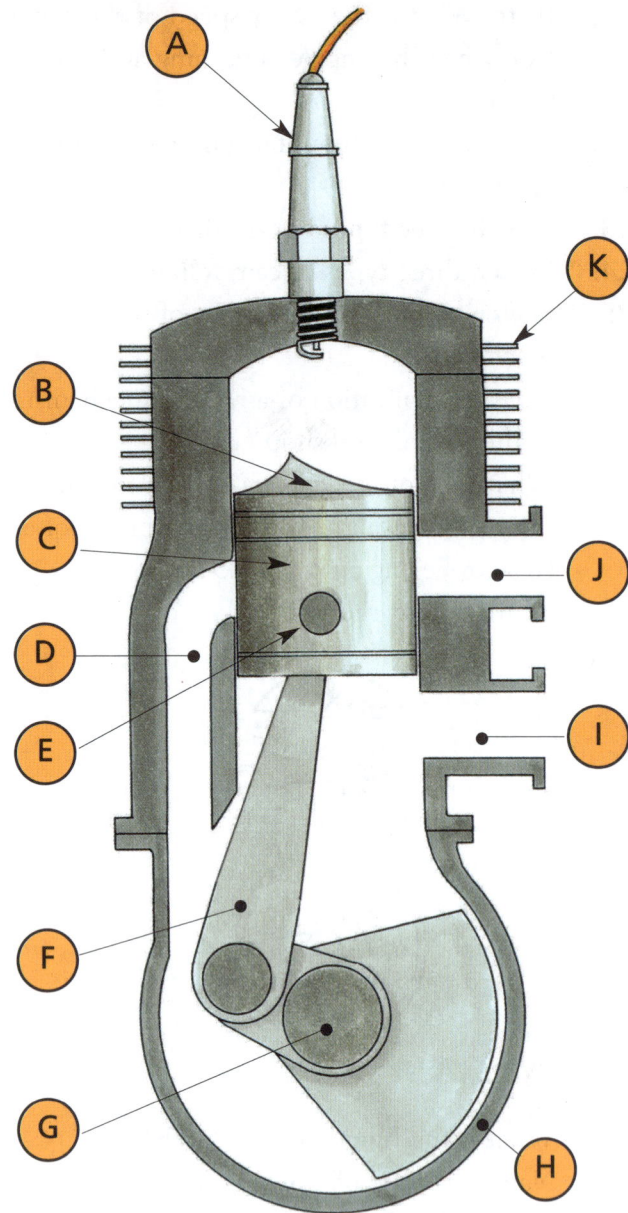

A

K

B

C

J

D

E

I

F

G

H

Fig. 15.60

## Drawing

Drawing, or graphics, is a very important form of communication. Visual images are a great aid in the description of objects. Drawings are used to show how things look, to describe how to make articles and to record, explain and develop ideas. They are, therefore, widely used in design work. Various forms of drawings are used in technology and some important ones are described here.

## Orthographic Projection (2D drawing)

This method of drawing, Fig. 16.1, enables objects to be shown in great detail. It consists of flat, two dimensional views from various sides of the object. This shows the object in a series of flat shapes.

The views projected from the front and sides are called elevations and the view from above is called a plan.

## Three Dimensional (3D) or Pictorial Drawing

Objects often have to be drawn so that they appear three dimensional, i.e. indicating length, height and depth. This helps to give a clearer idea

of their appearance and function. Two types are shown on page 228 — oblique projection and isometric projection.

## Oblique Projection (Fig. 16.2)

This consists of one face drawn as a true shape with the others projected from it, usually at 45°. Oblique drawings are useful when there is a lot of detail to be shown on the front face. Circles on the front face remain as they are, but circles on the other surfaces appear as ellipses.

A method of showing circular forms on the other surfaces is shown in Fig. 16.2 B. Ordinates are drawn at convenient distances in one quadrant of the circle and the heights of these are transferred to the four quadrants on the other surfaces.

## Isometric Projection (Fig. 16.3)

The main lines in isometric projection are vertical and at 30° to the left and to the right. All circles appear as ellipses and can be drawn as shown in Fig. 16.3 B.

Fig. 16.1
Orthographic projection

PLANES FOR ORTHOGRAPHIC PROJECTION

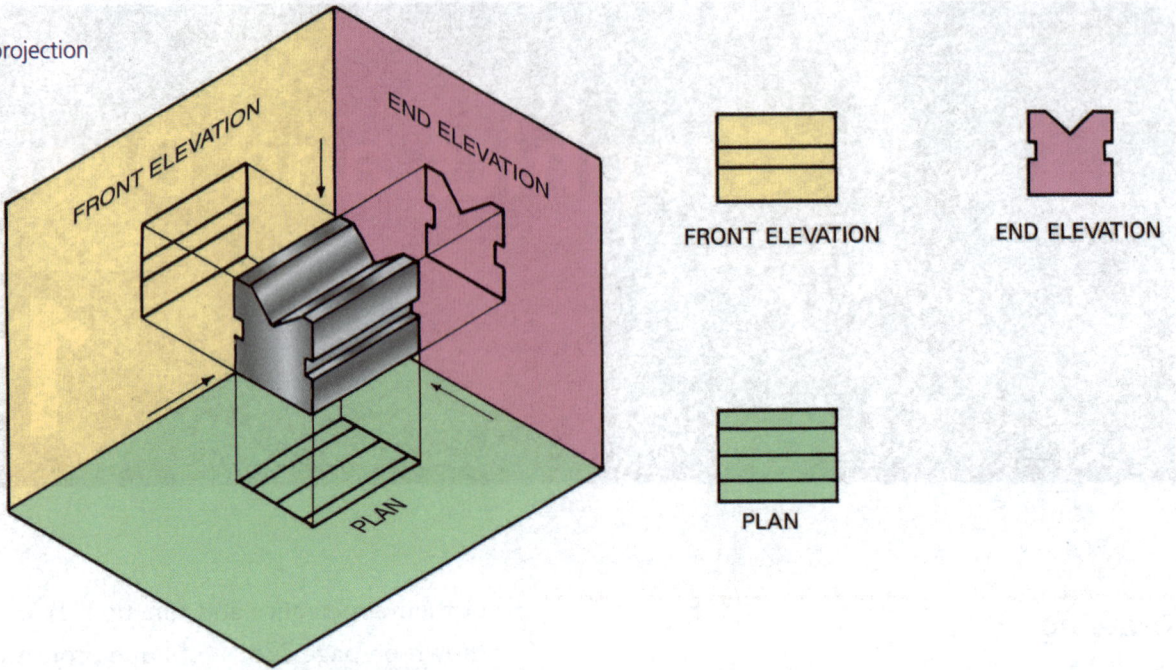

FRONT ELEVATION

END ELEVATION

PLAN

Fig. 16.2
Oblique drawing

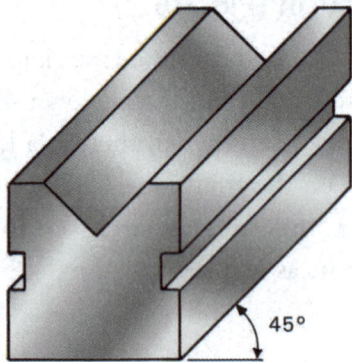

45°

A    OBLIQUE VIEW

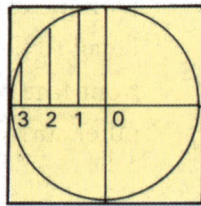

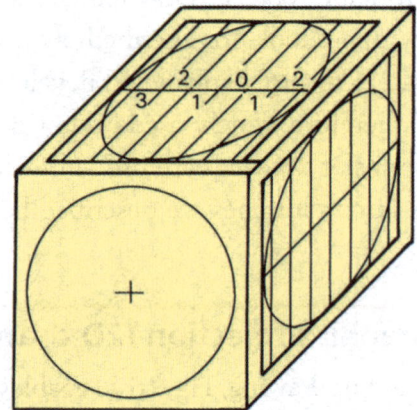

3 2 1 0

B    CIRCLES IN OBLIQUE PROJECTION

3 2 0 2
3 1 1

Fig. 16.3
Isometric drawing

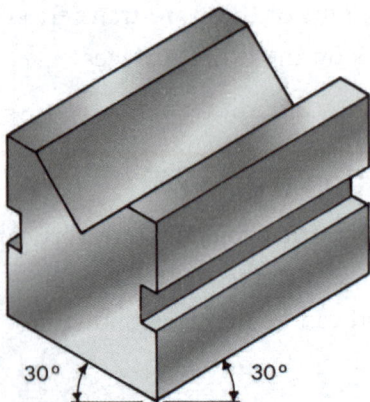

30°        30°

A    ISOMETRIC VIEW

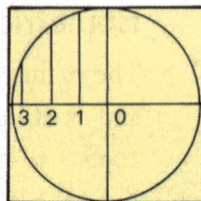

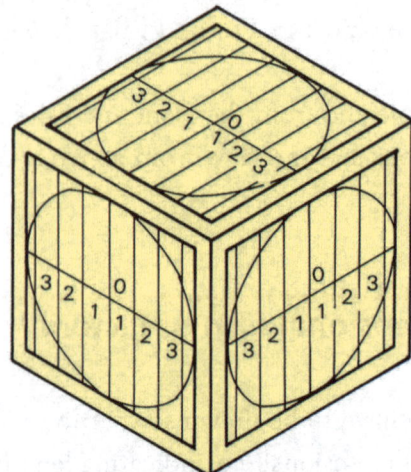

3 2 1 0

B    CIRCLES IN ISOMETRIC PROJECTION

3 2 1 0 1 2 3

3 2 0
3 1 1 2 3

0
3 2 1 1 2 3

## Freehand Sketching

Freehand sketching has widespread applications. For example, drawings often have to be made in locations where drawing instruments are not available or where it would be inconvenient to use them. Freehand sketches are also used to develop and explain designs and to explain and record ideas.

Sketches should be clear and neat, in good proportion and well spaced on the sheet. Freehand working drawings should include sufficient views to show the shape of the article and include measurements, centre lines and any other information required to make the article.

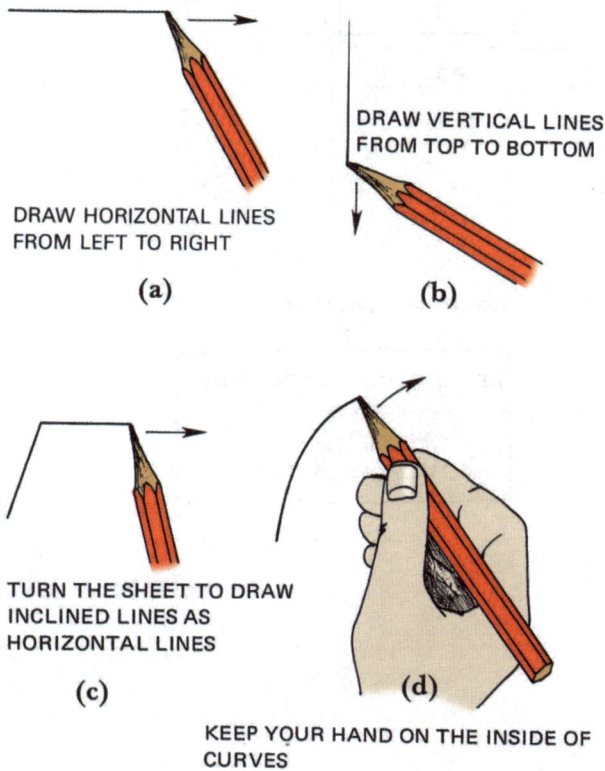

**Fig. 16.5**
Sketching a circle

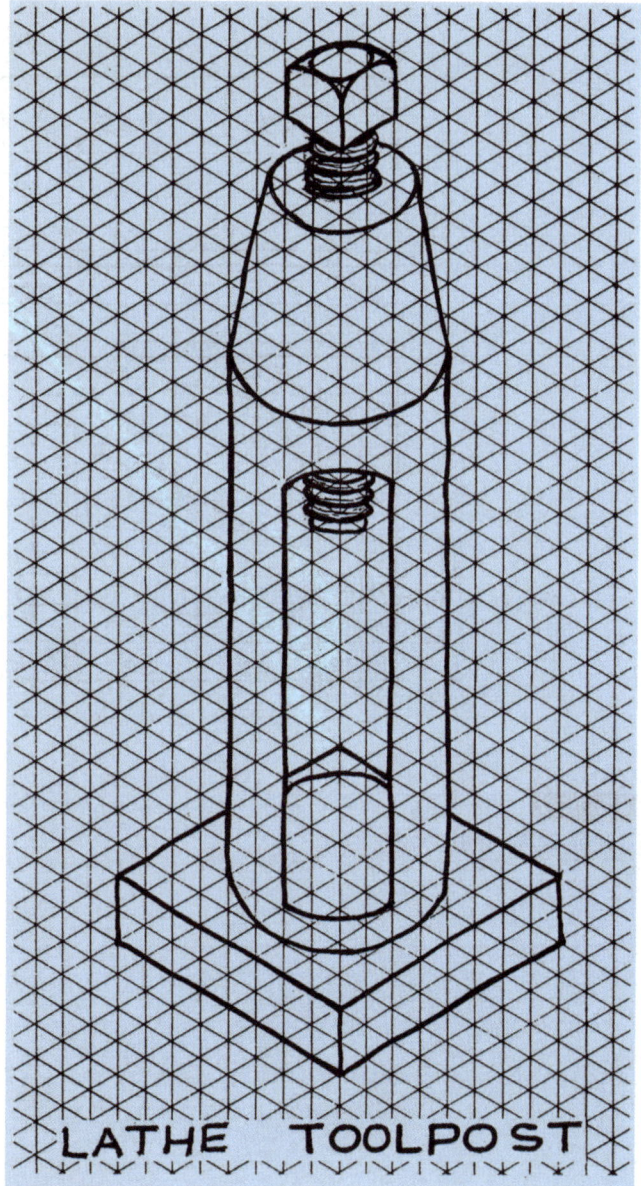

DRAW HORIZONTAL LINES FROM LEFT TO RIGHT

**(a)**

DRAW VERTICAL LINES FROM TOP TO BOTTOM

**(b)**

TURN THE SHEET TO DRAW INCLINED LINES AS HORIZONTAL LINES

**(c)**

**(d)**

KEEP YOUR HAND ON THE INSIDE OF CURVES

**Fig. 16.4**

## Hints for Freehand Sketching

Isometric grid paper and square grid paper, Figs. 16.6 and 16.7, are very useful for freehand sketching. They help to achieve straight lines and good proportion. A reasonably soft pencil, HB grade for instance, without too sharp a point, should be used.

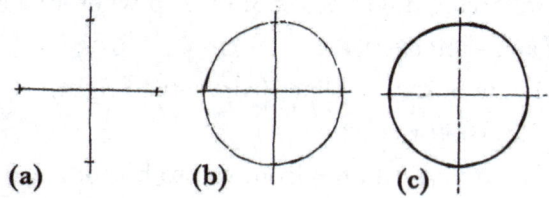

LATHE TOOLPOST

**Fig. 16.6**
Use of isometric grid paper

The following directions should help when making freehand sketches:

(a) Draw horizontal lines from left to right, Fig. 16.4(a).

(b) Draw vertical lines from top to bottom, Fig. 16.4(b).

(c) For inclined lines, turn the sheet so that they can be drawn horizontally, Fig. 16.4(c).

(d) Keep your hand on the inside of curves, Fig. 16.4(d). You may have to turn the sheet to do this.

(e) To draw a circle, first draw horizontal and vertical centre lines. Mark off distances equal to the radius on each side of the centre, Fig. 16.5(a). Join these points with light curved lines, Fig. 16.5(b). Draw in the circle, Fig. 16.5(c).

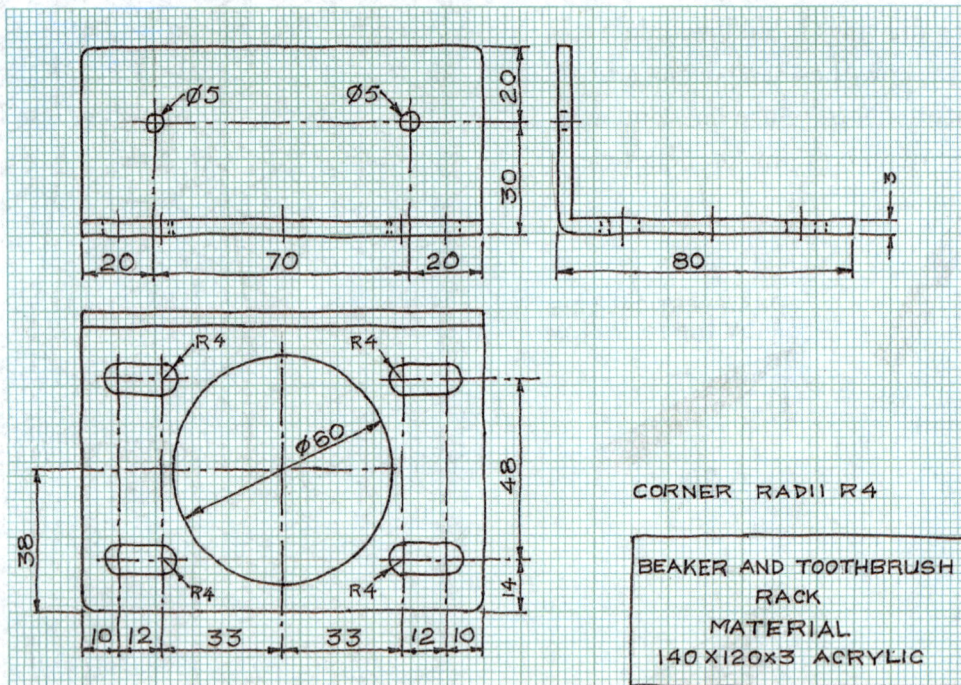

**Fig. 16.7**
Use of square grid paper

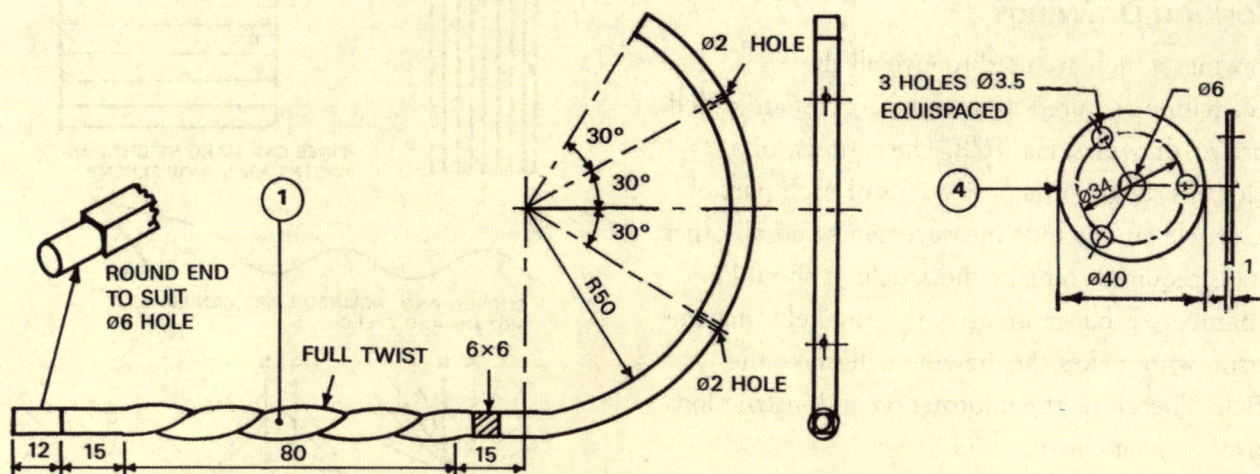

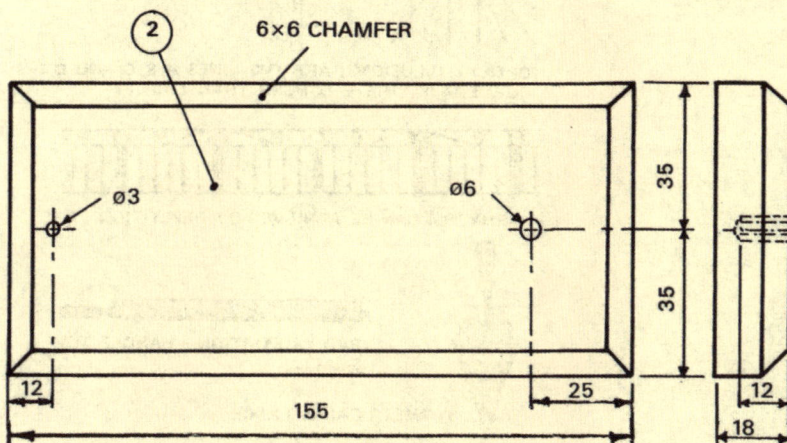

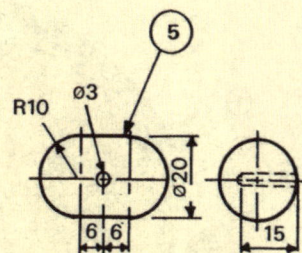

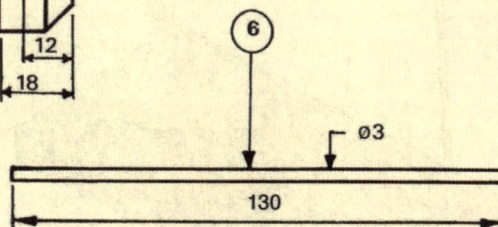

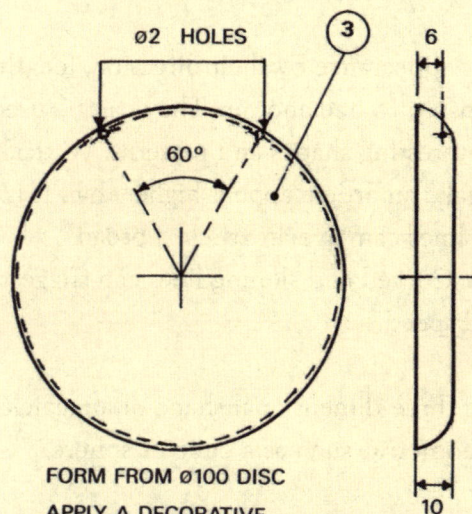

ø2 HOLE

3 HOLES ø3.5
EQUISPACED

ø6

30°

30°

30°

R50

ø2 HOLE

ROUND END
TO SUIT
ø6 HOLE

FULL TWIST

6×6

12  15  80  15

ø34

ø40

1

6×6 CHAMFER

ø3

ø6

35

35

12  155  25

18  12

R10  ø3

ø20

6  6

15

ø3

130

ø2 HOLES

60°

FORM FROM ø100 DISC

APPLY A DECORATIVE
DESIGN TO FACE BY
ETCHING, ENGRAVING
OR PUNCHING

6

10

| NO. | PART | NO. REQD. | MATERIAL |
|-----|------|-----------|----------|
| 1 | SUPPORT | 1 | 6 × 6 BLACK M.S. |
| 2 | BASE | 1 | HARDWOOD |
| 3 | GONG | 1 | 0.7 COPPER SHEET |
| 4 | SECURING PLATE | 1 | 1.0 BRASS SHEET |
| 5 | STIKER HEAD | 1 | ø20 HARDWOOD ROD |
| 6 | STIKER HANDLE | 1 | ø3 BRASS ROD |
| 7 | SCREWS | 3 | 12 × 3.5 BRASS ROUND HEAD |
| 8 | TIE | 2 | HEAVY NYLON LINE |

**Fig. 16.8**

Working drawings of a dinner gong

## Working Drawings

Drawings which are used to give all the information required for making articles are called working drawings, Fig. 16.8. They consist of a series of orthographic projections of each part of the article and include measurements and all other details required to make the article. It should be remembered that in industry it is unlikely that the person who makes the drawing will make the article. Therefore, the information and instructions must be given clearly.

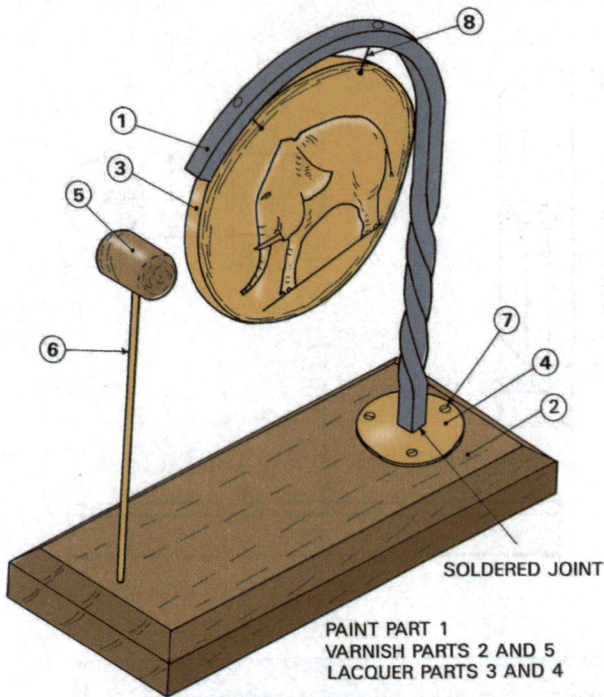

SOLDERED JOINT

PAINT PART 1
VARNISH PARTS 2 AND 5
LACQUER PARTS 3 AND 4

Assembly details of dinner gong

## Blending of Lines, Forms and Colours

When designing an article, appearance must be taken into account and lines, forms and colours must be considered. You should experiment with these until you find an attractive combination.

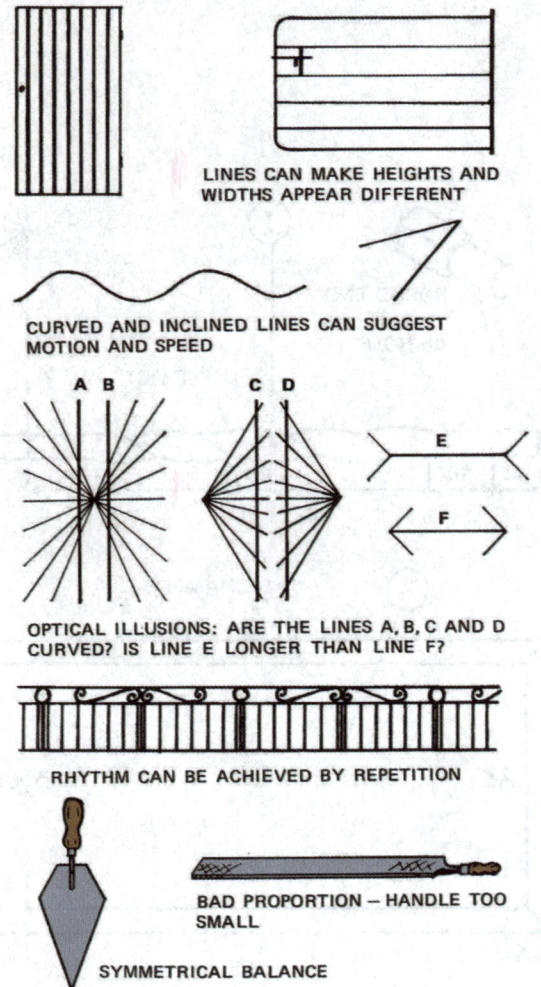

LINES CAN MAKE HEIGHTS AND WIDTHS APPEAR DIFFERENT

CURVED AND INCLINED LINES CAN SUGGEST MOTION AND SPEED

OPTICAL ILLUSIONS: ARE THE LINES A, B, C AND D CURVED? IS LINE E LONGER THAN LINE F?

RHYTHM CAN BE ACHIEVED BY REPETITION

BAD PROPORTION – HANDLE TOO SMALL

SYMMETRICAL BALANCE

**Lines** affect appearance by their direction, length and relationship to one another. They can be used to create interesting shapes and patterns. Vertical lines can make an article appear higher than it is. Horizontal lines can give an article a broad appearance. Curved and sloping lines can suggest motion and speed.

**Form** is the three-dimensional shape of an article. It can be geometric, such as a cube or sphere, or irregular.

**Colour** can make an article look bright, dark, dull, rich, warm or cool. **Materials** have their own natural colours, which are sometimes very attractive, but they can also be coloured by painting or enamelling. Colours can be matched so that they are either in harmony or in contrast with each other.

**Rhythm** can be achieved by the repetition of straight lines, curves, shapes, forms and colours.

**Proportion** is the relationship in size between parts of an article. Good proportion involves making parts the size that suits them best.

**Balance** can be achieved by having parts on each side of a centre line alike, but a sense of balance can also be achieved in other ways.

## Designing

Designing involves thinking, creating, problem-solving, decision-making, working on one's own initiative and putting knowledge, involving various subjects to practical use. Designing also provides an additional incentive to develop craft skills — we take special interest in the making of articles of our own design.

To help recognise good designs and know what to aim for in designing, examine some familiar articles such as can-openers, chairs, bicycles, toys, safety pins and paper clips. Note how well they fulfil their functions and their appearance, cost and construction. Usually, the more simple an article is the better, provided it fulfils its functions. You will also see that there can be a number of solutions to a problem — there are many different types of bicycles, chairs, cars.

At the beginning, you will need some help and guidance with designing. Start with simple problems and follow a definite procedure. The teacher may help you to identify the requirements involved and provide outlines of possible solutions.

As your designing ability improves, you will need less help and be able to undertake more complex problems. This will allow you more scope to use your initiative and to develop a personal approach. However, before making the article, ask your teacher to check the solution for suitability and practicality. Solutions must comply with your skills and also the availability of materials, tools, processes and time.

## The Design Process

This is a procedure, or route, to follow in order to solve a problem. Such a procedure is illustrated in Fig. 16.11. It involves breaking up the work into stages. Each stage must be worked through in turn, and the final one involves comparing the solution with the problem. It can, therefore, be called a design cycle or a design loop.

### Design Brief

This is a clear description of the problem to be solved. It may be based on identifying a problem, need or situation. It should give clear guidelines to help get started but still leave room for innovation.

### Search for Information

This is needed to get a closer understanding of the problem and the functions, properties, limits and restrictions involved. This is called a specification. Drawing up a list of questions that you need to find answers to will help structure your search for information. You could start with the five 'Ws' – what, where, who, when and why. You could formulate questions based on these and add more as appropriate.

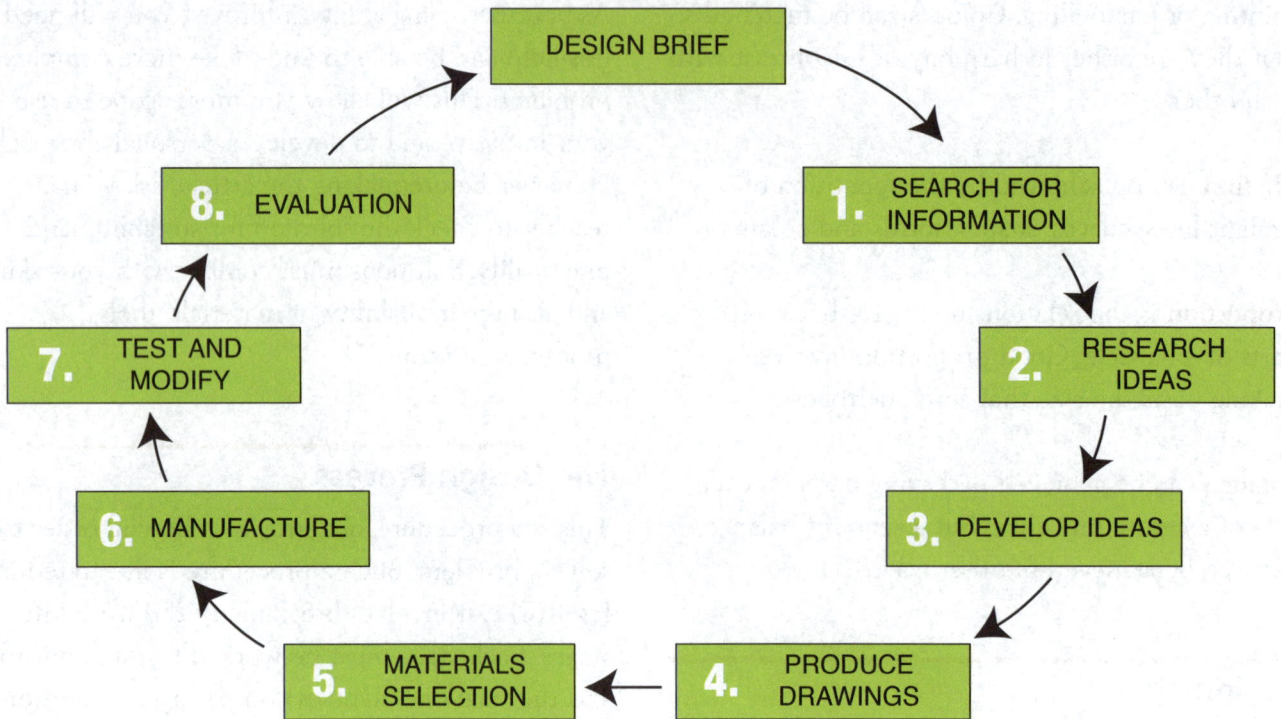

**Fig. 16.11**
A design loop

The following are some examples:
- What is the purpose of the solution?
- What are the limits and restrictions involved?
- What safety issues must be considered?
- Where will it be used?
- Who will use it?
- When will it be used?
- Why will it be used?
- How important is appearance?

Having drawn up a list of questions, you can now go in search of answers. Methods of gathering information include:
- Interviewing people.
- Visiting libraries and reading books and magazines.
- Visiting shops and exhibitions.
- Examining existing or related solutions.
- Writing to relevant companies.
- The Internet

A useful method of recording information during your search is to use a **bubble chart**.

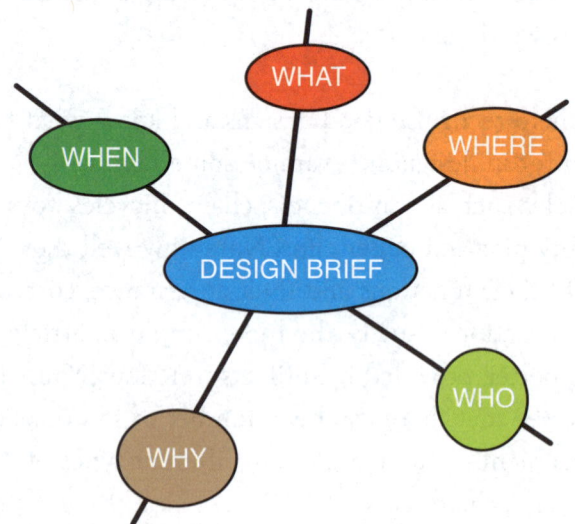

**Fig. 16.12**
A bubble chart

Look at Fig. 16.12. The information can be added outwards from the centre. You can go on adding information and ideas as they occur to you.

Articles should be made of such sizes and shapes that they are easy, comfortable and efficient to use. This involves **anthropometry** and **ergonomics**. Anthropometric data refer to the collection of human measurements which enable designers to work out suitable sizes for articles such as tables and chairs. Using anthropometric data in this way is called ergonomics.

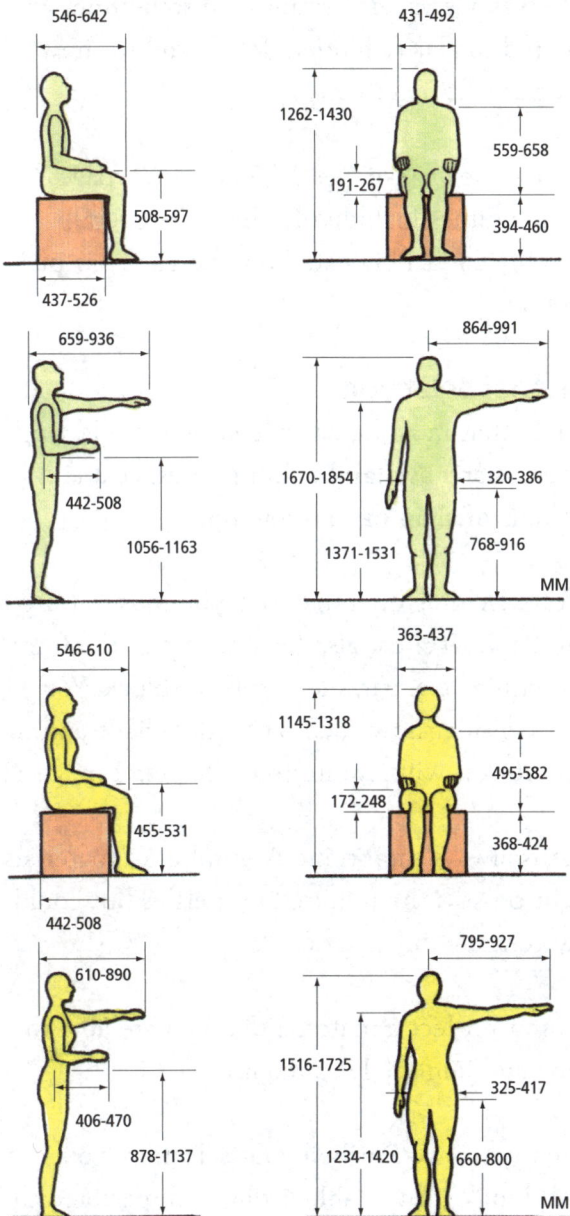

**Fig. 16.13**

Anthropometry and ergonomics

Having collected sufficient information, it is important to sort through it and decide what is relevant. You should then have a good understanding of the problem and be able to set out requirements, limits and restrictions.
You can also make out the criteria for the solution. Criteria do not change much from one technological problem to another and the following apply in most cases – safety, cost, reliability, ease of use, appearance and maintenance cost. However, their relative importance can vary considerably from task to task. For example, appearance would be very important in designing a piece of jewellery but not in designing a wheelbarrow.

## Research Ideas

The search for solutions involves thinking up completely new ideas, using new versions of old ideas and using ideas from other solutions.
You should also look at nature and see if you can find inspiration from the way any related problem has been solved naturally. Use sketches and notes for creating ideas and also for recording them.

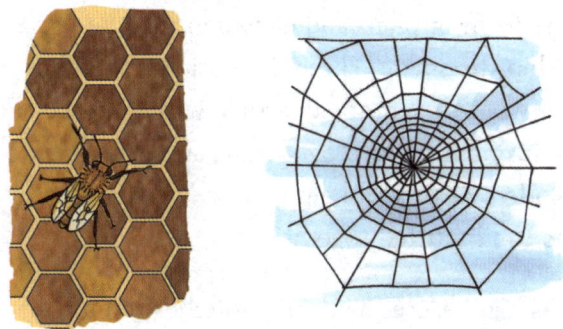

**Fig. 16.14**

Nature as a source for ideas

Brainstorming is a group activity where everyone is involved in thinking up ideas to solve the problem. The ideas are shared which can lead to further ideas and modifications. Do not spend too much time on details at this stage. Instead, try and find a large and varied number of solutions. If you spend a lot of time working out details, you will not be inclined to search further. Also, it is usually possible to evaluate a solution from general outlines.

A useful approach to the search is to break up the problem into sections. Then work on solutions to each section. Explore different combinations of the partial solutions to get a selection of complete solutions.

## Develop Ideas

Having found a number of ideas, you must now select the most suitable and develop them further. Finally, you must select your best idea and refine and modify it as far as possible. To evaluate ideas, you should compare the functions and properties of each one with those found in your **search for information** stage. Check how each idea meets your criteria and also compare the ideas with one another. Finally, check how each idea solves the problem stated in the brief.

In developing your ideas, sketches, notes and prototypes (models) are very important. **Sketches** in the form of plans and elevations can be used to develop the shape. Three-dimensional sketches show what the complete article will look like and how it might be improved. Cut-away views and exploded views will help to work out how the parts can be fitted together.

**Notes** can be used with the sketches to explain aspects of the design and to suggest changes and improvements as they occur to you.

**Prototypes** help to develop suitable proportions and size. They also show how the solution works or if modifications are needed to enable it to work or to improve its operation. Prototypes can often be made from simple materials such as cardboard, hardboard and pegs. They should be made full size if possible.

## Produce Drawings

This stage involves producing a set of drawings to enable the article to be made. These drawings are called **working drawings** (see Fig 16.8, page 231). They must show the shape of each part clearly and give all the necessary dimensions required to make the part. Orthographic projection — plans and elevations — are normally used. A number of views of the individual parts must be given. Cut-away views and sections are sometimes required to clarify hidden details and to show how parts fit together.

Pictorial views (see Figs 16.3 and 16.4, page 228) are sometimes included to show the overall assembly and to indicate how the parts are put together.

## Material Selection

Factors that must be considered when selecting materials are: **availability**, **properties**, **cost** and **methods of shaping and joining**.

Before deciding on a material, you must ensure it is available. It must also be available in the form you require, e.g. bar, sheet, tube or block. You must consider how each part will behave and the properties it will require (see Chapter 1, page 3).

Cost is always important. A number of materials might possess the required properties but could vary considerably in price.

You must select a material that you are able to shape and join safely as required.

When you have finished your selection, you should make out a table listing each part and the material from which it is to be made.

## Manufacturing

The following are procedures involved in the making of an article:

- Plan the sequence of operations for making the parts.
- Draw up a timetable for the completion of the various stages.
- Ensure that you have the necessary tools and equipment.
- Design and make any special tools required such as templates, jigs, formers and moulds.
- Observe the necessary safety precautions when using tools and equipment.
- Mark out the material accurately.
- Aim for a high degree of accuracy in making the parts and ensure that they fit together well.
- Protect the fine finishes on the materials and try to achieve a high quality finish on worked surfaces.

## Test and Modify

You must now test the article and see if it works. Check if it meets the requirements set out in the brief and fulfills its functions. If it fails to work satisfactorily, check each component and find the problem. You must then make whatever adjustments and modifications are necessary to make it work. In certain circumstances, it may involve redesigning and making a part.

## Evaluation

Test the article and see how it works and how well it solves the original problem. Check it against your specifications and criteria for the solution. This brings you back to the brief. If the solution is not satisfactory, you will have to modify it or go round the loop again.

## Example of Design Problems

## STUDENT'S PROJECT 1

Emma Coen, 3S, was given the following design brief.

**Design Brief** Design a teapot stand which is to be made in the school workshop.

## Search for Information

Emma was told that she had five weeks to complete the project. She examined teapots and stands in the school's Domestic Science room, in her friends' houses and in shops. She also read books and catalogues in her search for information. She came up with the following list of functions and requirements:

1. A teapot stand should normally be able to support teapots of various sizes.
2. It must be able to hold the teapot steady without risk of toppling over.
3. It must restrict the passage of heat to the table.
4. It must not mark or scratch the table.
5. It must be able to withstand the heat of the teapot.
6. It should be attractive.
7. The design must take into account the equipment available and also your skills.

After careful consideration, she decided that the following criteria would apply to the stand: safety, appearance, reliability, ease of use and cost.

## Research Ideas

Emma decided to break up the problem as follows:

1. Design the shape of the stand.
2. Find a method of preventing the table being marked.
3. Find a method of restricting heat transfer to the table.

## Ideas for Number 1:
She worked on shapes that would fulfill the requirements. The following were her ideas:

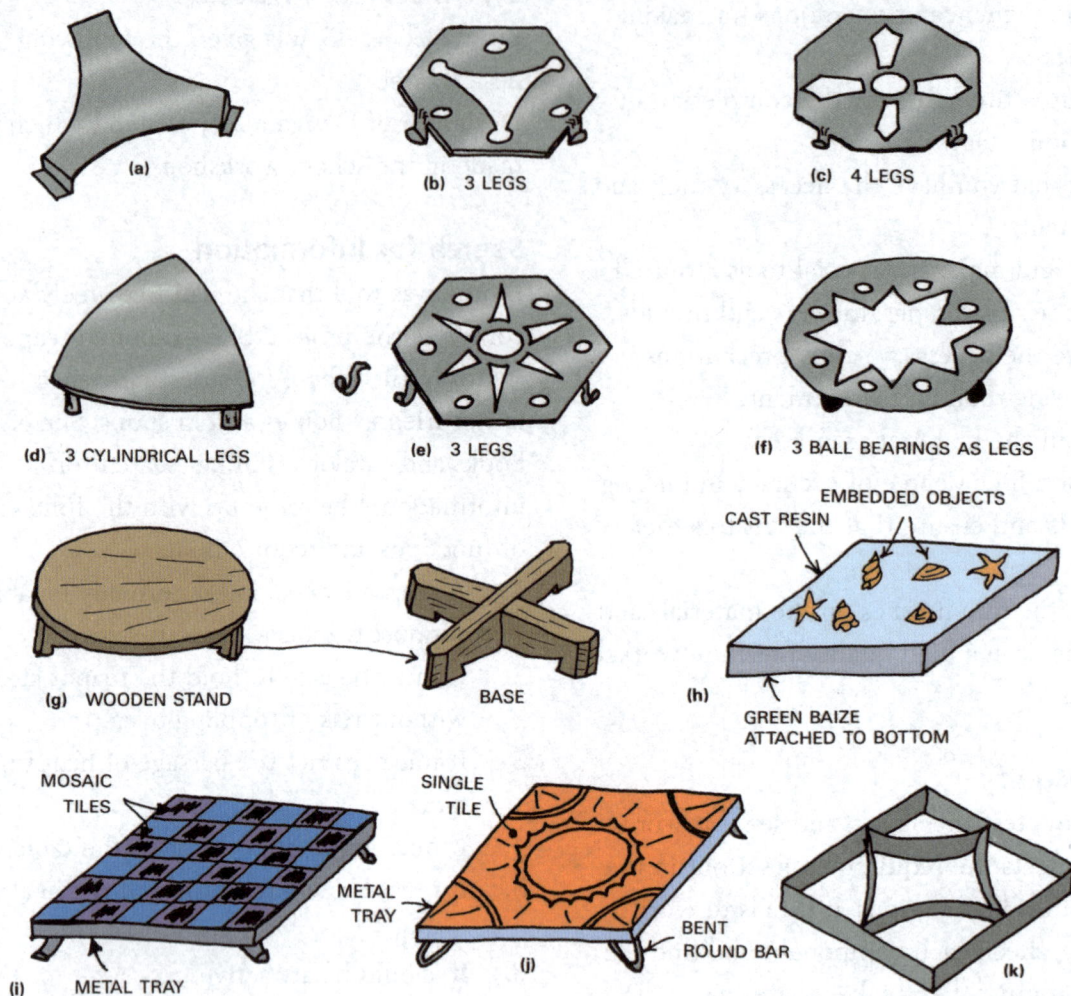

**Fig. 16.15**
Shapes of stand

## Ideas for Number 2:
(a) Make the stand from a non-scratching material.
(b) Attach a layer of soft material to the bottom of the stand.

## Ideas for Number 3:
(a) Make the stand from an insulating material such as wood.
(b) Attach a layer of insulating material to the bottom of the stand.

Attaching a layer of soft insulating material, such as cork, to the bottom of the stand could solve both problems.

## Develop Ideas
She now compared the functions and properties of each idea with those she had identified in the **Search for Information**. She also compared them with one another and with her criteria. As a result, she chose shape (b).

## Reasons

- The shape looked attractive.
- The shape would not be too difficult to produce.
- The bending was within her ability.
- The top and the legs could be made from one piece.
- With three legs properly placed, it would always be steady.

She made a number of models from cardboard to decide on the exact shape of the stand.

## Produce Drawings

She now made a working drawing for her chosen idea.

## Material Selection

Emma first consulted her teacher about the materials available and was told that there was brass, copper, mild steel and aluminium sheets in the school workshop store. She was also told that the cost would be small. She then considered the suitability of their properties. Brass would be very attractive but would tarnish quickly. It could easily be shaped and bent. Mild steel could rust. Aluminium could also be shaped and bent, would be attractive but would be more prone to scratching than mild steel or brass.

After careful consideration, she decided to use aluminium. For the leg insulation, she considered green baize and cork. After some investigation, she decided on cork. She would bond it to the bottom of the legs using a suitable adhesive.

| Part | Material |
|------|----------|
| Stand | 155 x 155 x 1.5mm Aluminium Sheet |
| Table Protection | Cork |
| Adhesive | Suitable for Aluminium and Cork |

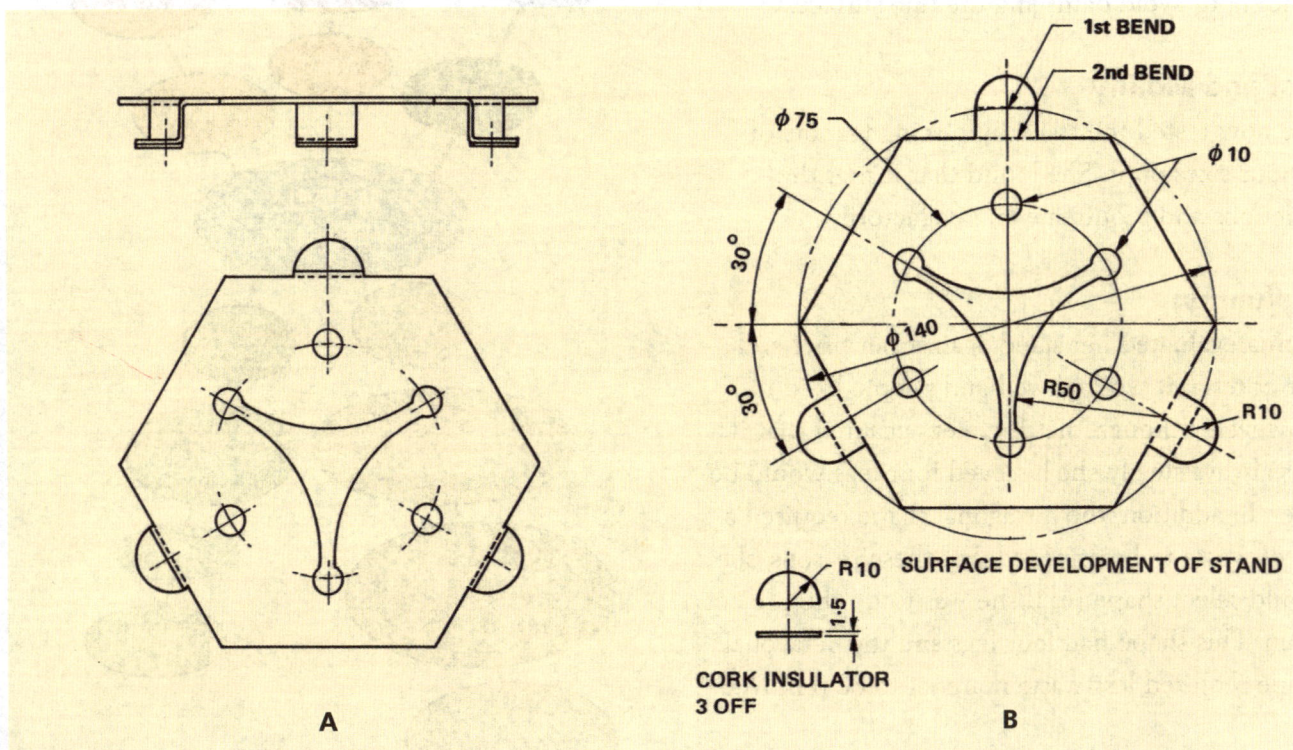

**Fig. 16.16**
Working drawing for stand

## Manufacture

Emma now drew up a sequence of the operations for making the stand:

1. Mark out the development on the aluminium blank. Outlines can be scribed but other lines must be drawn with a pencil.
2. Drill six Ø10 holes for the ornamentation.
3. Saw away the outer waste using a fine toothed saw.
4. Remove the central waste using a tension file.
5. File to the lines.
6. Draw-file the edges.
7. Form the bends for the legs.
   Make the outer bends first.
8. Polish the stand.
9. Mark out the cork insulators and cut them to size.
10. Bond the pieces of cork to the legs.

She familiarised herself with the special safety precautions to be observed while drilling sheet metal and take special care with the shaping and bending to avoid damaging the fine surface.

## Test and Modify

She now tested the stand by placing teapots of various sizes on it. She found that it met the functions and requirements satisfactorily.

## Evaluation

Emma evaluated her stand against her brief and her criteria. It worked well and people liked it. However, although the three legs ensured that it was always steady she believed four legs would be safer. In addition, the hexagonal shape required a lot of waste to be removed. For these reasons, she would select shape (c) if she was to do the project again. This shape had four legs and the octagonal shape required less waste material to be removed.

# STUDENT'S PROJECT 2

Niall Brown, 3R, was given the following design brief.

**Design Brief** Design and make a model vehicle that will be able to travel under its own power and have three different types of motion.

## Search for Information

Niall was told by his teacher that he had five weeks to complete the project and to keep its overall length between 150mm and 200mm. At this stage, Niall decided to draw a bubble diagram to record information.

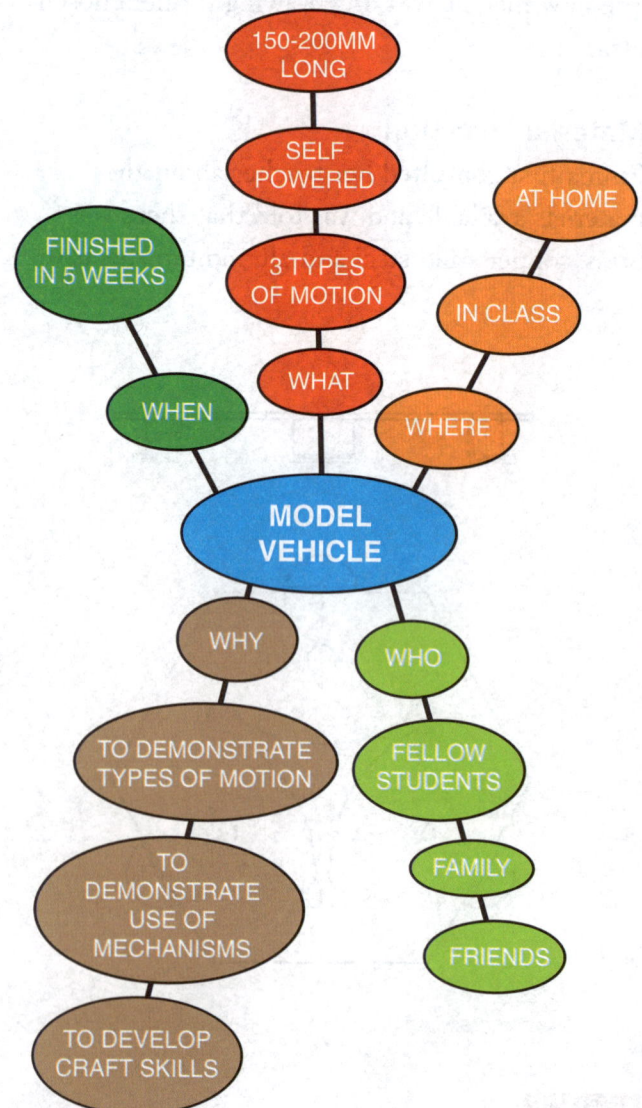

Fig. 16.17

Niall visited toy shops and examined toys at home and those belonging to friends. He read books and magazines on different types of vehicle and also checked the Internet and discussed his project with his fellow students, friends and parents.

He found that many of the toys with movements were powered by wind-up clockwork motors and friction motors while others were powered by batteries and small electric motors. They could also be powered by solar panels and solar motors.

He found that linear motion could be provided by the main movement of the vehicle and rotary motion by the wheels. Reciprocating motion could be produced by a cam or a crank. Oscillating motion could also be produced by a cam.

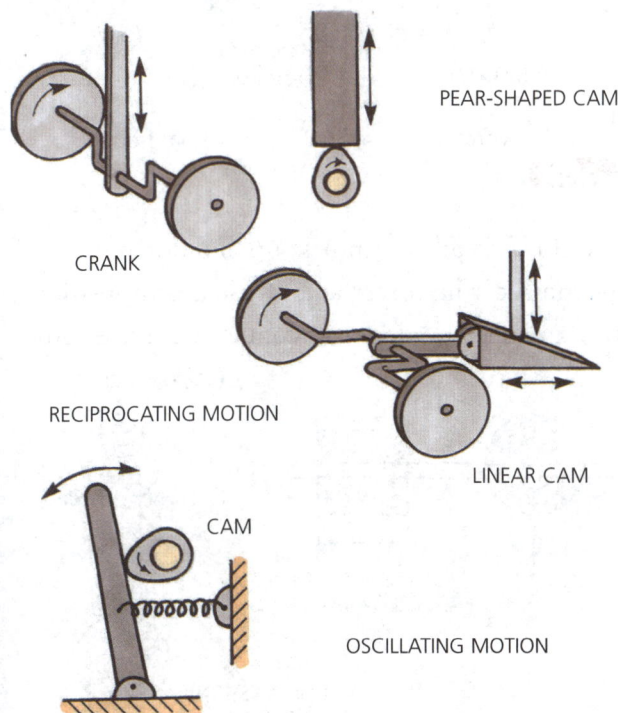

CRANK

PEAR-SHAPED CAM

RECIPROCATING MOTION

LINEAR CAM

CAM

OSCILLATING MOTION

**Fig. 16.18**
Methods of producing reciprocating and oscillating motion

With regard to criteria, Niall decided that appearance, ease of use and safety would need to be given a high priority. Cost would also be a major factor if he decided to use remote control.

## Research Ideas

Among the vehicles he considered were a steam engine, a racing car, a truck, a tractor, a JCB, a roller and an excavator.

**Fig. 16.19**
Ideas for vehicles

Niall now considered how to include the third type of motion. After some research, he came up with some methods.

By having the wheels off centre on the axle, he could make any of the vehicles move up and down.

With regard to the steam engine, the chimney could be made to move up and down by having a cam or crank on the axle.

MOVEMENT OF VEHICLE

WHEELS OFF CENTRE

The driver in the racing car could be made to move up and down by the same means.

CAM MOVING THE DRIVER UP AND DOWN

The arm of the excavator could be made to oscillate by means of a cam or crank on the axle.

By discussing the availability of components with his teacher and consulting catalogues which his teacher provided, Niall found that the following were readily available – small battery-operated motors, clockwork motors, friction motors, solar panels and solar motors, gears and gearboxes, pulleys, belts and springs.

## Develop Ideas

To decide on the type of vehicle to make, Niall compared the functions and properties of each idea with those he believe were required. He compared his ideas with one another, with his criteria and with the brief.

After careful consideration, he opted for the racing car. Making the driver move up and down would provide the third type of motion. He now made a number of models from cardboard to help him decide on the shape and size and the placement of components. Having considered the different options, he selected an electric motor to power the car. Having consulted with his teachers, he decided to use an eccentric cam to provide the reciprocating motion of the driver. This, he believed, would be easier to make than a cranked axle and a connecting rod.

He now had some other problems to solve:
(i)   how to reduce the speed of the motor and increase the torque;
(ii)  how to accommodate the motor, speed reduction mechanism and cam and also place the driver in the centre of the car if possible.

He again approached his teacher and discussed these problems with him. His teacher organised a class session to analyse the problems and try to produce solutions.

After considering the various suggestions, he decided to use a simple worm and wormwheel gearbox. He believed that it would be easier to achieve a large speed reduction with this than with a pulley and belt driver arrangement.

The motor could easily be attached to the gearbox and could be mounted on the side of the chassis using a motor mount with a self-adhesive base.

The easiest way to move the driver up and down would be to place the cam directly underneath it. However, the gearbox reached past the centre of the car model. He overcame this problem by replacing one of the spacers in the gearbox with the cam, making the cam the same width as the spacer.

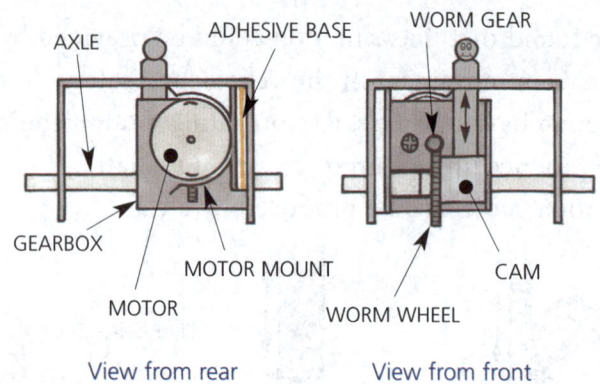

View from rear          View from front

**Fig. 16.20**

He decided to allow 4mm as up and down movement of the driver and to use a compression spring to keep the driver in contact with the cam.

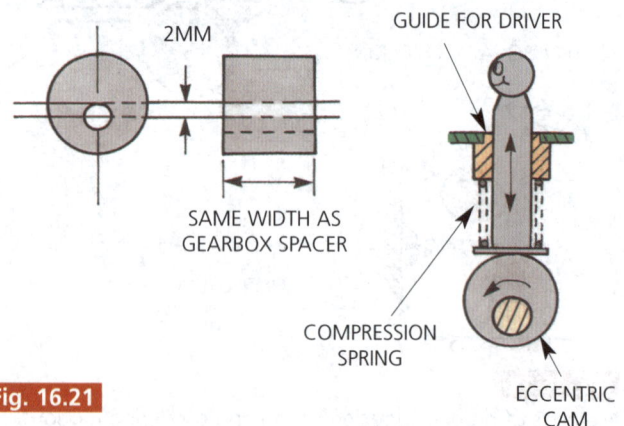

**Fig. 16.21**

He now discovered that the gearbox axle was too short for his model. As a result, he decided to make a longer one.

From checking his model, he found that he could fit the battery underneath the chassis.

# Produce Drawing

Niall now produced his working drawing.

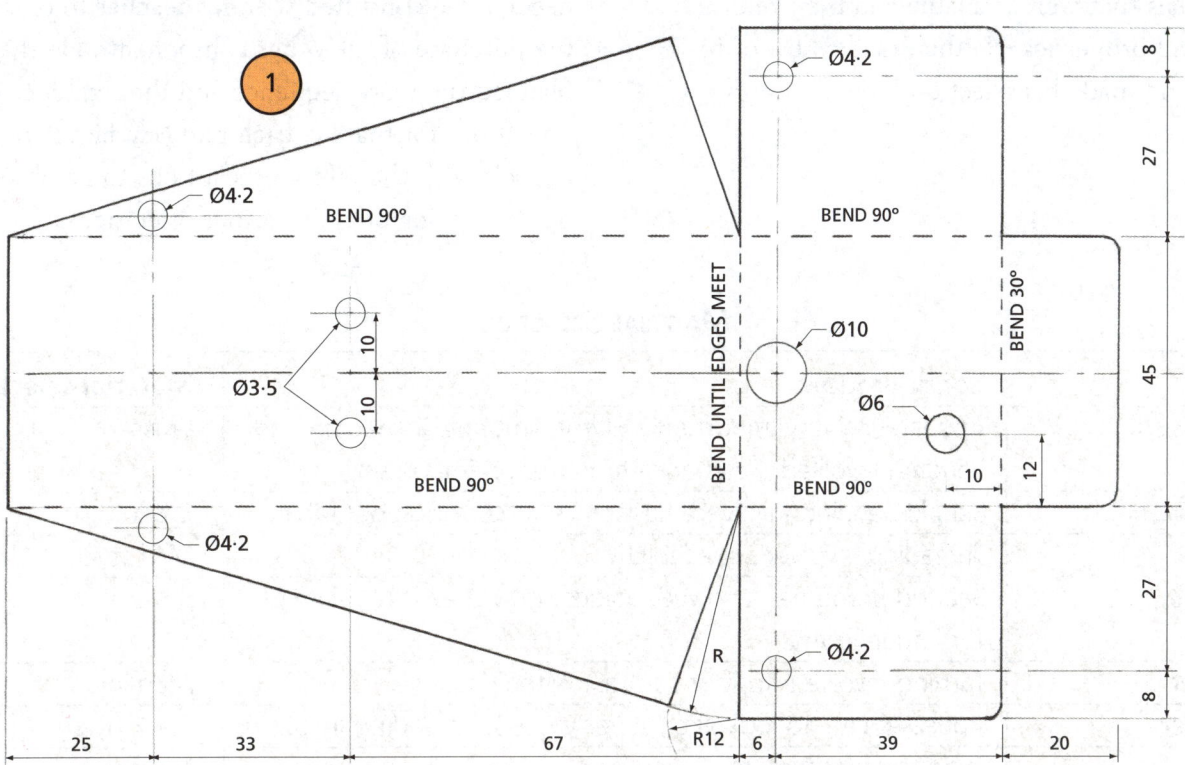

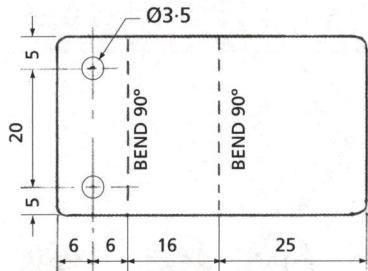

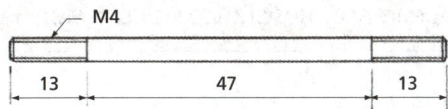

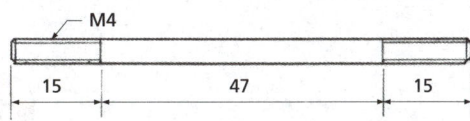

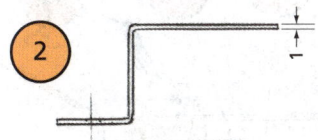

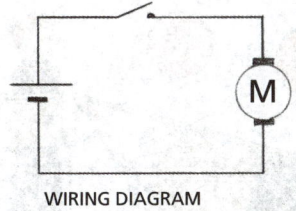

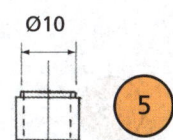

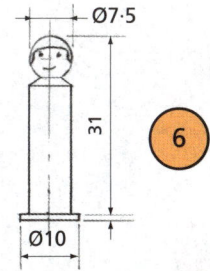

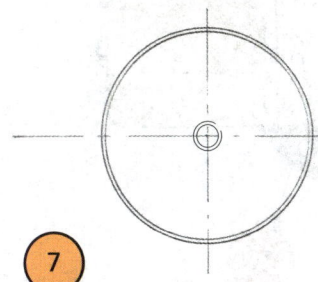

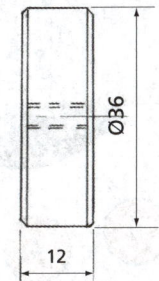

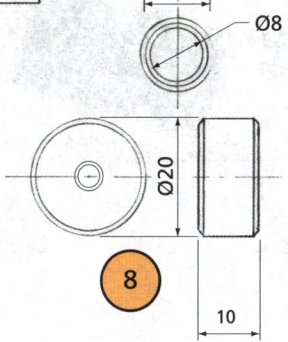

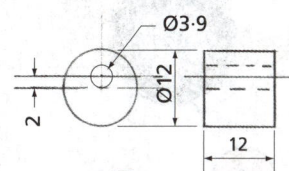

Ø4·2
BEND 90°
Ø4·2
8
27
BEND UNTIL EDGES MEET
Ø10
BEND 30°
BEND 90°
Ø3·5
10
10
Ø6
45
10
12
BEND 90°
BEND 90°
27
Ø4·2
R
Ø4·2
8
25
33
67
R12
6
39
20

Ø3·5
BEND 90°
BEND 90°
5
20
5
6
6
16
25

M4
13
47
13

M4
15
47
15

WIRING DIAGRAM
M

Ø10
Ø12
Ø8

Ø7·5
31
Ø10

Ø36
12

Ø20
10

Ø3·9
Ø12
2
12

1
2
3
4
5
6
7
8
9

Fig. 16.22

243

## Material Selection

Niall first checked with his teacher about the materials that were available and their relevant cost and properties. He then made a list of his parts and made his selection.

## Manufacture

Niall now made out a cutting list of the materials needed. He consulted with his teacher to organise the purchase of the other components. He then planned the work sequence and the sequence of operations for making each part. He familiarised himself with the safety precautions to be observed when carrying out the various operations.

### MATERIAL SELECTION

| Part | Considerations | Material selected |
|---|---|---|
| Chassis | Appearance very important. A large amount of shaping and bending involved. Resistance to corrosion important. | Brass |
| Battery holder | Simple bending involved. Resistance to corrosion desirable. | Brass |
| Axles | Threading involved. Availability. | Mild steel |
| Guide | Bearing properties involved. Soldering to chassis required. Turning involved. | Brass |
| Driver | Turning involved. Colour contrast with chassis. | Aluminium |
| Wheels | Appearance – to look like rubber wheels. Threading involved. | Black nylon |
| Cam | Bearing properties involved. | Nylon |
| Screws and nuts | Appearance. Resistance to corrosion. Availability. | Stainless steel |

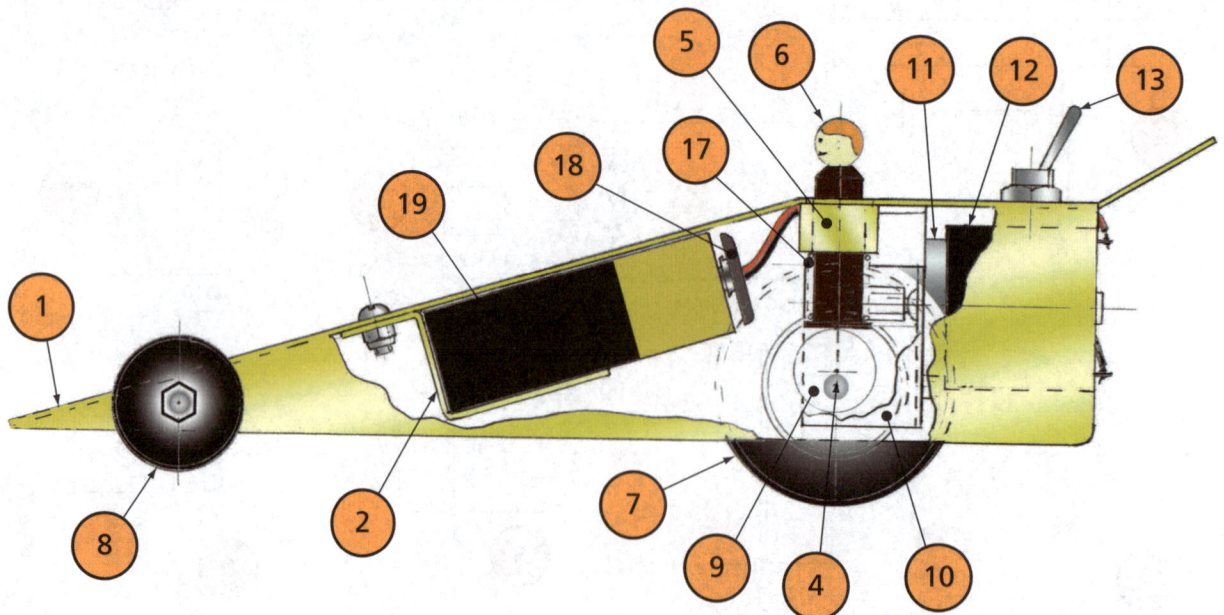

Fig. 16.23

## PARTS LIST

| Part Number | Part Name | Number Required | Material or Description |
|---|---|---|---|
| 1 | Chassis | 1 | 1.0mm brass sheet |
| 2 | Battery holder | 1 | 1.0mm brass sheet |
| 3 | Front axle | 1 | Ø4mm steel rod |
| 4 | Rear axle | 1 | Ø4mm steel rod |
| 5 | Guide | 1 | Ø12 brass rod |
| 6 | Driver | 1 | Ø10 aluminium rod |
| 7 | Rear wheels | 2 | Ø40 black nylon rod |
| 8 | Front wheels | 2 | Ø20 black nylon rod |
| 9 | Cam | 1 | Ø12 nylon rod |
| 10 | Gearbox | 1 | Worm and wormwheel unit |
| 11 | Motor | 1 | Ø24 x 27 (1.5V-3.0V) |
| 12 | Motor holder | 1 | Self-adhesive type |
| 13 | Switch | 1 | Miniature toggle switch |
| 14 | Set screws | 2 | M3 x 10 pan head, steel |
| 15 | Nuts | 2 | M3 lock nuts |
| 16 | Nuts | 4 | M4 cap nuts |
| 17 | Spring | 1 | Compression spring Ø10 x 15mm x Ø 0.5 wire |
| 18 | Battery snap | 1 | PP3 |
| 19 | Battery | 1 | PP3 |

He used a pencil for marking out the brass parts to avoid scratches. He took special care with the bending to ensure neat, accurate bands. He finally assembled the parts to complete the car.

## Test and Modify

When Niall turned on the switch, the car did not move. He then carefully checked the operation of each component. He eventually discovered that the worm and wormwheel unit were jammed due to lack of clearance between them. To free them, he had to carry out some slight modifications and adjustments to the gearbox attachment to the motor. On retesting, the car moved satisfactorily and the driver moved up and down. It fulfilled the functions required in the brief.

## Evaluation

Niall now evaluated his project against the brief and his criteria. Although it met the requirements satisfactorily, he felt that its appearance would be more attractive and realistic if the chassis had been painted with nice colours like a real racing car. By doing this, he could also have used mild steel instead of brass for the chassis. This would be easier to bend. However, he was very pleased with his project overall.

# Inventions and Discoveries

A selection of people who made outstanding contributions to technological developments is given below. There are, of course, many others. The approximate year of the invention or discovery is also given.

| Inventor | Year | Development |
|---|---|---|
| Robert Boyle (Ire.) | 1662 | Relation between gas, pressure and volume |
| Thomas Newcomen (Eng.) | 1712 | Steam engine |
| James Watt (Scot.) | 1769 | Steam engine with separate condenser |
| Eli Whitney (U.S.) | 1793 | Cotton gin. Mass production methods (1798) |
| Alessandro Volta (It.) | 1800 | Electric battery |
| Henry Maudslay (Eng.) | 1800 | Screwcutting lathe |
| Richard Trevithick (Eng.) | 1804 | Steam locomotive |
| Humphrey Davy (Eng.) | 1815 | Miner's safety lamp |
| Karl von Sauerbronn (Ger.) | 1816 | Bicycle |
| Joseph Niepse (Fr.) | 1822 | Camera |
| Charles Babbage (Eng.) | 1823 | Digital calculating machine |
| John Walker (Eng.) | 1827 | Match |
| James Neilson (Scot.) | 1828 | Preheating of air blast for blast furnace |
| Fr. Nicholas Callan (Ire.) | 1828 | Induction coil — had difficulty in getting his work recognised |
| Michael Faraday (Eng.) | 1831 | Electric motor and dynamo |
| Samuel Colt (U.S.) | 1836 | Revolver |
| Charles Goodyear (U.S.) | 1839 | Vulcanised rubber |
| Walter Hunt (U.S.) | 1849 | Safety pin |
| Isaac Singer (U.S.) | 1851 | Sewing machine |
| William Kelly (U.S.) | 1851 | Principle of steel production by blowing air through molten pig iron |
| Alexander Parkes (Eng.) | 1855 | Celluloid |
| Henry Bessemer (Eng.) | 1856 | Bessemer process for steel making |
| William Siemens (Ger.) | 1856 | Open hearth furnace |
| Cyrus W. Field (U.S.) | 1866 | Transatlantic cable between Newfoundland and Ireland |
| Alexander Graham Bell (Scot.) | 1876 | Telephone |
| Thomas Edison (U.S.) | 1877 | Phonograph, Incadescent electric lamp 1879, Edison patented more than 1,000 inventions |
| Nicholas Otto (Ger.) | 1876 | Four stroke engine |
| Dugald Clerk (Scot.) | 1878 | Two stroke engine |
| Joseph J. Thomson (Eng.) | 1879 | Discovered the electron |
| Marcus Daly (Ire.) | 1883 | Mining and smelting of copper ore |
| Charles A. Parsons (Ire.) | 1884 | Steam turbine |
| Gottlieb Daimler (Ger.) and Karl Benz (Ger.) independently | 1885 | Motor car engine |
| John B. Dunlop (Scot.) — lived in Belfast | 1888 | Pneumatic tyre |

| Inventor | Year | Development |
|---|---|---|
| Rudolf Diesel (Ger.) | 1892 | Diesel engine |
| Whitcomb Judson (U.S.) | 1893 | Zip fastener |
| Guiglielmo Marconi (It.) | 1895 | Wireless |
| John P. Holland (Ire.) | 1898 | Submarine |
| Wilbur and Orville Wright (U.S.) | 1903 | Aeroplane |
| Ambrose Fleming (Eng.) | 1904 | Radio valve (diode) |
| Albert Einstein (Swi.) | 1905 | Theory of relativity |
| Leo Bakeland (Belg.) | 1909 | Bakelite |
| Henry Ford (U.S.) | 1913 | Assembly line manufacture |
| John L. Baird (Eng.) and others | 1925 | Television |
| Frank Whittle (Eng.) | 1930 | Jet engine |
| Ernest Walton (Ire.) | 1932 | Splitting the atom |
| Heinrick Focke (Ger.) | 1937 | Helicopter |
| Wallace Carothers (U.S.) | 1938 | Nylon |
| J.P. Eckert and J.W. Mouchly (U.S.) | 1946 | Electronic computer |
| John Bardeen, Walter Brattain and William Hockley (U.S.) | 1948 | Transistor |
| Theodore Maiman (U.S.) | 1960 | Laser |

## Exercises

1. Draw an elevation and plan on square grid paper of a combination pliers, Fig. 16.24 below.

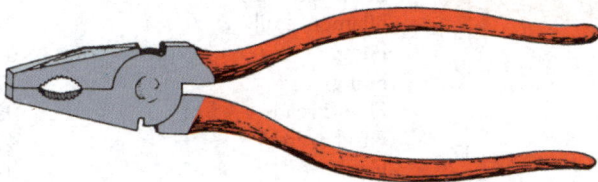

Fig. 16.24

2. Make a three dimensional drawing on isometric grid paper of a toolmaker's clamp.

3. The outline of a soldering iron stand is shown in Fig. 16.25 below. Complete the details and make a working drawing for the stand.

Fig. 16.25

4. Design a candlestick holder and make a working drawing of your solution.

# Index

| ISO METRIC COARSE THREADS | | | |
|---|---|---|---|
| Nominal size | Pitch (mm) | Tapping size drill (mm) | Clearance size drill (mm) |
| M2 | 0.40 | 1.60 | 2.05 |
| M2.5 | 0.45 | 2.05 | 2.60 |
| M3 | 0.50 | 2.50 | 3.10 |
| M4 | 0.70 | 3.30 | 4.10 |
| M5 | 0.80 | 4.20 | 5.10 |
| M6 | 1.00 | 5.00 | 6.10 |
| M8 | 1.25 | 6.80 | 8.20 |
| M10 | 1.50 | 8.50 | 10.20 |
| M12 | 1.75 | 10.20 | 12.20 |